AF352558

RESHAPING THE MOSAIC

Canadian Immigration Policy in the Twenty-first Century

Immigration remains a cornerstone of national policy, although it has undergone significant transformations across economic, family, and refugee admission streams in the past two decades. *Reshaping the Mosaic* offers an insightful exploration of Canada's immigration policy, ranging from its historical roots to contemporary developments.

The book examines the growth in permanent and temporary immigration to Canada. It explores changes in selection criteria and evaluates their impact on key policy objectives: contributing to Canadian economic prosperity, facilitating family reunification, providing refuge for those fleeing persecution, and enabling the integration of immigrants and their descendants into Canadian society. The book sheds light on the legal, political, economic, and social paradoxes inherent in Canadian immigration policy, highlighting shifts in exclusion powers, deportation practices, settlement support, and citizenship rules, as well as their implications for Canadian ideals of multiculturalism, fairness, and integration. It documents the lack of transparency and informed public engagement in policy formation and the implications this lack may have on maintaining public confidence and ensuring that immigration policies align with the national interests.

Driven by a conviction that the contemporary changes in immigration policy need to be examined in a comprehensive and inclusive way, *Reshaping the Mosaic* looks at recent shifts and their implications for society and offers invaluable insights for policymakers, scholars, and stakeholders, aiming to assist the development of a new immigration policy framework.

(UTP Insights)

NINETTE KELLEY is a lawyer and former official of the United Nations High Commissioner for Refugees (UNHCR).

JEFFREY G. REITZ is the R.F. Harney Professor Emeritus of Ethnic, Immigration, and Pluralism Studies, a professor emeritus of sociology, and an affiliated faculty member at the Munk School of Global Affairs & Public Policy at the University of Toronto.

MICHAEL J. TREBILCOCK is a university professor emeritus of law and economics at the University of Toronto.

UTP insights

UTP Insights is an innovative collection of brief books offering accessible introductions to the ideas that shape our world. Each volume in the series focuses on a contemporary issue, offering a fresh perspective anchored in scholarship. Spanning a broad range of disciplines in the social sciences and humanities, the books in the UTP Insights series contribute to public discourse and debate and provide a valuable resource for instructors and students.

For a list of the books published in this series, see page 417.

RESHAPING THE MOSAIC

Canadian Immigration Policy in the Twenty-first Century

Ninette Kelley, Jeffrey G. Reitz, and Michael J. Trebilcock

UNIVERSITY OF TORONTO PRESS
Toronto Buffalo London

© University of Toronto Press 2025
Toronto Buffalo London
utppublishing.com

ISBN 978-1-4875-6296-0 (cloth)   ISBN 978-1-4875-6299-1 (EPUB)
ISBN 978-1-4875-6297-7 (paper)   ISBN 978-1-4875-6298-4 (PDF)

Library and Archives Canada Cataloguing in Publication

Title: Reshaping the mosaic : Canadian immigration policy in the twenty-first century / Ninette Kelley, Jeffrey G. Reitz, and Michael J. Trebilcock.
Other titles: Canadian immigration policy in the twenty-first century
Names: Kelley, Ninette, author | Reitz, Jeffrey G., author | Trebilcock, M.J., author
Series: UTP insights.
Description: Series statement: UTP insights | Includes bibliographical references and index.
Identifiers: Canadiana (print) 20240537254 | Canadiana (ebook) 20240537262 |
    ISBN 9781487562960 (cloth) | ISBN 9781487562977 (paper) |
    ISBN 9781487562991 (EPUB) | ISBN 9781487562984 (PDF)
Subjects: LCSH: Canada – Emigration and immigration – Government policy – History – 21st century.
Classification: LCC JV7225.2 .K45 2025 | DDC 304.8/71–dc23

Cover design: Mary Beth MacLean
Cover image: "On the Road to Collingwood" by Jan Trebilock

We wish to acknowledge the land on which the University of Toronto Press operates. This land is the traditional territory of the Wendat, the Anishnaabeg, the Haudenosaunee, the Métis, and the Mississaugas of the Credit First Nation.

University of Toronto Press acknowledges the financial support of the Government of Canada, the Canada Council for the Arts, and the Ontario Arts Council, an agency of the Government of Ontario, for its publishing activities.

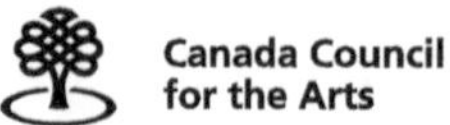

Contents

Acknowledgments

We extend our gratitude to experts in the fields of economics, law, political science, and sociology who generously reviewed earlier chapters of this book and contributed their insights to its refinement. Our sincere thanks go to Rupa Banerjee, David Beatty, Michael Casasola, Adèle Garnier, Tania Ghanem, Fen Hampson, Barb Jackman, Shauna Labman, Robin Seligman, John Shields, Colin Singer, Mikal Skuterud, Azadeh Tamjeedi, and David Vinokur. As well, we are grateful to Feng Hou of Statistics Canada for his kind assistance in accessing census data and relevant Statistics Canada research.

We express our gratitude to Maija Fiorante and Sophie Keller for their dedicated early research assistance, and to Zoe Hawkins for her meticulous attention to detail in verifying footnotes. We also thank Melissa MacAulay for her work on the index. Special appreciation is extended to Michael Hunter for his editing work on earlier drafts, ensuring not only consistency of style but also enhancing the accessibility of this book. Additionally, we are thankful to Beth McAuley for her scrupulous copy editing and to Dan Quinlan and Barb Porter for efficiently shepherding the book through the publication process with the University of Toronto Press.

Any errors or inaccuracies within this book are solely our responsibility.

Introduction: Canadian Immigration Policy at a Crossroads

Canada's rise from a minor colonial outpost into a dynamic, multicultural nation was powered by immigrants. Immigration policy was central to the country's transformation into one of the leading democracies in the world. As the country charts its course through the first quarter of the twenty-first century, immigration policy remains a key component of national policy. It has been far from static. Over the past twenty years, Canadian immigration policy has undergone seismic shifts.

Notably, the selection criteria for all three major immigrant streams – economic, family, and refugee – have been significantly revised and the process for selecting economic immigrants, constituting 60 per cent of admissions, thoroughly overhauled. As well, the rules and procedures governing the exclusion and removal of immigrants have been tightened as have the criteria for obtaining Canadian citizenship.

Throughout, annual immigration levels have swelled, amplifying the ramifications. Having hovered around 250,000 for two decades, they close to doubled by 2024. Despite the disruption of the COVID-19 global pandemic, 2023 saw 471,000 immigrants welcomed to Canada.[1] Simultaneously, the number of temporary

---

1 Immigration statistics in this paragraph are as presented in figures 2–7 in the appendix. The current annual immigration targets are published in Marc Miller, *2023 Annual Report to Parliament on Immigration* (Ottawa: Immigration, Refugees and Citizenship Canada, 2023), https://publications.gc.ca/collections/collection_2023 /ircc/Ci1-2023-eng.pdf.

foreign workers skyrocketed from under 70,000 in 2000 to 1,270,000 in 2023 (see figure 5). International student numbers surged from just under 125,000 to over 1 million during the same period (see figure 7).

Central to these policy shifts is the *Immigration and Refugee Protection Act 2001*, which provides the legal authority for immigration policy and change. This book aims to document and elucidate the transformations, seeking to comprehensively assess their broader impact. It highlights how the process of immigration policy-making has also changed. Over the past two decades, there has been a notable decline in public transparency. Unlike the structured hearings and extensive studies characterizing policy shifts from the 1960s to the 1990s, changes under the act have often been swift and less known, frequently directed by executive decisions.

The waning transparency in the immigration policy-making process is concerning. Public hearings, once forums for diverse views on immigration levels and criteria, have become less common. Consequently, many recent policy changes remain obscured from public scrutiny. It is within the historical tradition of public engagement that that this book emerges driven by the conviction that the contemporary overhaul in immigration policy needs a comprehensive and inclusive examination.

Historically, Canada has maintained a positive consensus on immigration.[2] Public opinion polls continue to reflect the recognition

---

2 Canada's consensus in favour of immigration has stood as a cornerstone of its immigration program, a remarkable strength that has been upheld despite decades marked by significant increases in immigrant numbers and their cultural and racial diversity. This resilience persisted even during the extended period of international tension following the terrorist attacks of 2001.While other nations grappled with contentious debates surrounding immigration, Canada's unique stance, often termed as "Canadian exceptionalism," has been fortified by the principles of multiculturalism, which are now deeply ingrained in the national identity. See Michael Trebilcock, "The Puzzle of Canadian Exceptionalism in Contemporary Immigration Policy," *Journal of International Migration and Integration* 20 (2019): 823–49; Irene Bloemraad, *Understanding "Canadian Exceptionalism" in Immigration and Pluralism Policy* (Washington, DC: Migration Policy Institute, 2012); Jeffrey Reitz, "The Distinctiveness of Canadian Immigration Experience," in "National Models of Integration and the Crisis of Multiculturalism: A Critical Comparative

of immigrants' contributions to Canada's growth and diversity,[3] and Canada remains a desired destination for migrants globally.[4] However, a new volatility of public opinion has emerged. The annual Environics poll published in 2022 showed continuity with the past. Seven in ten Canadians surveyed expressed support for current immigration levels – "the largest majority recorded on Environics surveys in 45 years."[5]

A survey the following year revealed that while most Canadians continue to hold a positive view of immigration overall, support for the immigration levels had plummeted. Forty per cent believed that Canada was taking in too many immigrants, a 17 per cent increase from the previous year, marking the largest single year change since 1977.[6] Survey responses suggest that this drop in support is attributed to concerns regarding the impact of permanent and temporary immigration on domestic housing, healthcare, and labour sectors, as well as their effects on Canada's declining economic productivity.[7]

Perspective," ed. Christophe Bertossi and Jan Willem Duyvendak, special issue, *Patterns of Prejudice* 46, no. 5 (2012): 418–35; Jeffrey Reitz, *Pro-immigration Canada: Social and Economic Roots of Popular Views*, IRPP Study, No. 20 (Montreal: Institute for Research on Public Policy, 2011).

3 Environics Institute, *Canadian Public Opinion about Immigration & Refugees*, Focus Canada Report (Fall 2023), 2, https://www.environicsinstitute.org/projects /project-details/public-opinion-about-immigration-refugees.

4 Anita Pugliese and Julie Ray, "Nearly 900 Million Worldwide Wanted to Migrate in 2021," *Gallup*, 24 January 2023, https://news.gallup.com/poll/468218/nearly -900-million-worldwide-wanted-migrate-2021.aspx; Neli Esipova, Julie Ray, and Dato Tsabutashvili, "Canada No. 1 for Migrants, U.S. in Sixth Place," *Gallup*, 23 September 2020, https://news.gallup.com/poll/320669/canada-migrants-sixth-place.aspx.

5 Environics Institute, *Canadian Public Opinion about Immigration and Refugees, Focus Canada* (Fall 2022), 1, https://www.environicsinstitute.org/projects/project-details /canadian-public-opinion-about-immigration-and-refugees---fall-2022.

6 Environics Institute, *Canadian Public Opinion about Immigration & Refugees*, Focus Canada Report (Fall 2023), 2.

7 Other 2023 and 2024 surveys echoed these concerns. The surveys used varying sample selection and interview methods and, unlike the Environics Focus Canada series, were less able to establish trends over time. A survey conducted in September 2023 by Nanos Research showed that 53 per cent of Canadians wanted Canada to accept fewer immigrants than the target of 465,000 for 2023, up from 34 per cent from the previous March. Nanos, "Canadians Prefer that Canada Accepts Fewer Immigrants

Given the significance of public support for immigration to the success of the immigration program, much is at stake here. As Canada grapples with defining its future immigration trajectory, public engagement and transparency in policy-making are paramount. The sustainability of past successes in immigration hinges on maintaining public confidence and ensuring that immigration policies align with the national interest.

Reshaping the Mosaic: Contemporary Canadian Immigration Policy aims to inspire deeper critical engagement on the central components of our immigration policy that directly affect hundreds of thousands of lives, and touch millions more. It is our hope that greater informed engagement in the shaping of immigration policy will help provide a sound basis for reform and ensure the public confidence necessary to sustain policies in the future.

This book draws from broad expertise on current global dynamics in migration and forced displacement. It covers the history of Canadian immigration policy and understandings of the path to integration of immigrants to Canada over the past fifty years. Given the pivotal positive role immigrants have played in Canada, and their future impact on the nation, we hope this book will help spark deeper engagement in how immigration policy is set, and how to best assess its impact over time.

---

and International Students than What Is Projected for 2023," 11 September 2023, https://nanos.co/canadians-prefer-that-canada-accepts-fewer-immigrants-and -international-students-than-what-is-projected-for-2023-globe-nanos/. See also, Marie Woolf, "Poll Finds More than Half of Canadians Want Fewer Immigrants than Ottawa's Target," *Globe and Mail*, 11 September 2023, https://www.theglobeandmail .com/politics/article-poll-finds-more-than-half-of-canadians-want-fewer-immigrants -than/; Mitchell Consky, "Mortgages, Inflation and Immigration among Top Concerns for Canadians in 2024: Nanos Survey," *CTV News*, 3 January 2024, https:// www.ctvnews.ca/canada/mortgages-inflation-and-immigration-among-top-concerns -for-canadians-in-2024-nanos-survey-1.6708433; Tyler Dawson, "Half of all Canadians Say There Are Too Many Immigrants: Poll," *National Post*, 12 March 2024, https:// nationalpost.com/news/canada/half-of-all-canadians-say-there-are-too-many -immigrants-poll; Jack Jedwab, "What Underlies Concern over Canada's Immigration Numbers?," Metropolis Institute and the Association for Canadian Studies, 11 March 2024, https://acs-metropolis.ca/studies/what-underlies-concern-over -canadas-immigration-numbers/.

Immigration and the Canadian Mosaic

In 2001, Canada made the most significant shift in its immigration policy in almost three decades. The new *Immigration and Refugee Protection Act 2001* stood in stark contrast to its 1976 predecessor, itself a marked departure from the past.

The *Immigration Act, 1976* eliminated remaining explicit forms of racial discrimination within Canada's immigration legislation. It significantly broadened the opportunities for Canadian permanent residents to sponsor their family members and introduced a distinct category for refugee admissions. It established enhanced independent review mechanisms to scrutinize immigration officers' decisions related to admission denials and deportation orders. The act also introduced greater transparency and accountability in the formulation of immigration policy, confirming parliamentary authority to review regulatory changes and providing for provincial and public engagement in the setting of annual immigration targets.[8]

The *Immigration Act, 1976* stands as one of the most progressive pieces of immigration policy in Canada's history. The expansive, inclusive, and transparent immigration policy established under the act underwent a significant overhaul twenty-six years later with the enactment of the *Immigration and Refugee Protection Act 2001*.

When the act was introduced in Parliament, the Minister of Immigration made clear that that it was designed to be "tough." She said it aimed to address abuses within the immigration system, impose severe penalties for human smuggling and trafficking, clarify and expand detention provisions, place limitations on family admissions, and facilitate economic immigration to give employers easier access to the "best and brightest" talent worldwide.[9] Introduced following the 2001 terrorist attacks on the

---

8 Details of the act and its significant departure from the past is extensively discussed in Freda Hawkins, *Critical Years in Immigration: Canada and Australia Compared*, 2nd ed. (Montreal: McGill-Queen's University Press, 1991), 70–9.

9 Canada, *House of Commons Debates (Hansard)*, 1 May 2000 (Hon. Elinor Caplan, Minister of Citizenship and Immigration).

United States, the act also gave the government extensive powers to restrict access, to detain, and to remove persons considered security threats.[10]

In a major departure from the *Immigration Act, 1976* (but in keeping with much of the legislation of the previous century), the *Immigration and Refugee Protection Act 2001* is largely skeletal, setting out the framework of immigration policy in broad terms. It provides for the details to be fleshed out with regulations. Regulations are statutory instruments, subject to a rigorous legal process and many must first be considered by Parliament.[11]

The *Immigration and Refugee Protection Act 2001* authorized the minister to issue instructions to immigration officers. Legislative amendments introduced in 2008 considerably widened the scope of this authority.[12] Ministerial Instructions are directives to immigration officers on matters the minister determines necessary to meet "immigration goals."[13] They encompass a wide range of areas, including assessment criteria, ranking systems, quotas, and processing measures for economic and family sponsorship programs. They do not require the same consultation and publication requirements as regulations.[14]

Notably, Ministerial Instructions can be subject to frequent changes and are generally not subject to parliamentary review, further reducing the level of scrutiny from both Parliament and the public.[15] This shift has led to an increased detachment of immigration policy from the oversight of elected representatives. The ability to modify Ministerial Instructions swiftly also introduces an

---

10 Ninette Kelley and Michael Trebilcock, *The Making of the Mosaic*, 2nd ed. (Toronto: University of Toronto Press, 2010), 417, 423, 448–51, 457–8.

11 Laurence Brosseau, *Immigration Policy Primer* (Ottawa: Library of Parliament, 2019), 4, https://lop.parl.ca/sites/PublicWebsite/default/en_CA/ResearchPublications /202005E.

12 *Budget Implementation Act*, 2008, S.C. 2008, c. 28, s. 118.

13 *Immigration and Refugee Protection Act*, S.C. 2001, c. 27, s. 44.1, 87.3 (Can.).

14 Brosseau, *Immigration Policy Primer*, 4.

15 In a few cases, the minister must include in its annual report to Parliament, instructions issued in relation to the ranking of eligible foreign nationals, and those relating to the issuing and revocation of work permits. See *Immigration and Refugee Protection Act 2001*, s. 94.

element of uncertainty regarding how the provisions of the act are applied and how they will be applied in the future.[16]

Compositional Shifts and Escalating Numbers

Since the enactment of the *Immigration and Refugee Protection Act 2001*, new admission avenues have largely supplanted the traditional route within the economic stream. This stream had itself increased from representing only 30-40 per cent of permanent immigration before 1990 to 60 per cent since 2021 (see figure 3).

Provinces and employers have been given substantially larger roles in the selection of economic immigrants. And persons with Canadian work experience as temporary immigrants or as international students have been given new opportunities to become permanent residents (see figure 4). The aim of these changes is to enhance the alignment between skilled immigrants and the demands of the Canadian labour market. However, due to the recent nature of these changes, existing evaluations do not make clear the extent to which improvements may or may not have been achieved.

In 2016, a government advisory group appointed by the Minister of Finance released a report recommending that immigration targets be increased very substantially, to 450,000, within five years.[17] This recommendation appears to have been accepted and has been in the process of implementation.

As well, the number of temporary foreign workers admitted to Canada annually has increased dramatically, particularly since 2015 when numbers grew from 260,000 to over 880,000 in 2023.[18]

---

16 Peter Carver, "A Failed Discourse of Distrust amid Significant Procedural Change: The Harper Government's Legacy in Immigration and Refugee Law," *Review of Constitutional Studies* 21, no. 2 (2016): 227; Triadafilos Triadafilopoulos and Zack Taylor, "The Domestic Politics of Selective Permeability: Disaggregating the Canadian Migration State," *Journal of Ethnic and Migration Studies* 50, no. 3 (2023): 702–25, https://doi.org/10.1080/1369183X.2023.2269785.

17 Government of Canada, Advisory Council on Economic Growth, "The Path to Prosperity: Resetting Canada's Growth Trajectory," 20 October 2016, https://www.budget.canada.ca/aceg-ccce/pdf/pathway-to-prosperity-eng.pdf.

18 The total number of temporary work holders in Canada (newly and previously issued) grew from 322,000 to over 1,270,000 in 2023. See figures 5 and 6.

In most cases, temporary foreign workers have arrived without an employer having to show that Canadian workers are not disadvantaged as a consequence.

There also has been a substantial increase in the number of international students admitted to Canada, from 219,000 in 2015 to 683,000 in 2023, many also holding work permits for temporary employment.[19] These changes require detailed analysis as part of a review of policy under the act.

In the 1990s, family sponsorships, which averaged 34 per cent of annual admissions, began to decline, falling to around 25 per cent in the past two decades. The number of refugees seeking protection within Canada or at its border averaged around 30,000 individuals per year from 2001 to 2021. For reasons discussed later, annual numbers have risen dramatically in the past two years.[20]

There has also been a rise in the number of refugees selected annually from abroad, up from 10,000 to 20,000 persons, consistently representing between 5 and 7 per cent of the total annual immigrant admissions. However, there has been a decline in the proportion of government sponsorships compared to private sponsorships in recent years, dropping from 70 per cent to approximately 40 to 50 per cent. Cumulatively, the total numbers of refugees granted permanent residency in Canada from 2001 to 2015 averaged 27,000 annually, rising to 54,000 in the period from 2016 to 2023 (see figure 3).

Conditions governing family sponsorships have tightened in the contemporary period as have processes to determine refugee claims in Canada. Additionally, the grounds for deporting permanent residents and foreign nationals have broadened and the scope of judicial review narrowed.

---

19 The total number of international student visa holders in Canada (new and previously issued) grew from 352,000 to 1, 041,000 in 2023. See figure 7.

20 Citizenship and Immigration Canada, *Canada Facts and Figures: Immigration Overview Permanent and Temporary Residents 2010* (Ottawa: Public Works and Government Services Canada, 2011), 6–10, https://publications.gc.ca/collections/collection_2011/cic/Ci1-8-2010-eng.pdf. The Immigration, Refugees and Citizenship Canada's *Annual Report to Parliament on Immigration* for the years 2011 to 2022 can be found at https://publications.gc.ca/site/eng/359079/publication.html.

Requirements for becoming a Canadian citizen are now more stringent. Alongside more onerous citizenship requirements, the percentage of permanent residents who become naturalized within ten years of arrival has dropped precipitously: from 75 to 46 per cent between 2001 and 2021.[21]

Demographic Impact

Canada admits more immigrants on a *per capita* basis than most other countries in the world[22] and from increasingly diverse countries of origin. Immigrants make up close to one quarter of the population,[23] and by 2036 this is expected to rise to 36 per cent. The proportion of immigrants to total population is the highest since Confederation, and a larger proportion than that of all other major industrial economies except Australia.[24]

From the turn of the twenty-first century, more than 60 per cent of immigrants to Canada have come from Asia (see figure 1)[25] and 25 per cent from Africa and the Middle East. Most immigrants settle in Toronto, Vancouver, and Montreal contributing to the population growth of

---

21 See Christian Collington, "Percentage of Permanent Residents Becoming Canadian Citizens in Decline, Statscan Data Shows," *Globe and Mail*, 15 February 2023, https://www.theglobeandmail.com/canada/article-percentage-of-permanent-residents-becoming-canadian-citizens-in/. While some speculate that there is a direct correlation between more stringent requirements and falling rates, the issue has not been fully studied. Further discussed in chapter 3.3, "Citizenship: Raising the Bar."

22 Organisation for Economic Co-operation and Development, *International Migration Outlook 2022* (PARIS: OECD Publishing, 2022), 22, https://doi.org/10.1787/30fe16d2-en.

23 Robin Levinson-King, "Canada: Why the Country Wants to Bring in 1.5m Immigrants by 2025," *BBC News*, 22 November 2022, https://www.bbc.com/news/world-us-canada-63643912. In comparison, the immigrant population of the United Kingdom and the United States is 14 per cent.

24 Organisation for Economic Co-operation and Development and European Commission, *Indicators of Immigrant Integration 2023: Settling In* (Paris: OECD Publishing, 2023), https://doi.org/10.1787/1d5020a6-e; Immigration, Refugees and Citizenship Canada, "Canada Welcomes Historic Number of Newcomers in 2022," News Release, 3 January 2023, https://www.canada.ca/en/immigration-refugees-citizenship/news/2022/12/canada-welcomes-historic-number-of-newcomers-in-2022.html.

25 In recent years the leading source countries were India, the Philippines, and the People's Republic of China.

these cities. Nearly half the population of Toronto and Vancouver are of non-European origin compared to 23 per cent for Montreal.

In 2022, Statistics Canada reported that international migration accounted for over 97 per cent of population growth[26] compared to 44 per cent in the 1990s. This trend is expected to continue. The government estimates that, by the year 2032, immigrants will account for 100 per cent of the growth in Canada's population.[27]

Public Support

Over the last decade, in the United States and across Europe, elections have been fought and often won on populist, anti-immigration rhetoric. It was a major factor in Britain's vote to leave the European Union.[28] In contrast, for decades Canada has enjoyed a high level of public support for immigration, notwithstanding current concerns over the dramatic increase in annual admission levels. This "Canadian exceptionalism"[29] is reflected in higher proportions of the population saying that immigrants make the country stronger rather than being a burden.[30]

---

26 Statistics Canada, "Canada's Population Estimates: Record-High Population Growth in 2022," *The Daily*, 22 March 2023, https://www150.statcan.gc.ca/n1/daily-quotidien/230322/dq230322f-eng.htm.

27 Immigration, Refugees and Citizenship Canada, "An Immigration Plan to Grow the Economy," News Release, 1 November 2022, https://www.canada.ca/en/immigration-refugees-citizenship/news/2022/11/an-immigration-plan-to-grow-the-economy.html.

28 Hungary, Austria, Denmark, Holland, France, Germany, Italy, Sweden, and Britain (with the latter's decision to exit from the EU in a referendum in June 2016 prompted in part over concerns with unrestricted internal EU immigration). See Rita Chin, *The Crisis of Multiculturalism in Europe: A History* (Princeton, NJ: Princeton University Press, 2017). In 2016, US President Donald Trump was elected on a conservative immigration platform and again in 2024, promising mass deportations of illegal aliens and to clamp down on authorized arrivals through the southern and northern borders.

29 Bloemraad, *Understanding "Canadian Exceptionalism" in Immigration and Pluralism Policy*.

30 Ana Gonzales-Barrera and Philipp Connor, "Around the World, More Say Immigrants Are a Strength Than a Burden," Pew Research Center, 14 March 2019, https://www.pewresearch.org/global/2019/03/14/around-the-world-more-say-immigrants-are-a-strength-than-a-burden/.

Political parties have sought support from immigrant voters by adopting policies that appealed to them. As experts on Canadian multiculturalism, Keith Banting and Will Kymlicka, put it, "political parties in Canada now understand that running against immigrants is a short route to political oblivion."[31]

But it is also the case that there remains a sizable minority – some thirty per cent of those polled – who do not agree that immigrants enhance their communities. Among this minority, many are concerned that Canada accepts too many immigrants from racialized cultures, posing a threat to prevailing culture and identity. This minority view has remained stable over the past decades, despite increases in immigration numbers in the 1990s, fears raised by terrorist attacks in 2001, and subsequently, the global recession of 2008.[32]

Aside from debates over the number of immigrants Canada needs, criticism of immigration policy also focuses on specific aspects raised by individuals and groups most directly impacted. Examples range from the tightening of family sponsorship requirements, the expansion of temporary worker programs, raising citizenship requirements, and placing limitations on the legal rights of immigrants and refugees in matters affecting their status. The federal government has also been criticized for failing to ensure settlement services are adequately resourced while annual immigration levels rise.

As noted at the outset, a new volatility in Canadian attitudes towards immigration in general has appeared in 2023. Evidently, critics of immigration have become more numerous, and concerns are being raised. Recent shifts in some programs show sensitivity to public opinion but not to calls for greater transparency. Declining public support for high annual immigration levels underscore the importance of looking more closely at the justifications for

---

31 Keith Banting and Will Kymlicka, "Introduction: The Political Sciences of Solidarity in Diverse Societies," in *The Strains of Commitment: The Political Sources of Solidarity in Diverse Societies*, ed. Keith Banting and Will Kymlicka (Oxford: Oxford University Press, 2017), 27–8.

32 Environics Institute, *Canadian Public Opinion about Immigration and Refugees – Focus Canada* (Fall 2022), 3.

increased numbers, at the impact of selection policies, and at the underlying policy decision-making processes.

Canadian Exceptionalism

Geography

There are various explanations for Canada's uniquely positive views on immigration.[33] One is geography. Canada has natural geographic impediments to the kind of large-scale, unauthorized migration in other countries, where anti-immigrant sentiment runs high. Even in Canada, however, relatively small influxes of refugees and unauthorized migrants have provoked public furor and exaggerated concerns over the integrity of borders. But such episodes have been short-lived and limited in size.[34] Political and public apprehensions of "losing control of our borders" are not nearly as intense in Canada as in many other Western countries.[35]

Inclusive Yet Controlled Admission Policies

As immigration became more diverse in the years following the Second World War, Canada was able to maintain public support by its careful approach to immigrant selection. In the aftermath of the war, Canada experienced strong economic growth and faced a labour shortage that could not be fulfilled solely by immigrants from "preferred countries" in the United Kingdom and Europe. It also faced a steady exodus of skilled Canadians to the rapidly growing US economy.

As a result, there was a partial easing of admission criteria to enable immigration from a larger number of source countries, though still primarily from within Europe. Restrictions remained

---

33 Trebilcock, "The Puzzle of Canadian Exceptionalism."
34 Discussed further throughout Part I: An Historical Reprise.
35 Robert Kaplan, *The Revenge of Geography: What the Map Tells Us About Coming Conflicts and the Battle Against Fate* (New York: Random House, 2012).

in place for immigrants from most other parts of the world, including British subjects other than those from the United Kingdom, Australia, New Zealand, or the Union of South Africa.[36]

The international human rights and anti-discrimination treaties that emerged after the war were inconsistent with Canada's racially selective admissions criteria. Canada came under increasing external and internal pressure to bring its immigration policies into line with its international obligations.[37]

Internally, various faith-based groups, ethnic associations, academics, and legal advocates – later joined by Members of Parliament, some trade unions, and members of the press – insisted that Canadian immigration policy be reformed. Officials within the Department of External Affairs had long observed that the country's discriminatory immigration policy was not in keeping with "Canada's carefully crafted image as a progressive 'middle power.'"[38]

The combined pressures from these different sources and an ongoing demand for immigrant labour eventually led to Canada opening its immigration policies in the early 1960s to more areas of the world. By 1976, all remaining explicit racial and ethnic based selection was removed from the *Immigration Act*.

At the same time, Canada adopted a points-based immigration selection process for most immigrant applicants, allowing it to still carefully choose immigrants based on the likelihood that they would be able to successfully establish themselves. The number

---

36 Order in Council, P.C. 1956–785 and P.C 1956, 785.

37 Triadafilos Triadafilopoulos, *Becoming Multicultural: Immigration and the Politics of Membership in Canada and Germany* (Toronto: University of Toronto Press, 2012), 65–6. According to Triadafilopoulos, Jamaica, Barbados, Trinidad, and the other island states in the West Indies were among the most vocal critics of Canadian immigration policy. See also Jeffrey G. Reitz, "The Institutional Structure of Immigration as a Determinant of Inter-Racial Competition: A Comparison of Britain and Canada," *The International Migration Review* 22, no. 1 (1988): 117–46, https://doi.org/10.2307/2546399.

38 Triadafilopoulos, *Becoming Multicultural*, 70. To control the immigration to Canada of non-white British immigrants, Canada passed regulations that specified the source countries of admissible immigrants limited them to British "white dominions." See Part I: An Historic Reprise.

and location of visa offices also reflected preferences for immigrants from certain regions over others, as did family sponsorship provisions that were more restrictive for immigrants from certain regions.

So, while the elimination of overt racial and ethnic preferences opened admissions from more regions of the world, selection processes meant that the doors were not entirely wide open, which helped to forestall fears of unregulated immigration.[39]

Provincial and Local Engagement

Provincial involvement in immigrant selection in itself may also contribute to ongoing positive attitudes over immigration, even if the selection process being used in each province is not widely known. As discussed later in this book, earlier periods of history saw significant friction between various provinces and the federal government over federal immigration policy. This began to change in the 1970s with the first federal-provincial agreement with Quebec, an agreement that has evolved to give Quebec increased autonomy in managing immigration to the province.

Under the agreement with the federal government, Quebec maintains its own point system for evaluating economic immigrant applicants, giving priority to French-speaking individuals and skilled workers in high-demand sectors. Quebec also maintains exclusive jurisdiction over immigrant integration services and mandates French-language instruction in the public school system for most immigrant children. The agreement has allowed Quebec to tailor its immigration policies and services to its specific cultural and economic needs.

---

39   Reitz, "The Institutional Structure of Immigration." In this respect the Canadian and British postwar experiences were different. British policy was to permit admission without distinction from anyone from the former British Empire and all members of the British Commonwealth. This stoked fears of unrestricted admission from the developing world. Black and brown immigrants faced increased hostility. Negative perceptions of immigrants eventually led Britain to change its policy and introduce criteria like that in Canada in the late 1960s, though many in Britain regarded those criteria as racially discriminatory.

The Provincial Nominee Program, embodied in federal-provincial agreements signed over the period 1998 to 2009, permits other provinces and territories to identify a certain number of immigrants destined for their regions. The aim has been to give more devolved control over the selection of immigrants aligned with specific regional labour-force requirements.[40] This may help to explain their ongoing support for immigration policy. The operation of the program, the characteristics of provincially nominated immigrants, and their integration in the labour market and society are examined in chapter 2.1, "Economic Stream."

Similarly, federal partnerships with civil society organizations in delivering settlement support and integration services may also contribute to fostering a broad social and political consensus in favour of an expansive immigration policy.[41]

Role of Public Information

In this context, we would raise a question about the role of public information in immigration policy-making. The popularity of immigration in Canada, supported by the idea of "multiculturalism" as part of the national identity, may have helped to insulate immigration policy-making from more intense public scrutiny. A system that has enjoyed broad support for decades may become less concerned to provide detailed data on its operation. Consequently, positive perceptions of immigration are more likely to predominate due to a lack of data that could illuminate areas of difficulty.

An absence of compelling evidence may mask problems. Significant changes to immigration levels and to admission and removal policies have largely been made without rigorous transparent studies or evaluations of possible impacts. Often, changes have

---

40 F. Leslie Seidle, *Canada's Provincial Nominee Immigration Programs: Securing Greater Policy Alignment*, IRPP Study, No. 43 (Montreal: Institute for Research on Public Policy, 2013).

41 Daniel Hiebert, *What's So Special about Canada? Understanding the Resilience of Immigration and Multiculturalism* (Washington, DC: Migration Policy Institute, 2016), 1, https://www.migrationpolicy.org/sites/default/files/publications/TCM-Trust -Canada-FINAL.pdf.

been justified as necessary to address demographic needs, curb abuse, or maintain border and internal security without providing in-depth analysis in support of the changes. Impact targets are not built into policy shifts to assess their effect, and detailed data to conduct independent analyses and reviews are increasingly hard to find and often inaccessible.

The absence of information and the potential insights derivable from such information are particularly important in a period of very rapid policy change, such as we have seen in Canada in recent years. As systems have become more complex, review and analysis by independent researchers has become more difficult. As a result, the public does not benefit from a robust and informed public discourse.

Rising numbers of immigrants, temporary workers, and international students have captured headlines, but the potential impacts of these changes are only discussed superficially. Public information about the performance of various expanding immigration programs remains limited and many problems are not brought to light. While it remains premature to draw definitive conclusions, there are indications that the once-solid consensus on immigration policy is showing signs of stress.

Fault Lines

Numbers and Impact

The plan to substantially increase annual admissions of permanent residents had not been immediately conveyed in the immigration ministers' annual reports to Parliament.[42] Although, as mentioned, an Advisory Council on Economic Growth report had recommended in 2016 that Canada move to an annual immigration target

---

42 The Immigration, Refugees and Citizenship Canada's *Annual Report to Parliament on Immigration* for the years 2014 to 2023 can be found at https://www.canada.ca /en/immigration-refugees-citizenship/corporate/publications-manuals/annual -reports-parliament-immigration.html.

of 450,000 admissions within five years, the targets set in annual reports to Parliament rose only slowly from year to year. In some cases, actual numbers exceeded the stated targets (except of course 2020, when the COVID-19 pandemic restricted immigration and numbers were extraordinarily low; see figure 2). The first annual report to include a target greater than 400,000 was in 2020 for the following year. Fully embracing the target of 450,000 was included in the 2022 report, projected for 2024, though it was exceeded in 2023.

In announcing the 2022 annual admissions plan, Minister Sean Fraser explained that higher immigration levels were necessary to accelerate economic growth and meet labour market needs.[43] He pointed to Canada's aging population and declining birthrates, suggesting that younger immigrants will not only meet gaps in labour supply but also help support social service programs. Immediately following the government's announcement, the Business Council of Canada enthusiastically supported it.

The new and elevated levels since 2015 have been the focus of considerable critiques. Economists have long questioned the rationale, suggesting that the economic benefits of immigration have been exaggerated. They point to evidence showing that while significant increases in immigration expand the economy, immigration has little effect on per capita gross domestic product, which in effect measures how well-off people are.[44]

In 2021, the Organisation for Economic Co-operation and Development reported that Canada had relatively low GDP per capita growth and predicted it would be the worst performing advanced economy for the 2020–30 period.[45]

---

43 Sean Fraser, *2022 Annual Report to Parliament on Immigration* (Ottawa: Immigration, Refugees and Citizenship Canada, 2022), https://publications.gc.ca/collections/collection_2022/ircc/Ci1-2022-eng.pdf.

44 For a review of the literature, see Matthew Doyle, Mikal Skuterud, and Christopher Worswick, "Optimizing Immigration for Economic Growth," C.D. Howe Institute Commentary No. 662 (Toronto: C.D. Howe Institute, 2024).

45 Yvan Guillemette and David Turner, "The Long Game: Fiscal Outlooks to 2060 Underline Need for Structural Reform," *OECD Economic Policy Papers*, No. 29 (Paris: OECD Publishing, 2021), https://doi.org/10.1787/a112307e-en; Business

There are numerous factors contributing to Canada's current and anticipated decline in economic productivity, including competition, education, infrastructure, immigration, foreign investment, and research and development policies. Isolating the individual impact of each presents a challenge. The influence of immigration policy on the productivity of the Canadian labour force hinges on whether immigrants bring skills or work experience that are consistently in short supply.

Economists and leading Canadian banks suggest that the surge in permanent and temporary immigration is contributing to slow productivity growth. They point to the fact that employers have an abundant supply of low-cost labour that has helped less productive or uncompetitive firms stay in business. Moreover, this has dampened incentives to invest in technological and processes improvements and in education and skills development to enable the local work force to meet labour demand.[46]

Council of British Columbia, "OECD Predicts Canada Will Be the Worst Performing Advanced Economy over the next Decade … and the Three Decades after That," *Business Council of British Columbia* (blog), 14 December 2021, https://bcbc.com /insight/oecd-predicts-canada-will-be-the-worst-performing-advanced-economy -over-the-next-decade-and-the-three-decades-after-that/; Philip Cross, "Canada's Per-Person GDP Growing at Slowest Rate Since the Great Depression," *The Quarterly* (Fall 2023), 2–3, https://www.fraserinstitute.org/sites/default/files/quarterly -fall-2023.pdf.

46 Rebekah Young, "Raising the Bar, Not Just Lowering the Number: Canada's Immigration Policy Confronts Critical Choices," Scotia Bank, 21 March 2024, https:// www.scotiabank.com:443/content/scotiabank/ca/en/about/economics/economics -publications/post.other-publications.insights-views.canada-s-immigration-policy --march-21--2024-.html; David Dodge, "Economic Outlook: The Long Term Is Now," Bennett Jones, 11 December 2023, https://www.bennettjones.com/Events-Section /Economic-Outlook-The-Long-Term-is-Now; Tristen Hopper, "How Record-High Immigration Could Be Hurting Canadian Productivity," *National Post*, 13 December 2023, https://nationalpost.com/opinion/first-reading-how-record-high -immigration-could-be-hurting-canadian-productivity; Matt Lundy, "Canada Stuck in 'Population Trap,' Needs to Reduce Immigration, Bank Economists Say," *Globe and Mail*, 15 January 2024, https://www.theglobeandmail.com/business/article -canada-stuck-in-population-trap-needs-to-reduce-immigration-bank/; David Green, "No, Immigration Is Not Some Magic Pill for Saving the Economy," *Globe and Mail*, 25 December 2022, https://www.theglobeandmail.com/business/commentary /article-no-immigration-is-not-some-magic-pill-for-saving-the-economy/; Matt Lundy, "Canada Wants to Welcome Immigrants," *Globe and Mail*, 26 November 2022, https://

Aging Population

Some critics have also raised questions about the demographic justification behind the escalation of annual immigration targets. The government argues that as the baby boomer generation reaches retirement age, there will be a decline in the ratio of working individuals to non-working individuals in the coming years. Consequently, a higher number of younger immigrants is necessary to mitigate the negative effects of an aging population.[47]

However, immigration as a solution to population aging has been debunked by demographers. A major comparative United Nations Study published in 2000 concluded that only extremely high levels of immigration would be able to offset population aging.[48]

Contemporary commentators have also cast doubt on whether the government's planned increase will be able to significantly mitigate the negative effects of an aging population. Immigrants are only somewhat younger than the current resident population, and the projected increase in young immigrants will not be enough to substantially change the overall dependency ratio. As well, immigrants might not offset population aging because they are only slightly younger, have fewer children, and live longer.[49]

---

www.theglobeandmail.com/business/article-canada-immigration-population-boom
/; Jim Stamford, "Interrogating the Labour Shortage Hypothesis," The Center
for Future Work, 11 October 2023, https://centreforfuturework.ca/2023/10/11
/interrogating-the-labour-shortage-hypothesis/.

47 Lundy, "Canada Wants to Welcome Immigrants."

48 United Nations, *Replacement Migration: Is It a Solution to Declining and Ageing Populations?* (New York: United Nations, Population Division, Department of Economic and Social Affairs, 2000). For a brief summary, see Leon F. Bouvier, "Replacement Migration: Is It a Solution to Declining and Aging Populations?," *Population and Environment* 22, no. 4 (2001): 377–81. The study examined the following eight countries: France, Germany, Italy, Japan, Republic of Korea, Russian Federation, United Kingdom, and United States. An analysis confirming the applicability of the findings to Canada was provided by Roderic Beaujot, "Effect of Immigration on Demographic Structure," in *Canadian Immigration Policy for the 21st Century*, ed. Charles M. Beach, Alan G. Green, and Jeffrey G. Reitz (Montreal: McGill-Queen's University Press, and John Deutsch Institute for the Study of Economic Policy, 2003), 49–91.

49 Beaujot, "Effect of Immigration on Demographic Structure."

Housing

Many commentators critical of high immigration levels voice concern over the impact of significant immigration on an already-strained housing supply. Home prices continue to rise and the rental vacancy rate is the lowest since 1988 when national records were first compiled.[50]

Rising home prices, and too few rental options, have led to what is commonly described as an "affordability crisis." This was one of the chief issues raised by candidates in the 2023 Toronto mayoral elections and echoed in immigrant-receiving areas across the country. A 2003 national poll on immigration showed that concern about the effect of immigration on housing prices was the most important factor in the decline in support for current immigration levels.[51]

A lack of housing options presents deep challenges for the existing working population. And, as the Canada Mortgage and Housing Corporation points out, it is also a disincentive to potential skilled immigrant workers.[52] The government's response is that labour gaps in the construction trades will be met by more skilled immigrants. Others claim that the problem is complex and cannot be solved with more construction workers alone.

The problem itself is located where the authority of federal, provincial, and municipal government intersects. Demand for housing is increased through immigration, run largely at the national level, with some provincial devolution. The supply of housing is heavily dependent on municipal and provincial policies.

---

50 Canada Mortgage and Housing Corporation, "Canada's Vacancy Rate Reaches New Low as Demand Outpaces Supply," News Release, 31 January 2024; Joe Hood, "Housing Affordability Woes Have Spilled over to Rental Market, CMHC Report Finds," *Financial Post*, 26 January 2023, sec. Real Estate, https://financialpost.com/real-estate/cmhc-rental-vacancy-rate-lowest-two-decades; Kelly Cryderman, "Alberta, and the Rest of Canada, Are Woefully Unprepared for the Coming Immigration Boom," *Globe and Mail*, 25 July 2023, https://www.theglobeandmail.com/opinion/article-alberta-and-the-rest-of-canada-are-woefully-unprepared-for-the-coming/.

51 Environics Institute, *Canadian Public Opinion about Immigration and Refugees* (Fall 2023).

52 Lundy, "Canada Wants to Welcome Immigrants."

This can create a mismatch in accountability for the impact of immigration on housing. Increasing the supply of affordable homes often involves adjusting provincial and municipal regulations. That can take years. Meanwhile, immigration and housing policies are developed in isolation, and some predict that, without better coordination, the housing crisis will continue to deepen.[53]

Other factors also contribute to housing shortages, including disruptions in supply chains and high interest rates, which more immigration does not alleviate.

Health Services

Concerns about the capacity of health services to accommodate the growth in new arrivals have been increasingly raised. Shortages in family, specialized, and emergency health care services are prevalent throughout the country.[54] Critics argue that relying solely on immigration to bring in more medical personnel will not effectively address the issues related to service delivery and infrastructure.

Commentators also point out that stringent recognition requirements for foreign credentials, which differ across provinces, also create obstacles. Unless these requirements are significantly eased and harmonized, the influx of foreign-trained health care workers may not effectively address the gaps in health care delivery. There is also a risk that these immigrants may end up working in positions that are below their qualified level, rather than filling the

---

53 Steve Lafleur and Josef Filipowicz, "Canada's Housing and Immigration Policies Are at Odds," *Globe and Mail*, 10 April 2023, https://www.theglobeandmail.com/opinion/article-canadas-housing-and-immigration-policies-are-at-odds/.

54 A Royal Bank of Canada study points out that Canada falls below the OECD average in number of physicians per capita and the shortage is anticipated to grow to 40,000 by 2028. See Ben Richardson, Yadullah Hussain, and Naomi Powell, "Canada Needs More Doctors – and Fast," RBC Thought Leadership, 23 November 2022, https://thoughtleadership.rbc.com/proof-point-canada-needs-more-doctors-and-fast/; Tony Keller, "Canada Has a Doctor Shortage. But If Governments Wanted, We Could Have a Doctor Surplus," *Globe and Mail*, 4 August 2023, https://www.theglobeandmail.com/business/commentary/article-canada-has-a-doctor-shortage-but-if-governments-wanted-we-could-have-a/.

more critical gaps in health care services. This can result in more immigrants working in jobs that they are overqualified to do.[55]

Integration

Support for the integration of immigrants into society is another area that is often highlighted as underfunded and ill-prepared to meet current demands, let alone increased needs. Integration services are provided by federal, provincial, and civil society partners, relying on various sources of funding, most of which are short-term. The lack of coordination among federal, provincial, and municipal governments has long been a point of frustration for front-line workers, who consistently find themselves having to secure funds for projects with limited long-term sustainability.

Criticism is also directed at funding models that prioritize the meeting of targets rather than the proper measurement of long-term success. Increased immigration levels have raised concerns among many settlement service providers, who emphasize the need to scale resources to ensure that newcomers have help to secure employment, find suitable housing, and receive necessary support, including language training, mentorship, and connection with services in the community.[56] Chapter 3.2 on immigrant integration considers both short-term and long-term processes of integration and government policies intended to affect each.

Processing

As the government has expanded annual immigration admissions, attention has been drawn to persistent administrative backlogs that could grow further.

Each year the government reports on its ability to meet its own processing standards for applications across all immigrant

---

55   Green, "No, Immigration Is Not Some Magic Pill."
56   David Moscrop, "Canada Must Support the Migrants It's Letting in to Fill Jobs," *Washington Post*, 18 November 2022, https://www.washingtonpost.com/opinions /2022/11/18/canada-migrants-economy-jobs/.

streams. In May 2023, Immigration Refugees and Citizenship Canada revealed that 51 per cent of all its permanent residence applications were in a backlog of cases that have not met service standards. This does not bode well for its ability to meet processing standards for future annual admissions,[57] nor do the findings of a recent Auditor General of Canada report issued in October 2023.

The report highlighted substantial backlogs within all major immigration programs as of the close of 2022. The Auditor General's findings revealed disparities in both the magnitude and age of application backlogs, varying depending on the country of citizenship. Moreover, several overseas offices handling significant immigration workloads had notably fewer staff compared to others with considerably lighter workloads.

Backlogs were found to be higher in the refugee and humanitarian class than in the family class, and lowest in the economic class. While the report confirmed that the implementation of "Express Entry," an online system for management of applications from skilled workers introduced in 2015 (described in chapter 2.1, "Economic Stream") had reduced backlogs as intended, the backlogs were far from eliminated. Importantly, the Auditor General also found that the government had not monitored the impact of the automated eligibility-assessment tool for economic immigrants. This prevented it from assessing whether the tool was effectively reducing processing times for all applicants as originally intended, or from identifying and rectifying any unintended disparities in outcomes for applicants.[58]

This book does not intend to evaluate directly the pros and cons of higher or lower annual immigration levels. However, any such assessment should rely on evidence and analysis of the efficacy of underlying policies rather than on arbitrary targets that drive the

---

57 Edana Robitaille, "IRCC Inventory Stands at 2 Million Applications," *CIC News*, 27 May 2023, https://www.cicnews.com/2023/05/ircc-inventory-stands-at -2-million-applications-0535128.html.

58 Auditor General of Canada, "Report 9 – Processing Applications for Permanent Residence – Immigration, Refugees and Citizenship Canada," *Report of the Auditor General of Canada* (Ottawa: Office of the Auditor General of Canada, 2023).

policies. And the apparent absence of that is a source of additional concern, to which we now turn.

Information, Transparency, and Public Debate

As mentioned above, the availability of information concerning immigration selection processes and admissions, trends, and impact is a key aspect of administrative transparency with important implications for the quality of public debate. Many researchers have experienced increasing difficulty in accessing clear and consistent data on all aspects of Canada's immigration program.

Longitudinal data – collected repeatedly from the same subjects over an extended duration – that was once made easily accessible by the government is no longer readily available and access to information requests go unanswered. This despite the passage of the *Access to Information Act* forty years ago, which granted individuals the right to request access to records under the control of federal government institutions. It also mandated the government institutions to respond within a specific period, commonly within thirty days.

But the government is exempt from providing certain sensitive or confidential material, although it must justify reasons for withholding it. Decisions to withhold information can be appealed to the Canadian Information Commissioner. In 2023, investigative reporting by the *Globe and Mail* revealed the extent to which the access to information system had broken down.[59] These were also revealed in a House of Commons Standing Committee report, *The State of Canada's Access to Information System*, published in June 2023.[60]

Delays are endemic, ranging from months to years. Critics claim that the information released is often heavily redacted without

---

59   "Secret Canada Is a Freedom of Information Project from The Globe and Mail," Secret Canada, accessed 28 June 2024 from https://www.secretcanada.com.

60   Standing Committee on and Access to Information, Privacy and Ethics, *The State of Canada's Access to Information System*, 9 June 2023, https://www.ourcommons .ca/DocumentViewer/en/44-1/ETHI/report-9/. The committee began its work in October 2022. It received twelve briefs and heard forty-two witnesses. The committee's ninety-nine-page report includes thirty-eight recommendations.

convincing justification and that enforcement mechanisms are weak, while penalties for non-compliance are insufficient.

The number of access requests received by Immigration, Refugees, and Citizenship Canada is disproportionately high, around 80 per cent of all such requests to the federal government. And over the past decade, there has been an increase of over 760 per cent in the number of these requests. Almost 90 per cent of them relate to specific cases where applications have either been refused or experienced significant processing delays. In 2024, the Information Commissioner updated her findings of the previous year, noting the lack of progress by Immigration Refugees and Citizenship Canada "on providing applicants with an alternative method of obtaining information related to their file."[61]

This trend emerges because immigration applicants are typically provided with limited information throughout the application and determination process. In many instances, if their case encounters delays, they are left uninformed, and if their application is rejected, they may receive only a brief and perfunctory explanation. As a result, filing an access to information request becomes the only avenue for them to gain insight into the reasons behind the issues they encountered with their case.[62]

Immigration, Refugees, and Citizenship Canada has reportedly been aware of the lack of capacity to handle the increasing volume of access to information requests for some time. Critics claim that no substantial efforts have been made to address the problem, which is expected to worsen as the number of unanswered requests continues to rise. Critics also question why the government does

---

61 Carolyn Maynard, *Access at Issue: the Unsustainable Status Quo*, Special Report to Parliament (Ottawa: Information Commissioner to Canada, 2024), 3, https://www.oic-ci.gc.ca/en/resources/reports-publications/access-issue-unsustainable-status-quo.

62 In October 2023, Treasury Minister Anita Anand acknowledged that the government shared many of the committee's concerns but that the federal access to information regime would not be reviewed until 2025. In the meantime, it would focus on some priority areas. See Tom Cardoso and Robyn Doolittle, "Canada's Immigration System Is Overwhelmed with Information Requests. Ottawa Was Warned – but Did Nothing," *Globe and Mail*, 16 June 2023, https://www.theglobeandmail.com/canada/article-immigration-applications-access-requests/.

not systematically provide applicants with reasons for processing delays or rejected decisions, which would significantly alleviate the problem and introduce greater transparency and accountability into the process.[63]

While policy-related access to information requests constitute only one per cent of the total requests made to Immigration, Refugees, and Citizenship Canada, they still represent a significant number of inquiries.[64] Researchers and analysts also complain of long delays in responses and requests that go unanswered or that are only partially met. These obstacles greatly hinder efforts to gain a deeper understanding of the rationale behind policy changes and to conduct thorough evaluations of their performance and impact.

The importance of fostering public dialogue on future immigration plans is clear in commentary covering immigration levels, targets, integration capacity, and the absence of comprehensive data and evidence. That significance is matched by the need for mechanisms to assess their effectiveness. Without the means for proper scrutiny, it is not possible to effectively evaluate government policies and determine the validity of the criticisms leveled against them. This concern is a central theme throughout this book.

In the debate surrounding projected immigration levels, for example, many observers point to the lack of informed public discussion that would enable a thorough analysis of the underlying rationale. There is also a growing demand for a comprehensive review and deeper discussion on the goals of immigration policy. Policy formation should be closely aligned with these goals and accompanied by concrete measures to assess the impact of policy changes.[65]

---

63 Cardoso and Doolittle, "Canada's Immigration System Is Overwhelmed."

64 For example, in 2022, 177,000 access to information requests were made to Immigration Refugees and Citizenship Canada. Cardoso and Doolittle, "Canada's Immigration System Is Overwhelmed."

65 The Editorial Board, "Canada's Immigration Plan Should Involve More than Just Big Numbers," *Globe and Mail*, 7 January 2023, https://www.theglobeandmail.com /opinion/editorials/article-canadas-immigration-plan-should-involve-more-than -just-big-numbers/. The Editorial Board of the *Globe and Mail* suggests that a goal for economic immigration could be that the earnings of economic immigrants should outstrip the national average. It then should ensure reliable data to measure progress and adjust immigration levels based on whether the benchmark is being met.

We agree with these calls for action. Immigration continues to enrich Canada and public support for immigrants is evident. But as we enter the next transformative era in Canadian immigration history, it is crucial to have confidence that contemporary policies are grounded in sound reasoning, with proper measures in place to evaluate their impact.

As one commentator wisely warns, we must carefully analyse the situation to determine if we are exacerbating critical problems for which we have yet to find solutions.[66] Without such analysis, we run the risk of pursuing a policy where the benefits of planned immigration levels may not ultimately outweigh the costs, potentially straining the enduring support for immigration in Canada.

Ideas, Interests, and Institutions in Policy Evolution

In describing and evaluating contemporary immigration policy, we have tried to identify the key ideas, interests, and institutions across all immigration-related dimensions. As in other Western democracies, immigration policy has always reflected complex sets of interactions between ideas or values, interests, and the institutions – political, bureaucratic, and legal – through which ideas and interests or values are mediated. Elsewhere, we have looked at how these have shaped Canadian immigration policy over time.[67]

At the heart of debates over immigration policy are two core ideas that stand, to some irreducible degree, in opposition to each other: liberty and community. Liberalism prioritizes individual rights and freedoms. That includes the right of the individual to move, to own property, and to be treated equally. Applied to migration, principles of liberalism have underpinned arguments

66 Gary Mason, "It's Not Racist or Xenophobic to Question Our Immigration Policy," *Globe and Mail*, 5 January 2023, https://www.theglobeandmail.com/opinion/article-its-not-racist-or-xenophobic-to-question-our-immigration-policy/.
67 Kelley and Trebilcock, *Making of the Mosaic*.

in favour of the free movement of people. Proponents of this view claim that this increases individual productivity and often enhances trade, financial, knowledge, and technology flows between home and host countries through networks that reduce information costs and enhance trust.

In opposition to these liberal values stand the core values of community. In the context of immigration policy, communitarians assert that controlling which strangers might enter is a powerful expression of a nation's identity and autonomy. Sovereignty means the unlimited power of a nation, like that of a free individual, to decide whether, under what conditions, and with what effect it will consent to enter a relationship with a stranger.[68]

In Canada's case, Indigenous peoples found their traditional ways of life radically disrupted by successive waves of immigrants in ways to which they never consented. Finding ways to redress the gross injustices perpetrated on them remains a challenge that Canada continues to grapple with to this day.

There are two prominent controversial features of communitarian theories of immigration. One is that political sovereignty is a near-absolute value. This view is increasingly challenged by the evolution of international human rights norms. The second is that the only communities of character are those that reflect ethnic, religious, cultural, or ideological commonalities. Many liberals would oppose this notion, arguing that communities of character can also be sustained through shared dedication to liberal civic institutions and toleration of other cultures.

However, many communitarian concerns are echoed in contemporary critiques of multiculturalism. These stress that liberal immigration policies may entail the admission of immigrants often from fragile or conflicted states. These people may have discordant religious, cultural, social, political, or economic values that may compromise national unity in receiving countries. This has the

---

68 Peter Schuck, "The Transformation of Immigration Law," *Columbia Law Review* 84, no. 1 (1984): 6, https://www.jstor.org/stable/1122369.

potential to hinder the effective response to new domestic and foreign policy challenges, weaken the social cohesion that supports widely endorsed social policies, and diminish social cohesion that generates valuable forms of community involvement.[69]

In any political community, the ideas of liberty and community are typically articulated by interest groups. Some interest groups will have a reasonably well-defined material self-interest in relation to the issues in question. Other interest groups will include community, church, and public interest groups with no direct self-interest in relation to the issue but a commitment in principle to particular ideas or values.

Canadian immigration history reveals that business groups have tended to favour a permissive immigration policy. They view a growing population base as likely to increase aggregate demand for goods and services, and thus enhance the prosperity of the business sector. A steady and abundant supply of labour helps minimize risks of labour shortfalls and helps to constrain local wage levels.

Labour groups have traditionally favoured an immigration policy that prioritizes family reunification and ensures that the admission of economic immigrants does not adversely affect local workers. Ethnic groups too have tended to support generous family reunification processes and lobbied for admission of those with similar ethnic, cultural, religious, or political backgrounds.

Ethno-nationalists – who, in contemporary times, often avoid racist language – argue that some groups of immigrants are less inclined to integrate with the broader community and so weaken common social bonds and purposes. Arrayed against them are

---

69 See, for example, Paul Brimelow, *Alien Nation: Common Sense about America's Immigration Disaster* (New York: Random House 1995); Patrick Buchanan, *The Death of the West: How Dying Populations and Immigrant Invasions Imperil Our Country and Civilization* (New York: St. Martin's Press, 2002); Samuel Huntington, *Who Are We? Challenges to America's National Identity* (New York: Simon and Schuster, 2005); Arthur Schlesinger, *The Disuniting of America: Reflections on a Multicultural Society* (New York: W.W. Norton, 1992); Brian Barry, *Culture and Equality: An Egalitarian Critique of Multiculturalism* (Boston: Harvard University Press, 2002); and Paul Collier, *Exodus: How Migration Is Changing Our World* (New York: Oxford University Press, 2013).

various civil liberties and human rights organizations and advocates who oppose any form of discriminatory immigration policies. They have pressed for firmer and ongoing commitments to admitting forcibly displaced and persecuted people.

Most interest groups prefer immigrants who will be productive members of the community and contribute more, in the way of taxes, than the costs they impose in terms of increased educational, health, unemployment, housing, law enforcement, and social welfare expenditures. Related to this are concerns that admissions policies do not place undue strain on housing and health care or necessitate major new public expenditures.

While ideas and interests are clearly important in determining public policy outcomes, they must be mediated through institutions to be translated into public policy. Institutions often exert an independent influence on which interests and ideas in particular domains of policy are marginalized or accommodated and what information or data are relevant to policy decisions. They assume an important role in the explanation of policy outputs.[70] This is especially true in the contemporary period.

Immigration, Refugees and Citizenship Canada administers the *Immigration Refugee Protection Act 2001* and the *Citizenship Act* and reports to the Minister of Citizenship, Immigration, and Refugees.[71] The *Immigration Refugee Protection Act* confers broad discretion upon the minister in the setting and administration of immigration policy. As a result, the executive branch has once again assumed a dominant role in the immigration domain at the expense of greater parliamentary and judicial oversight.

---

70   Michael M. Atkinson, *Governing Canada: Institutions and Public Policy* (Toronto: Harcourt Brace & Company Canada, 1993).

71   Also of note is that, soon after the *Immigration and Refugee Protection Act 2001* came into force, the Canadian Border Services Agency (CBSA) was created by regulation. CBSA is responsible for border control and reports to the Minister of Public Safety and Emergencies. It replaced the Canadian Customs and Revenue Agency, the enforcement branch of the Department of Immigration and the border examination responsibilities of the Canadian Food and Inspection Agency. CBSA works closely with Immigration Refugees and Citizenship Canada in carrying out its responsibilities for border control and removal of inadmissible immigrants and refugees.

Structure of the Book

This book has three parts.

Part I provides an overview of the history of Canadian immigration policy. Canadians often note with pride that they are a nation of immigrants. What is not as readily acknowledged is that, throughout much of our history, immigration policies were designed to exclude individuals based on their race, aiming to admit only those considered of "superior stock." They were also designed to expedite removal of immigrants who were found to be unfit due to their political beliefs, reliance on social assistance, or involvement in criminal activities.

In contrast to past periods, current immigration policies are relatively open and non-discriminatory. At the same time, elements of reactionary policies of the past – often the result of unchecked exercise of executive discretion – have resurfaced in contemporary times. Part 1 explains how and why immigration policy has changed over time and raises caution as to how elements of previously discredited policies have re-emerged.

Part 2 examines contemporary admissions policies, focusing on the three primary streams of permanent admissions to Canada: economic, family, and refugee. Each stream is given a separate chapter, outlining the transformations that have taken place within that stream over the past two decades and assessing the alignment of these changes with the objectives outlined in the *Immigration and Refugee Protection Act 2001.* Each chapter explores how interested stakeholders have viewed and/or experienced these changes and makes recommendations to guide current and future policy decisions.

Part 3 examines the concepts of membership and belonging within the context of Canadian immigration policy. Since 1976, one of the explicit objectives of Canadian immigration policy has been to facilitate the successful integration of immigrants into Canadian society. This took on broader significance in the 1980s with the national commitment to multiculturalism. The preservation and enhancement of Canada's multicultural heritage became a recognized imperative, enshrined in the 1982 *Canadian Charter of Rights and Freedoms* and the *Multiculturalism Act* of 1988. These legislative measures aim to promote the full and equitable participation of individuals from diverse backgrounds in Canadian society.

The *Immigration and Refugee Protection Act 2001* builds upon these principles by emphasizing the importance of respecting Canada's bilingual and multicultural nature. It highlights the goal of facilitating the successful integration of permanent residents and emphasizes the significance of family reunification. In part 3, we look at whether immigration settlement programs and associated human rights, multiculturalism, and employment equity policies facilitate the integration of immigrants in an effective and equitable manner.

We also examine the changes to deportation policies over the past two decades. Immigrants and refugees with permanent resident status have traditionally enjoyed many of the rights of Canadian citizens. However, they do not have an unqualified right to remain or to return to Canada once they have left. During the past two decades, the criteria for losing permanent resident status and facing removal from Canada have been significantly expanded. In part 3, we review the factors and justifications behind this policy shift and its implications for the notions of membership and belonging.

Securing Canadian citizenship is the end of a long journey for immigrants. Part 3 concludes with an examination of the policy shifts around citizenship in the twenty-first century and their underlying rationale. We look at some of the possible implications of the change in policies and point to areas where more information is needed to properly assess impact.

Immigration remains a valued and pivotal force in the ever-evolving Canadian mosaic. Our conclusion synthesizes the main changes in immigration policy covered in this book. We conclude with recommendations for helping to ensure that immigration policy is aligned with Canadian values and responsive to the demographic, economic, and social requisites of the future.

PART 1

An Historical Reprise

Immigration has been part of Canada's story ever since British colonies in North America came together to form a nation in 1867. Immigrants have helped the country advance and develop ever since, and immigration policy has been a central component of national strategies.[1] In part 1, we trace the historical patterns and the shifting political and social forces that shaped Canada's policies on who it let into the country – and who it did not – moving up to contemporary times.

Outlining the changes in the direction of immigration policy, and showing how they came about, reveals longer-term patterns, which are often reminiscent of current debates over immigration. Our understanding of Canada's contemporary immigration policy, and the discourse around it, is enhanced by an awareness of the historical legacy of immigration into a young country.

Broadly speaking, for Canada's first 100 years, its immigration rules were highly selective and racially exclusionary. It then moved towards the more open, diverse, and egalitarian policies of the past several decades. This shift in attitudes is exemplified in the stances of the two prime ministers who bookend the period.

Sir John A. Macdonald, Canada's first prime minister, strongly advocated a robust yet highly selective immigration policy. Immigrants were welcome to remain permanently, provided they were useful and culturally compatible. To allow the permanent settlement of non-"Aryan" immigrants, in his view, would dilute British values and interests and not be successful.[2]

Around 130 years later, Prime Minister Justin Trudeau extolled the benefits of diversity, forged over a century of immigrant settlement. What for Macdonald would have been a singular weakness, for Trudeau is one of Canada's key strengths: a society that is "open, diverse and inclusive." According to Trudeau, most

---

1 Kelley and Trebilcock, *Making of the Mosaic*. The following is an abridged history drawing primarily from this resource. This book has a more comprehensive set of references, each of its chapters contain detailed footnotes and there is an extensive bibliography.

2 *House of Commons Debates*, 4 May 1885, 1582. Indigenous persons also faced franchise restrictions with limited exceptions. They would not have universal suffrage until the 1960s; see John F. Leslie, "Indigenous Suffrage," *The Canadian Encyclopedia*, 31 March 2016, https://www.thecanadianencyclopedia.ca/en/article/indigenous-suffrage.

Canadians "refuse to see a contradiction between individual liberty and collective identity ... we have created a society where both thrive, and mutually reinforce one another."[3]

In part 1, we trace the road between these two ideals. Most Canadians take pride in their openness to immigrants and their commitment to multiculturalism. However, the path leading us to this point has not always been smooth or without its challenges. In fact, it has been marked by periods of insularity and even moments of shame.

The philosopher George Santayana's warning – that those "who cannot remember the past are condemned to repeat it" – is as relevant today as when it was first stated in 1905.[4] By examining our history, we not only discover the valuable lessons we have learned from it, but also recognize the resurgence of certain discredited policies in contemporary times. It is through this examination that we can best ensure that the policies we adopt today will enhance our future social and economic prosperity.

Pre-Confederation

New archaeological discoveries have expanded our understandings of the earliest migrations to North America. The most recent scientific findings suggest that human settlements on the continent date back as far as 30,000 years, although their exact paths remain unclear.[5] What is certain is that when Europeans arrived in

---

3 Right Honourable Justin Trudeau, Prime Minister of Canada, "Diversity Is Canada's Strength," Address, London, UK, 26 November 2015, https://pm.gc.ca/en/news/speeches/2015/11/26/diversity-canadas-strength.

4 George Satayana, *The Life of Reason: The Phases of Human Progress*, vol. 1, *Reason in Common Sense* (n.p., 1905), chap. 12.

5 Lorena Becerra-Valdiva and Thomas Higham, "The timing and Effect of the Earliest Human Arrivals in North America," *Nature* 584 (2020): 93–7. Evidence of a very early human settlement discovered at Bluefish Caves in Yukon, Canada, led many archeologists to conclude that such settlements existed much earlier than previously believed. See Lauriane Bourgeon, Ariane Burke, and Thomas Higham, "Earliest Human Presence in North America Dated to the Last Glacial Maximum: New Radiocarbon Dates from Bluefish Caves, Canada," *PLoS One* 12, no. 1 (2017): e0169486.

the fifteenth century, the land now known as Canada was already home to hundreds of thousands of Indigenous people with diverse languages and customs.[6]

Excavated remains of Viking settlements in Newfoundland from the eleventh century are the earliest evidence of European settlement in Canada. Several centuries later, John Cabot founded a British presence in Newfoundland in 1497. Within fifty years, Jacques Cartier established French settlements along the St. Lawrence River. Both the British and French interests were focused on exploiting natural resources such as fish and fur rather than on colonization.

It was not until a century later that permanent European settlements were established, starting with French settlements in Quebec. Growth was slow, but by the 1760s the French-speaking population was close to 70,000 settlers in Quebec, with smaller numbers across the Maritimes. Most were farmers.

English and French colonial settlements in North America were frequently embroiled in territorial battles between the two European powers. Each colonial outpost tried to populate its settlements with co-nationalists. In 1749, Britain took the extraordinary step of expelling all French-speaking settlers in Acadia. Over 10,000 Acadians were forced to leave and transported to British colonies further south. Many died during their passage.

The battles for control over North American colonies ended in 1763 when the Treaty of Paris brought an end to the Seven Years' War and France ceded its colonial possessions to the British. Under the terms of the treaty, French settlers were allowed to remain and become British subjects. Those who wished to join the public service had also to take an oath of loyalty to the British monarch and renounce their Catholic faith.

These terms were a source of resentment among the French-speaking settlers who comprised nearly the entire settler community

---

6 Russell Thornton, "Population History of North American Indians," in *A Population History of North America*, ed. Michael R. Haines and Richard H. Steckel (Cambridge: Cambridge University Press, 2000), 13. See also John Douglas Belshaw, *Canadian History: Pre-Confederation*, 2nd ed. (Victoria, BC: BCampus, 2020), https://opentextbc.ca/preconfederation2e/.

in Quebec. Despite subsequent concessions made by the British to French settlers there,[7] their concerns over English dominance grew with the arrival of over 30,000 British Loyalist refugees from the United States, beginning with the War of Independence in 1775.[8] In response, the British government passed the *Constitution Act* in 1791 to establish more stable governance. This act divided Quebec into Lower and Upper Canada (modern-day Quebec and Ontario), with each having its own elected assembly yet also with a more powerful legislative council appointed by Britain.[9]

The War of 1812, between Britain and the United States, marked a turning point in settlement policies in British North America. In its aftermath, anti-American sentiments intensified, particularly in Upper Canada, where the United States was perceived as a looming threat.[10] The fear of American expansion influenced immigration policy for more than a century and, in the immediate term, fuelled the desire to focus the promotion of immigration into Canada of potential migrants from Great Britain.

Push factors in Great Britain aided these efforts. Poor economic conditions, land scarcity, and the 1847 potato famine in Ireland

---

7   Such as the *Quebec Act* of 1774 that expanded the territorial boundaries of the colony, permitted Catholics to hold public office, and reinstated the right of the Roman Catholic Church to impose tithes. However, it also imposed English law in public and criminal law.

8   Maya Jasanoff, *Liberty's Exiles: American Loyalists in the Revolutionary World* (New York: Vintage Books, 2012), 52. The British Loyalist refugees arrived between 1775 and 1883. Aside from the 2,000 slaves who were forced to move north, most of the Loyalists were white settlers, soldiers, and individuals. Among the movement were 5,000 Iroquois and roughly 3,000 Black Loyalists who had been promised various concessions by the British in exchange for their loyalty. These promises were often broken.

9   *Constitution Act*, 1871, 34-35 Vict., c. 28 (1871).

10   The conclusion of the war also altered the relationship between settlers and Indigenous communities. The latter were no longer considered as needed military allies. Responsibility for "Indian" policy transferred from military to civil authorities who prioritized measures to eliminate their culture and traditions and integrate them into the settler society. Government of Canada, *Report of the Royal Commission on Aboriginal Peoples*, vol. 1 (Ottawa: Canada Communication Group, 1996), 130 (hereafter Canada, *Royal Commission Report*), https://www.bac-lac.gc.ca/eng /discover/aboriginal-heritage/royal-commission-aboriginal-peoples/Pages /final-report.aspx.

propelled thousands of people to leave for British North America. Within twenty-five years, the European population of Canada doubled to over 3 million people in 1871, with the most significant increase experienced in Upper Canada. By this time, Canada was a self-governing federated state created by the *British North America Act* in 1867. The push for more immigrants would accelerate.

During the 1860s, between 30,000 and 40,000 American slaves came to Canada through the largest anti-slavery movement in North America,[11] the Underground Railroad, a network of safe houses and secret routes out of the United States. By this time, slavery had been banned in the British Empire for close to thirty years. Subsequent Canadian nativist policies in the twentieth century would eventually ban black and brown immigrants on the grounds that they were unsuitable to the climate and conditions of Canada.

Two prominent negative legacies from pre-Confederation immigration history would cast long shadows. One was enmity between French- and English-speaking settlers. The push by British Colonial authorities to ensure the numerical superiority of English-speakers through immigration would stoke resentment among the French-speaking populations for over a hundred years. The relative autonomy that Quebec exercises today over immigration has roots in its early history.

Another harm was the disastrous impact that European settlers had on Indigenous populations. Europeans introduced infectious diseases that ravaged entire Indigenous communities, who were also decimated by territorial wars, forced relocation, loss of livelihoods, and famine.[12] Scholars estimate that, prior to sustained contact with Europeans, the Indigenous population in Canada was around half a million. By 1871, this figure had plummeted to just over 100,000.[13]

---

11 Natasha Henry-Dixon, "Underground Railroad," *The Canadian Encyclopedia*, last edited 3 March 2023, https://www.thecanadianencyclopedia.ca/en/article/underground-railroad.

12 Canada, *Royal Commission Report*, vol. 1, 42. Successive *Indian Acts* authorized relocations, the establishment of residential schools, and the outlawing of Aboriginal cultural practices.

13 Canada, *Royal Commission Report*, vol. 1, 21.

Over time, the Canadian government acquired most Indigenous lands between Ontario and British Columbia. Oral agreements often preceded formal written treaties. As described by the Royal Commission on Aboriginal Peoples, Indigenous parties "understood they would maintain their traditional governments, their laws and their customs" and were promised economic and social benefits in exchange for "the continued use of their land and resources."[14]

But the written treaties often placed limits on these commitments and had political and legal implications unfamiliar to Indigenous parties. Moreover, successive governments were not committed to meeting their obligations.[15]

The *Indian Act* of 1876 formalized the loss of the autonomy of Indigenous people as their lives became regulated by federal agents. They lost rights to self-government, to freely practise their religion, to educate their children, to own land or property, and to move freely. They were denied the vote. It was a bitter legacy of the government's desire to obtain prime agricultural land for new settlement and its disregard for the rights of those who were its first inhabitants. The scars of European conquest and subsequent marginalization of Indigenous communities continue to be unresolved to this day.[16]

---

14 Canada, *Royal Commission Report*, vol. 1, 161.

15 Canada, *Royal Commission Report*, vol. 1, 163–4. The Royal Commission noted several flaws in the treaty meeting process: only the Crown's version of the treaty negotiations and agreements were recorded; the Crown failed to establish the necessary laws to uphold the treaties; sufficient money to meet its obligations was not set aside for that purpose; and there was no appointed office in government responsible for fulfilling Crown treaty commitments.

16 In 2008, the Canadian government established a commission to review the history and impact of the Canadian residential school system on Indigenous persons in Canada. It heard from students and their families in private meetings across the country. The commission concluded in 2015 with several reports, including 94 Calls to Action: Truth and Reconciliation Commission of Canada, *Calls to Action* (Winnipeg: TRCC, 2015), https://ehprnh2mwo3.exactdn.com/wp-content/uploads/2021/01/Calls_to_Action_English2.pdf. In 2022, it was reported that just thirteen of the Commission's 94 Calls to Action had been completed: Eva Jewell and Ian Mosby, *Calls to Action Accountability: A 2022 Status Update on Reconciliation* (Toronto: Yellowhead Institute, 2022), https://yellowheadinstitute.org/wp-content/uploads/2023/12/YI-TRC-C2A-2023-Special-Report-compressed.pdf. According to a Canadian Broadcasting Corporation study, over sixty others were underway: "Beyond 94: Truth and Reconciliation in Canada," *CBC News*, 19 March 2018, last updated 1 May 2024, https://www.cbc.ca/newsinteractives/beyond-94/.

The First Hundred Years: 1867–1967

1867–1914: Consolidating the Dominion

The *British North America Act* (*Constitution Act*) of 1867 created a federated union of Canada's provinces, aiming to fulfil the political aspirations of the different regions and foster greater economic cooperation and prosperity.[17] At a time when leading Americans were eyeing Canada as part of the US's "Manifest Destiny," Confederation was also seen as an essential bulwark against American expansion northwards.

The *Constitution Act* recognized federal jurisdiction over immigration policy and provincial responsibilities for settlement and land distribution in their jurisdictions. Two years later, the *Immigration Act, 1869* was passed, which gave Cabinet the authority to issue orders and proclamations regulating immigrant arrivals.[18] Heavy reliance on executive discretion would remain a distinctive feature of Canadian immigration policy for the next hundred years.

Unity among the provinces alone could not deliver on the promise of Confederation. Thus, soon after winning a national election in 1878, Prime Minister John A. Macdonald began implementing a comprehensive set of strategies to create a prosperous political and national economy. Known as the National Policy, it had three pillars: high tariffs to protect domestic manufacturing; massive investment in transportation infrastructure linking all parts of the country; and significant population growth through immigration. Immigrants would create demand for consumer goods and provide an abundant supply of labour to help settle the West. This was made possible by claiming land occupied by Indigenous communities and the construction of a transcontinental railway.

As Indigenous people were being divested of their title to lands in the West, migrants from Eastern Canada and abroad were entering the area to take their place. They were often enticed by promotional campaigns that included transportation assistance and free

---

17 The first to join were Nova Scotia, New Brunswick, Quebec, and Ontario, soon followed by Prince Edward Island and British Columbia.

18 *An Act Respecting Immigration and Immigrants*, c. 10, 32-33 Vict. (1869).

grants of land to males over twenty-one years of age. Substantial areas of land were also set aside for group settlement.[19]

Public and private agents travelled widely to Great Britain, the United States, and Western Europe, extolling and often exaggerating the benefits of Canada. Immigrants were led to believe that they could establish themselves with ease and readily profit from their homesteads. But the reality was far different. Hardships were legion. Ocean voyages were frequently overcrowded and the ships not seaworthy, lacking in clean water and adequate food. In Canada, settlers confronted the difficulties of homesteading in a cold climate, with poor accommodation, limited food, and an absence of medical care.

Life for immigrant labourers in manufacturing and resource extraction held different challenges, often no less onerous. Many arrived through special private immigration schemes that advanced loans for transportation. Federal immigration agents acted as middlemen, selecting eligible workers, and making the necessary employment contracts with them.

Canadian and immigrant labourers worked long hours, six days a week, in grim conditions, with no job security. Discipline was harsh, the rate of industrial accidents was high, and compensation for work-related injuries uncommon. Foreign-born people lacked political leverage, were often unable to speak English and, desperate for work, often experienced severe forms of exploitation, abuse, and discrimination.

Chinese immigrants were particularly marginalized. Admitted to Canada primarily to construct the transcontinental railroad, they were paid less than others and subjected to an array of discriminatory taxes and policies that restricted where they could reside, how long they could remain, and that denied those born or naturalized in Canada the right to vote. Their numbers were regulated and a "head tax" was imposed on each person arriving in Canada.[20]

---

19   Among those to benefit were Hungarians and Scandinavians as well as Jewish and Mennonite refugees from Russia. They would later be joined by other persecuted minorities from across Eastern Europe.

20   *An Act to Restrict and Regulate Chinese Immigration into Canada*, c. 71, 48-49 Vict. (1885). The head tax would be raised over the years from $50 to $500 by 1903.

Further restrictions would later prohibit Chinese immigration as well as limit immigrants from Japan and India.

Poor and destitute children were brought to Canada by British philanthropic organizations to work on farms, in factories, and in domestic service. Over 100,000 children immigrated to Canada this way in the late nineteenth and early twentieth centuries.[21] Poorly monitored, they were subject to considerable abuse.

Promotional efforts did not meet the desired impact. Despite twenty-five years of vigorous attempts to attract newcomers, the population of Canada grew below its rate of natural increase. Most of the estimated 1.5 million immigrants to Canada during this period did not remain, and many Canadians also left during this time, most to the United States. As a result, in every decade until the turn of the century, more people left Canada than arrived.[22]

Factors contributing to the exodus included better economic opportunities in the United States and other immigrant-receiving countries with less harsh climates.[23] Additionally, farming practices were not yet suitable for the Canadian terrain and climate, resulting in numerous failed farming efforts. Hundreds of farmers in Manitoba and the Northwest saw their efforts disappear in floods, early frosts, drought, and grasshopper plagues. Prosperity would not come to the Prairies until the turn of century when new, more suitable strains of wheat and new cultivation practices were introduced.[24]

By 1900, these new farming practices helped fuel economic growth. So too did declining transportation rates, increased foreign

---

21　*The Canada Year Book, 1914* (Ottawa: Dominion Bureau of Statistics, 1915), 88; Annual Report of the Department of Immigration and Colonization for 1918, *Sessional Papers, 1919*, no. 18, 88.

22　Roderic P. Beaujot and Kevin McQuillan, *Growth and Dualism: The Demographic Development of Canadian Society* (Toronto: Gage, 1982), 83; Kenneth Norrie and Douglas Owram, *A History of the Canadian Economy* (Toronto: Harcourt Brace Jovanovich, 1991), 296. Kenneth Norrie and Douglas Owram estimate that between 1870 and 1900 net emigration from Canada was approximately 485,000.

23　Apart from the United States, Brazil, Argentina, New Zealand, and Australia were among the most significant competitors faced by the Canadian government.

24　Norrie and Owram, *History of the Canadian Economy*, 296.

demand for Canadian exports, and new technologies for profitable power generation and manufacturing. Immigration to Canada swelled and, this time, many remained. Between 1896 and 1914, Canada experienced six of the ten largest annual immigration levels to be registered until contemporary times: over 3 million people immigrated to Canada, twice as many as during the preceding thirty years.[25] In virtually every area of economic expansion, immigrant workers were found in substantial numbers.

The Canadian population increased by 30 per cent to 7 million people in 1910. Economic growth boomed throughout the Prairies and, across the country, urban areas grew exponentially. Cities now accounted for 50 per cent of the total population, up 20 per cent from the preceding decade.[26]

Immigrants from Britain, the United States, and Western Europe continued to be prioritized. The need for more immigrants, however, led the government to expand promotion efforts to other parts of Europe. As a result, the proportion of British immigrants fell from 60 per cent in the years following Confederation to 38 per cent by 1914. Immigration from Europe, in contrast, grew to 25 per cent: most arriving from the central, eastern, and southern parts of the Continent.[27]

This more expansive immigration policy was met with concerns from various quarters. Unions feared that unrestricted immigration would jeopardize the jobs and wages of local workers, while municipal authorities called for tighter controls to prevent overcrowding and strains on social assistance. Church groups and social service providers also sounded the alarm as they struggled to keep up with the influx of needy immigrants. Meanwhile, medical and law enforcement officials claimed that impoverished immigrants led to increased vice and criminality, threatening the vitality of the nation.

Eugenics theory also influenced public opinion with its claim that certain races were superior to others. Human development

---

25 "Report of the Department of Immigration and Colonization," *Annual Departmental Reports, 1929–30*, 8–9.

26 Montreal, Toronto, Winnipeg, Edmonton, and Vancouver experienced exponential growth, see *The Canada Year Book, 1932* (Ottawa: Dominion Bureau of Statistics, 1933), 103.

27 "Report of the Department of Immigration and Colonization."

was enhanced through selective breeding of the fit over the unfit. Eugenicists argued that Canada should prioritize the immigration of genetically superior individuals from the British Isles and white immigrants from the Americas, while limiting the entry of those from Eastern and Southern Europe and excluding those from Asia. Racial bans, they argued, should be accompanied by stricter medical exams and intelligence tests to ensure that only the "fit" were granted entry into Canada.

1910–1914: Selective Restrictions

Despite dissenting voices, the Liberal and Conservative governments of the time heeded the calls of employers, who supported robust immigration levels. Economic prosperity was the primary goal. A comprehensive immigration policy was seen as necessary to secure a reliable and adaptable workforce and for the continued settlement of Western Canada.

As a concession to those who argued for more restrictive policies, the *Immigration Act* of 1910 gave Cabinet broad authority to block admission to Canada for those belonging to "any race deemed unsuitable to the climate or requirements of Canada" and to prohibit other classes for reasons of occupation or character.[28] Cabinet was also authorized to impose landing money requirements, the amount of which could depend on the race, occupation, or destination of the immigrant.

Chinese immigrants were among the first to feel the impact as the head tax was progressively raised following the completion of the trans-Canada railway in the late 1880s. Japanese immigrants were also limited through a special agreement with Japan.[29] East

---

28 *The Immigration Act*, c. 27, 9-10 Edw. VII., s. 38 (1910).

29 *House of Commons Debates*, 21 January 1909, 1611. The 1908 "Gentleman's Agreement" was negotiated by Minister of Labour Rodolphe Lemieux. Japan agreed to voluntary limit the number of passports to its citizens wishing to immigrate to Canada to 400 annually (based on specific agreed criteria such as close family members, domestic servants, or persons with prearranged employment) providing that the agreement was portrayed as a voluntary restraint and that the number would remain secret.

Indian immigrant arrivals were subject to a relatively high head tax as well, and their arrival was effectively stopped through an Executive Order that barred immigrants who did not come to Canada on a continuous journey from their native land or country of citizenship. Black immigrants from the United States and the Caribbean were refused entry on the grounds that they were unsuitable to Canada.[30]

General admissibility criteria were tightened to exclude those considered medically or morally unfit. The grounds for inadmissibility were wide, encompassing serious health conditions like tuberculosis to more minor afflictions such as foot ailments. Those who were deemed financially impoverished, destitute, or lacking in moral fortitude could also be turned away. Expenses associated with repatriating inadmissible immigrants were borne by the transportation company responsible for their arrival in Canada.

The legislation governing naturalization was also tightened. Following Confederation to 1946, the highest available status in Canada was that of British subject. This meant that immigrants from Britain with three years domicile (residence) in Canada had the same rights and privileges as those born here. Non-British immigrants had to undergo the process of naturalization, which initially involved acquiring domicile before applying for naturalization.

By 1914, the prerequisites for naturalization had expanded. Residency requirements for domicile were raised to five years, applicants had to be fluent in English or French, and they had to provide evidence of good character. The latter injected a degree of subjectivity into the decision. Asian applicants and labour advocates were frequently rejected.

Under the *Naturalization Act, 1914*, once naturalized, immigrants had the right to vote in federal elections, sit in Parliament, and could not be excluded from entering the country unless their certificates had been revoked. Persons found to have obtained

---

30 Kelley and Trebilcock, *Making of the Mosaic*, 158; David Scott FitzGerald and David Cook-Martín, *Culling the Masses: The Democratic Origins of Racist Immigration Policy in the Americas* (Cambridge, MA: Harvard University Press, 2014), 156–7.

naturalization through misrepresentation or fraud could have their naturalization revoked. This provision had broad application, as being not to be of good character at the time of the application could be considered as misrepresentation.[31] Revocation left people liable to deportation.

Prior to acquiring domicile, a person could be deported for an expanding set of reasons. In 1906, deportation grounds included criminality, moral turpitude, hospitalization, or having relied on public or private charity. By 1910, additional grounds included advocating the overthrow of governments by force or attempting to cause a riot or public disorder in Canada.[32] Even naturalized citizens were vulnerable to removal if the grounds for it could be said to have existed at the time of their arrival.[33]

By the outbreak of the First World War, Canadian immigration policy had been transformed. The great waves of immigrants of the early 1900s were premised on a belief that prosperity depended on a rapid rise in population contingent on an expansionist approach to immigration. By 1914, immigration was still a national priority, but the focus shifted to managing it in a way that ensured a steady supply of labour and desirable settlers, while preventing the arrival or naturalization of those believed to undermine political and social mores. Successive immigration acts broadened the authority of Cabinet to meet these priorities flexibly.

1914–1930: Between Two Extremes

The period between 1914 and 1929 marks a significant transition between two eras in immigration policy: from the most expansive to the most restrictive. Straddling these two poles, the immigration

---

31 Since the *Naturalization Act* was a federal statute, it could confer only entitlements that were within federal jurisdiction. Rights within provincial jurisdiction, such as the right to vote in provincial elections, were thus not guaranteed upon naturalization.

32 The *Immigration Act*, ss. 3, 40, 41 (1910).

33 The reasoning being that they would have been inadmissible at that time and therefore not eligible.

policy of this period showcased several characteristics that distinguished the eras on either side of it. During economic downturns, the government became more discerning and curtailed immigration promotion, while periods of economic prosperity witnessed a relatively more lenient policy. Yearly admissions, therefore, tended to fluctuate sharply.

In 1913, Canada welcomed over 400,000 immigrants. During the First World War, however, the number plummeted to an average of 55,000 annually due to European emigration restrictions and costly transatlantic transportation. Most immigrants during the war were from the United States.

First World War: Declining Admissions and Internment

During the First World War, nearly half a million residents of Canada were considered enemy aliens. These people, who originated from countries with which Canada was at war, faced widespread hostility and government restrictions on their liberties, as authorized by the *War Measures Act, 1914*. Thousands were fired from their jobs and many deported. Orders and regulations were passed requiring them to register with authorities, prohibiting the possession of material in an enemy language, restricting their movements, and authorizing the government to intern and deport those considered a threat to national security.[34]

Despite no evidence of widespread subversive activities, over 8,500 enemy aliens were interned in camps across the country, mostly Germans and Ukrainians. Appeals for judicial review were typically unsuccessful. An acute shortage of labour led to internees being released from camps prior to the conclusion of the war, again illustrating the power of economic interests.

In 1919, the *Immigration Act* was amended, broadening the reasons for which an immigrant could be denied admission to Canada.[35] In the aftermath of the war, and during a period of sluggish economic activity, the executive continued to exercise its

---

34   The *War Measures Act*, S.C. 1914, 15 George V, c. 2 (1914).

35   *An Act to Amend the Immigration Act*, 1919, 9-10 George V, Chapter 25.

broad authority through regulations to require most immigrants to show they had funds with which to establish themselves upon arrival, to prohibit immigrant workers from entering Canada via the coastal ports of entry in British Columbia and to bar undesirable groups such as the Mennonites, Hutterites, and Doukhobors from entering the country.[36]

1920s Cautious Expansion

As the Canadian economy began to show signs of recovery in the 1920s, there was growing pressure to ease immigration restrictions. With many Canadian and American workers in Canada leaving for the United States, there was a shortage of workers. Although Canada began to open its doors wider, its admission policy remained highly selective.

Various initiatives were employed to encourage selective immigration to Canada. The *Empire Settlement Agreement* between Canada and Britain provided incentives to British farmers, farm workers, and domestic servants to migrate to Canada. However, of the 130,000 immigrants who came through the program, fewer than 10 per cent ended up working in the agricultural sector.[37] Additionally, the *Railway Agreement* allowed the national railways to recruit European farmers and farm labourers, resulting in nearly 200,000 mostly Eastern and Central Europeans arriving in Canada by the end of the decade.[38]

Another means was through the permit system, which allowed the entry under permit of any immigrant "whose labor or service was required in Canada."[39] Employers could apply for permits based on their labour needs, which helped open the door to European immigrants from non-preferred countries. Tens of thousands of

---

36 Order in Council, P.C. 1204 (9 June 1919). Various factors contributed to this decision: their pacifism and refusal to join the Armed Forces, their communal lifestyle that was seen to illustrate their unwillingness to assimilate. The ban was eventually lifted a few years later.

37 FitzGerald and Cook-Martín, *Culling the Masses*, 164.

38 Kelley and Trebilcock, *Making of the Mosaic*, 198–200.

39 P.C 534 (8 April 1926).

European labourers were admitted through this permit system. By 1929, immigration from Continental Europe had increased from 25 per cent in 1914 to 46 per cent of annual arrivals.[40]

Not all European immigrants were treated equally. Jewish refugees fleeing brutal pogroms in Eastern Europe were subjected to additional requirements, including literacy tests and proof of origin. They were often rejected by recruiters in both the public and private sectors. Similarly, Armenian refugees were unwelcome. Between 1915 and 1916, over 1.5 million Armenians were killed, and hundreds of thousands expelled from Turkey. Canada admitted relatively few and, throughout the 1920s, considered Armenians as Asians and, therefore, subject to the same barriers to entry.[41]

In 1923, the Cabinet signed an order excluding immigrants of "any Asiatic race" with limited exceptions.[42] Chinese immigrants continued to be regulated by the *Chinese Immigrant Act*. In 1923, it too was tightened. Only fifteen Chinese immigrants were admitted to Canada between 1923 and 1947 when the restrictions were lifted.[43]

Deportation provisions were also expanded. In 1919, the *Immigration Act* was amended. As noted above, domicile now required five years residence and the grounds for which a person could be removed prior to that time were expanded. They included those who advocated the unlawful destruction of property or were

---

40   "Report of the Department of Immigration and Colonization," 8, table 1.

41   Isabel Kaprielian-Churchill, "Armenian Refugees and Their Entry into Canada, 1919-30," *The Canadian Historical Review* 71, no. 1 (1990): 80–108, https://muse-jhu-edu.myaccess.library.utoronto.ca/article/573505/pdf. This included having to meet the restrictive occupational requirements, narrow family-class definition, continuous journey stipulation, and $250 landing-money regulations.

42   Order in Council, P.C. 182 (1923). The exceptions were for genuine farmers or farm labourers, female domestic servants or wives and dependent children of legal residents. Japanese immigrants were governed by a special agreement with Japan that had limited their numbers.

43   "Oriental Immigration to Canada, 1906 to 1946," Statistics Canada, 7 August 2009, https://www65.statcan.gc.ca/acyb02/1947/acyb02_19470136011-eng.htm; *An act to Amend the Immigration Act and to Repeal the Chinese Immigration Act*, S.C. 1947, c. 19.

affiliated with any organization "entertaining or teaching disbelief in or opposition to organized government."[44] Sedition laws were changed along similar lines.[45]

Together with deportation powers, these laws were used against political dissidents and labour activists. The government worked with employers to identify and remove labour reformers resulting in the deportation of hundreds of alleged anarchists and revolutionaries, severely dampening radical labour politics in Canada.

1930–1950: Retrenchment

From the onset of the Great Depression in 1929,[46] and for the following two decades, Canada had the harshest admission, removal, and naturalization policies of any period – before or since. A combination of factors contributed to this legacy.

Depression: Closing the Doors

The economic cataclysm of 1929 prompted a severe tightening of admission criteria. Employers could no longer apply for special permits to admit immigrant workers. Admissible classes were reduced to immediate relatives of Canadian residents, farmers with means, and white immigrants from Britain and the United States with sufficient finances.[47] All government promotion efforts stopped, and health criteria were stringently enforced. As a result, annual immigrant arrivals plunged to 11,000 in 1936, a drop of over 93 per cent within the space of six years.[48]

---

44 *An Act to Amend the Immigration Act*, S.C. 1919, 9-10 George V, c. 25, s. 15 (1919).

45 *An Act to Amend the Criminal Code*, S.C. 1919, c. 46, 0; *The Canadian Annual Review of Public Affairs: 1917* (Toronto: Annual Review Publishing, 1918), 438.

46 Michiel Horn, "The Great Depression: Past and Present," *Journal of Canadian Studies* 11, no. 1 (1976): 42, 45. By 1933, more than 32 per cent of Canadian wage earners were unemployed, and 15 per cent of the population was dependent on public relief.

47 Order in Council, P.C. 695 (21 March 1931).

48 "Report of the Department of Mines and Resources," *Annual Departmental Reports*, 1944–45, 200.

As admissions to Canada plummeted during the 1930s, deportations rose. Close to 6,000 persons each year were deported in the first half of the decade, six times higher than the yearly average of the preceding twenty-five years. Most were non-naturalized immigrants who had relied on social assistance within five years of their arrival.[49]

Many Canadians were searching desperately for employment and had to wait for hours in lines for relief. They supported the removal of those who placed additional demands on shrinking resources. And for those who already resented and feared the changing ethnic composition of the country, tighter immigration restrictions and enhanced removals were viewed as long overdue.

Although smaller in number, thousands of naturalized immigrants were also removed during this time if found to have been inadmissible when they arrived. This applied to persons with health issues and alleged character flaws as well as those accused of attempting to create a public disturbance or advocating the overthrow of the government by force.[50] Many socialist and communist organizations and affiliated unions lost their leaders and supporters, some of whom were removed to fascist countries where their lives were at risk.[51]

In parallel, naturalization requests were denied in increasing numbers. In 1934, a time of both high unemployment and increased labour militancy, 90 per cent of the 18,379 naturalization applications made were rejected.[52]

Second World War: Selectivity and Internment Revisited

As the economy recovered in the late 1930s, the number of deportations declined. Contrary to historical patterns, however, a surge in economic activity did not translate into a significant uptick in

---

49   "Report of the Department of Mines and Resources," 220, table 14.

50   The *Immigration Act, 1910* as amended, s. 41.

51   *Canadian Forum*, February 1934, 165. One deported labour activist, Hans Kist, reportedly died of torture in a German concentration camp.

52   Shin Imai, "Deportation in the Depression," *Queen's Law Journal* 7, no. 1 (1981): 70.

immigrant admissions. Canada's wartime economy boomed, with escalating demand for agricultural and industrial goods propelling the nation towards a new era of prosperity.

Within two years of entering the Second World War in 1939, the gross national product surged by nearly 50 per cent, and unemployment largely disappeared.[53] By the end of the war, industry supplanted agriculture as the dominant sector driving the economy.

Despite this period of relative prosperity, stringent measures governing immigrant admissions remained firmly in place, primarily to impede the entry of Jewish refugees seeking sanctuary from the genocide unfolding across Europe.[54] Employers were able to secure immigrant labour through special permits granted by the government. However, even Jewish individuals possessing sought-after skills and capital were routinely rejected.

Of the approximately 100,000 immigrants who arrived in Canada between 1937 and 1945, fewer than 5,000 were Jewish. Canada had one of the worst records of providing safety to Jewish refugees of any Western democracy.[55]

Canada's allies urged it to do more for the millions of Jewish refugees in distress. Within Canada, the Canadian Commonwealth Federation admonished the government in Parliament. Various faith-based groups, non-governmental organizations, and media outlets also lobbied heavily for an easing of restrictions and condemned the racist policies of the government that ran counter to the ideals for which Canadians were fighting in the war.

The government refused to yield on the basis that, despite occasional expressions of sympathy, most Canadians were not willing to open their doors to Europe's outcasts.[56] There was ample

---

53 For more on the Canadian economy at this time, see K.H. Norrie, Douglas Owram, and J.C. Herbert Emery, *A History of the Canadian Economy*, 4th ed. (Toronto: Thomson/Nelson, 2008).

54 As revealed in public debates and internal government documents and memoranda.

55 Irving Abella and Harold troper, *None Is Too Many*, 4th ed. (University of Toronto Press, 2023), preface.

56 Several senior Cabinet ministers and officials within the immigration branch were opposed to opening avenues for Jewish refugees and Prime Minister King also read public opinion as equally unsupportive.

evidence to support this view. Several public opinion polls conducted throughout the war revealed a widely held belief that European Jews would not adapt well to Canada. And, at the same time, Jews across the country faced restrictions from entering certain professions and advancing in others. There were prohibitions on buying property, living in certain areas, and participating in recreational centres and private clubs.

The only special movement that got significant public support was temporary refuge provided to 4,500 British children and 1,000 British mothers. Canada also agreed with Britain to admit and detain 2,500 suspect German-aliens, 3,000 German prisoners of war, and 2,000 refugees[57] from the United Kingdom. Critics accused the government of administering the program as insensitively as its admission policy, for the government interned the refugees in the same camps as those who were their oppressors.[58]

As with the First World War, the outbreak of hostilities in Europe triggered a surge of public animosity towards "enemy aliens." Many were fired from their jobs and vigilantes emerged, vowing to act against immigrants suspected of engaging in subversive activities. Once again, the *War Measures Act* was invoked, allowing for the arrest and internment of individuals without warrant or trial if they were believed to harbour subversive intentions.

Organizations associated with Nazi, fascist, and communist ideologies were prohibited, and immigrants from countries with which Canada was at war were required to report to local police monthly, regardless of their naturalized status.[59] Initially, around 2,500 individuals of Italian or German descent accused

---

57 There were a few other special programs for refugees from the Sudetenland and the Iberian Peninsula, but they were small commitments that became bogged down by the selective and cumbersome approach taken by Canada Immigration.

58 Eric Koch, *Deemed Suspect: A Wartime Blunder* (Toronto: Methuen, 1980), xiii. In his moving memoir of the years spent in Canadian internment camps, one Jewish refugee, Eric Koch, recalled that among the hardest things the refugees experienced was having to live in the same quarters as those they considered their grievous enemies, and, to be treated as enemies themselves.

59 *Defence of Canada Regulations* (Ottawa: King's Printer, 1939), 47; and Order in Council, P.C. 3751 (13 August 1940).

of harbouring pro-fascist sympathies, were interned. A smaller group of individuals suspected of communist sympathies and labour activism were also detained.[60] Even after the Soviet Union joined the Western Allies, Canada upheld the ban on the Communist Party and carried on incarcerating those suspected of having communist sympathies. It was not until 1943, after a series of victories by the Allied forces, that these internment measures started to loosen.

There was a much larger second wave of internments aimed at the ethnic Japanese community. Among the approximately 22,500 individuals of Japanese descent, a significant portion – about 60 per cent – were born and educated in Canada. Of the remaining population, two-thirds had resided in Canada for more than twenty-five years, and one-third had acquired naturalization before 1923. After that time, Asian immigrants encountered mounting challenges in obtaining approval for their applications, making naturalization exceedingly difficult.

The majority of Japanese Canadians were in British Columbia, where anti-Japanese sentiment was particularly pervasive. Unsubstantiated rumours of gun-running and coastal surveillance by individuals of Japanese descent proliferated in the province.[61] They reached a fever pitch following the Japanese bombing of Pearl Harbor and the fall of Hong Kong in December 1941.

Historians disagree on whether there was sufficient evidence to justify the forced evacuation of all persons of Japanese ancestry from the West Coast to internment camps in the interior of the province.[62] However, there is scholarly consensus that the other

---

60 Reg Whitaker, "Official Repression of Communism during World War II," *Labour/ Le Travail* 17 (1986): 145–6. Government records suggests that some 65 per cent were alleged fascists of Italian and German descent, 30 per cent were considered pro-Japanese, and 5 per cent were alleged communist sympathizers.

61 Board of Review [Immigration], *Final Report*, 29 September 1938, 38, quoted in Ramdeo Sampat-Mehta, *International Barriers: A Critique* (Ottawa: Canada Research Bureau, 1973), 244-6.

62 See Kelley and Trebilcock, *Making of the Mosaic*, 310–12, where this debate is discussed.

actions against ethnic Japanese residents were unjustifiable. These included the confiscation of their property and measures taken to remove them to Japan at the end of the war.

Proceeds from confiscated land, houses, and personal possessions were used to offset the costs of internment camps. Critics pointed out that this approach violated international humanitarian law and drew comparisons to the Nazi regime's expropriation of Jewish property.[63] Attempts to seek judicial redress often resulted in denials.[64] Over time, some internees were granted permission to work outside the camps, particularly in industries experiencing severe labour shortages.[65] Others were compelled to fill job vacancies in eastern parts of the country, often encountering discriminatory laws that restricted their choice of residence and employment opportunities.

In 1944, Prime Minister Mackenzie King acknowledged that "no person of Japanese race born in Canada has been charged with any act of sabotage or disloyalty during the years of war."[66] Despite this acknowledgment, the policy of King's government was to remove as many as possible to Japan at the war's conclusion. To that end, all residents of Japanese descent were offered financial incentives to sign voluntary removal requests. Less than half the population agreed,[67] although most subsequently tried to rescind their requests and remain in Canada. In response, Cabinet passed a regulation to make the initial requests binding, with limited exceptions. Other regulations were passed to include wives and dependent children in deportation orders and to authorize the

---

63 Maryka Omatsu, *Bittersweet Passage: Redress and the Japanese Canadian Experience* (Toronto: Between the Lines, 1992), 74–5, 93–4.

64 Ann Gomer Sunahara, *The Politics of Racism: The Uprooting of Japanese Canadians during the Second World War* (Toronto: Lorimer, 1981), 109–10; *Nakashima et al. v R*, [1947] 4 D.L.R. 487; Ken Adachi, *The Enemy That Never Was: A History of Japanese Canadians* (Toronto: McClelland and Stewart, 1976), 261.

65 Order in Council, P.C. 946 (5 February 1943); see Adachi, *Enemy That Never Was*, 261.

66 *House of Commons Debates*, 4 August 1944, 5915.

67 Sunahara, *Politics of Racism*, chap. 6, https://japanesecanadianhistory.ca/chapter -6-deportation/. Their motives were mixed: financial destitution, ongoing discrimination, coercion, and some believed Japan would win the war.

revocation of citizenship of deported naturalized or natural-born Canadians of Japanese descent.

The regulations were judicially challenged on the grounds that they were a crime against humanity. In 1946, the federal government referred the matter to the Supreme Court of Canada to decide whether the regulations were lawful.[68] The Court upheld the regulations, except for the provisions that included wives and dependent children in deportation orders.[69]

The decision of the Court was subsequently endorsed by the British Privy Council.[70] It underscored the tenuous hold naturalized immigrants had in their adopted country, and for the first time permitted the deportation of Canadian-born citizens, arguably in contravention of international law.[71] Strong public criticism eventually led the Government to repeal the regulations in 1947 by which point around 4,000 individuals had already been deported to Japan.[72]

During the Great Depression and the Second World War, admission, removal, and internment policies were generally supported by the public. They were to leave lasting scars. One was from Canada's refusal to provide safety to Jewish refugees. A senior

---

68 *Reference to the Validity of Orders in Council in relation to Persons of Japanese Race*, [1946] SCR 248.

69 *Re Persons of Japanese Race*, para. 281. Justice Hudson noted that noted that a person could withdraw their request up to a deportation order being issued. The signing of the request, in his opinion, was akin to signing "a firm contract."

70 *Co-operative Committee on Japanese Canadians et al. v The Attorney-General of Canada et al.*, [1947] AC 87.

71 International human rights law and international humanitarian law provide protections to individuals against arbitrary or unlawful deprivation of their nationality, arbitrary expulsion, and forced displacement. See UN General Assembly, Resolution 217A, *Universal Declaration of Human Rights* (UDHR) (10 December 1948), Article 12; UN General Assembly, Resolution 2200A (XXI), *International Covenant on Civil and Political Rights* (16 December 1966), Article 12.

72 W. Peter Ward, *The Japanese in Canada. Canada's Ethnic Groups*, Booklet No. 3 (Ottawa: Canadian Historical Association, 1982), 15. Most of the internees were settled in the eastern part of the country. Just 7,000 eventually returned to British Columbia once the wartime prohibitions were lifted, 30 per cent of the prewar population. In 1988, Prime Minister Brian Mulroney issued a formal apology and announced a compensation for each surviving internee. Canada also reinstated the citizenship of those Japanese Canadians who were deported at the conclusion of the war.

government official summed up the position with words that would become emblematic of the country's record. Asked in 1945 how many Jews Canada would admit, he replied that "none is too many."[73]

The second was from the internment operations. While genuine concerns of subversive activities influenced Canada's wartime internment policies, the measures taken were disproportionate to the perceived threats.

Restrictive policies revealed deep-rooted racial and political prejudices. The internment of the ethnic Japanese population in British Columbia found support in a province that had long held negative views towards persons of Japanese descent, considering them as an alien and undesirable race. The crackdown on communists, socialists, and union activists was advocated and backed by security officials and powerful business interests seeking to suppress ideologies that called for improved worker protections.

1950–1966: Shifting Emphasis

The prejudices that shaped Canadian war-time policies endured for an extended period. Except for the repeal of the *Chinese Immigration Act* in 1947, immigration selection processes based on race continued to prevail for some time.[74] Additionally, the politics of the Cold War influenced responses to refugees and decisions on deportations. Nevertheless, as this period ended, the need for a move from an executive-driven, race-based immigration policy to one with greater inclusivity and transparency received broad support.

---

73 Abella and Troper, *None Is Too Many*, preface.

74 Repeal of the *Chinese Immigration Act* followed sustained pressure from various fronts. The Chinese diplomatic mission in Canada, several faith-based groups, government officials and various Members of Parliament pointed to the fact that Canada's legislation was inconsistent with the principles of the UN Charter and the *Universal Declaration of Human Rights*. FitzGerald and Cook-Martín further observe that Liberal democracies like Canada were "laggards in doing away with their explicit ethnic discrimination, long after undemocratic Latin American countries such as Uruguay (1936), Chile (1936), Paraguay (1937), Cuba (1942), and Argentina (1949)." See FitzGerald and Cook-Martín, *Culling the Masses*, 7.

After the war and well into the 1970s, the Canadian economy continued to experience sustained prosperity. Annual immigration levels averaged 150,000 persons annually between 1950 and 1975.[75] In 1952, a new *Immigration Act* authorized the Cabinet to issue regulations prohibiting admission to Canada for a range of reasons. They included nationality, ethnicity, occupation, class, and even peculiar customs, habits, modes of life, or methods of holding property.

Cabinet was also authorized to prohibit the entry of those who were unsuitable "having regard to the climatic, economic, social, industrial, educational, labour, health or other conditions in Canada" or the person's "probable inability to become readily assimilated."[76] The immigration regulations authorized senior immigration officers to use their discretion in a similar manner. The Supreme Court of Canada struck down this aspect of the regulations on grounds that the act did not authorize Cabinet to delegate its discretion.[77]

More precise criteria followed in regulations. Admissions were limited to individuals from white British Dominions, France, and the United States provided they had the means to establish themselves upon arrival.[78] Immigrants from certain European countries were admissible provided they had reasonable prospects for employment. Immigrants from other parts of the world could only enter if sponsored by a family member, and in the case of African or Asian immigrants, the

---

75 Statistics Canada, "150 Years of Immigration in Canada," last updated 17 May 2018, https://www150.statcan.gc.ca/n1/pub/11-630-x/11-630-x2016006-eng. htm; Statistics Canada, *Immigrants in Canada: Selected Highlights* (Ottawa: Statistics Canada, 1990), https://publications.gc.ca/site/eng/9.816566/publication. html. Between 1945 and 1962, Canada admitted on average 126,000 per year, increasing to over 150,000 in the early 1970s, peaking at over 200,000 in 1976, after which they began to fall before rising again in the 1990s.

76 *Immigration Act*, R.S.C. 1952, s. 61. Race as an explicit ground was removed but wide discretion to screen, along with quotas applied to certain countries and limitations on who could sponsor extended relatives led to ongoing racially based selection.

77 *A.G. of Canada v. Brent* [1956] S.C.R. 318, 2 D.L.R. (2d).

78 White British Dominions included Australia, New Zealand, the United Kingdom, or the Union of South Africa.

sponsor had to be an immediate family member. Immigration from India, Pakistan, and Ceylon was limited to a few hundred per year.[79]

The permit system was revived, allowing employers to apply to the government for the admission of immigrant workers. Employers were required to show that the job was genuine, could not be filled locally, and was valid for at least one year at the prevailing wage rate in the locality of employment. If approved, private companies were often part of the selection process.

All admissible classes had to meet health, morality, and security requirements. Medical prohibitions remained extensive, and immorality exclusions were extended to bar homosexuals and drug addicts. Security grounds continued to be used to deny admission and deport suspected communists.[80] Even distinguished visitors like the academic W.E.B. Du Bois and concert and film star, Paul Robeson, were denied admission on this basis.[81] Security screens were not as rigorously applied to fascist sympathizers, a number whom turned out to be war criminals.[82]

In 1947, Prime Minister King made it clear that Canadian immigration policy would remain selective. He characterized admission to Canada as a "privilege" and not a "right," noting that Canadians did not want to see through immigration a "fundamental alteration in the character of our population."[83]

The same approach applied to refugee policy. The emphasis was on those whom the government considered would assimilate well and be able to establish themselves in Canada. Consistent with prevailing popular opinion and government directives, Canadian

---

79 These are discussed in Kelley and Trebilcock, *Making of the Mosaic*, 333–4, and David Corbett, *Canada's Immigration Policy: A Critique* (Toronto: University of Toronto Press, 1957), 39–41.

80 Reg Whitaker, *Double Standard: The Secret History of Canadian Immigration Policy* (Toronto: Lester & Orpen Dennys, 1987). Other Western democracies like Britain and the United States also imposed security checks on the same basis. See *Double Standard* for more on inadmissibility and removal on security grounds.

81 Whitaker, *Double Standard*, 62. Close to 9,000 persons were deported on similar grounds.

82 Whitaker, *Double Standard*, 89–93.

83 Prime Minister Mackenzie King, in *House of Commons Debates*, 1 May 1947, 2644–7.

policy was to restrict the admission of Jewish refugees even after the revelations of Nazi atrocities were well known.[84]

Canadian immigration officers participated in international efforts to help resettle hundreds of thousands of refugees who could neither remain in displacement camps nor return home. A quarter of this population were holocaust survivors.[85] Canada, along with other participating countries, approached the resettlement efforts as an immigration exercise, to the frustration of the United Nations, which accused them of focusing on the most skilled and employable and rejecting those who did not fit their immigration priorities.[86]

Many of the 157,000 displaced persons that Canada admitted came under contract labour schemes. Others were admitted through public and private sponsorship programs.[87] Jewish refugees were often screened out by government and participating industries. Government restrictions meant that even Jewish-dominated industries, like the needle trades, could not have more than 50 per cent of their recruits be Jewish.[88]

Initially, private humanitarian and faith-based sponsors played a role in the selection process. However, this involvement was later eliminated because they tended to prioritize individuals in the greatest need rather than focusing on their employability.[89] It

---

84 A public opinion poll in 1946 revealed that 50 per cent of Canadians objected to Jews immigrating to Canada. Sixty per cent also objected to admitting Japanese immigrants. Canadian Institute of Public Opinion, Public Opinion News Service Release, 30 October 1946.

85 Ninette Kelley, *People Forced to Flee: History, Change and Challenge* (Oxford: Oxford University Press, 2022), 194. Among the others were hundreds of thousands of Eastern Europeans with diverse backgrounds, including displaced persons forced to work in Germany, prisoners of war, and Nazi collaborators.

86 Ben Shephard, *The Long Road Home: The Aftermath of the Second World War* (New York: Anchor Books, 2012), 5, 346–83. Sheppard provides a detailed account of how this process was handled in the displaced persons camps.

87 "The Arrival of Displaced Persons in Canada, 1945-1951," Government of Canada, 15 February 2016, https://www.canada.ca/en/parks-canada/news/2016/02/the-arrival-of-displaced-persons-in-canada-1945-1951.html.

88 Abella and Troper, *None Is Too Many*, 258–71.

89 Freda Hawkins, *Canada and Immigration: Public Policy and Public Concern*, 2nd ed. (Montreal: McGill-Queen's University Press, 1988), 304–6. This involvement was eliminated in 1958 through a government directive.

would take another decade before Canada agreed to accept 26,000 refugees who did not meet strict eligibility requirements and remained stranded in camps for displaced persons.

Selectivity and geopolitical considerations also influenced Canada's other refugee responses during this period. Canada did not sign the 1951 UN *International Convention Relating to the Status of Refugees* until 1969. It was concerned that signing the convention would restrict Canada's ability to reject or deport refugees, particularly those suspected of being communists.

Canada responded promptly to the Hungarian refugee crisis that arose after the Soviet invasion of Hungary in 1956. Within a year, Canada welcomed over 37,000 Hungarian refugees, primarily consisting of working-age Roman Catholics. Similarly, in 1969, within a year of the Soviet suppression of the Czech uprising, Canada accepted 12,000 Czechoslovakian refugees who had favourable prospects for employment. Additionally, in 1972, in response to a request from Britain, Canada admitted 8,000 skilled East-Indian British subjects who had been expelled from Uganda.[90]

These efforts contrasted with Canada's rather slow and painstaking response to Chilean refugees, following the 1973 military coup that toppled the democratically elected socialist government of President Allende.[91] In the first six months, Canada issued just 780 visas, its processing weighed down by intensive security screening, a lack of translators, and no relaxation of immigration criteria. Pressure from various civil society groups, faith-based organizations, labour unions, and Members of Parliament, helped to ease the policy with Canada eventually accepting close to 7,000 Chilean refugees.[92]

Pressures for Change

Both internal and external pressure would eventually lead Canada to broaden admissible categories and shift away from race-based

---

90 "The Ugandan Asian Refugees in Canada–Uganda Collection," accessed 22 July 2023, https://carleton.ca/uganda-collection/the-ugandan-asian-refugees-in-canada/.

91 To be admitted refugees had to have "reasonable prospects for employment."

92 Canadian Museum of Immigration at Pier 21, https://pier21.ca/research/immigration-history/canadas-response-chilean-crisis.

selection. Internationally, experiences during the Second World War led to the establishment of the United Nations in 1945 and the adoption of the *Universal Declaration of Human Rights* the following year. Canadian immigration policies were not consistent with the non-discriminatory principles that underpinned the UN and were enshrined in many of the international instruments that followed in the wake of its creation.[93] Canadian diplomats frequently felt uneasy with the misalignment between Canadian policy and international norms. However, this discrepancy alone was inadequate to prompt a shift in the orientation of Canadian immigration policy.

Pressure also came from elsewhere. Members of the British Commonwealth, many having recently won their independence, firmly objected to Canada discriminating against their nationals. Britain too urged reform. It permitted any British subject to immigrate to the United Kingdom. By 1961, there were annual arrivals of 60,000 from the West Indies alone. It was having trouble ensuring adequate housing and employment and urged Canada to open its policy to accept people from these countries as labourers, for which there was a need.[94]

Within Canada, ethnic groups, advocacy organizations, and several trade unions also lobbied for reform.[95] In 1960, the federal Parliament enacted the *Canadian Bill of Rights* recognizing

---

93   UN General Assembly, United Nations Charter (26 June 1945); UN General Assembly, UDHR (1948). For example, Article 1(3) of the UN Charter reads: "respect for human rights and for fundamental freedoms for all without distinction as to race, sex, language, or religion." Similarly, Article 2 of the UDHR recognize the principle of equal rights and dignity without distinction of any kind, such as race, colour, sex, language, religion, political or other opinion, national or social origin, property, birth, or other status. Among the other human rights treaties of the 1960s are the *International Convention on the Elimination of All Forms of Racial Discrimination* of 1965, the *International Covenant of Civil and Political Rights* of 1966, and the *International Covenant on Economic, Social, and Cultural Rights* of 1966.

94   In the mid-1950s, Canada extended the contract labour scheme to include domestic workers from the Caribbean. Initially, only a small number of individuals with "exceptional merit" were permitted. The success of the program led it to be expanded to several hundred people per year. The program was criticized as being exploitive as the domestic workers had to live with their employers and were required to work much longer and for far less than expected.

95   Including leading representatives of the Canadian Congress of Labour, which represented less-skilled industries with a large immigrant membership.

individual human rights and fundamental freedoms without discrimination by reason of race, national origin, colour, religion, or sex.[96] Canadian immigration policy could not be reconciled with these commitments.

In 1962, the government responded with measures that reduced discrimination, without eliminating it completely. Independent immigrants who were able to successfully establish themselves in Canada were admissible without regard to their nationality, ethnicity, or race. Immigration officers were instead to consider education, skills, qualifications, finances, or secured employment in making their decision.[97] They had considerable discretion in determining the weight to give these factors and in deciding what skills were relevant in the determination.

Race-based preferences continued in several areas. All Canadian citizens and permanent residents could sponsor immediate family members. However, the sponsorship of more extended family members was limited to individuals from preferred countries in the Americas, Europe, and the Middle East.[98] Quotas were also retained on immigrants from Ceylon, India, and Pakistan. Refugee responses also remained partial. Although Africa and Asia were experiencing the most severe refugee crises in the world, Canada did not participate in international efforts to resettle refugees from these continents.[99]

It would take several more years before all race-based preferences were eliminated. Canada was not alone among liberal democracies in this regard. It was, however, far behind less democratic

---

96 *An Act for the Recognition and Protection of Human Rights and Fundamental Freedoms*, S.C. 1960, c. 44, s. 1 (1960). And the right not to be deprived thereof except by due process of the law.

97 Order in Council, P.C. 1962–86 (18 January 1962), s.31(a)

98 Middle Eastern countries included Egypt, Israel, Lebanon, and Turkey.

99 Department of External Affairs file 5475-EA-140, internal memorandum, 14 February 1962, cited in Gerald Dirks, *Canada's Refugee Policy: Indifference or Opportunism?* (Montreal: McGill-Queen's University Press, 1977), 225. The Department of External Affairs took the position that at "this stage it would seem unrealistic to us to consider taking in African and Asian refugees, at least until such time as the necessity of such efforts is apparent and other countries have begun to share our concern."

countries in the Americas as FitzGerald, Cook-Martín, and García have documented:

> While all countries in the Americas eventually adopted ethnic selection policies, undemocratic regimes in Cuba, Argentina, Chile, Uruguay, Paraguay, and Mexico reversed their discriminatory laws and pioneered the explicit deracialization of immigration policy in the late 1930s and '40s, a generation or more before liberal-democratic Canada, the United States, Australia, and New Zealand.[100]

In 1963, the Liberals came to power under Lester Pearson. The new government launched a major review of immigration policy amid concerns that Canada was admitting more unskilled immigrants than could be absorbed into an economy where there was a shortage of skilled labour.

In 1966, public hearings of a Joint House of Commons Senate Committee discussed a government position paper on immigration known as the White Paper.[101] Around the same time, the government commissioned a report on the arrest, detention, and deportation policies and the exercise of discretion under the *Immigration Act*.

The main thrust of the White Paper was that Canada's longterm labour needs should be integrated into Canada's immigration policy. Family sponsorship should be open to all Canadians and permanent residents on equal terms, but assessed more stringently. Relatives outside the immediate family should be selected based on literacy, education, and skills. It also recommended a means to appeal deportation decisions.

The public hearings revealed considerable opposition to proposals to limit family sponsorships along with support for an end to race-based selection, and more due process protections for

---

100 FitzGerald and Cook-Martín, *Culling the Masses*, 334. They provide the following dates: Uruguay (1936), Chile (1936), Paraguay (1937), Cuba (1942), and Argentina (1949).

101 Government of Canada, *White Paper on Immigration* (Ottawa: Queen's Printer, 1966).

immigrants detained or under removal orders. Business interests were in favour of economic admissions being more closely tied to economic needs. As is the case today, there were differences of opinion regarding whether Canada should admit more immigrants or fewer.[102]

Policy Transformed: 1967–2001

1967–1975: Towards a New Immigration Act

In 1967, new regulations were passed,[103] introducing features that would remain in place for the next forty years. Explicit prohibitions based on nationality, ethnicity, or racial identity were removed from all immigration streams. The admissible categories for immigration were simplified and reduced to three: independent, sponsored, and nominated immigrants.

Independent immigrants were required to meet a specific threshold of points focused on the ability of a person to establish themselves in Canada. Points were assigned based on a person's age, education, training, finances, skills, family in Canada, knowledge of English or French, and secured employment.

Sponsored immigrants included close family members of Canadian citizens or permanent residents. They were exempt from the points system, with sponsors remaining responsible for their settlement.

Nominated immigrants were more distant relatives. They had to clear a points threshold but needed fewer than independent applicants. Points were assigned based on factors like age, education, skills, and long-term suitability.

The points system represented a significant departure from the previously wide-ranging discretion granted to immigration officers, but certain aspects still allowed for subjective evaluation. For

---

102   FitzGerald and Cook-Martín, *Culling the Masses*, 176–7; Kelley and Trebilcock, *Making of the Mosaic*, 354–5.
103   Order in Council, P.C. 1967-1616 (16 August 1967).

instance, up to fifteen of a total of 100 points were allocated based on the immigration officer's assessment of qualities, including adaptability, motivation, initiative, and resourcefulness.[104]

Furthermore, the minister had the authority to reject applicants who met the required points threshold while admitting those who did not. This was also delegated to immigration officers provided they had the approval of a superior officer.[105] Between 1963 and 1976, approximately 4,000 to 7,000 individuals per year who did not meet established criteria were nonetheless admitted on a temporary or permanent basis via this discretionary power.[106] It is unclear how many were rejected in this manner.

The 1967 regulations opened immigration to Canada in two significant ways. First, they eliminated remaining explicit exclusions based on race and ethnicity, and further opened immigration to Canada from more diverse source countries. Second, they expanded opportunities for Canadians and permanent residents to sponsor their relatives, thus contributing to a significant shift in the composition of immigrants.

Immigration from traditional sources in the United Kingdom, Europe, and the United States declined from 80 per cent in the 1960s to 49 per cent in the 1970s, 22 per cent in the 1980s, and 20 per cent in the 1990s, while immigration from the rest of the world – Asia, the Caribbean, Central and South America, Africa, and the Middle East – increased (see figure 1). Just between 1962 and 1976, European immigration to Canada fell from 78 per cent of annual admissions to 38 per cent. British immigration fell from 28 per cent to 16 per cent in the same period. Meanwhile, the proportion of immigrants from Asia increased from 3 per cent to 22 per cent.[107]

Also, by 1976, immigrants coming through the family and nominated categories made up 62 per cent of annual admissions, economic

---

104 Order in Council, P.C. 1967–1616, schedules A and B.
105 Louis Parai, "Canada's Immigration Policy, 1962–74," *International Migration Review* (1975): 459.
106 Kelley and Trebilcock, *Making of the Mosaic*, 363.
107 R. Douglas Francis, Richard Jones, and Donald B. Smith, *Destinies: Canadian History Since Confederation* (Toronto: Holt, Rinehart, and Winston, 1988).

immigrants comprised 30 per cent, and refugees made up less than 8 per cent of the total.[108] Immigrants from new source countries were often recruited for jobs in urban areas that Canadians were unwilling or unable to fill. Various ethnic groups often were concentrated in low-wage sectors in specific occupations and industries. The combined effects of economic segregation and shared cultures contributed to the formation of cohesive ethnic communities that survived over time.[109]

By the mid-1970s, the country entered a period of rising interest rates and flatlining economic growth – stagflation – in part due to the rising cost of oil. Unemployment rates rose as did prices. A wave of rising prosperity lasting close to thirty years was over and the economy lapsed into a deep and persistent recession. Immigration became the focus of attention and debate.

The scrutiny was also fuelled by the delays experienced in immigration processing, which dated back to the creation of the Immigration Appeal Board in 1967. Authorized to hear appeals from Canadian citizens whose sponsorship applications were denied and from immigrants ordered to be removed from Canada, it survives to this day. Before it was established, potential immigrants had to apply to Canada from outside the country. In 1966, the law was changed to allow for applications within its borders. Shortly afterwards, the Immigration Appeal Board was overwhelmed.

To cope with the backlog, the potential immigrant's right to apply from within Canada was revoked in 1972 and the size of the board expanded the following year. Appeal rights were no longer extended to those in the country unlawfully or to those from countries that Canada did not require a visa to enter, such as the United States and the United Kingdom. In parallel, the government allowed a limited grace period for people who were in Canada irregularly, to adjust their status. These applications were judged on humanitarian and compassionate grounds, including how well they had become established in Canada. Thirty-nine thousand people became permanent residents under this amnesty.

---

108   Kelley and Trebilcock, *Making of the Mosaic*, 353.
109   Jeffrey Reitz, *The Survival of Ethnic Groups* (Toronto: McGraw Hill-Ryerson, 1980), chap. 2.

The difficulties encountered by the Immigration Appeal Board put more attention on immigration policy, just as the economy was slowing down. In 1974, the government commissioned a study, known as the Green Paper. It concluded that large-scale immigration was not desirable, that it exacerbated the negative impacts of increased urbanization, heightened racial tensions, and contributed to a declining proportion of francophones in Canada.[110] Recommendations in the Green Paper included reducing immigration, tying admissions to labour market needs, requiring immigrants to settle in designated areas, creating a separate category of refugees based on Canadian definitions, and not becoming a signatory to the *International Refugee Convention*.[111]

The Green Paper provoked widespread criticism. A Joint Senate-House of Commons Committee was commissioned to conduct cross-country public hearings on it.[112] A broad constellation of stakeholders joined in the debate: politicians, church groups, ethnic associations, business alliances, other special interest groups, individual Canadians, academics, and the media. By this time, sizeable ethnic political constituencies had developed, particularly in the major urban areas. Members of Parliament from those areas were increasingly attentive to immigration policy that affected these constituents.

The 1975 hearings revealed that there was relatively broad consensus in favour of a liberal immigration policy, although there was some divergence of opinion on whether it should be based on short- or long-term economic factors. Representatives of the legal community argued for enhanced due process protections in admission, removal, and appeal processes.

---

110 Canada, Department of Manpower and Immigration, *Report of the Canadian Immigration and Population Study (The Green Paper)* (Ottawa: Information Canada, 1974). It was comprised of several volumes all of which were published by the Department of Manpower and Immigration.

111 Department of Manpower and Immigration, *The Green Paper*, 119–28.

112 Not, however, in Quebec which appreciated the recognition that large-scale immigration was diluting the francophone population. Between 1946 and 1971, only 15 per cent of immigrants to Canada settled in that province, and of that number only 5 per cent were francophone.

Among its many recommendations, the committee called for the setting of annual immigration quotas in consultation with the provinces and subject to parliamentary approval. Immigration applications should be assessed on a first-come first-served basis. Criteria for economic immigrants should place greater emphasis on life experience, personal competence, and having relatives in Canada, and less on education and personal assessment.

The committee recommended eliminating the nominated category and permitting the sponsorship of parents of any age. Additionally, it called for a separate regime for refugees, and the removal of the ban on the admission of homosexuals. Among the enhanced due process protections, it recommended greater due process protections in deportation procedures.[113] Sixty of the committee's sixty-five recommendations were implemented in new legislation – the *Immigration Act, 1976* – which set a new trajectory for Canadian immigration policy.

1976–1987: Greater Inclusion and Transparency

The *Immigration Act, 1976* was passed following extensive political and public debate. It reflected broad consensus for transparent and points-based admission criteria for independent immigrants, generous family reunification policies, due process protections for individuals facing deportation, and a reasonably generous refugee policy. It was the most inclusive admissions policy in Canadian history.

The act set out who would be included under the various admission streams while leaving the detailed selection criteria and processes to regulations that were subject to parliamentary review.[114] It provided for increased provincial engagement

---

113 Canada, *Report to Parliament by the Special Joint Committee on Immigration Policy*, First Session, Thirtieth Parliament, 1974–75 (Ottawa: Information Canada, 1975), 21–2, 32, 36–7, 42–4.

114 Some vestiges of executive discretion remained. Cabinet could admit or deny entry to individuals or groups that did not meet the requirements of the act or its regulations, but it could not overturn a deportation order unless it had been successfully appealed.

in immigration policy, not least in mandating that the minister responsible for immigration consult with provinces, individuals, and institutions regarding future immigration levels.[115] Immigration levels during most of this period closely aligned with economic conditions.

Following the economic downturn that started in 1974, annual admissions declined from 201,000 to 86,000 over the course of four years. Subsequently, as the economy recovered, immigration numbers began to rise, only to decrease again during the 1980s recession, reaching just over 84,000 in 1985, the lowest point since 1962. However, sustained economic growth throughout the 1990s resulted in a significant increase in annual admissions, more than doubling to over 200,000 for most of the decade.[116]

Expansive admission criteria contributed to the changing composition of new arrivals. Immigrant arrivals had shifted from Europe and the United States to elsewhere by the late 1970s. Initially, many new arrivals were from the Caribbean (predominantly Afro-Caribbean).[117] This source declined in the 1980s and, by 1990, approximately 50 per cent of arriving permanent residents were from the Middle East and Asia. Arrivals from countries within the European Union accounted for 25 per cent, down from over 50 per cent twenty years before.[118]

Under the *Immigration Act, 1976* immigrants to Canada continued to come through the three main streams: economic, family,

---

115 *Immigration Act, 1976*, SC 25-26 Elizabeth II, c. 52, s. 7 (1977).

116 Citizenship and Immigration Canada, *Canada Facts and Figures: Immigration Overview – Permanent and Temporary Residents, 2010* (Ottawa: Public Works and Government Services Canada, 2010), 3–4, https://www.canadianimmigration.com/media/facts2010.pdf.

117 Jeffrey G. Reitz, "Canada: Continuity and Change in Immigration for Nation-Building," in *Controlling Immigration: A Comparative Perspective*, 4th ed., ed. Wayne A. Cornelius, Philip L. Martin, James F. Hollifield, and Takeyuki Tsuda (Stanford, CA: Stanford University Press, 2022), 125.

118 Jane Badets and Tina W.L. Chui, *Canada's Changing Immigrant Population: Focus on Canada* (Ottawa: Statistics Canada, and Toronto: Prentice Hall Canada Inc., 1994), 12–13; Monica Boyd and Michael Vickers, *100 Years of Immigration in Canada*, Canadian Social Trends 58 (Ottawa: Statistics Canada, 2000). The top five countries accounting for one third of all admissions were Hong Kong, the People's Republic of China, India, the Philippines, and Sri Lanka.

and assisted relative. To this was added a separate humanitarian category and a much smaller business stream.[119]

Economic immigrants were still required to meet a minimum threshold of points, which were adjusted to prioritize individuals with occupations in high demand. Employers could apply for permits to bring in immigrant workers but, as of 1978, they had to demonstrate that there were no qualified Canadian or permanent-resident candidates available for the position. During the recession of 1982–6, all independent immigrants had to have a firm job offer to be admissible.[120]

The family class was broadened under the 1976 act to include spouses, fiancé(e)s, unmarried children under twenty-one years of age, parents, and minor unmarried orphaned relatives.[121] The assisted relative category was also broadened to include brothers, sisters, aunts, uncles, nieces, nephews, and grandparents. Like economic immigrants, individuals in these categories were required to meet specific point requirements. Notably, some points were awarded for having a family member already residing in Canada.

The use of points-based criteria in the economic and assisted relative stream gave authorities the ability to carefully choose immigrants based on the likelihood that they would successfully establish themselves. The number and location of visa offices also reflected preferences for immigrants from certain regions over

---

119 "Report of the Department of Employment and Immigration," *Annual Departmental Reports, 1990–91*, 39. Several programs were initiated for business class immigrants and investors. They aimed to attract individuals with experience and capital and the ability to create jobs in Canada. The programs admitted just a few thousand individuals annually and were criticized for being laxly monitored and used as a means of selling Canadian passports to wealthy buyers. The investor program was eventually cancelled in 1994.

120 *Annual Report to Parliament on Future Immigration Levels, 1985* (Ottawa: Ministry of Supply and Services, 1985), 3, https://publications.gc.ca/collections/Collection /Ci1-2005E.pdf. A similar condition was imposed in the postwar period.

121 This brought the regulations in line with the definition of a child under the UN *Convention on the Rights of the Child*. See UN General Assembly, Resolution 44/25, *Convention on the Rights of the Child*, 20 November 1989, ss. 1(1)(2), https://www .ohchr.org/en/instruments-mechanisms/instruments/convention-rights-child. Parents were initially limited to over sixty years of age or disabled but in 1978 parents of any age could be sponsored.

others. So, while the elimination of overt racial and ethnic preferences opened admissions from more regions of the world, selection processes meant that the doors were not entirely wide open, which helped to avoid fears of unregulated immigration.

The humanitarian stream provided for the admission of displaced and persecuted persons. The regulations provided for the selection of refugees abroad, through resettlement, as well as for the determination of refugee claims made from within Canada or at Canadian ports of entry. For the first time, the government included refugee admissions in its detailed planning. It established dedicated overseas resettlement processes and inland refugee determination procedures.

Refugees selected from abroad had to meet the international refugee definition,[122] show that they could successfully establish themselves in Canada and have a Canadian sponsor. The federal government set annual numbers for the refugees it would sponsor, and established processes for private groups to sponsor refugees. Sponsors were required to provide lodging, care, maintenance, and resettlement assistance for one year.[123]

The government also established special humanitarian classes in response to specific circumstances in Eastern Europe and Latin America. The requirements for admission varied depending on the class, reflecting the prevailing ideological influences during the Cold War era. The most lenient criteria were applied to individuals from Eastern Europe, who only needed to demonstrate that they were outside their country and willing to immigrate to Canada.[124]

---

122 As set out in the 1951 *Convention Relating to the Status of Refugees* and its 1967 Protocol. UN General Assembly, A/RES/429, "Draft Convention Relating to the Status of Refugees," 14 December 1950, https://www.refworld.org/docid/3b00f08a27 .html; UN General Assembly, A/RES/2198, *Protocol Relating to the Status of Refugees*, 16 December 1966, https://www.refworld.org/docid/3b00f1cc50.html.

123 Hawkins, *Critical Years in Immigration*, 78–9.

124 *Regulations Respecting the Designation of a Self-Exiled Persons Class*, S.O.R./78–933. In contrast, to come within the *Regulations Respecting the Designation of Political Prisoners and Oppressed Persons Designated Class*, S.O.R./82–977, which applied to Latin America (S.O.R./82-977), individuals had to meet the definition of a Convention refugee or provide evidence of being detained for exercising their civil liberties or freedom of thought. They also had to demonstrate their ability to successfully establish themselves in Canada.

Another program was established for the admission of refugees from the communist regimes in Vietnam, Cambodia, and Laos following the end of the Vietnam War in 1975.[125] It was part of a larger international effort to respond to a growing refugee crisis in the region where fleeing refugees were often pushed from the borders of neighbouring states.

Tens of thousands of refugees had died in flight and many thousands were stranded in the South China Sea in overcrowded, leaky vessels with inadequate food and water and vulnerable to pirate attacks.[126] Initially, the Canadian government committed to accepting 12,000 Indochinese refugees for resettlement, most through government sponsorship. Strong public support and advocacy for the government to do more led to a promise by the government that it would sponsor one refugee for every refugee sponsored privately.

The response was unprecedented. By 1982, more than 60,000 refugees from Vietnam, Laos, and Cambodia were resettled in Canada, most of whom subsequently integrated well into Canadian society.[127] With the onset of a recession in the early 1980s, the number of both federal and private sponsorships fell.

Other refugees were admitted through the exercise of ministerial exceptions. This was used to benefit 10,000 Lebanese fleeing the 1976 civil war and 8,000 Chinese refugees following the 1989 Tiananmen Square massacre in Beijing.[128]

---

125 *Regulations Respecting the Designation of an Indochinese Designated Class*, S.O.R./78–931.

126 In 1979, the United Nations negotiated an agreement between countries in the region and resettlement countries. The former agreed to provide temporary protection to refugees, pending their resettlement abroad. The plan was revised in 1989. By the end of the program, in the early 1990s, 1.4 million refugees were resettled. Kelley, *People Forced to Flee*, 197–9.

127 Morton Beiser, *Strangers at the Gate: The "Boat People's" First Ten Years in Canada* (Toronto: University of Toronto Press, 1999), preface.

128 Salvadorans faced with deportation from the United States were also admitted in this way as Canada's recognition rate of refugees from El Salvador was much higher than the United States. For further information, see "Report of the Department of Employment and Immigration," *Annual Departmental Reports*, 1982–83; Gerald E. Dirks, *Controversy and Complexity: Canadian Immigration Policy During the 1980s* (Montreal: McGill-Queen's University Press, 1995), 74.

Many significant refugee situations did not benefit from special measures and accounted for a small proportion of the government's annual plans. For example, of the over 6.5 million Afghan refugees in Pakistan and Iran in 1986, Canada provided resettlement places for just 300.[129] Similarly, of the 5 million refugees in Africa, no more than 1,000 were selected in any year in the 1980s despite a continually worsening refugee situation.[130] Between 1975 and 1990 annual admissions of refugees selected abroad rose from 7,300 in 1977 to more than 52,000 in 1992. A similar increase was experienced in the number of refugees who sought Canada's protection either at the border or from within Canada. Annual numbers increased from a few hundred annually in the 1970s, to a few thousand in the 1980s, eventually reaching 37,000 in 1992.[131]

The refugee determination process was designed to handle a few hundred cases a year. It involved multiple steps and layers of decision-making. Claims were determined based on a written submission with limited rights to seek judicial review of a negative decision.[132] Persons who received a positive determination were subsequently subject to health and security admissibility checks. The very lengthy procedure, coupled with the increase in annual refugee claims, led to serious backlogs in the mid-1980s and calls for better management of the system.

By this time, concerns were also being raised regarding the other admission streams. In the family admission category, allegations circulated of high default rates on family sponsorship undertakings

---

129 The total number of government-assisted refugees in 1986 was set at 12,000 from "other world areas." See the *Annual Report to Parliament on Future Immigration Levels, 1985*, 5.

130 Based on statistics in the *Annual Report to Parliament on Future Immigration Levels*, 1980 to 1989, available in the Library and Archives Canada.

131 Employment and Immigration Canada, *Refugee Perspectives, 1985–86* (Ottawa: Employment and Immigration Canada, 1985), 39.

132 The claims were reviewed by an advisory committee to the minister. The minister decided the claim. Negative decisions could be reviewed by a special committee on compassionate and humanitarian grounds. An unfavourable decision could then be reviewed again by the Immigration Appeal Board. A further review by the Federal Court with permission of the court and on the narrow grounds of errors in law or jurisdiction. *The Immigration Act, 1976*, ss. 47(1), 70–2.

and weak federal oversight. Meanwhile, low employment rates among recent immigrants triggered debates on whether the selection criteria in the economic stream aligned with the country's economic needs. Several provinces, seeing a surge in annual immigrant arrivals, voiced growing disaffection with what they perceived as inadequate federal support to meet settlement costs.

1988–2001: Calls for Change

Failings in immigration processing were addressed by a patchwork of changes to the *Immigration Act* from 1987 onward leading to a full-scale review in 1994. Several in-depth reports had been published on how best to reform the refugee determination system. All called for a simplified process and for refugee claims to be heard orally by an independent tribunal with an opportunity to appeal that decision.[133] The Supreme Court of Canada's decision in the 1985 *Singh* case was the catalyst for change.[134] The Court held that, given the gravity of the issues at stake in refugee determinations, fundamental justice required that the claimant have an opportunity to an oral hearing.[135]

In 1989, the Immigration Appeal Board was replaced by the Immigration and Refugee Board, a change that has endured to this day. Initially, the board consisted of two divisions: the Refugee Determination Division focused on determining refugee claims in

---

133   Walter G. Robinson, *The Refugee Status Determination Process: A Report of the Task Force on Immigration Practices and Procedures* (Ottawa: Minister of Supply and Services, 1981). Another report was published in 1984 by Ed Ratushny, *A New Refugee Status Determination Process for Canada* (Ottawa: Minister of Supply and Services, 1984). The following year the government commissioned a study led by Rabbi Plaut whose report was issued the same year: W. Gaunther Plaut, *Refugee Determination in Canada* (Ottawa: Minister of Supply and Services, 1985).

134   *Singh v. Minister of Employment and Immigration,* [1985] 1 S.C.R. 177.

135   The government responded with some temporary measures such as expanding the size of the Immigration Appeal Board and implementing a partial amnesty in 1987 to deal with the backlog of cases. This gave permanent residence status to refugee claimants who were likely to establish themselves successfully in Canada. Eighty-five per cent of the 28,000 applicants gained immigrant status under this measure.

an oral hearing, while the Immigration Appeal Division handled appeals related to denied family sponsorship applications and removal orders. The members of both divisions were appointed by the Cabinet and operated independently from the Department of Immigration. In 1993, the Adjudication Division was introduced, tasked with conducting admissibility hearings and detention reviews for foreign nationals suspected of being inadmissible to or removable from Canada.[136]

The creation of the Immigration and Refugee Board marked a significant milestone, providing greater transparency and due process protections to Canadians, permanent residents, and foreign nationals who received unfavourable immigration decisions. However, it also coincided with other changes to the *Immigration Act* aimed at reducing the number of refugees arriving in Canada.

Although the number of refugee claims per year was rising, it was relatively small compared to the countries that received far larger numbers of refugees with far fewer resources to care for them. Most of the 11 million refugees around the world were hosted in low- and middle-income countries, where refugee influxes were measured in the hundreds of thousands of arrivals in a short span of time. Nonetheless, for many Canadians, an increase in spontaneous arrivals raised concerns over the ability to control national borders.

For some, the arrival of 173 East Asian refugee claimants off the coast of Nova Scotia in 1987 was a case in point. Most were Sikhs claiming refuge from religious persecution in India. They had spent three weeks at sea in a crowded vessel and, once close to land, told to jump ship and swim to shore. Responding to public outcry, the government recalled Parliament to on the basis that the arrival was a matter of grave importance.[137] Over the next few years, the *Immigration Act* and regulations were amended to deter arrivals, tighten admissibility, and secure borders.[138]

---

136 David Vinokur, "30 Years of Changes at the Immigration and Refugee Board of Canada," *CIHS Bulletin*, no. 88 (2019): 8, https://cihs-shic.ca/wp-content/uploads/2019/04/Bulletin-88-Final.pdf. Its members are from the Canadian civil service.

137 *House of Commons Debates*, 11 August 1987, 7910.

138 Changes were introduced to Parliament in a series of bills: Bill C-84 (1987), Bill C-55 (1987), and Bill C-86 (1992).

Increased fines and jail terms were imposed on transportation companies and individuals who brought to Canada individuals without the required prior authorization. Moreover, refugee claimants who came to Canada through the United States were required to wait there until the date of their Canadian refugee determination hearing. Provision was made for Cabinet to proscribe certain countries as "safe" based on their compliance with international refugee protection principles.[139] Refugees who came to Canada through one of these countries would be removed there without their claim being heard in Canada. Mandatory detention was imposed for all persons whose identities were in doubt.

To critics, such changes put the lives of refugees at risk. They noted that refugees often flee without visas and documentation and that penalizing them for it was contrary to international law. Additionally, they highlighted interpretive differences between Canadian and American jurisprudence such that certain claims of persecution might be recognized in Canada but not in the United States. As a result, refugees with valid claims could face the risk of being deported from the United States to potentially harmful situations while awaiting their appointments in Canada. Within Parliament, members of the Opposition made nearly 100 motions to amend the provisions, most of which were defeated by the Conservative majority.

Another controversial change was introduced in the early 1990s. It involved admissibility criteria for live-in caregivers. Applicants were required to have the equivalent of a Canadian grade-twelve education; six months' formal training related to the job; and the ability to speak, read, and understand French or English.[140] Critics argued that

---

139   *Immigration Act*, s. 46.01(1) (b), as enacted by R.S.C. 1985 (4th Supp.), c. 28. For over fifteen years no country was proscribed as "safe." This was partly due to significant opposition to invoking the concept. Advocates pointed out that even among Western countries with good human rights records, the recognition rates of refugee asylum claims still varied widely. Therefore, individuals who could be recognized as refugees in Canada might be rejected in another country. To remove them would implicate Canada in *refoulement* (or forcible return), which is prohibited by international law.

140   Canada, Department of Employment and Immigration, *The Live-In Caregiver Program* (Ottawa: Ministry of Supply and Services, 1992), 9.

such requirements created unnecessary barriers for otherwise qualified individuals. The policy was somewhat eased in subsequent years with evidence that there was a shortage of caregivers in Canada.[141]

Less controversial was the broadening of general inadmissibility provisions. In 1992, medical officers were provided with wider latitude to reject applicants if they were likely to endanger public health or safety or be too great a burden on health or social services. Persons convicted of crimes prohibited under Canadian law continued to be inadmissible and the provisions were broadened to include those suspected of committing such crimes or being members of an organized criminal group. An actual conviction was no longer necessary to trigger the ban.

In the early 1990s, the ability of family members to sponsor their relatives was curtailed. In 1992, the age limit of a sponsored child was lowered from twenty-one years to nineteen years and the nominated class provision was abolished the following year.[142] Criteria in the economic stream was also reviewed. Through the late 1980s and into the 1990s, there were several studies on the impact of immigration on the Canadian economy.[143] The majority view was that immigrants did not displace Canadian workers and had small but positive economic benefits for the host community.[144]

---

141 Eliminating the requirement that foreign "nannies" have six months of formal training and replacing this with at least a year of related experience.

142 Exceptions were made for children older than nineteen but "dependent" on their parents for reasons of full-time study or a disability. Employment and Immigration Canada, *Annual Report to Parliament: Immigration Plan for 1991–1995, Year Two* (Ottawa: Minister of Supply and Services, 1991), 3.

143 W.L. Warr and M.B. Percy, "Immigration Policy and Canadian Economic Growth," in *Domestic Policies in the International Economic Environment*, ed. John Whalley (Toronto: University of Toronto Press, 1985). Their research was commissioned by the Royal Commission on the Economic Union and Development Prospects for Canada (Ottawa, 1985). See also Don J. DeVoretz, "Immigration and Employment Effects," Discussion Paper 89.B.3 (Ottawa: Institute for Research on Public Policy, 1989); Neil Swann et al., *The Economic and Social Impacts of Immigration: A Research Report Prepared for the Economic Council of Canada* (Ottawa: Minister of Supply and Services, 1991); Don DeVoretz, ed., *Diminishing Returns: The Economics of Canada's Recent Immigration Policy* (Toronto: C.D. Howe Institute, 1995).

144 Another finding, generally accepted, was that increased contact between persons of different races reduces racial discrimination and animus over time.

During the 1990s, the employment rates and earnings of recently arrived immigrants were closely examined. Despite higher education levels and language proficiency compared to the Canadian-born population, evidence indicated that immigrants faced lower employment rates and earned lower average incomes.[145] These findings supported growing calls for an assessment of criteria that prioritized immigrants with skills that were in demand in the Canadian labour market. The Canadian government incorporated this approach into the first multi-year immigration plan submitted to Parliament in 1990. The plan aimed to attract immigrants whose skills and expertise would contribute to the country's economic growth and development. The plan set specific immigration targets for a period of five years, outlining the levels for each admission stream. It was developed through extensive consultations involving more than 4,000 individuals representing a diverse range of stakeholders, including businesses, labour groups, various levels of government, and community organizations.

Since the mid-1980s, annual immigration levels had steadily risen from below 100,000 to over 200,000 annually in 1990.[146] The consultations revealed widespread support for a continued increase in immigration from 200,000 annually in 1990 to 250,000 by 1995. This was notable as the country was experiencing a recession at the time. The plan marked the first time the government, backed by the major political parties, made a commitment focusing on long-term growth rather than short-term fluctuations in the economic cycle.

As part of the plan, the government consulted with the provinces and businesses and developed a list of occupations in short

---

145　Garnett Picot and Andrew Heisz, "The Performance of the 1990s Canadian Labour Market," Analytical Studies Branch–Research Paper Series (Ottawa, ON: Statistics Canada, 2000). Subsequent studies point to the same: Marc Frenette and René Morissette, "Will They Ever Converge? Earnings of Immigrant and Canadian-Born Workers over the Last Two Decades," Analytical Studies Branch–Research Paper Series (Ottawa, ON: Statistics Canada, 2003); Jeffrey G. Reitz, "Immigrant Skill Utilization in the Canadian Labour Market: Implications of Human Capital Research," *Journal of International Migration and Integration* 2, no. 3 (2001): 347–78.

146　Reitz, "Canada: Continuity and Change in Immigration," 125.

supply in particular areas. Applicants who qualified for those positions received extra selection points.[147] Additional points were also awarded for those with a relative in Canada.[148] Within a few years, a new Provincial Nominee Program was introduced that gave participating provinces a greater role in the selection of economic immigrants based on their labour market needs.[149]

By this time, the *Immigration Act, 1976* had been amended many times and, in the government's view, had become overly cumbersome and inadequate. In 1996, it commissioned a three-member committee to review the act with a view to arriving at less complex legislation and a more streamlined refugee determination process. The panel was also asked to study the scope and depth of ministerial discretion.

The panel's report was released in 1997 and presented recommendations for two new pieces of legislation. One focused on immigrants and the other concerned refugees and individuals in need of protection. It also proposed the implementation of legal ceilings on the number of immigration visas issued annually, while emphasizing the need for the federal government to allocate adequate resources for settlement services.

The panel recommended expanding the scope of family class sponsorship. However, it also proposed that all sponsored and independent immigrants meet a prescribed language proficiency level in English or French. The report further recommended consolidating the skilled worker, entrepreneur, and investor categories into a unified self-supporting class, considering language proficiency, education, age, and work experience as significant factors for assessment. Specifically, it proposed that applicants in the investor program be no older than forty-five years and possess a minimum of half a million dollars for investment purposes.

---

147 Employment and Immigration Canada, *Immigration Plan 1991–1995, Year Two*, 13.

148 Employment and Immigration Canada, "Helping a Relative Immigrate to Canada," Immigration Fact Sheet No. 2, January 1993.

149 The Provincial Nominee Program is discussed more in chapter 2.1: "Economic Stream: Accelerated Change and Growth." In 1978 Quebec had the first federal-provincial agreement with Quebec, which over time was revised giving Quebec increased autonomy in managing immigration destined for the province.

The panel advanced recommendations concerning the requirements for citizenship. In addition to the existing criteria, prospective citizens should also be required to know an official language and have actively participated in Canadian society through holding a job, going to school, raising a family, or doing volunteer work.[150]

The report received a critical reception from business associations, immigrant and faith-based groups as well as bar associations and international humanitarian agencies. Following its publication, the Minister of Immigration chaired public hearings across the country and received over 2,000 written submissions.[151] The language recommendations received the most criticism as being unsound and unworkable given that over two-thirds of all immigrants to Canada spoke neither English nor French. The panel's suggested changes to the investor program were said to be so strict that they would lead to the collapse of the program. The panel was also criticized for recommending that decisions on refugee claims be transferred to civil servants. And the proposed elevated requirements of citizenship were seen as so onerous most Canadians would be unable to meet them.

Over the next two years, a series of events helped to maintain public focus on immigration policy and fuel demands for reform. One was the arrival of 600 Chinese migrants off the coast of British Colombia in the summer of 1999. The migrants were largely from Fujian province and had paid thousands of dollars to go to North America where they believed jobs awaited them. A significant number were children between eleven and eighteen years of age. Many of the arrivals were detained, most were returned to China, and a small number received refugee status. The smugglers were criminally prosecuted. Several aspects of the handling of the incident came under scrutiny, including the fact that a number of arrivals made refugee claims and then disappeared. It was characterized as a further example of a failing process.

---

150 Susan Davis, Roslyn Kunin, and Robert Trempe, *Not Just Numbers: A Canadian Framework for Future Immigration* (Ottawa: Minister of Public Works and Government Services Canada, 1997).

151 Jennifer Hyndman, "Gender and Canadian Immigration Policy: A Current Snapshot," *Canadian Woman Studies* 19, no. 3 (1999): 6, https://cws.journals.yorku.ca/index.php/cws/article/view/7868.

Also in 1999, a case before the Federal Court of Canada revealed that many failed refugee claimants were making repeat claims in a manner the presiding judge characterized as "a scandalous abuse of our border." The minister was quick to note that the practice was under review.[152]

The following year, the Auditor General's report to Parliament added pressure to reform. The report pointed to multiple weaknesses in the immigration system: long processing times, overly vague medical, criminal, and security inadmissibility criteria; insufficient quality control over immigration decisions; and inadequate rights of appeal. The report concluded that the failings limited "Canada's ability to maximize the economic and social benefits that immigration affords."[153]

Pressure also came from the United States. The chief of the Central Intelligence Agency, among others, alleged that Canada's immigration system and relatively porous border made it a haven for terrorists. This apprehension was amplified following the 11 September 2001 terrorist attacks.

All these concerns influenced the drafting of a new legislation, introduced to Parliament in 2001. The *Immigration and Refugee Protection Act 2001* marks another pivotal inflection point in Canadian history and is the bedrock of contemporary immigration policy.

Main Historical Shifts

Throughout its history, Canadian immigration policy has had three broad trajectories. First, for close to 100 years, it was racially selective, designed and executed in a manner that gave close to

---

152   Estanislao Oziewicz, "Ottawa Reconsidering Refugee Process: Immigration Act Provision Allowing for Multiple Claims under Review," *Globe and Mail*, 6 November 1999.

153   Auditor General of Canada, "Citizenship and Immigration Canada – The Economic Component of the Canadian Immigration Program," *Report of the Auditor General of Canada* (Ottawa: Office of the Auditor General of Canada, 2000), 9–11; Benjamin Dolin and Margaret Young, "Canada's Immigration Program," Background Paper (Ottawa: Parliamentary Information and Research Service, 2004).

unfettered discretion to the executive branch of government. Permanent residents could be removed from the country relatively easily, on broad grounds and with limited rights of judicial review. Naturalization criteria and naturalization decisions reflected prevailing racial and political prejudices.

Second, from the late 1960s, admission policies were no longer defined by ethnicity and race. The design of immigration policy became more consultative. Annual admissions levels were set in consultation with the provinces, interest groups, and individuals. Structured public hearings preceded major shifts in policies. The details of immigration policy were set out in regulations and subject to parliamentary review. The rights of immigrants and Canadian sponsors to seek judicial review of immigration officers' decisions were expanded.

Then came the third main shift in the country's immigration history: the *Immigration and Refugee Protection Act 2001*. It is the main foundation of national immigration policy, which also features vestiges of both earlier periods, as the subsequent chapters reveal. They will also show how Canada continues to be a country of opportunity for immigrants from all over the world. Public support for immigrants is high. Nonetheless, immigration policy and selection criteria shift frequently and are more removed from parliamentary and public scrutiny than was the case at the end of the twentieth century. These changes and their implications are the focus of the remainder of this book.

PART 2

Immigration to Canada: Rapid Change and Expansion

Part 2 analyses contemporary admission policies, focusing on Canada's three primary streams for permanent admissions: economic, family, and refugee. Each stream is explored in a separate chapter, outlining the changes observed over the past two decades and evaluating how these align with the goals set forth in the *Immigration and Refugee Protection Act 2001*.

The economic stream (chapter 2.1) is the primary avenue for permanent resident admissions. While the precise percentage of economic immigrants has experienced minor fluctuations, it has consistently represented around 60 per cent of all admissions throughout the contemporary era (see figure 3).

The proportion of immigrants entering via family sponsorship (chapter 2.2) has also displayed some variability since 2001, yet has constituted approximately a quarter of annual permanent resident admissions on average. In more recent years, however, its contribution has diminished to around 21 per cent (see figure 3).

The number of refugees (chapter 2.3) granted permanent residency each year has seen a steep rise in the past several years. From 2001 to 2015, approximately 29,000 refugees received permanent resident status on average each year. Since then, the yearly average has increased to 50,000 persons (see figure 3).

Immigration, Refugees and Citizenship Canada administers the *Immigration Refugee Protection Act* and the *Citizenship Act*[1] and reports to the Minister of Immigration Refugees, and Citizenship. Immigration officers assess immigration applications. Shortly after the *Immigration and Refugee Protection Act* came into force, the Canadian Border Services Agency was created and given responsibility for border control. The Agency reports to the Minister of Public Safety, Democratic Institutions, and Intergovernmental Affairs.[2] It works closely with Immigration Refugees and Citizenship

---

1 *Citizenship Act* R.S.C., 1985, c. C-29.
2 It replaced the Canadian Customs and Revenue Agency, the enforcement branch of the Immigration Department and the border examination responsibilities of the Canadian Food and Inspection Agency.

Canada in carrying out its responsibilities for border control and removal of inadmissible immigrants and refugees.

Eligibility Criteria

Immigrants who seek permanent residence in Canada are assessed according to the criteria applicable to the immigration stream in which their application is made. These are discussed in more detail in the following chapters. The failure to meet the criteria can lead to rejection of their application.

Inadmissibility Grounds

In addition to meeting the eligibility criteria for the relevant immigration stream, applicants must also be found to be otherwise admissible to Canada.[3] Canadian immigration legislation has always set out who is inadmissible to Canada. For over a century, criminal, security, medical, financial, or misrepresentation have been grounds for inadmissibility. Some of these grounds have been expanded over the past two decades. As discussed in the chapter on refugee admissions, there are additional grounds pertaining to refugee exclusion.

Inadmissibility decisions can be made in various circumstances. They are considered in the context of an immigration application decision. They can also be used to deny a foreign national or permanent resident admission at a Canadian port of entry. And they can be the basis for an inquiry into whether a foreign national or permanent resident in Canada has contravened the *Immigration and Refugee Protection Act 2001* and should be detained and removed from Canada. These last two circumstances are discussed in chapter 3.1: "Deportation."

---

3 *Immigration and Refugee Protection Act*, S.C. 2001, c. 27, ss. 33–43.

Criminality

Criminality bars are broad and apply to actions committed both inside and outside Canada. For example, a person is inadmissible if convicted in Canada of a serious crime. A serious crime is defined as one with a possible sentence of ten years or more, or one where the person was sentenced to more than six months in prison. In the former case, actual time served is not relevant.[4]

For crimes committed outside Canada, the bar is lower as it applies to persons who have been convicted and/or for whom there is reason to believe they have committed a crime which would carry a sentence of ten or more years in Canada. In other words, an actual conviction is not necessary, merely a reasonable belief that the person has committed a serious crime. Inadmissibility provisions also cover persons believed to be involved in organized crime, people smuggling, human trafficking, money laundering, or any other act that is transnational in nature.[5]

Inadmissibility for criminality is a lifelong bar to permanent residency unless the person applies for and receives a "record of suspension" (pardon) from the Parole Board of Canada or files an application to be admitted on the grounds that they have been rehabilitated. The immigration regulations set out the process for determining if a person has rehabilitated.[6]

For some less serious offences, a person may be deemed to have rehabilitated with the passage of time. In other instances, decisions on the rehabilitation of an applicant are considered by an immigration officer or, in very serious cases, by the minister. Relevant factors include time passed since the criminal offence, number of crimes committed, stability of lifestyle, and likelihood of reoffending. Critics claim that a person can wait decades for such a decision by the minister.

---

4 *Immigration and Refugee Protection Act*, S.C. 2001, s. 36.
5 *Immigration and Refugee Protection Act*, S.C. 2001, s. 37.
6 *Immigration and Refugee Protection Regulations* (S.O.R./2002-227), s. 18.

Security

The basis for inadmissibility on security grounds include engaging in an act of espionage against Canada or Canadian interests; subversion by force of any government; and subversion of any kind against a democratic government, institution, or process.

A person is also inadmissible on security grounds for engaging in terrorism, being a danger to the security of Canada, or engaging in acts of violence that might endanger the lives or safety of persons in Canada. Membership in any organization believed to be engaged in any of the security grounds enumerated in the act is also grounds for inadmissibility.[7]

The membership provisions have been criticized as overly broad and harsh since they include individuals who may not be aware of the criminal activities of the association to which they belong. They may have become members because of the cultural, social, or humanitarian activities of the group.

Human or International Rights Violations

Individuals who have participated in or held senior positions within a government involved in the following acts are considered inadmissible: terrorism, systematic or severe human rights violations, genocide, war crimes, or crimes against humanity. Additionally, individuals originating from countries subjected to international sanctions are also deemed inadmissible.[8]

Non-Compliance

A person may also be deemed inadmissible if they fail to meet the requirements of the act, whether through an act or omission. This failure can encompass various aspects, including the omission

---

7   *Immigration and Refugee Protection Act*, S.C. 2001, s. 34(1).
8   *Immigration and Refugee Protection Act*, S.C. 2001, s. 35.1(1).

of necessary information, such as dependent family members, criminal activities, or a previous refugee determination. It also can encompass fraud, such as where a person submits false documents in support of an immigration application. A permanent resident who has not fulfilled their obligations, such as maintaining continuous residency, may also be considered inadmissible on these grounds.[9]

Medical Reasons

Medical evaluations are required for most persons who apply to visit, study, work, or live permanently in Canada. They are not required for refugees, protected persons and sponsored spouses, common-law partners, and dependent children.[10] A person can be inadmissible for health reasons if their condition is likely to be a danger to public health or safety or might reasonably cause excessive demands on health or social services. Relevant factors include whether the person suffers from an infectious disease or other malady that might lead to sudden mental or physical incapacity or unpredictable or violent behaviour.[11]

In considering whether a condition will cause an excessive demand on health or social services, two factors are most salient. One is if the treatment will extend wait times for services in Canada. Another is whether the cost of treatment exceeds a specified threshold over five years. Critics have raised ongoing concerns regarding the inconsistency of the excessive demand criterion with the *Canadian Charter of Rights and Freedoms* and Canada's obligations under the *Convention on the Rights of Persons with Disabilities*.[12]

---

9   *Immigration and Refugee Protection Act*, S.C. 2001, s. 41.

10   *Immigration and Refugee Protection Act*, S.C. 2001, s. 38.

11   Immigration, Refugees and Citizenship Canada, "Medical Inadmissibility," last modified 8 January 2024, https://www.canada.ca/en/immigration-refugees-citizenship/services/immigrate-canada/inadmissibility/reasons/medical-inadmissibility.html.

12   United Nations, "Convention on the Rights of Persons with Disabilities," Treaty Series, 2515 (2006): 3.

They argue that this criterion unfairly discriminates against individuals with disabilities and perpetuates outdated and discriminatory perspectives towards people living with conditions such as HIV/AIDS. Furthermore, they argue that the provision fails to recognize the significant contributions that people with disabilities make to Canadian society.[13]

In response to some of these concerns, the government raised the threshold for determining excessive demand in 2018. As of 2022, the threshold amount became $120,000 over five years. This is reportedly three times what an average Canadian costs health and social services for the same period. The government also amended the definition of social services by removing special education, social and vocational rehabilitation services, and personal support services.

For some commentators, the changes are not fully responsive to concerns and have injected a degree of unnecessary complexity in medical assessments. The criteria and complicated process favour those with financial resources to help overcome the obstacles. Critics point to the high cost of medical assessments and administrative reviews as well as having to obtain evidence that a family can help offset the costs of medical care.

Financial Reasons

A foreign national is inadmissible for financial reasons if they are unable or unwilling to support themselves or their dependents or if they do not have a sponsor who can meet the requirements.

Avenues of Appeal and Review

Legal avenues to contest a decision to refuse an application for permanent residency vary.

---

13 For more detailed analysis of the medical inadmissibility process related to persons with disabilities, see Valentina Capurri, *Not Good Enough for Canada: Canadian Public Discourse around Issues of Inadmissibility for Potential Immigrants*

Reconsideration by an Immigration Officer

Persons whose immigration applications are refused can make a request to the immigration officer for a reconsideration of the decision. However, this is rarely done in the applicant's favour as immigration officers are instructed that "reconsideration should only be done, where warranted, in exceptional cases."[14]

Appeal to the Immigration Appeal Division

Canadian citizens and permanent residents whose family sponsorship applications have been denied can appeal the decision to the Immigration Appeal Division provided that the grounds for refusal were not based on serious criminality, security concerns, organized criminality, or international crimes. As discussed in the chapter on the family stream, certain forms of misrepresentation can also be a bar to an appeal before the Immigration Appeal Division.

The Immigration Appeal Division is part of the Immigration and Refugee Board. It is a quasi-judicial tribunal with the authority to review errors of law or fact and to consider whether there are sufficient humanitarian and compassionate grounds to justify granting an exemption or permanent resident status.

Appeal to the Refugee Appeal Division

The Refugee Appeal Division considers appeals from decisions of the Refugee Protection Division to allow or reject claims for refugee

---

with Diseases and/or Disabilities, 1902–2002 (Toronto: University of Toronto Press, 2020), 67–8, 171–2; Robert Wilton, Stine Hansen, and Edward Hall, "Disabled People, Medical Inadmissibility, and the Differential Politics of Immigration," *The Canadian Geographer* 61, no. 3 (2017): 389–400, https://doi.org/10.1111/cag.12361; and Constance MacIntosh, "Medical Inadmissibility, and Physically and Mentally Disabled Would-Be Immigrants: Canada's Story Continues," *Dalhousie Law Journal* 42, no. 1 (2019): 138.

14 Refugees and Citizenship Canada Immigration, "Reconsideration after Refusal," last modified 30 October 2023, https://www.canada.ca/en/immigration-refugees-citizenship/corporate/publications-manuals/operational-bulletins-manuals/service-delivery/reconsideration-after-refusal.html.

protection. This right is not extended to refugee claimants whose claims were withdrawn or abandoned. The Refugee Appeal Division can consider errors of fact and law. It can uphold or overturn the decision of the Refugee Protection Division as well as send the case back for a redetermination.

There is no right of appeal to the Refugee Appeal Division of refugee sponsorship applications that are refused.

Judicial Review by the Federal Court of Canada

Leave to judicially review a refusal in the Federal Court is available to other rejected applicants for permanent residency within a prescribed time period.[15] It also extends to individuals whose appeals have been rejected by the Immigration Appeal Division or the Refugee Appeal Division of the Immigration and Refugee Board.

Permission is required of a judge on the court to hear the case. This is only given in rare cases such as where the applicant can show there is clear error, or if the case raises a significant legal issue warranting further consideration.

Humanitarian and Compassionate Applications

The *Immigration and Refugee Protection Act 2001* also has provisions for some rejected applicants to apply for permanent residency on humanitarian and compassionate grounds. The process is not available to persons who are inadmissible on the grounds of security, organized criminality, human or international rights violations. As well, failed refugee claimants must wait one year after receiving a negative decision from the Immigration and Refugee Board before making a humanitarian and compassionate application.

The application for humanitarian and compassionate consideration is made online to Immigration Refugees and Citizenship

---

15 *Immigration and Refugee Protection Act*, S.C. 2001, s. 72(1).

Canada. The application form requires extensive information, and it is up to the applicant to ensure that it is comprehensively provided. This includes setting out all the reasons why they would face disproportionate hardship if removed from Canada. Relevant considerations include how well the person has become established in Canada, the impact of removal on remaining family members, the effect on the applicant's health, the best interests of dependent children, and conditions in the country of origin other than those considered as part of a refugee claim. The decision is made by an immigration officer.

Obtaining permanent residency status based on humanitarian and compassionate considerations is a discretion that has been in existence for decades. It is not intended to be a rarely used remedy, but one which is to be granted where there are humanitarian and compassionate grounds to support it.[16] Approximately 4,000 applications have been granted each year over the past two decades. The process can take several years, and a person who is ordered removed from Canada is not entitled to remain in the country pending the outcome of the humanitarian and compassionate application.

We now turn to a more detailed examination of the criteria and processes for immigration to Canada under the economic, family, and refugee streams.

---

16 *Kanthasamy v. Canada (MCI)*, 2015 SCC 61, para. 13, 31–2. The minister argued that the discretion was exceptional. The majority did not accept this, rather it adopted the dictionary understanding of humanitarian and compassionate articulated years before in the *Chirwa* decision: *Chirwa v. Canada (MMI)*, [1970] I.A.B.D. No. 1.

Economic Stream: Accelerated Change and Growth

Canada's immigration policy has been consistently influenced by economic priorities: nation-building and boosting economic prosperity. In national surveys three in four Canadians express agreement that immigration has a positive impact on the economy.[1] Economic priorities have shaped the decisions taken on the annual number of immigrants accepted and the selection criteria.

This chapter is about the economic stream, the largest of the three main immigration streams (see figure 3). We look at how

---

1 Environics Institute, "Focus Canada – Fall 2023: Canadian Public Opinion about Immigration and Refugees," *Focus Canada* (Toronto: Environics Institute for Survey Research, 2023), 10. Among economists, the extent of economic benefits from immigration is a matter of debate. Various scenarios have been theorized and investigated. George Borjas, a prominent American immigration economist, has argued that benefits of immigration arise from underpaying immigrants, because the goods and services created by immigrants cost less. George J. Borjas, "The Economic Benefits from Immigration," *Journal of Economic Perspectives* 9, no. 2 (1995): 3–22, https://doi.org/10.1257/jep.9.2.3. Economists also emphasize that skilled immigration is beneficial not only in creating more wealth for immigrants and their families but also because their greater spending power stimulates economic benefits more generally. See Anthony Edo et al., "An Introduction to the Economics of Immigration in OECD Countries," *Canadian Journal of Economics* 53, no. 4 (2020): 1365–1403, https://doi.org/10.1111/caje.12482. An economic simulation for Canada provided a detailed analysis supporting this hypothesis, suggesting that higher wages for immigrants increases their economic contribution. Peter Dungan, Tony Fang, and Morley Gunderson, "Macroeconomic Impacts of Canadian Immigration: Results from a Macro Model," *British Journal of Industrial Relations* 51, no. 1 (2013): 174–95. See also Matthew Doyle, Mikal Skuterud, and Christopher Worswick, "Optimizing Immigration for Economic Growth," C.D. Howe Institute Commentary No. 662 (Toronto: C.D. Howe Institute, 2024).

policy choices have affected the flow of permanent admissions, and consider the arrival of temporary foreign workers, a category also defined by essentially economic considerations.

The economic stream is central to the national immigration program. It has various interconnections with the other two, which cover family-class admissions and refugees. Economic criteria have also shaped selection within the family stream and the balance between it and the purely economic stream. For example, Canadian citizens or permanent residents sponsoring family members to join them must meet financial requirements, although spouses, partners, or dependent children are exempt. There are additional economic considerations with other family applicants designed to ensure new arrivals can establish themselves in Canada.[2] Refugees with private sponsorship are admitted only if their sponsors have sufficient financial resources for proper support, which is considered alongside the refugee's ability to establish themselves in the country.[3]

The chapter is focused on the economic aspects of immigration policy since the *Immigration and Refugee Protection Act 2001*. It covers three basic shifts in policy that have attempted to address a perceived need to strengthen the economic component of immigration.

First, from 2006, there were significant changes to the traditional points-based system used since the 1960s. These changes followed the election of a Conservative government but have been kept almost entirely by the Liberal government formed in 2015. The overhaul brought in new official assessments of language knowledge and educational qualifications alongside greater scrutiny of specific occupational skills. Previous work experience in Canada was emphasized, as were recommendations from provincial governments. In 2015, an online administrative innovation called "Express Entry" replaced the traditional "first-come, first-served" process. It set up an annually renewable pool of prioritized prospective candidates.

---

2 Such as the permanent immigration of parents or grandparents. See chapter 2.2: "Family Sponsorship: Raising Requirements," 159–93.

3 See chapter 2.3: "Refugees Greater Selectivity and Barriers to Asylum," 163–7.

Second, the numbers of temporary immigrants grew steadily under both Liberal and Conservative governments during this period. The number of work permit holders in Canada increased from less than 70,000 in 2000 to about 353,000 in 2016, surging to 1,270,000 in 2023 (see figure 5). International students with study permits also grew very rapidly, to more than 1 million in 2023 (see figure 7).[4]

And third, from 2015 onwards, the Liberal government has dramatically ramped up the number of permanent residents admitted annually, virtually doubling it from an average of roughly 250,000 over two decades to 471,000 in 2023 (see figures 2 and 3), targeting 485,000 for 2024.

Cumulatively, these changes have shifted selection priorities for permanent settlement to addressing short-term labour market needs in specific occupational categories, and to preferring candidates with previous Canadian work experience and those who meet requirements set by provincial governments.

This chapter takes a closer look at how each of these shifts has transpired. It assesses their demonstrated and potential impacts, both in terms of practical outcomes and precedents created. As ever, these contemporary transformations were set up by the experience that led up to them, and so that is where we begin.

Context

Throughout Canadian history, the significance of economic immigration has been revealed by the ways that policy defining it has changed in response to the development of the economy itself.

---

4   Numbers in figure 5 refer to those with valid temporary work permits at the end of each year, including those whose visas were granted in the specified year, as well as those granted in previous years whose visas remain valid. Numbers of temporary work permits issued from 2015 to 2023 are given in figure 6. Numbers in figure 7 refer to those with valid study permits at the end of each year, and, for 2015 to 2023, the numbers granted in each year. There may be overlap in that some study permit holders also have work permits. See sources in figures, and also Immigration, Refugees and Citizenship Canada, *Annual Report to Parliament on Immigration 2023*, and previous years at https://publications.gc.ca/site/eng/359079/publication.html.

During the late nineteenth century, immigration policy focused on agricultural development and settlement of the vast western part of the country to exploit economic opportunities and consolidate the Dominion. The construction of the Canadian Pacific Railway was central to those ambitions. It depended on immigrant labour and so did the mining industry. With the onset of industrialization and urban development in the early twentieth century, emphasis shifted towards recruiting immigrants for factory labour and construction. This trend continued strongly after the Second World War.

In the 1960s, Canada experienced a significant shift in its immigration policy. It moved from low-skilled to high-skilled immigration to align with the emerging post-industrial economy. The government introduced a points-based selection system designed to ensure that immigrants possessed the highest level of employability. Economic necessity also contributed to the decision to open immigration to applicants from around the world, also taken in the 1960s.[5] Immigration into Canada from Europe, which was still being rebuilt, had dropped. Diversifying sources of immigration helped to meet the demand for labour and kept the economy growing.

Federal Skilled Worker Program's Initial Point System

Ever since Canada's points-based immigration system began in 1967, the Federal Skilled Worker Program has been central to the economic stream. It has been the defining characteristic of the country's immigration policy, at least until recently. The program scores candidates for their employability in the general labour market based on points awarded for indicators of employability such as language fluency, education, youth, and previous work experience. Points are also given for having an actual job offer in hand. Over nearly four decades, the Federal Skilled Worker Program comprised most of the economic stream. The two other

---

5 As discussed in part 1, history, human rights considerations, and pressures from Commonwealth nations also played a role in the decision to open immigration to Canada from other parts of the world.

components of the economic stream were the business class – including self-employed, entrepreneurs, and investors – and the Live-In Caregiver program (formerly "Foreign Domestics" along with other precursors).[6]

Initially, the point system focused on age, language proficiency, secured employment in a high-demand area like Toronto, and "personal suitability" as assessed by an immigration officer. The threshold level of points required was relatively low. An applicant could pass with no education or occupational qualifications. The impact of the points system was also relatively modest as, in its earliest years, the number of admissions through the economic stream made up a relatively small proportion of overall admissions.

Over time, both the numbers of economic immigrants and their proportion of the total have increased (see figure 3). Between 1971 and 1990, overall numbers of immigrants admitted annually averaged 140,000. This number jumped to over 250,000 in 1992, an increase of 75 per cent over the earlier average, and it remained at about that level until recently.

The percentage of economic immigrants also increased. From 1980 to 1990, the economic stream averaged about 40 per cent of the total. From 1993 to 2001, however, under a Liberal government, there was a steady increase to about 60 per cent, with corresponding percentage reductions in the family class and refugee categories. This proportion has been maintained consistently ever since then.

The points system also evolved to give greater weight to educational qualifications, work experience, occupational skills, and other employability factors.[7] This led to a shift towards skilled individuals who were seen as more likely to contribute to economic growth and development.

---

6 See Jan Raska, "Recruiting Domestic Workers and Live-in Caregivers in Canada," Canadian Museum of Immigration at Pier 21, accessed 8 July 2024, https:// pier21.ca/recruiting-domestic-workers-and-live-caregivers-canada.

7 From the implementation of the points system in the 1960s, refined further in 1978. Monica Boyd, "Immigration Policies and Trends: A Comparison of Canada and the United States," *Demography* 13, no. 1 (1976): 83–104; Hawkins, *Critical Years in Immigration*, 107.

The 1976 *Immigration Act* mandated the government to engage in regular and transparent immigration planning. The decision in the 1990s to present five-year immigration plans was the first time the government moved to such a long-term planning horizon.[8] The basic program structure of the economic stream was maintained. A new and quite small Provincial Nominee Program was introduced in 1998, giving participating provinces the right to select economic immigrants based on their local labour market needs. It followed earlier special agreements with Quebec.[9] By 2001, six provinces were part of the Provincial Nominee Program.[10] Still, in that year, provincial nominees comprised less than 1 per cent of the economic stream; skilled workers were 88.1 per cent, business class 9.4 per cent, and live-in caregivers 1.7 per cent.

Employment Problems of Skilled Immigrants

While Canada's points-based immigrant selection system impressed other countries, internal scrutiny revealed its weaknesses. One was that immigrants experienced significant difficulties in getting jobs that matched the qualifications on which their permanent residence status had been granted. Another was a pervasive downward trend in employment rates and relative

---

8 Citizenship and Immigration Canada, *A Broader Vision: Immigration and Citizenship Plan, 1995–2000, Annual Report to Parliament* (Ottawa: Citizenship and Immigration Canada, 1995), 10.

9 Since the 1970s, Quebec had a special agreement with the federal government that underwent revisions over the years. By 1991, the province was authorized to determine immigration levels for its jurisdiction, select all economic immigrants bound for Quebec, and receive integration support with assistance from the federal government. See discussion in Part 1: An Historical Reprieve.

10 Yukon joined in 2001, Alberta and Nova Scotia in 2002, Ontario in 2005, and Northwest Territories in 2009. See Seidle, *Canada's Provincial Nominee Immigration Programs*, 5. See also Citizenship and Immigration Canada, *Facts and Figures 2005: Immigration Overview–Permanent and Temporary Residents* (Ottawa: Citizenship and Immigration Canada, 2006), 2; Immigration, Refugees and Citizenship Canada, "Immigrate as a Provincial Nominee," last updated 8 August 2024, https://www.canada.ca/en/immigration-refugees-citizenship/services/immigrate-canada/provincial-nominees.html.

earnings of newly arrived immigrants since the 1970s. A considerable body of research showed that, while immigrants selected on the points-system had higher earnings than those selected in the family class or refugee streams,[11] many faced difficulties in using their skills effectively within the labour market. This phenomenon, often referred to as "brain waste," became increasingly evident from the late 1990s onwards.

Various potential barriers were identified, including employers' lack of familiarity with foreign qualifications, professional licensing processes predicated on Canadian qualifications, limited professional networks for immigrants, and the perception of inadequate "Canadian experience."[12] Discrimination based on race, country of origin, or cultural differences were recognized as playing a role as well. The underuse of immigrant skills imposes large costs on the Canadian economy.[13] It is also one of the most

---

11 These studies were facilitated by the creation in 1981 of an Immigration Data Base linking immigration records to tax filling data on employment earnings through subsequent years. See, for example, Citizenship and Immigration Canada, *The Economic Performance of Immigrants: Immigration Category Perspective* (Ottawa: Citizenship and Immigration Canada, 1998), https://publications.gc.ca /collections/Collection/MP22-18-2-2000E.pdf. Another important source is the Longitudinal Survey of Immigrants to Canada (LSIC), see Arthur Sweetman and Casey Warman, "Canada's Immigration Selection System and Labour Market Outcomes," *Canadian Public Policy* 39, Supplement 1 (2013): S141–64, https://doi .org/10.3138/CPP.39.Supplement1.S141. Many of the recent evaluations of immigration policy change have used these data sources.

12 See the review by Jeffrey G. Reitz, "Immigrant Employment Success in Canada, Part I: Individual and Contextual Causes," *Journal of International Migration and Integration / Revue de l'integration et de La Migration Internationale* 8, no. 1 (2007): 11–36.

13 Michael Bloom, *Brain Gain: The Economic Benefits of Recognizing Learning and Learning Credentials in Canada* (Ottawa: The Conference Board of Canada, 2001); Jeffrey G. Reitz, "Immigrant Success in the Knowledge Economy: Institutional Change and the Immigrant Experience in Canada, 1970–1995," *Journal of Social Issues* 57, no. 3 (2001): 579–613; Reitz, "Immigrant Skill Utilization in the Canadian Labour Market," 347; Peter S. Li, "The Market Worth of Immigrants' Educational Credentials," *Canadian Public Policy* 27, no. 1 (2001): 23–38; Jeffrey G. Reitz, Josh Curtis, and Jennifer Elrick, "Immigrant Skill Utilization: Trends and Policy Issues," *Journal of International Migration and Integration* 15, no. 1 (2014): 1–26.

common and important complaints from immigrants about their experiences in Canada.[14]

Studies also revealed that immigrant employment rates and earnings were falling, beginning in the 1970s. While there was a partial improvement in the 1990s, the downward trajectory continued well into the first decade of the twenty-first century.[15] The pattern to some degree tracked changes in the economy, such as the recession of the early 1980s and weak labour demand in the early 1990s. But it extended across several business cycles, suggesting various other factors were at play.

First, there was a general reduction in employment opportunities for all new labour force entrants, not solely limited to immigrants. However, immigrants were more frequently pushed into poverty when opportunities became limited. Second, several changes affected immigrants specifically. The educational levels of the native-born workforce started increasing more rapidly compared to immigrants, putting arrivals at a competitive disadvantage. In the new "knowledge economy," many employers placed a premium on formal education, making it more challenging for immigrants with foreign-acquired credentials to secure work. Furthermore, analysts observed a decrease in the appeal

---

14 Statistics Canada, "Longitudinal Survey of Immigrants to Canada: A Portrait of Early Settlement Experiences" (Ottawa: Statistics Canada, 2005). Lack of recognition of immigrant credentials is a problem in many countries. See A. Schuster, M.V. Desiderio, and G. Urso, eds., *Recognition of Qualifications and Competences of Migrants* (Brussels: International Organization for Migration, 2013). The problem looms larger in Canada because of the significance of immigration and its economic value to the country.

15 Frenette and Morissette, "Will They Ever Converge?" See also Jeffrey G. Reitz, *Warmth of the Welcome: The Social Causes of Economic Success for Immigrants in Different Nations and Cities* (Boulder, CO: Westview Press, 1998); and Reitz, "Immigrant Success in the Knowledge Economy." These studies have shown that, despite substantial increases in immigrant educational levels and taking account of business cycle fluctuations in labour demand, average entry-level earnings have declined perhaps 20 per cent for newly arriving immigrants, for both men and women. Along with this, there has been a decline in employment rates.

of foreign work experience to employers, though the precise reasons were not clear.[16]

Efforts to Remove Labour Market Barriers

From the 1990s on, there have been efforts to alleviate the underemployment of immigrants. They include federal, provincial, business, and community-based programs to help employers better assess foreign-acquired qualifications. There have also been programs to support immigrants to obtain the necessary licences to practise their professions in Canada, improve language skills, gain networks through mentorships, and eliminate barriers to their full participation in the labour market. In 2003, the federal government launched the Foreign Credential Recognition Program[17] to improve recognition of foreign-acquired qualifications. It engaged regulatory authorities, industry sectors, and institutions responsible for non-regulated occupations to develop strategies to address underemployment of immigrants.[18]

Provinces with the largest number of immigrants have established services to assess their credentials over the past two decades and to help match qualifications and skills to jobs.[19] For example, in 2006, Ontario passed the *Fair Access to Regulated Professions and Compulsory Trades Act* to help immigrants receive fair access to licensing. Many provinces have also introduced best practices

---

16 David Green and Christopher Worswick, "Entry Earnings of Immigrant Men in Canada: The Roles of Labour Market Entry Effects and Returns to Foreign Experience," in *Canadian Immigration: Economic Evidence for a Dynamic Policy Environment*, ed. Ted McDonald et al. (Montreal: McGill-Queen's University Press, 2010), 77–110.

17 This was established under Human Resources and Skills Development Canada (HRSDC). The current website is https://www.canada.ca/en/employment -social-development/programs/foreign-credential-recognition-program.html.

18 Reitz, Curtis, and Elrick, "Immigrant Skill Utilization," 4.

19 For example, World Education Services, established in Ontario with a government mandate and start-up subsidy, now operates as an independent business, preparing over 10,000 assessment reports annually. Quebec's provincial government provides assessment services, and the federal government has its own program to develop the assessment concept further.

models to streamline the process, and further efforts are underway to improve policy.[20]

To address the "Canadian experience" barrier, the Ontario Human Rights Commission recommended that employers frame job qualifications in terms of competencies and job-related knowledge and skills, rather than in terms of the location of previous work experience.[21] In 2023, the Ontario government announced its intention to ban requirements for Canadian work experience in job postings and application forms.[22]

Non-governmental agencies also exist in most provinces to provide credential assessments. Training programs in specific occupations aim to top-up foreign-acquired skills, and to offer a bridge into Canadian jobs and enable immigrants to acquire work experience in the country. Mentorship systems help immigrants network with professionals in their field, and many websites offer helpful advice for newcomers.

Despite the range of these programs and the engagement of governmental and non- governmental actors, their effectiveness remains in question. This is in part due to the difficulty in identifying the relative importance of the various factors which lead to the problem of immigrant underemployment.

Temporary Foreign Workers

Canada's use of migrant farm labour represents the first of its temporary foreign worker policies and dates back at least to the First World

---

20　An example is the *International Credentials Recognition Act* introduced as Bill 38 in British Columbia Legislative Assembly, https://www.leg.bc.ca/parliamentary-business/legislation-debates-proceedings/42nd-parliament/4th-session/bills/first-reading/gov38-1

21　Ontario Human Rights Commission, *Policy on Removing the "Canadian Experience" Barrier* (Toronto: OHRC, 2013), https://www.ohrc.on.ca/sites/default/files/policy%20on%20removing%20the%20Canadian%20experience%20barrier_accessible.pdf.

22　Ontario Ministry of Labour, Immigration, Training and Skills Development, "Ontario to Ban Requirements for Canadian Work Experience in Job Postings," News Release, 23 November 2023, https://news.ontario.ca/en/release/1003798/ontario-to-ban-requirements-for-canadian-work-experience-in-job-postings.

War.[23] Migrant farm labour was regularized in the Seasonal Agricultural Worker Program created in 1966 to allow the employment of farm workers from Jamaica in Canada during the growing season when sufficient local workers were unavailable, and later expanded to include workers from Mexico and other Caribbean countries.[24] A broader Canadian Temporary Foreign Workers program was created in 1973.[25]

Temporary foreign workers in Canada before 2000 were generally fewer than 100,000 in any year. During the early 1980s, the number of temporary foreign workers arriving annually was about 60,000, according to official statistics published in 2006, rising to 85,000 by 1990, and to 97,000 by 2000; in 2000 the number in the country at the end of the year was given as 102,000.[26] It is notable that these statistics for 2000 were later revised downward; at least since 2016 the number of temporary foreign workers in the country at the end of 2000 has been given as 67,000.

Foreign workers came in under the terms of programs designed to fill gaps in the Canadian workforce that were unlikely to affect Canadian workers. The *Immigration Act 1976* permitted the admission of "visitors" to Canada for the purpose of work but provided no guidelines. As will be seen, the number of temporary work permits granted without consideration of labour market impacts has increased considerably in recent years.

Relevant Legislative Provisions

The current *Immigration and Refugee Protection Act 2001* reiterates the age-old objective of Canada's immigration policy: to support

---

23 Victor Satzewich, *Racism and the Incorporation of Foreign Labour: Farm Labour Migration to Canada since 1945* (New York: Routledge, 1991).

24 Jenna Hennebry, *Permanently Temporary?: Agricultural Migrant Workers and Their Integration in Canada*, IRPP Study, No. 26 (Ottawa: Institute for Research on Public Policy, 2012), 4.

25 Bryan May, *Temporary Foreign Worker Program: Report of the Standing Committee on Human Resources, Skills and Social Development and the Status of Persons with Disabilities* (Ottawa: House of Commons, 2016), 1, https://publications.gc.ca/collections/collection_2016/parl/xc67-1/XC67-1-1-421-4-eng.pdf.

26 Citizenship and Immigration Canada, *Facts and Figures 2005*, 62–3.

the development of a strong and prosperous Canadian economy, of benefit to all regions of the country.[27] The act contains provisions for the admission of foreign nationals through the economic stream based on their ability to become economically established in Canada,[28] while at the same time recognizing the need to remove barriers to immigrant employment arising from inadequate recognition of foreign credentials.[29] It also provides for the admission of foreigners on a temporary basis to work with authorization.[30]

In this chapter, we will look at how each of the main changes to policy have been shaped by the act and amendments to it. The most extensive changes cover the program structure of the economic class and associated changes in selection criteria. The significant expansion of temporary immigration during the past two decades is also of considerable importance, partly because changes to selection criteria for permanent residents provided new opportunities for temporary immigrants to transition to permanent status. The details of the economic stream, the various programs, criteria, and application processes are specified in the regulations,[31] which are subject to parliamentary review and in Ministerial Instructions.

Ministerial Instructions were expanded in 2008 through amendments to the *Immigration and Refugee Protection Act 2001*. They are not statutory instruments and so, unlike regulations, they need not be brought before Parliament or discussed in House or Senate committees before they are adopted. They can be used to cap, pause, and eliminate economic immigration programs. They set eligibility criteria, guide how the criteria should be applied in selection decisions and fast-track applications for high-demand occupations.[32]

---

27 *Immigration and Refugee Protection Act*, S.C. 2001, c. 27, s. 3(c).

28 *Immigration and Refugee Protection Act*, S.C. 2001, s. 12(2).

29 *Immigration and Refugee Protection Act*, S.C. 2001, s. 3(j).

30 *Immigration and Refugee Protection Act*, S.C. 2001, ss. 22, 24, 30.

31 *Immigration and Refugee Protection Regulations* (S.O.R./2002-227).

32 *Immigration and Refugee Protection Act*, S.C. 2001, s. 14.1. Immigration, Refugees and Citizenship Canada, "Ministerial Instructions Related to Other Immigration

In 2013, the scope of Ministerial Instructions was broadened to enable the minister to create new economic class pilot programs without having to formalize them through a lengthy regulatory review process. They are limited to five years, after which time the program must be discontinued or made permanent through regulations.

In reviewing the expansion of overall immigration numbers since 2015, we ask whether evaluations of the impact of changing selection priorities and temporary immigration are sufficiently positive to justify a major program expansion.

Changing Priorities and Programs

Shortly after winning the federal election in 2006, the Conservative government launched an effort to improve immigrant employment with several revisions to the selection policy.[33] As described above, previous efforts focused on removing barriers to immigrant employment in the labour market. The new revisions to the selection policy were based on the supposition that many immigrant employment problems were traced to matters of selection that could be improved. Initially, relatively simple adjustments were made to the points criteria for selection in the traditional Federal Skilled Worker Program, including a return to priority occupation lists that had been used in the past.

Over time, program structures also changed. The Provincial Nominee Program became more significant, and a new economic stream

---

Programs and Goals," last updated 25 July 2024, https://www.canada.ca/en/immigration-refugees-citizenship/corporate/mandate/policies-operational-instructions-agreements/ministerial-instructions/other-goals.html.

33 Reitz, "Canada: Continuity and Change in Immigration"; Rupa Banerjee, "Introduction to the Special Issue: Canada's Economic Immigration Policy: Opportunities and Challenges for the Road Ahead," *Journal of International Migration and Integration* 24, no. 3 (2023): 585–97, https://doi.org/10.1007/s12134-023-01068-y; Ana M. Ferrer, Garnett Picot, and William Craig Riddell, "New Directions in Immigration Policy: Canada's Evolving Approach to the Selection of Economic Immigrants," *International Migration Review* 48, no. 3 (2014): 846–67, https://doi.org/10.1111/imre.12121.

admission category was added in 2008, called the "Canadian Experience Class." This class provided new opportunities for successful temporary immigrants, and international students, to transition to permanent status. Temporary immigration itself was increased, not only to address labour shortages as they arose but also to provide Canadian work experience to those who would become eligible for permanent status. A new Federal Skilled Trades Class was also introduced.

Further, in 2015, an administrative process for admitting economic immigrants called "Express Entry" was introduced. As described in detail later in this chapter, Express Entry was designed to improve selection in two ways. First, it would eliminate delays resulting from the extensive accumulated backlog, replacing the "first-come, first-served" process with a continuously renewing candidate pool. Selection from this pool was based on a new "Comprehensive Ranking System," which could be adjusted to allow flexibility in the selection of the most attractive candidates available at any given time. Second, it would allow employers to review and make offers to candidates in the pool.[34]

A key feature of both Express Entry and the Canada Experience Class was that they provide employers with a more direct say in the immigrant selection process. The Provincial Nominee Program provided similar opportunities through processes set up within each province.

The points system previously awarded more points to candidates with job offers, but the intention of these changes in the structure of programs was to significantly increase the numbers of immigrants arriving with either an approved job offer or with previous successful Canadian experience, showing a capacity to satisfy employers in the country.

---

34 Prospective immigrants may use Express Entry if they qualify for access to the Federal Skilled Worker Program, the Canadian Experience Class, and the Federal Skilled Trades Program, and those eligible for one of these programs also can use Express Entry for access to the Provincial Nominee Program. See Immigration and Citizenship Canada, "How Express Entry Works," last updated 13 June 2024, https://www.canada.ca/en/immigration-refugees-citizenship/services/immigrate-canada/express-entry/works.html.

Bringing employers into the immigrant selection process may be seen as a shift from supply driven selection to demand-driven selection.[35] Policy had long relied on admitting candidates based on indicators of employability. Essentially, it brought into the country a large supply of employable people who were then obliged to seek employment after arrival. When these immigrants encountered difficulties finding jobs, policy-makers began focusing attention on removing social barriers they believed might be restricting their access to employment.

The new approach brought employers into the selection process to reflect the idea that the qualities they sought were often not reflected in the formal selection indicators of employability previously used by policy-makers. If employer involvement allows for a more accurate understanding of employer demand, then it should select immigrants more likely to become successful workers in Canada.

Such changes in the program structure (current features are summarized in table 1) have affected the overall composition of the economic stream. Since 2006, the Provincial Nominee Program and Canada Experience Class have gradually supplanted the points-selected Federal Skilled Worker category[36] in terms of numbers of immigrants admitted (see figure 4). Whereas in 2006, the Federal Skilled Worker Program comprised 77 per cent of economic immigrants (including principal applicants, spouses, and dependent children arriving at the same time), by 2023 it had shrunk to 24 per cent.

In 2006, only 10 per cent of economic immigrants entered Canada through a Provincial Nominee Program, and the Canadian Experience Class did not yet exist. By 2023, these two programs

---

35 Jeffrey G. Reitz, "The Role of Employers in Selecting Highly Skilled Immigrants: Potentials and Limitations," *Journal of International Migration and Integration* 24, Supplement 3 (2023): 621–39, https://doi.org/10.1007/s12134-023-01030-y.

36 Note that the term "skilled workers" is used differently in regulations published under the authority of the act to include these new categories and others; see Immigration and Citizenship Canada, "How Express Entry Works." Here we adopt the terminology as it appears conventionally in the Immigration, Refugees and Citizenship Canada's reports and websites.

together grew to account for fully 71 per cent of all economic immigrants. Three other categories remained small: business class, skilled trades, and live-in caregivers made up less than 5 per cent of the total.[37]

The structural changes continued. By 2023, the economic stream consisted of no less than fourteen components.[38] Long-standing components remained in place: the Federal Skilled Worker Program, the business class, and caregiver class, the Quebec economic classes, and the new Provincial Nominee Class, Canadian Experience Class, and Skilled Worker Class. There was also the Atlantic Immigration Program, Temporary Resident to Permanent Resident Pathway, and four pilot programs (Atlantic Immigration Pilot, Rural and Northern Immigration Pilot, Agri-food Pilot, and Economic Mobility Pathways Pilot).

Federal Skilled Worker Program

Initial adjustments made to the points criteria in the traditional Federal Skilled Worker Program were significant. Official language knowledge was tested rather than self-reported, and points for fluency were increased. Points for previous work experience were reduced but not eliminated. Points allocated to younger applicants were increased, while points awarded for age decreased for older applicants. More highly educated applicants continued to receive significant points based on their education credentials. From 2013, a requirement was added that education credentials

---

37 Program instability during the COVID-19 pandemic is evident in the figures for 2021 and 2022. Overall immigration numbers were down in 2020. As well, the program in 2021 relied more heavily than usual on the Canada Experience Class, since those selected were already in the country and not barred from entry by travel restrictions. Numbers for 2022 show the previous pattern had resumed.

38 The structure of the current "Economic Classes" is given on the website: Immigration, Refugees and Citizenship Canada, "Permanent Resident Program: Economic Classes," https://www.canada.ca/en/immigration-refugees-citizenship /corporate/publications-manuals/operational-bulletins-manuals/permanent -residence/economic-classes.html.

obtained abroad must be assessed for Canadian equivalence by a designated organization.

As for work experience, it would be counted only in certain skilled occupation categories defined in the Canadian National Occupational Classification (NOC) and requiring post-secondary education or training. The previous use of occupational preferences was abandoned because of the shifting demand in the labour market and difficulties getting foreign applicants into the workforce in a timely manner,[39] but the hope was that, in the current period, this difficulty could be overcome.

Priority processing went to applicants with experience in certain in-demand occupations. Specific occupational preferences, a feature of the points system since its inception, were eliminated with the passage of the *Immigration and Refugee Protection Act 2001*, based on research indicating that highly educated immigrants' ability to adapt to labour market changes was an advantage in the long run.[40] But occupational preferences were reintroduced in 2008 under the authority of Ministerial Instructions. Initially, there were thirty-eight occupations on the government priority list of in-demand occupations. In 2011, this was reduced to twenty-nine.[41]

In June 2023, the government introduced an eighty-two-occupation priority list in various fields. They ranged from high- to low-skilled jobs in healthcare; science, technology, engineering, and mathematics (abbreviated to STEM); trades; transport; and agriculture and agri-food. Applicants were required to have at least six months experience in one of the occupations within the past three years.[42]

---

39 Ferrer, Picot, and Riddell, "New Directions in Immigration Policy," 851.

40 Ferrer, Picot, and Riddell, "New Directions in Immigration Policy."

41 The initial list included physicians, nurses, geologists, and petroleum engineers, as well as less-skilled occupations such as plumbers, electricians, and workers in specific industries such as mining and oil or gas drilling. Immigration, Refugees and Citizenship Canada, "Ministerial Instructions (MI1): Federal Skilled Workers," last updated 20 December 2019, https://www.canada.ca/en /immigration-refugees-citizenship/corporate/mandate/policies-operational -instructions-agreements/ministerial-instructions/other-goals/mi1.html.

42 Government of Canada, "Express Entry Rounds of Invitations: Category-Based Selection," 31 May 2023, https://www.canada.ca/en/immigration-refugees

Provincial Nominee Program

The Provincial Nominee Program was initially small but has grown considerably since 2006: from 10 per cent of the immigrants in the economic class to 42 per cent in 2023 (see figure 4; data include Atlantic Immigration Programs). Excluding Quebec – which has its own arrangements with Ottawa under the Quebec-Canada Accord – Alberta, British Columbia, and Manitoba receive the largest number of immigrants through this program.[43]

Provinces nominate immigrants based on their own criteria. Provincial selection accounts for a significant number of points awarded under the Comprehensive Ranking System described below. Although the final decision rests with the federal government, provincial choice is given considerable weight, and usually prevails.[44] While the Federal Skilled Worker Program selects those intending to work in professional occupations, provincial nominees have tended to seek work in "skilled or technical" occupations.[45] As the share of provincial nominees has risen, those within the Federal Skilled Worker Program has dropped. With that, so has the proportion of skilled professionals selected.

In line with their intended occupations, fewer provincial nominees have a university degree compared to immigrants in the Federal Skilled Worker Program, but there is an upward trend. In 2005, 80 per cent of principal applicants in the Federal Skilled

---

-citizenship/services/immigrate-canada/express-entry/submit-profile/rounds -invitations/category-based-selection.html; Colin R. Singer, "Canada Express Entry Draws to Target 82 Occupations in 5 Fields Starting in Summer 2023," Immigration.ca, 31 May 2023, https://www.immigration.ca/canada-express-entry -draws-to-target-82-occupations-in-5-fields-starting-in-summer-2023/.

43 Ontario is the largest immigrant-receiving province, but it was the last to negotiate an agreement. A significant motivation for doing so was to negotiate federal funds transfers in support of immigration programs. These were part of the Quebec-Canada Accord, with Quebec receiving as much as four times the amount of federal transfer money than Ontario received.

44 Garnett Picot, Feng Hou, and Eden Crossman, "The Provincial Nominee Program: Its Expansion in Canada," Statistics Canada, 26 July 2023, 3,https:// www150.statcan.gc.ca/n1/pub/36-28-0001/2023007/article/00004-eng.htm.

45 Picot, Hou, and Crossman, "The Provincial Nominee Program," 8.

Worker Program had university degrees, compared to 48 per cent of those in the Provincial Nominee Class, increasing to 68 per cent in 2015.[46] The primary source countries were China, India, and the Philippines.[47]

Additionally, in line with the growing emphasis on Canadian work experience, the proportion of provincial nominees with previous employment earnings in Canada has significantly increased, from 6 per cent in 2000 to 61 per cent in 2019.[48] Research indicates that recent immigrants who had previous medium- or high-paying jobs in the country tend to achieve more favourable economic outcomes compared to those without such prior experience.[49] According to the findings of an evaluation by Immigration, Refugees and Citizenship Canada, people who arrived through the Provincial Nominee Program initially earned more than those in the Federal Skilled Worker Program. But after seven years in the country, that flipped around.[50] Other research shows that employment rates and earnings of provincial nominees were less impressive when compared to the Canadian Experience Class.[51]

The Provincial Nominee Program is credited with helping to decentralize settlement destinations of new economic immigrants. For example, Ontario's share has dropped from 61 per cent to 42 per cent between 2000 and 2019, with the share in British Columbia and the Atlantic provinces rising.[52]

---

46 Education data are not reported for provincial nominees who have landed since 2011; see Picot, Hou, and Crossman, "The Provincial Nominee Program," 9.

47 See also Immigration, Refugees and Citizenship Canada, *Evaluation of the Provincial Nominee Program* (Ottawa: IRCC, Research and Evaluation, Evaluation Division, 2017), https://www.canada.ca/content/dam/ircc/documents/pdf/english/evaluation/e1-2015-pnp-en.pdf.

48 Picot, Hou, and Crossman, "The Provincial Nominee Program," 11. The proportion grew to 72 per cent in 2021 but this was an anomaly because the global pandemic restricted travel from outside Canada.

49 Picot, Hou, and Crossman, "The Provincial Nominee Program," 11.

50 Immigration, Refugees and Citizenship Canada, *Evaluation of the Provincial Nominee Program*, 26.

51 Discussed below in the section "Impact of Changes."

52 Picot, Hou, and Crossman, "The Provincial Nominee Program," 11. As this study notes, other factors also contributed, notably changing source countries and economic conditions.

Areas in need of improvement have also been highlighted. For example, each province has its own criteria and mechanisms for selection, creating a need for greater coordination and sharing of experiences, according to independent assessments.[53] The program has also been criticized for a lack of federal supervision, which has contributed to the emergence of integrity issues in several provinces, particularly regarding business investor programs where it was found that requirements were inadequately applied, and fraudulent documents were accepted.[54]

Most commentators point to the need for better monitoring and systematic impact evaluations to reveal how provincial nominees fare overtime and the impact of the program on provincial labour markets.[55]

Canadian Experience Class

The Canadian Experience Class was established in 2008. It provides opportunities for persons at certain skill levels who have Canadian work experience to be considered for permanent residence. Applicants must have at least one year of full-time skilled work experience in Canada within the last three years before applying, or an equivalent amount of part-time experience. This class draws applicants who come to Canada on temporary work permits as well as those who come to study in Canada. The requirements are slightly different for both. For temporary workers to be eligible, their Canadian work must fall within managerial occupations, professional, skilled trades, or technical occupations. International students must have completed their studies at a Canadian post-secondary institution and have one year of post-graduation work experience in the country.[56]

---

53 Seidle, *Canada's Provincial Nominee Immigration Programs*.

54 Seidle, *Canada's Provincial Nominee Immigration Programs*, 1, 10.

55 Picot, Hou, and Crossman, "The Provincial Nominee Program"; Seidle, *Canada's Provincial Nominee Immigration Programs*.

56 Immigration, Refugees and Citizenship Canada, "Eligibility to Apply for the Canadian Experience Class (Express Entry)," last updated 13 June 2024, https://www.canada.ca/en/immigration-refugees-citizenship/services/immigrate -canada/express-entry/eligibility/canadian-experience-class.html.

The education levels required vary. Some qualifying occupations require a university degree. Others specify apprenticeship training of at least two years, although shorter apprenticeships in some occupations may be sufficient if there is accumulated on-the-job training of at least six months.[57] In the past, "skilled immigrant" generally referred to those with a university degree. The term now has broader application and includes those who are skilled in a trade. This reflects the perception that the Canadian labour market has a need for immigrants with skills in key trades.

Note that temporary foreign workers who have skill levels below those required for the Canadian Experience Class (that is, below skilled trades, and including clerical workers and manual labourers) may nevertheless qualify for transition to permanent residence status through the one of the Provincial Nominee Programs, the Live-in Caregiver Program, or the family class. Approximately 30% of low-skilled temporary workers made this transition after five years during the period 2000 to 2014, generally a somewhat higher rate than for the higher skilled temporary workers.[58] It remains to be seen if immigrants recruited with qualifications in skilled trades will have employment and earnings profiles comparable to those with higher education degrees over the longer term.

Growth in the Canadian Experience Class was initially slow. But it started to rise in 2014 where it comprised 14 per cent of the economic class (see figure 4). It fluctuated in the years that followed but picked up significantly between 2020 and 2021 in part because of the slowdown in selecting immigrants from abroad due to the

---

57 Immigration, Refugees and Citizenship Canada, "Find Your National Occupation Classification (NOC)," last updated 23 August 2023, https://www.canada .ca/en/immigration-refugees-citizenship/services/immigrate-canada/express -entry/eligibility/find-national-occupation-code.html. For the Canadian Experience Class, the occupation must fall between TEER 0 and TEER 3 of the National Occupational Classification.

58 Low-skilled temporary foreign workers comprised between 30 and 45 per cent of the total; see Garnett Picot, Feng Hou, Eden Crossman, and Yuqian Lu, "Transition to Permanent Residency by Lower- and Higher-Skilled Temporary Foreign Workers," *Economic and Social Reports* 2, no. 1 (2022), https://www150 .statcan.gc.ca/n1/en/pub/36-28-0001/2022001/article/00002-eng.pdf?st =YCPN-IQW.

global COVID-19 pandemic. As of 2023, the Canadian Experience Class still comprised close to 29 per cent of the economic stream.

Processing: Express Entry

In 2015, the government launched Express Entry, a new administrative procedure for processing most applications in the economic class.[59] Express Entry is an online system used to assess candidates for the Federal Skilled Worker Program, the Canadian Experience Class, and the small Federal Skill Trades Program. In addition, those eligible for one of those can apply for the Provincial Nominee Program through Express Entry, and many have done so.[60]

Candidates must first complete an online profile. It is screened to determine whether the applicant is eligible for one of the programs. Screening criteria are set out in the regulations with further guidance in Ministerial Instructions. They vary according to the program. The points assigned are subject to change.

Eligible profiles are then ranked using what is called the "Comprehensive Ranking System."[61] It amounts to a second points system, designed to further enhance selection of those most likely to

---

59 At the time Express Entry was launched, the Migration Policy Institute considered it as a possible model for managing migration in the European Union. See Maria Vincenza Desiderio and Kate Hooper, *The Canadian Expression of Interest System: A Model to Manage Skilled Migration to the European Union?* (Brussels: Migration Policy Institute Europe, 2016).

60 Immigration, Refugees and Citizenship Canada, "How Express Entry Works." Other provincial nominees, as well as those seeking entry in the business class or as live-in caregivers (a program currently suspended), and all those seeking entry in the family class or as refugees, do not use Express Entry.

61 Immigration, Refugees and Citizenship Canada, "Eligibility for Express Entry Program: Comprehensive Ranking System (CRS) Criteria," last updated 13 June 2024, https://www.canada.ca/en/immigration-refugees-citizenship/services /immigrate-canada/express-entry/eligibility/criteria-comprehensive-ranking -system/grid.html. See also Aneta Bonikowska, Feng Hou, and Garnett Picot, *Which Human Capital Characteristics Best Predict the Earnings of Economic Immigrants?* Catalogue no. 11F0019M – No. 368 (Ottawa: Statistics Canada, 2015), https://www150.statcan.gc.ca/n1/en/pub/11f0019m/11f0019m2015368-eng. pdf?st=BCoNEdoz; and Garnett Picot, Feng Hou, Li Xu and Aneta Bonikowska,

succeed in the labour market. The scheme ranks candidates on two sets of factors. There are "core" criteria covering skills, experience, education, and spousal characteristics that are part of the traditional points system. Then, "additional" criteria are considered, including job offers, the nomination of a province or territory, Canadian education certification, French language skills, and any siblings living in Canada. Each candidate could receive up to 600 points on each of the two sets of criteria, for a total possible score of 1,200. There is no "passing" score to qualify; instead, those with the highest rankings are invited to apply for permanent residence.[62]

Invitations for full applications under the scheme, valid for sixty days, are sent out at regular intervals, with the number set by the minister. Registered candidates without an invitation after twelve months, and who wish to stay in the scheme, must resubmit their profile. Employers can view the candidate pool, and if they find someone suitable for a job offer, that is reflected in ranking and can make an invitation more likely. When Express Entry was introduced, this feature of the system was expected to enable employers to play a "key role" in selecting economic immigrants.[63] However, points awarded for job offers were quickly reduced, based on the desire to invite more highly skilled candidates who had not received job offers.[64] This change reflected a lack of participation in Express Entry by employers seeking to fill their most highly skilled positions.

Which Immigration Selection Factors Best Predict the Earnings of Economic Principal Applicants? (Ottawa: Immigration, Refugees and Citizenship Canada, 2020), https://www.canada.ca/content/dam/ircc/documents/pdf/english/corporate/reports-statistics/research/immigration-selection-factors-predict-earnings-economic-principal-applicants/r3c-2020_ee_eng.pdf.

62 Immigration, Refugees and Citizenship Canada, "Eligibility for Express Entry Program: Comprehensive Ranking System."

63 Citizenship and Immigration Canada, *Annual Report to Parliament on Immigration 2014* (Ottawa: Citizenship and Immigration Canada, 2014), 5, https://www.canada.ca/content/dam/ircc/migration/ircc/english/pdf/pub/annual-report-2014.pdf.

64 Immigration, Refugees and Citizenship Canada, *Express Entry Year-End Report 2016* (Ottawa: Immigration, Refugees and Citizenship Canada, 2016), 4, https://www.canada.ca/content/dam/ircc/migration/ircc/english/pdf/pub/ee-2016-eng.pdf.

Express Entry stopped the accumulation of a backlog because of the expiry date on profiles without invitations. The government has reported that the system has reduced processing times, because an application can only be submitted once the candidate has received a provisional acceptance through an invitation, by which time the assessment of the candidate has been completed. However, an Auditor General's report in 2023 concluded that application backlogs continued to exist. In 2022 only 3 per cent of Express Entry applications had been processed within the service standard of six months.[65]

From the immigrants' point of view, the system can be frustrating. Even those who satisfy the minimum points criteria may have to submit and resubmit their profile for many years and may never to be invited to apply.

The criteria for eligibility of an Express Entry profile varies from program to program. For the Federal Skilled Worker Program, eligibility remains based on the traditional points system. The Comprehensive Ranking System introduces additional criteria as indicated above. For the Canada Experience Class, a main eligibility requirement is Canadian work experience instead of education. This experience must be in a "skilled" occupation, defined as an occupation requiring at least a post-secondary diploma, apprenticeship training, or at least six months on-the-job training.

In the Federal Skilled Trades Program, experience in a skilled trade is required from a list of trades typically requiring only a secondary school diploma. A valid job offer is required and certification of qualification from the relevant Canadian authority. While this program, like the Canadian Experience Class, provides opportunities for those without a university education to qualify for eligibility, few have been admitted under this program (about 1 per cent of the economic stream).

The fact that invitations to apply depend on rankings made against other candidates, rather than an overall passing score, adds a level of uncertainty for candidates. It makes it difficult

---

65   Auditor General of Canada, "Report 9."

for those eligible to know their chances of receiving an invitation during the year their profile is active. The government does provide a lot of information, including the dedicated website, "How Express Entry works,"[66] with a page "How We Rank Your Express Entry Profile"[67] and a "Summary of Maximum Points per factor for Express Entry Candidates."[68] There is also a "Comprehensive Ranking System (CRS) Tool" to help candidates cope with the complexities.[69]

However, the calculations are not definitive since the underlying rules may be changed at any time according to Ministerial Instructions, a fact which is clearly posted on the government website. Further, in 2023, "category-based Express-Entry draws" were established, in which the minister would specify categories of qualification for highest priority.[70] And, as mentioned, the precise number of points needed to qualify for an invitation to apply is unknown because it depends on the points allocated to others in the candidate pool, which always varies.[71]

---

66 Immigration, Refugees and Citizenship Canada, "How Express Entry Works."

67 Immigration, Refugees and Citizenship Canada, "How We Rank Your Express Entry Profile," last updated 13 June 2024, https://www.canada.ca/en/immigration-refugees-citizenship/services/immigrate-canada/express-entry/eligibility/criteria-comprehensive-ranking-system.html.

68 Immigration, Refugees and Citizenship Canada, "Eligibility for Express Entry Program: Comprehensive Ranking System."

69 Immigration, Refugees and Citizenship Canada, "Comprehensive Ranking System (CRS) Tool: Skilled Immigrants (Express Entry)," last updated 27 February 2024, https://ircc.canada.ca/english/immigrate/skilled/crs-tool.asp.

70 Immigration, Refugees and Citizenship Canada, "Express Entry Rounds of Invitations: Category-Based Selection," last updated 13 June 2024, https://www.canada.ca/en/immigration-refugees-citizenship/services/immigrate-canada/express-entry/submit-profile/rounds-invitations/category-based-selection.html.

71 The posted CRS score cut-offs for programs and occupations show that they vary considerably over time. Prospective immigrants are advised as follows: "The way Express Entry works has changed over time. Make sure you check which ministerial instructions respecting the Express Entry system apply to your round to see how to calculate your CRS points." Immigration, Refugees and Citizenship Canada, "Ministerial Instructions Respecting Invitations to Apply for Permanent Residence under the Express Entry System," last updated 28 May 2024, https://www.canada.ca/en/immigration-refugees-citizenship/corporate/mandate/policies-operational-instructions-agreements/ministerial-instructions/express-entry-rounds.html.

The inability to know immigration selection priorities at any given time leaves the system rather closed to public scrutiny.[72] Moreover, the flexibility of the system, including the ability of the government to adjust ranking criteria and establish priority categories frequently, makes evaluation of it more difficult.[73]

Express Entry provides expanded opportunities for employers to participate in the selection process, but their involvement has been somewhat disappointing, as mentioned above. The Express Entry report in 2016 noted that points for having a valid job offer have been substantially reduced across several categories, including management, professional, and technical occupations, and in lower skilled categories.[74] Subsequently, invitations to apply for permanent residency to those with arranged employment have been significant but they remain a relatively small proportion of the economic stream's total.[75]

Express Entry procedures for filling skilled positions may not always align perfectly with employers' preferences. Employers may not wish to be limited to those who have already expressed an interest in working in Canada via this system, particularly for top-level positions where employers seek to search internationally. Express Entry may not include candidates who excel in their respective professional fields in their home countries.[76]

---

72 Daniel Hiebert, *The Canadian Express Entry System for Selecting Economic Immigrants: Progress and Persistent Challenges* (Washington, DC: Migration Policy Institute, 2019), 12–14.

73 Hiebert, *Canadian Express Entry System*, 13.

74 Immigration, Refugees and Citizenship Canada, *Express Entry Year-End Report 2016*, 4.

75 In the years 2019–21, invitations to apply issued to candidates with arranged employment numbered 10,905, 17,249, and 20,299, respectively; these were 5 per cent, 16 per cent, and 8 per cent of the economic stream, respectively. See Immigration, Refugees and Citizenship Canada, *Express Entry Year-End Report 2021* (Ottawa: Immigration, Refugees and Citizenship Canada, 2021), 17. See also Immigration, Refugees and Citizenship Canada, *Express Entry Year-End Report 2019* (Ottawa: Immigration, Refugees and Citizenship Canada, 2019), 15.

76 A broader search, such as is possible under the US EB visa program, may seem preferable. Still, even a US-type system would seem unlikely to increase participation in Express Entry significantly.

Surge in Temporary Foreign Workers

The *Immigration and Refugee Protection Act 2001* provides for the admission of temporary foreign workers to Canada with authorization. Like the permanent economic stream, the details of the program are set out in the regulations.[77] Temporary work permits are issued under two programs: the Temporary Foreign Worker Program and the International Mobility Program. The Temporary Foreign Worker Program is intended for periods of labour shortages when qualified Canadians are not available.[78] The International Mobility Program was created following a comprehensive program review of the Temporary Foreign Worker Program conducted in 2014.[79] The review, discussed in detail below, concluded that the Temporary Foreign Worker Program henceforth should be restricted to work permits requiring a Labour Market Impact Assessment, conducted by Employment and Social Development Canada, to ensure that Canadian workers would not be adversely affected. The International Mobility Program is exempt from the impact assessment and had the stated intention to "advance Canada's broad economic and cultural interests."[80]

Numbers of temporary foreign workers in Canada have grown by more than an order of magnitude over the past two decades. Temporary work permit holders expanded from just over 65,000 in [81] to over

---

77 *Immigration and Refugee Protection Act*, S.C. 2001, s. 87.31; *Immigration and Refugee Protection Act Regulations*, ss. 194–209.

78 Employment and Social Development Canada, "Temporary Foreign Worker," last updated 9 March 2023, https://www.canada.ca/en/employment-social-development/programs/temporary-foreign-worker.html.

79 Employment and Social Development Canada, "Government of Canada Overhauls Temporary Foreign Worker Program Ensuring Canadians Are First in Line for Available Jobs," News Release, 20 June 2014, https://www.canada.ca/en/news/archive/2014/06/government-canada-overhauls-temporary-foreign-worker-program-ensuring-canadians-are-first-line-available-jobs.html.

80 Immigration, Refugees, and Citizenship Canada, *Annual Report to Parliament on Immigration 2014*, 2.

81 Note that for data prior to 2014, the government has retroactively assigned work permits not requiring a Labour Market Impact Assessment to the International Mobility Program.

1,270,000 in 2023 (see figure 5).[82] Work permits not requiring a Labour Market Impact Assessment account for most of that growth. Between 2015 and 2023 alone, the number of new work permits issued in the Temporary Foreign Worker Program increased by 40,000, while those in the International Mobility Program increased by 580,000, almost fifteen times as many (see figure 6).

Temporary Foreign Worker Program Review in 2014

The Temporary Foreign Worker Program has a long history in Canada. Until 2006, before a work permit was authorized, every employer was required to obtain a Labour Market Impact Assessment from the government confirming that the job was genuine, and the employment would not adversely affect the Canadian labour market.[83] Relevant factors included proof of efforts made to recruit or train Canadian citizens or permanent residents, wages consistent with the prevailing regional wage, and working conditions that met generally accepted Canadian standards.

In 2006, Canada introduced lists of regional occupations facing labour shortages, exempting employers from the requirement to demonstrate efforts to recruit Canadian workers for those positions. Additionally, the government established dedicated recruitment sites in Calgary and Vancouver. These were intended to

---

82 Census-based estimates of work permit holders are somewhat lower. For example, there was an estimate of 502,000 in 2021, according to Catherine Tuey and Nicolas Bastien, "Non-Permanent Residents in Canada: Portrait of a Growing Population from the 2021 Census," Statistics Canada, Catalogue no. 75-006-X, 2021, https://www150. statcan.gc.ca/n1/pub/75-006-x/2023001/article/00006-eng.htm; with the difference possibly because of permit holders leaving the country or because of their deaths. However, census undercounting is also potentially quite significant, particularly for work permit holders; there was 46 per cent undercounting of work permit holders in the 2011 National Household Survey, according to Julien Bérard-Chagnon, Stacey Hallman, and Genevieve Caron, *Recent Immigrants and Non-Permanent Residents Missed in the 2011 Census*, Catalogue no. 89-657-X2019008 (Ottawa: Statistics Canada, 2019), https:// www150.statcan.gc.ca/n1/pub/89-657-x/89-657-x2019008-eng.htm. See also Mikal Skuterud, "Canada's Missing Workers: Temporary Residents Working in Canada," C.D. Howe Institute e-Brief 345, 2023, https://www.ssrn.com/abstract=4569515.

83 Formerly called a "Labour Market Opinion."

streamline the hiring process especially for Alberta's oil sands development, and for construction-related work in British Columbia related to its preparations to host the 2010 Paralympic Games.

The following year, a new expedited Labour Market Impact Assessment process was introduced to accelerate approvals for various occupations. This fast-track option was made available to employers with a proven track record of complying with the program's conditions. The government also extended the validity of work permits from one year to two years.[84] These changes reduced processing times and led to increasing annual admissions of temporary foreign workers. By 2013, the annual number of admissions was reported to have doubled to over 200,000. Most were exempt from Labour Market Impact Assessments.[85]

Alongside the increase in annual numbers of foreign workers admitted to Canada were criticisms that the program was loosely monitored and subject to abuse. Employers were accused of not making efforts to hire locally, using foreign temporary workers to avoid obligations mandated by law and collective agreements, and treating foreign workers as indentured servants.[86]

In some sectors, family members were not permitted to accompany temporary foreign workers. While some temporary foreign workers have recently been allowed to bring family members, who may be able to apply for work permits, the regulation against bringing family still applies to the Seasonal Agricultural Workers Program.

A 2009 Auditor General's report uncovered significant weaknesses in the program. Among the problems highlighted were the issuance of favourable labour market opinions without adequate

---

84 Opportunities to apply for further extensions also have been announced. Immigration, Refugees and Citizenship Canada, "Extend or Change the Conditions on Your Work Permit: About the Process," last modified 5 June 2024, https://www.canada.ca/en/immigration-refugees-citizenship/services/work-canada/permit/temporary/extend.html.

85 Immigration, Refugees and Citizenship Canada, *Annual Report to Parliament on Immigration 2014*, 16.

86 Karl Flecker, "Building 'The World's Most Flexible Workforce': The Harper Government's 'Double-Doubling' of the Foreign Worker Program," *Briarpatch*, 1 November 2007, https://briarpatchmagazine.com/articles/view/building-the-worlds-most-flexible-workforce. See also Yasmeen Abu-Laban, Ethel Tungohan,

evidence, permits being granted for non-genuine job offers, and a lack of systematic monitoring of employer compliance with terms and conditions, without consequences for employers found in breach. The report concluded that these failings undermined the integrity of the program, with foreign temporary workers left vulnerable to abuse and exploitation.[87]

Several changes were made. New agreements were reached between the federal government and several provinces to improve enforcement. Employers who violated the terms and conditions of their employment of foreign temporary workers were banned from the program for two years. Nonetheless, serious abuses continued to be reported.

In 2014, Justin Trudeau, as Leader of the Opposition, wrote that the temporary foreign worker program was broken. He called for it to be "scaled back dramatically" and refocused on its original purpose: "to fill jobs on a limited basis when no Canadian workers can be found."[88] The political backlash led to suspension of program activity and a general review, which began in June 2014 and was completed after the government transition in 2015.

Inspections were increased, as were the fees for a Labour Market Impact Assessment. Restrictions were placed on when an expedited assessment could be issued. Caps were also imposed on the number of low-wage foreign temporary workers an employer could hire in order to lower the number of annual applications of low-skilled immigrant workers. A fall in the number of annual admissions in the Temporary Foreign Worker Program followed – from 118,000 persons in 2013 to less than 100,000 for the next several years.[89]

---

and Christina Gabriel, *Containing Diversity: Canada and the Politics of Immigration in the 21st Century* (Toronto: University of Toronto Press, 2022).

87 Auditor General of Canada, "Chapter 2 – Selecting Foreign Workers under the Immigration Program," *Report of the Auditor General of Canada* (Ottawa: Office of the Auditor General of Canada, 2009).

88 Justin Trudeau, "How to Fix the Broken Temporary Foreign Worker Program," *Toronto Star*, 5 May 2014, https://www.thestar.com/opinion/commentary/2014/05/05/how_to_fix_the_broken_temporary_foreign_worker_program_justin_trudeau.html.

89 Immigration, Refugees and Citizenship Canada, *Facts and Figures 2016*, 17. See also figure 6.

However, once again the changes proved insufficient, according to a 2017 Auditor General's report, which highlighted poor monitoring of employer compliance with regulations of the foreign worker program. It also noted the lack of government evaluation of the program's impact on Canadian workers, potentially allowing lower-paid foreign workers to take jobs that unemployed Canadians could fill.[90]

Beyond this lack of regulation, there are significant additional downsides to the program itself. If many of the labour shortages cited as requiring "temporary" foreign workers are likely to be permanent, longer-term solutions may be needed.[91] In any case, temporary immigrants are inherently a vulnerable workforce. Their formal workplace equality rights are difficult to enforce. Employers may exercise undue influence in setting working conditions and rates of pay. Although opportunities for temporary workers to transition to permanent status are increasing, the majority do not make the transition.[92] Those who participate in the temporary program with that goal in mind are under greater pressure to satisfy their employers.

---

90 Auditor General of Canada, "Report 5 – Temporary Foreign Worker Program – Employment and Social Development Canada," *Report of the Auditor General of Canada* (Ottawa: Office of the Auditor General of Canada, 2017), https://www.oag-bvg.gc.ca/internet/English/att__e_42263.html.

91 Hennebry, "Permanently Temporary?" Creating pathways to permanent status for low-skilled temporary workers would likely not solve the problem of the temporary worker category itself, since if transition was not accompanied by improvements in the terms of employment in temporary-worker jobs, transitioned workers would likely seek other more attractive jobs for which they would become eligible. As a result, new temporary workers would be needed.

92 About 33 per cent of temporary foreign workers arriving in 2005 to 2009 made the transition to permanent status within ten years. For those arriving between 2010 and 2014, pathways used were provincial programs (by 48 per cent), Canadian Experience Class (by 30 per cent), the family class (by 10 per cent), and the Federal Skilled Worker Program (by 8 per cent), and other categories (by 4 per cent). Higher-skilled workers are no more likely to make the transition than lower-skilled workers, though they entered by different pathways (provincial programs, the Canada Experience Class, or the Federal Skilled Worker Programs, for the more highly skilled, Live-In Caregiver Program or family class for the less skilled).

There are also negative long-term effects from periods of precarious legal status, including lower job quality.[93] For example, temporary foreign workers often face challenges such as lack of union representation, limited access to the same benefits as permanent workers, absence of formal contracts, and unpredictable working hours.[94]

There are no reliable data on the number of immigrants admitted on a temporary visa who overstay their visas. A government statement on undocumented immigrants noted academic estimates of between 20,000 and 500,000 people with suggestions that there may be more.[95]

There are indications that more structured temporary foreign worker programs can create incentives for foreign workers to return home when their permits expire. Canada's Seasonal Agricultural Worker Program, though not without continuing criticism,[96] has been regarded as relatively successful due to the strong incentives it offers for workers to go back to their home countries at the end of the season. They are aware that future participation can be arranged indefinitely and that there are opportunities for promotion to supervisory roles.[97] However, without

---

93 Luin Goldring and Patricia Landolt, *Producing and Negotiating Non-Citizenship: Precarious Legal Status in Canada* (Toronto: University of Toronto Press, 2013).

94 These job attributes are typically measured through an index that considers factors such as unionization rates, benefit packages, the presence of formal contractual agreements, and the predictability of working hours.

95 Immigration, Refugees and Citizenship Canada, "Minister's Statement on Undocumented Migrants, November 18, 2022, to House of Commons Standing Committee on Citizenship and Immigration (CIMM)," 18 November 2022, https://www.canada.ca/en/immigration-refugees-citizenship/corporate/transparency/committees/cimm-nov-18-2022/undocumented-migrants.html.

96 For example, United Food and Commercial Workers and the Agricultural Workers Alliance, *The Status of Migrant Farm Workers in Canada* (Toronto: UFCW and AWA, 2015), https://www.ufcw.ca/templates/ufcwcanada/images/directions15/october/1586/MigrantWorkersReport2015_EN_email.pdf.

97 Audrey Macklin, "And Just like That, You're an Illegal Immigrant: Thanks to a Bad Regulation, Thousands of People Living and Working Here Are about to Become Outlaws," *National Post*, 19 March 2015, https://nationalpost.com/opinion/audrey-macklin-poof-now-youre-an-illegal-immigrant.

more reliable data, the extent to which foreign temporary workers return home at the expiration of their permits remains unknown. Related to this is the absence of rigorous evaluation of the program more generally, which is also a concern, as discussed in a separate section below.

In 2022, the government introduced several changes to the Temporary Foreign Worker Program that resulted in more admissions. It extended the validity of a Labour Market Impact Assessment from nine to eighteen months.[98] For certain skilled categories, the maximum period of employment was raised from two to three years. Employers in various seasonal low-skilled industries were no longer limited in the number of temporary foreign workers they could hire. And the maximum period of employment in these sectors was increased from six to nine months per year.[99]

As it has expanded, the Temporary Foreign Worker Program has attracted increased controversy. A United Nations expert visited Canada to review the program in 2023, and he concluded that the agricultural and low-wage streams "constitute a breeding ground for contemporary forms of slavery." He noted that the migrant workers are disproportionately racialized, that the policies that regulate migrant workers' immigration status, employment, and housing in Canada make them vulnerable to exploitation and abuse, and he expressed concern that the program is "sharply on the rise." He urged that the closed work permit system be

---

98   Validity was extended further to three years in an experimental program called the Recognized Employer Pilot (REP), available to employers with a record of compliance with program regulations. Immigration, Refugees and Citizenship Canada, "Hire a Temporary Foreign Worker through the Recognized Employer Pilot: Overview," last updated 27 June 2024, https://www.canada.ca/en/employment-social-development /services/foreign-workers/recognized-employer.html.

99   Employment and Social Development Canada, "Government of Canada Announces Workforce Solutions Road Map – Further Changes to the Temporary Foreign Worker Program to Address Labour Shortages across Canada," 4 April 2022, https://www.canada.ca/en/employment-social-development/news/2022/04 /government-of-canada-announces-workforce-solutions-road-map--further-changes-to-the-temporary-foreign-worker-program-to-address-labour-shortages -ac.html.

ended, and that the status of foreign migrant workers should be regularized.[100]

Policy review in Canada is underway, though the extent to any resulting change remains unclear. In early 2024, the government reversed course to some degree, reducing the validity of Labour Market Impact Assessments to six months, and placing certain other restrictions on the use of the Temporary Foreign Worker Program.[101] It also planned to set targets for temporary residents as well as permanent residents.[102] In May 2024, a Senate committee released a report on temporary and migrant labour programs in Canada, recognizing the need for change. Entitled *Act Now: Solutions for Temporary and Migrant Labour in Canada*, the report recommended phasing out employer-specific visas possibly by shifting to sector-specific visas, eliminating notifications prior to inspections of workplaces, and expanding information about accessing health care.[103]

---

100 United Nations Office of the High Commissioner on Human Rights, "Canada: Anchor the Fight against Contemporary Forms of Slavery in Human Rights, a UN Expert Urges," Press Release, 6 September 2023, https://www.ohchr.org/en/press-releases/2023/09/canada-anchor-fight-against-contemporary-forms-slavery-human-rights-un. See also "End of Mission Statement," Tomoya Obokata, Special Rapporteur on contemporary forms of slavery, including it causes and consequences, 6 September 2023, https://www.ohchr.org/sites/default/files/documents/issues/slavery/sr/statements/eom-statement-canada-sr-slavery-2023-09-06.pdf.

101 Government of Canada, "Government of Canada to Adjust Temporary Measures under the Temporary Foreign Worker Program Workforce Solutions Road Map," 21 March 2024, https://www.canada.ca/en/employment-social-development/news/2024/03/government-of-canada-to-adjust-temporary-measures-under-the-temporary-foreign-worker-program-workforce-solutions-road-map.html. Minister of Employment Randy Boissonnault announced on social media in the summer of 2024, that further restrictions in the use of temporary foreign workers are being introduced to curb "abuse and misuse." Tony Keller, "How Can the Trudeau Government Fix Its Immigration Mess? Press 'Rewind,'" *Globe and Mail*, 9 August 2024.

102 Immigration, Refugees and Citizenship Canada, "Speaking Notes for the Honourable Marc Miller, Minister of Immigration, Refugees and Citizenship: Announcement Related to Temporary Residents," 21 March 2024, https://www.canada.ca/en/immigration-refugees-citizenship/news/2024/03/speaking-notes-for-the-honourable-marc-miller-minister-of-immigration-refugees-and-citizenship-announcement-related-to-temporary-residents.html.

103 Canada Senate, *Act Now: Solutions for Temporary and Migrant Labour in Canada*, Report of the Standing Committee on Social Affairs, Science and Technology (Ottawa: Canada Senate, 2024), https://sencanada.ca/content/sen/committee

However, it also stated that it while migrant work may be temporary, it is "here to stay."

The final report of the UN expert (who had testified before the Senate committee), released in August 2024, maintained its criticism, noting that exploitative working conditions have not yet been addressed meaningfully, that reducing the numbers of temporary residents in Canada does nothing to address problems faced by those who continue to enter in the same programs, and that any migrant worker program should involve open work permits and accessible pathways to permanent residency.[104] The immigration minister responded by acknowledging abuses cited in the UN report, while objecting to the use of the term "contemporary slavery" as applicable to the Temporary Foreign Worker Program.[105]

International Mobility Program Features

The International Mobility Program, as introduced in 2014, permits employers to hire certain categories of temporary workers without obtaining a Labour Market Impact Assessment. Many workers that come through this stream are not tied to a single employer. They can work for any industry and anywhere in Canada regardless of whether there are available Canadian workers or whether unemployment rates are high.[106]

/441/SOCI/reports/2024-05-17_SOCI_Migrant_Report_e.pdf. The report also called for the establishment of a Migrant Work Commission and for improved data on migrant workers in Canada.

104 United Nations General Assembly, Human Rights Council, "Visit to Canada: Report of the Special Rapporteur on Contemporary Forms of Slavery, Including Its Causes and Consequences, Tomoya Obokata," 22 July 2024, https://documents .un.org/doc/undoc/gen/g24/120/97/pdf/g2412097.pdf.

105 CBC News, "UN Report on Canada's Temporary Foreign Workers Details the Many Ways They've Been Abused," *CBC News*, 14 August 2024, https://www .cbc.ca/news/politics/un-report-abuse-temporary-foreign-workers-canada -1.7293495.

106 Hadrian Mertins-Kirkwood, "The Hidden Growth of Canada's Migrant Workforce," in *The Harper Record 2008–2015*, ed. Tersea Healy and Syeart Trew (Ottawa: Canadian Centre for Policy Alternatives, 2015), 152, https://policyalternatives.ca/publications /report/harper-record-2008-2015.

While in Opposition, the Liberals called for a drastic reduction in foreign workers. However, after winning the 2015 federal election and coming into power, they significantly increased the numbers. Annual admissions of temporary foreign workers grew significantly from 260,000 in 2015 to approximately 879,000 in 2023 (see figure 6). The numbers in the country at year end rose from 322,000 in 2015 to 1,270,000 in 2023 (see figure 5). As mentioned, the International Mobility Program covering work permits that did not require a Labour Market Impact Assessment accounted for most of this increase (see figure 6).

Within the International Mobility Program are various streams.[107] They cover different groups such as international students, students with a post-graduation work permit,[108] young people in international youth exchange programs,[109] those covered by international trade agreements,[110] and individuals coming to Canada as part of intra-company transfers,[111] among others all of which are considered to bring with them "broader economic, cultural or other competitive advantages for Canada," or "reciprocal benefits enjoyed by Canadians and permanent residents."[112]

---

107 Reitz, "Canada: Continuity and Change in Immigration for Nation-Building," 139.
108 Study permit holders in general are a distinct category of temporary resident, not part of the International Mobility Program.
109 Such as the International Experience Class.
110 Such as the United States-Mexico-Canada Agreement (USMCA), the Trans-Pacific Partnership, and the Canada–European Union Comprehensive Free Trade Agreement (CETA).
111 The Intra-company Transfer Program.
112 This phrase is used to define the purpose of the International Mobility Program; see Immigration, Refugees and Citizenship Canada, "Temporary Workers," last updated 4 July 2024, https://www.canada.ca/en/immigration-refugees-citizenship /corporate/publications-manuals/operational-bulletins-manuals/temporary -residents/foreign-workers.html; and Immigration, Refugees and Citizenship Canada "Significant Benefit to Canada [R205(a) – C10] – Canadian Interests – International Mobility Program," last updated 7 March 2023, https://www.canada .ca/en/immigration-refugees-citizenship/corporate/publications-manuals /operational-bulletins-manuals/temporary-residents/foreign-workers/exemption -codes/canadian-interests-significant-benefit-general-guidelines-r205-c10.html.

While the government intends that "the impact on Canada's labour market should be neutral or positive," the only rationale for exempting so many foreign workers from the requirement of a Labour Market Impact Assessment is that the benefits to Canada are "so clear and compelling" as to override the need for such an assessment.[113] Note that the number of such "clear and compelling" cases for assessment-exempt work permits increased by 813,000 between from 2014 when the International Mobility Program was introduced and 2023, while the increase in cases of less compelling benefits in the Temporary Foreign Worker Program, where impact assessments were still required, was only 85,000.[114] No explanation for the difference has been offered.

Given the lack of transparency, it comes as no surprise that labour leaders have expressed criticism of the International Mobility Program, arguing that it exempts employers from regulations that protect Canadian workers. Unions have long argued that government should focus on enhancing employers' recruitment efforts for Canadian citizens and permanent residents, including those facing labour market barriers.[115]

The government has defended the program by noting that most who come through it are post-graduate students, spouses of students, high-skilled workers, and people on working holiday visas.[116] They

---

113   Quotations from website of IRCC, "Significant Benefit to Canada."

114   See sources for figure 5.

115   As early as 2014, the Canadian Labour Congress had already highlighted the inadequately monitored nature of the International Mobility Programs and called for a comprehensive review and stricter data collection protocols moving forward. See Canadian Labour Congress, "Labour Mobility in Canada: Issues and Policy Recommendations," 8 December 2014, https://canadianlabour.ca/research/issues-research-labour-mobility-canada-issues-and-policy-recommendations/. See also Canadian Labour Congress, "Submission to the Standing Committee on Human Resources, Skills and Social Development and Status of Persons with Disabilities, Review of the Temporary Foreign Worker Program," 31 May 2016, https://www.ourcommons.ca/Content/Committee/421/HUMA/Brief/BR8360140/br-external/CanadianLabourCongress-e.pdf.

116   J.J. Nuttall, "Increase in Foreign Workers through Federal Program Still a Problem, Says Union," *Tyee*, 17 July 2017, https://thetyee.ca/News/2017/07/27/Increase-in-Foreign-Workers-Still-a-Problem/. Note that the data presented earlier (see figures 5 and 6) incorporate revisions to the data on the International Mobility Program announced in 2023.

fall within the "competitiveness and public policy" category. However, in addition to the vagueness of the category itself, it remains unclear why there was a need to significantly increase the number admitted through the stream over a relatively short period of time.

The lack of clarity in the administration of the International Mobility Program adds to the perception of a haphazard program operating with little oversight. This was reinforced in 2023 when the government announced a revision of statistics to retroactively clarify categories of foreign workers that require a Labour Market Impact Assessment.[117] There is no available impact evaluation for the International Mobility Program. Overall, the lack of clarity and comprehensive oversight of the program has fuelled scepticism and criticism from labour leaders and others, who have urged the government to address these issues and ensure a more robust and transparent approach to managing foreign worker employment in the country.

Many international students are permitted to work while they study, contributing to the Canadian workforce though not included in temporary foreign worker statistics. Their numbers have increased very substantially in recent years, parallel to the increase in temporary work permits. In 2000, there were 123,000 study permit holders in Canada, rising to 225,000 in 2010, and then more than quadrupling to 1,040,000 in 2023 (see figure 7). New study permit holders in 2023 were up by over 100,000 from 2022 totalling nearly 683,000. In 2022, Ottawa removed limits on foreign students' work hours but reintroduced restrictions in 2024.

Foreign students who work while they are in Canada are not included in the published data on temporary foreign workers. In some cases, work permits are included with study permits, while in other cases study permit holders are permitted to work without permits.[118] As indicated above, the International Mobility Program

---

117 Matt Lundy, "Ottawa Revises Downward Two Decades of Data on Temporary Foreign Workers," *Globe and Mail*, 22 June 2023, https://www.theglobeandmail.com/business/article-temporary-foreign-workers-data-revision/.

118 See Immigration, Refugees and Citizenship Canada, "Work Off Campus as an International Student," last updated 21 June 2024, https://www.canada.ca/en/immigration-refugees-citizenship/services/study-canada/work/work-off-campus.html#after.

figures include post-graduates and student spouses, but they do not include international students while they are students.[119] Data from 2018 showed that over half of Canadian full-time under-graduates work at least part time.[120] If that rate applied to international students, the number of additional foreign workers would be 500,000, and the total of all temporary foreign workers would be nearly 1.8 million.

The rapid growth of the temporary resident population in Canada has created controversy for several reasons, including the impact many fear it may be having on straining urban housing markets. A focus is on international students, and one concern is that many of the students seem to have enrolled in educational institutions of dubious standing. An incentive for international students to enrol in such programs may be the prospect of transition to permanent status, but the prospects seem uncertain. While roughly three in ten of international students who arrived in the early 2000s became permanent residents within ten years,[121] this rate was established before the more recent expansion of international student numbers. The same rate of transition to permanent status applied to the current population of 1 million international students would produce 300,000 permanent residents annually, more than the total of economic stream immigrants in 2023.

In response, the government announced early in 2024 that it would temporarily cap international study permits, reducing their

---

119 The International Mobility data include work permits issued to study permit holders after they have completed their degrees, for example, as post-doctoral students. Spouses of persons with study permits are counted among the International Mobility Program foreign workers.

120 Eden Crossman, Youjin Choi, Yuqian Lu, and Feng Hou, "International Students as a Source of Labour Supply: A Summary of Recent Trends," *Economic and Social Reports* 2, no. 3 (2022), https://www150.statcan.gc.ca/n1/en/pub /36-28-0001/2022003/article/00001-eng.pdf?st=l-7CorVs. See also Canadian University Survey Consortium, "2011 Undergraduate University Student Survey," 2011, https://www.cusc-ccreu.ca/publications/CUSC_2011_UG _MasterReport.pdf.

121 Crossman et al., "International Students as a Source of Labour Supply."

numbers by roughly 50 per cent.[122] Whether the new policy would address concerns about the abuses in the program itself is unclear, and many universities and colleges have objected, based on the current budgetary significance of international students.[123]

Shortly thereafter, the government announced a further plan to set targets for the entire temporary resident population, beginning in the annual report to Parliament for 2025.[124] An October 2023 release from Statistics Canada reported that Canada's total temporary resident population was 2.5 million, 6.2 per cent of the total population.[125] The plan was to reduce the temporary resident population to 5 per cent of total population over three years. In 2023 that would have meant 2 million temporary residents, still considerably increased over recent years. Much of the reduction could be accomplished by the previously announced cap on international students.

Pressure on the government to improve data on the numbers of foreign workers in Canada continues. Many of those with temporary work permits based on administrative data may not be working in Canada, or may have left the country, as suggested by analyses of the Labor Force Survey.[126] Census data provide an

---

122 Immigration, Refugees and Citizenship Canada, "Canada to Stabilize Growth and Decrease Number of New International Student Permits to Approximately 360,000 for 2024," News Release, 22 January 2024, https://www.canada.ca/en/immigration-refugees-citizenship/news/2024/01/canada-to-stabilize-growth-and-decrease-number-of-new-international-student-permits-issued-to-approximately-360000-for-2024.html.

123 Laura Stone, "Groups Representing Canadian Universities and Colleges Raise 'Significant Concerns' about International Student Cap," *Globe and Mail*, 31 January 2024.

124 Immigration, Refugees and Citizenship Canada, "Speaking Notes for the Honourable Marc Miller." In addition to temporary foreign workers and international students, temporary residents include asylum seekers, who represent 5 per cent of the total.

125 Statistics Canada, "Canada's Population Estimates, Third Quarter 2023," 19 December 2023, https://www150.statcan.gc.ca/n1/en/daily-quotidien/231219/dq231219c-eng.pdf?st=Eg1RYeVw.

126 Skuterud, "Canada's Missing Workers." See also Yuqian Lu and Feng Hou, "Foreign Workers in Canada: Changing Composition and Employment Incidences of Work Permit Holders," *Economic and Social Reports* 3, no. 10 (2023), https://www150.statcan.gc.ca/n1/pub/36-28-0001/2023010/article/00004-eng.htm.

alternative source of data, but analyses suggest that census data may undercount both recent immigrants and temporary residents.[127] And, of course, all sources do not count those who reside in Canada without a valid visa.

Expansion of Permanent Immigration Admissions

Increasing total permanent migration was an early priority for the Trudeau government when it was elected in 2015. An Advisory Council on Economic Growth in 2016 called for expansion of immigration as one of its first three recommendations.[128] Immigration policy was to be updated to address both the aging workforce and the need for more "senior and specialized talent" in support of technology-based firms. Annual permanent immigration targets would be increased by 150,000 to a total of 450,000. Admission procedures would be streamlined to make it easier for businesses to recruit managers and highly skilled workers and to allow more international students to qualify for permanent residency. Annual targets for immigration began to increase almost immediately,[129] and despite the setback of the COVD-19 pandemic, the recommended target was surpassed in 2023 when permanent immigrants numbered 471,000 (see figure 3). An even higher target of 485,000 is set for 2024.[130]

---

127 Bérard-Chagnon, Hallman, and Caron, "Recent Immigrants and Non-Permanent Residents Missed in the 2011 Census."

128 Appointed on 18 March 2016, the council membership included "Canadian and international business and academic leaders." See Advisory Council on Economic Growth, "Attracting the Talent Canada Needs Through Immigration," 2016, https://www.budget.canada.ca/aceg-ccce/pdf/immigration-eng.pdf; and Advisory Council on Economic Growth, "The Path to Prosperity – Resetting Canada's Growth Trajectory: Executive Summary," 2017, https://www.budget.canada.ca/aceg-ccce/pdf/summary-resume-eng.pdf.

129 Immigration, Refugees and Citizenship Canada, *Annual Report to Parliament on Immigration, 2017.*

130 Immigration, Refugees and Citizenship Canada, *Annual Report to Parliament on Immigration, 2022,* 34.

Such increases in immigration numbers are not entirely new. The most recent similar rise occurred during 1987 to 1992 (see figure 3). In the previous period from 1980 to 1986, annual immigration numbers averaged 107,000. But by 1992, the figure had jumped to 253,000, an increase of 136 per cent. Higher numbers have been maintained since, and from 2001 until 2016, the average was 253,000. From there to 485,000 in 2024 is almost another doubling.[131] According to the 2023 annual targets, the number of immigrants would stabilize in future years.

This earlier increase between 1987 and 1992 was reasonably well-received by the Canadian population. Popular approval of immigration numbers increased at the end of the 1990s.[132] Today views are more mixed. Some groups have been campaigning publicly for more immigration. For example, the organization Century Initiative[133] advocates increasing the Canadian population to 100 million by 2100 using immigration with various supportive policies.

The government has been consulting on immigration levels with "stakeholders" from a range of institutional sectors, including businesses and local governments along with various community groups. For example, a 2023 stakeholder report showed remarkable support for expanded immigration numbers.[134] But the report did not describe the procedure for drawing the sample for the survey, and the response rate was quite low at 16 per cent. That makes it difficult to gauge the significance of the results.

---

131 The Canadian population is projected to grown to an estimated 41 million by 2025, a 46 per cent increase from the 1992 level of 28 million.

132 Environics surveys, summarized in Reitz, "Canada: Continuity and Change," 145.

133 Century Initiative, "Why 100 Million?," accessed 29 August 2024, https://www .centuryinitiative.ca/why-100m. See also Doug Saunders, *Maximum Canada: Why 35 Million Canadians Are Not Enough* (Toronto: Knopf, 2017).

134 The report states, "When asked about the current notional target of 447,055 newcomers for 2023, 45 per cent of respondents indicated that it was 'too few' immigrants, and 42 per cent felt the number was 'about right.'" See Immigration, Refugees and Citizenship Canada, "2022 Consultations on Immigration Levels – Final Report," last updated 6 March 2023, https://www.canada.ca/en /immigration-refugees-citizenship/corporate/transparency/consultations /2022-consultations-immigration-levels.html#annexc.

These reports do not contain enough information to be comparable to public consultations that include opportunities for in-depth analysis and debate. Representative surveys of the Canadian population have shown an almost opposite opinion, with solid majorities opposed to the recent expansion of expanded immigration numbers.[135] It may also be noted that labour union representation has been absent from both the Advisory Council on Economic Growth, and from the government's consultations with stakeholders.

Tracking trends in public opinion on immigration requires periodic surveys that ask a general question of whether Canadians approve of the numbers of immigrants entering the country, rather than asking respondents to assess specific numerical targets as the stakeholder surveys have done. Such tracking surveys have for several decades shown majority support for immigration policy.

Very recently, these surveys have shown signs that the national consensus supporting immigration levels in Canada may be changing. As discussed in our introduction, an Environics survey released in October 2023 showed that support for immigration numbers, a solid 69 per cent majority in 2022, had declined to a slim majority of only 51 per cent.[136]

Other recent survey data (cited in our introduction) also suggested that the Canadian public was critical of current immigration

---

135   In September 2023, respondents were informed that immigration targets for the year were 465,000, and were asked if Canada should accept more, accept about the same, or accept fewer; 53 per cent replied "accept fewer." See Nanos Research and the Globe and Mail, "Canadians Prefer That Canada Accepts Fewer Immigrants," September 2023, https://nanos.co/wp-content/uploads/2023/09/2023 -2450-Globe-Aug-Populated-report-A-Immigration-with-tabs.pdf.

136   Environics Institute, "Focus Canada (Fall 2023)." Survey respondents agreeing "there is too much immigration to Canada" increased from 27 per cent in 2022 to 44 per cent in 2023; those disagreeing declined from 69 per cent to 51 per cent over the same period. Some studies have asked respondents about specific immigration targets for future years, and generally show greater opposition. For example, a Nanos survey informed respondents that the immigration target for 2023 was 465,000, and asked whether Canada should accept more, showed 53 per cent wanting to accept fewer immigrants. See Nanos, "Canadians Prefer that Canada Accepts Fewer Immigrants and International Students than What Is Projected for 2023."

policy. Many opinion surveys do not use randomly selected respondents, so their representativeness is in question. As well, they are not able to show a change over time in attitudes regarding immigration if they are not part of a series of periodic surveys using similar methods.

Annual immigration levels have been set based primarily on consultations such as those described above, rather than on empirical studies such as have been used extensively to determine criteria for the selection of immigrants. One reason is that understanding how immigration levels affect the Canadian economy requires a very complex analysis, because of the large number of factors involved. As mentioned at the outset of this chapter,[137] the Canadian public expresses confidence that immigration has positive economic effects, but economists have not reached a clear evidence-based consensus on how immigration levels affect the economy.[138]

Previous increases in immigration levels, including during the period between the mid-1980s and the early 1990s, had the effect of lowering the wages paid to immigrants, according to one study.[139] The authors suggested that immigrants tend to work in labour market niches within which they compete with each other. Overcoming this effect might require efforts to enable immigrants to compete in a broader range of occupations.

---

137 See page 96 of this volume.

138 See note 1, page 96, in this volume. Theoretically, one might set immigration levels indirectly by first setting minimum selection standards, and then taking whatever number of immigrants might meet those standards at a given time. However, no studies have explored either the significance of a possible numbers-quality trade-off, or the potential economic effects of such a policy. See Parisa Mahboubi, *Quality over Quantity: How Canada's Immigration System Can Catch Up with Its Competitors*, Commentary No. 654 (Toronto: C.D. Howe Institute, 2024), https://www.cdhowe.org/sites/default/files/2024-02/For%20advance%20 release%20Immigration%20Commentary_654.pdf.

139 Feng Hou and Garnett Picot, "Annual Levels of Immigration and Immigrant Entry Earnings in Canada," *Canadian Public Policy* 40, no. 2 (2014): 166–81. Note that Hou and Picot did not find any numbers-quality trade-off in the period they studied. Immigrant education levels increased despite increased numbers during the late 1980s and early 1990s.

Impact of Changes

Permanent Economic Immigration

There are somewhat mixed results from research into efforts made to address the employment problems of permanent immigrants, either via the removal of labour market barriers or by the improved selection of immigrants. The task of such research is complex, given that numerous policy changes have been phased in over time, and some are quite recent.

Express Entry, for example, was introduced in 2015, so at the present time the longest that immigrants admitted in that program have been in the country is nine years, and for most it is much less. In some cases, short-term outcomes – such as employment rates in the first years after arrival – may be quite meaningful. In other cases – such as admission of workers with previous Canadian experience in the Canadian Experience Class and Provincial Nominations Programs – their head start virtually guarantees early employment after arrival as permanent residents, but not longer-term outcomes. These are the most significant factors in any assessment.

First, the big picture view. Overall trends in the labour market gaps between immigrants and the Canadian-born population – based on census and national household survey data over the period 2001 to 2021[140] – reveal the overall employment status of successive cohorts of immigrants. The most recent immigrants in each period are of special interest since their characteristics and experiences may be most affected by recent changes in selection policy. Notably, these data show that new immigrants have continued to be highly educated and to come from diverse countries of origin.[141]

---

140   Eden Crossman, Feng Hou, and Garnett Picot, "Are the Gaps in Labour
      Market Outcomes between Immigrants and Their Canadian-Born Counterparts
      Starting to Close?," *Economic and Social Reports* 1, no. 4 (2021), https://doi
      .org/10.25318/36280001202100400004-eng. The study provided Labour Force
      Survey data for the most recent period from 2015 and 2019. Parallel census data
      for 2021 were provided to the authors by Feng Hou.
141   Some shifts in origins have occurred, but the overall proportions of those from
      origins outside Europe have increased.

Employment rates and earnings of recent immigrants in the most recent five-year period appear to be slightly improved over those of recent immigrants in similar periods since 2001. "Slight" improvement is good news, although it is not at the level of good news policy-makers hoped for.

Education levels are up, as recent immigrants more often have university degrees compared to those arriving two decades earlier, particularly among women. New immigrants arriving in the most recent five-year period prior to the 2001 census held university degrees at a rate of 48 per cent for men and 40 per cent for women. Twenty years later in the 2021 census, similar new immigrants had university degrees at the rate of 61 per cent for men and 67 per cent for women.

These increases in levels of formal education of new immigrants ensured that they would maintain an education advantage over the Canadian-born, whose education levels also were increasing. In 2001, the rates of holding university degrees for the Canadian-born was 19 per cent among men and 22 per cent among women; in 2021 the rates had increased to 26 per cent among men and 40 per cent among women.

New selection procedures for permanent immigrants have focused attention on labour market demand, but with some exceptions, have continued to emphasize demand for the most highly educated. As mentioned earlier, the new category-based selections include certain low-skilled occupations such as in trades and transport.

Immigrants are getting into employment more quickly than previously, but an earnings gap has persisted. New immigrants – living in Canada for five years or less – could enter the labour market more quickly than in previous cohorts. Nevertheless, the earnings gaps with the Canadian-born has persisted, in an uneven pattern over time. A deterioration in the relative earnings of immigrants occurred through the period from 2001 to 2016, followed by a recovery in the most recent period from 2016 to 2021.[142]

---

142 For recent immigrant men, earnings reported in 2001 fell 20 per cent below those of the Canadian-born; in 2016, earnings were 24 per cent below; and in 2021, they were 16 per cent below. For immigrant women, the earnings gap in 2001 was 24 per cent below; in 2016, it was 25 per cent below; and in 2021, it was 19 per cent below.

Analysis showed that these earnings trends were mostly not due to shifts in immigrant profiles regarding education, source region, urban residence, or other socio-demographic characteristics.[143] Rather, they were due to trends in the success that immigrants with similar characteristics had in securing well-paying jobs. That applied to both the deterioration over the period 2001 to 2016 and the improvement in the most recent period. In other words, immigrant under-employment got worse during the period 2001 to 2016, and then improved in the subsequent period.

Longer-term outcomes must still be assessed, of course, to see if new selection procedures provide new immigrants with more than just a head start in job hunting. For long-term outcomes, the data cited immediately above are helpful in showing longer-term outcomes only for immigrants affected by policies in place relatively early, by 2006. For both men and women, the data show improvements followed by deterioration, with no net change at all over the period.[144] The data provide no indication of the longer-term impact of changes since 2011.

The uneven trend over time suggests the possibility of different effects for policies introduced at different times. Early changes – such as modifications to the points awarded to applicants in the Federal Skilled Worker Program, and the requirement for language tests – seem to have made little difference since the immigrants admitted during the period 2001 to 2016 had lower earnings than those admitted in the five years before 2001.

The later expansion of the Canadian Experience Class and the Provincial Nominee Program, or the advent of the Express Entry system, might have contributed to the improvements later because they became most significant in the period 2016–21. The requirement for a formal assessment of foreign educational qualifications

---

143 Official language, mother tongue, age, and year of immigration were also considered.

144 For a policy introduced in 2006, the first cohorts affected with six to ten years of experience in Canada will be in the 2016 and 2021 data, with our interest in the comparison to data from 2011 and before. The data show improvements between 2011 and 2016, and deterioration between 2016 and 2021. This could indicate that policy changes introduced between 2006 and 2011 were having no net effect on the employment earnings of immigrants living in the country between six and ten years.

to show equivalence to Canadian qualifications, introduced in 2013, also may partly explain the better performance of the recent cohort. But even with credential equivalence, immigrants from origins outside Europe and the United States have continued to experience disadvantage.[145]

We focus now on what is known about the impact of specific programs. Government evaluations of each program have been conducted.[146] But there are caveats on the government's use of data. The earnings of immigrants in a particular admission category are compared with those in another category or with those in the same category but at an earlier point in time. Key comparisons are lacking, such as those that could show how a particular program affected overall immigrant earnings compared to the mainstream workforce.[147]

A 2010 review of the Federal Skilled Worker Program showed that educational levels and employment outcomes for immigrants selected in this program were better after the passage of the *Immigration and Refugee Protection Act 2001*, when points were no longer given for specific occupations but rather for general education.[148] The report stated, "The new selection approach emphasizing human capital is viewed by stakeholders as being more effective than the previous approach because it facilitates better economic success and integration of skilled workers, there is broader diversity in the occupational and professional backgrounds of FSWs,

---

145   Rupa Banerjee, Feng Hou, Jeffrey G. Reitz, and Tingting Zhang, "Evaluating Foreign Skills: Effects of Credential Assessment on Skilled Immigrants' Labour Market Performance in Canada," *Canadian Public Policy* 47, no. 3 (2021): 358–72.

146   Immigration, Refugees and Citizenship Canada, "Program Evaluations — Immigration, Refugees and Citizenship Canada," last updated 24 June 2024, https://www.canada.ca/en/immigration-refugees-citizenship/corporate/reports-statistics/evaluations.html.

147   For example, the Immigration Database, which is a source of longitudinal data that links immigrant admission records with tax filings, and is useful in program evaluation, does not provide comparisons to the mainstream workforce. See the Longitudinal Immigration Database, https://www23.statcan.gc.ca/imdb/p2SV.pl?Function=getSurvey&SDDS=5057.

148   Note that points awarded for specified characteristics were not set by the act itself, but rather by Immigration and Refugee Protection Regulations.

and skilled workers are generally more adaptable to changing labour market conditions."[149]

Another analysis pointed to the disadvantages of selecting immigrants based on specific occupations. It showed that increased number of immigrants working in engineering and information technology occupations produced a decline in earnings for the entry cohorts 2000–4, related to the downturn in employment demand in those fields.[150] Two evaluations of the Provincial Nominee Class found that while those selected are less educated on average, they more often have previous Canadian work experience, particularly in the most recent cohorts as the program has expanded.[151] Their initial employment earnings have been higher than for the Federal Skilled Worker Program, likely for that reason. But they fall behind after a few years – five years in the 2011 evaluation,[152] seven years in the 2017 equivalent.[153]

A study of the early earnings of a more recent arrival cohort, those arriving in 2015–19, shows that even initial earnings of Provincial Nominees had become lower compared to the earnings among Federal Skilled Worker and Canadian Experience Class immigrants.[154] The authors pointed out that the impact of this difference is larger because of the increased size of the Provincial Nominee Program,

---

149 Immigration, Refugees and Citizenship Canada, "Evaluation of the Federal Skilled Worker Program – Conclusions, Part C," 24 October 2010, https://www.canada.ca/en/immigration-refugees-citizenship/corporate/reports-statistics/evaluations/federal-skilled-worker-program/section-6.html.

150 Garnett Picot and Feng Hou, *Immigrant Characteristics, the IT Bust, and Their Effect on Entry Earnings of Immigrants* (Ottawa: Statistics Canada, 2009).

151 Picot, Hou, and Crossman, "The Provincial Nominee Program."

152 Immigration, Refugees and Citizenship Canada, "Evaluation of the Provincial Nominee Program," September 2011, https://www.canada.ca/en/immigration-refugees-citizenship/corporate/reports-statistics/evaluations/provincial-nominee-program.html.

153 Immigration, Refugees and Citizenship Canada, "Evaluation of the Provincial Nominee Program," November 2017, https://publications.gc.ca/site/eng/9.848797/publication.html.

154 Garnett Picot, Eden Crossman, and Feng Hou, "Provincial Nominee Program: Recent Trends and Provincial Differences in Earnings Outcomes," *Economic and Social Reports* 3, no. 12 (2023), https://www150.statcan.gc.ca/n1/pub/36-28-0001/2023012/article/00004-eng.htm.

and attributed at least some of the difference as being related to the selection process for Provincial Nominees. Provincial Nominees are not required to have their educational credentials assessed prior to admission, and many are not selected through the Express Entry system. Complicating assessments of the Provincial Nominee Program is the right of nominees to move provinces once admitted as permanent residents. How many do this is unknown.

Apart from earnings, the Provincial Nominee Program may be judged by two other benefits: fostering more geographical distribution of immigrants and incurring lower administrative costs for the federal government, although costs to provincial governments have not been assessed.

Immigrants with previous Canadian work experience now dominate the economic stream, because of the expansion of both the Canadian Experience Class and the Provincial Nominee Program (see figure 4). The growth of this "two-step" selection, involving transition from temporary to permanent status, was taking place just as the supply of temporary workers was increasing (see figure 5). Setting a preference for previous work experience is intended to ensure immigrants' skills are relevant to Canada. It also gives employers an opportunity to review a potential immigrant's performance before extending a longer-term job offer paving the way for permanent residence status.[155]

Evidence suggests that immigrants with skilled pre-migration work experience in Canada earned considerably more than those without, net of relevant control characteristics. The advantage declined sharply with years in Canada but for men was still relatively high – 12 per cent more – after ten years.[156] This longer-term benefit is smaller, but still significant.

---

155 Feng Hou and Aneta Bonikowska, "Selections before the Selection: Earnings Advantages of Immigrants Who Were Former Skilled Temporary Foreign Workers in Canada," *International Migration Review* 52, no. 3 (2018): 695–723.

156 Hou and Bonikowska, "Selections before the Selection," 731. The true difference may be less than 12 per cent if adjustments could be made for possible errors in measuring years since arrival. Years since arrival are counted since the first year of submitting tax records for those with pre-migration experience, and since the year of becoming a permanent resident for those without. Hou and Bonikowska

In this two-step process, previous Canadian work experience tends to lead to comparatively higher earnings mostly for a small group whose previous experience was also in the highest earnings categories.[157] The composition of this elite group is revealing. A significant majority were found to have English as their first language and originated from Northern and Western European countries as well as the United States.[158]

The reasons for higher earnings trajectories of those with the highest pre-migration earnings need to be clarified. It may be that pre-migration work experience and job offers lead to immigrants with better job-related skills, but more prosaic factors may be involved, such as less time being spent looking for employment, or less time spent convincing employers of skills equivalence. If so, then immigrant employment difficulties might be resolved by addressing how these immigrants are searching for jobs, or by improving foreign credential recognition, rather than by requiring immigrants to have had previous Canadian work experience.

---

acknowledge in a note that rates of tax filing for temporary immigrants are likely to be lower, potentially boosting their apparent earnings trajectory (701). For a related discussion, see Mikal Skuterud, "Canadian Stats and Two-Step Immigration," *Policy Options*, 19 December 2016, https://policyoptions.irpp.org /magazines/december-2016/in-search-of-better-statistics-on-immigration/.

157 Feng Hou and Garnett Picot, "Changing Immigrant Characteristics and Pre-Landing Canadian Earnings: Their Effect on Entry Earnings over the 1990s and 2000s," *Canadian Public Policy* 42, no. 3 (2016): 308–23. The authors compare 1999 and 2007 arrivals and show that an increase in the proportion of immigrants in the high pre-migration earnings category resulted in an increase in the overall earnings of the immigration cohort. Similar findings were found in more recent studies: Feng Hou, Eden Crossman, and Garnett Picot, "Two-Step Immigration Selection: Recent Trends in Immigrant Labour Market Outcomes," *Economic Insights*, no. 113 (2020), https://www150.statcan.gc.ca/n1/pub/11-626-x /11-626-x2020011-eng.htm; Feng Hou, Eden Crossman, and Garnett Picot, "Two-Step Immigration Selection: An Analysis of Its Expansion in Canada," *Economic Insights*, no. 112 (2020), https://www150.statcan.gc.ca/n1/pub/11-626 -x/11-626-x2020010-eng.htm. See also Garnett Picot and Feng Hou, "The Effect of Pre-immigration Canadian Work Experience on the Returns to Human Capital among Immigrants," *Journal of International Migration and Integration* 24, no. 3 (2023): 661–79, doi:10.1007/s12134-023-01025-9.

158 Hou and Bonikowska, "Selections before the Selection," 709.

Analysis of the period from 1980 to 2011 showed that increases in the proportion of immigrants with previous Canadian work experience boosted the overall earnings across all immigrants in the economic stream.[159] Of course, earnings among Canadian-born workers also increased, so the immigrant shortfall remained.

It may also be useful to consider how the two-step process affects the economic integration of family members who accompany a principal applicant for permanent status. Australian experience suggests family members of two-step immigrants do less well possibly because of family disruptions during periods of temporary migration.[160]

Evaluations of the two-step immigrant selection process suggest the possibility that increasing the proportions of immigrants with previous Canadian work experience may help reduce overall earnings gaps between immigrants and the Canadian-born. The increase in immigrants with previous work experience could be a reason for the increase in overall immigrant entry earnings for the cohort arriving in Canada during the five years prior to the 2021 census. If so, however, the evaluation studies also indicate that the effect likely will fade over time.

Increasing the size of the elite group producing the most positive effects may prove challenging. Among immigrants with previous Canadian work experience, it is the less well-paid that are becoming more numerous. And the small group whose previous Canadian experience was in the most highly paid jobs were also in a relatively small demographic category – of US and European origin – which is not likely to increase. Data on immigrant employment generally show that racialized minorities experience the greatest barriers. Further analysis is needed to fully understand the root causes. Do foreign-trained minority groups – particularly those from Asia, Africa, the Caribbean, and Latin America – often lack qualifications required in the Canadian labour market, or do minorities face significant discrimination based on origins or race?

---

159   Hou and Picot, "Changing Immigrant Characteristics."
160   Jeffrey G. Reitz, "Selecting Immigrants for the Short Term: Is It Smart in the Long Run?," *Policy Options* 31, no. 7 (2010): 12–16.

Related to this is whether ethno-racial biases influence employer selection.

An evaluation of Express Entry, focused on the period 2015–18,[161] showed that among the principal applicants admitted by the program, 84.1 per cent had university degrees. That indicated that human capital criteria remained a priority, although it is not clear to what extent the flexibility of Express Entry had boosted education levels.[162] Early earnings of those admitted under Express Entry also were higher than those not admitted under Express Entry. Much of the difference was related to their higher educational levels.[163] Finding employment somewhat earlier may have contributed, showing the potential impact of the scheme's early treatment for job offers. As mentioned above, ranking points awarded for job offers have been reduced to give more priority to more highly skilled workers.[164] Employers surveyed[165] showed some satisfaction with Express Entry, but also complained about its bureaucratic processes and requirements.

In all the program evaluations, a more general and basic question about immigrant employment remains unresolved: To what

---

161 Immigration, Refugees and Citizenship Canada, "Evaluation of Express Entry: Early Impacts on Economic Outcomes and System Management," Immigration, Refugees and Citizenship Canada, 2020.

162 A group processed outside Express Entry during the same period was used as a comparison group; in this group 71.0 per cent had university degrees, but the difference is not relevant enough to establish the impact of Express Entry.

163 Immigration, Refugees and Citizenship Canada, "Evaluation of Express Entry," 30, 69. The comparison group included immigrants admitted during the study period who had applied before the launch of Express Entry (and hence screened under the former process), but also included provincial nominee applicants who did not qualify for programs covered by Express Entry. The reason for inclusion of these provincial nominee applicants was not explained and may have biased results in favour of the Express Entry admissions.

164 Higher early employment rates were related to having received points for prearranged job offers; however, many of the job offers were for lower-skilled work such as chefs and cooks, and a reduction in points for job offers reduced the admission of such less skilled workers. Immigration, Refugees and Citizenship Canada, "Evaluation of Express Entry," 34, 85.

165 Employers were recruited from among users of the Job Bank and were not claimed to be representative. Immigration, Refugees and Citizenship Canada, "Evaluation of Express Entry," 23.

extent is the problem of immigrant underemployment a result of poor selection or of labour market barriers experienced by well-qualified immigrants? Both avenues of policy development have been pursued, and evidence of progress on each remains sketchy. If there are basic labour market barriers facing minority groups, new selection procedures will be unlikely to change those barriers.

So far, evaluations of the economic stream have focused on the economic integration of immigrants, and their employment success, rather than on the overall "economic benefits of immigration," as specified in the objectives of the *Immigration and Refugee Protection Act*, and as expected by the Canadian public. The assumption that the two are closely related might be usefully assessed in program evaluations.[166]

Temporary Immigration

The terms of evaluation for temporary immigrants are different from those for permanent immigrants, creating issues with evaluation. Temporary foreign workers are admitted to help employers be more productive while at the same time respecting Canadian employment standards and without negatively affecting Canadian workers. An additional issue is visa compliance by the workers themselves – whether they remain in Canada after the end of the term of their work permit to become undocumented immigrants.

Evaluation studies followed each of the two Auditor General's reports mentioned above which were critical of the Temporary Foreign Worker Program, and were published in 2013 and 2021,

---

166 See note 1 in this chapter (p. 96) on the overall economic benefits of immigration. A 1991 report of a government advisory body assessing the economic impacts of immigration noted the complexity of the issues but concluded that regarding the impact on per capita incomes, "an increase in immigration has a positive effect, but it is very small." Neil Swann et al., *The Economic and Social Impacts of Immigration: A Research Report Prepared for the Economic Council of Canada* (Ottawa: Minister of Supply and Services Canada, 1991), 131. The report also drew several related conclusions, for example, that the effect of using immigration to fill labour market gaps is "almost certainly exceedingly small."

respectively.[167] Both evaluations were based on surveys and focus groups of employers and other informants, including temporary foreign workers themselves, as well as government documents and statistics.

The evaluations found that employers and key informants were satisfied that the program did not negatively impact Canadian workers. Temporary Foreign Workers themselves indicated that their job was as expected or better than expected; few said it was worse. Readers may question whether such reported interview responses can be taken at face value. The evaluation report did not discuss their validity.

Regarding potential negative wage-suppression effects on Canadian workers, both evaluations cited more direct evidence of no negative effects, though without reporting details. However, the 2021 evaluation acknowledged the complexity of the required analysis,[168] and indicated that two research projects had been commissioned to examine the matter further.

The first of these studies[169] found that when a firm employs more temporary foreign workers, earnings of low-skill and low-earning Canadians at the same firm are lower. The finding did not apply to the agricultural sector. It also found the same negative correlation both before and after the reforms to the Temporary Foreign Worker Program adopted in 2014. The second study confirmed

---

167 Human Resources and Skills Development Canada, Citizenship and Immigration Canada, and Corporate Affairs Branch Canada Border Services Agency, *Evaluation of the Labour Market Opinion Streams of the Temporary Foreign Worker Program: Final Report* (Ottawa: Government Works and Public Services Canada, 2013), https://publications.gc.ca/collections/collection_2013/rhdcc-hrsdc/HS28-207-2012-eng.pdf; Employment and Social Development Canada, *Evaluation of the Temporary Foreign Worker Program*, June 2021, https://www.canada.ca/content/dam/esdc-edsc/documents/corporate/reports/evaluations/temporary-foreign-worker/SSPB-ED-TFWP-Report-PPTVersion-ENG-20220217-V08-Final-PDF.pdf.

168 Human Resources and Skills Development Canada et al., "Evaluation of the Labour Market Opinion Streams," 23.

169 Miguel Cardoso et al., "Research on Labour Market Impacts of the Temporary Foreign Worker Program," Working Paper Series, Canadian Labour Economics Forum, 2023, https://clef.uwaterloo.ca/wp-content/uploads/2023/06/CLEF-057-2023.pdf. A footnote on the title page states: "Prepared for Employment and Social Development Canada as part of an evaluation into the Temporary Foreign Worker Program."

these findings.[170] Both studies, conducted by researchers external to government, showed that firms hiring temporary foreign workers experienced economic benefits, with higher wages for better paid workers and lower wages for those already earning less. In other words, inequality within the firms increased.

The International Mobility Program, which admits a far larger number of foreign workers, has not been included in the evaluations because it covers workers exempt from the requirement for a Labour Market Impact Assessment. As mentioned above, the explanation for the exemption mentioned on government websites is that the workers admitted under the International Mobility Program "provide broad economic, cultural or other competitive advantages for Canada,"[171] so "clear and compelling" as to override the importance of the labour market assessment, with the presumed impact on the labour market being "neutral or positive." Yet the research cited above shows negative effects on the least well-paid Canadian workers even for the Temporary Foreign Worker Program in which labour market assessments are required and conducted. Clearly, the rapid growth of the International Mobility Program raises questions about potential effects on Canadian workers, as with those raised regarding the Temporary Foreign Worker Program.

The recent and very rapid increase in numbers of international students in Canada – many of whom can work both while they are students[172] and after,[173] and who may become eligible for

---

170   Fabrizio Valenti and Susan Bennett, *Labour Market Impact of the Temporary Foreign Worker Program: Final Report* (Ottawa: KSAR Consulting Group, 2022).

171   Immigration, Refugees and Citizenship Canada, "Canadian Interests – International Mobility Program," last modified 3 July 2023, https://www.canada.ca/en/immigration-refugees-citizenship/corporate/publications-manuals/operational-bulletins-manuals/temporary-residents/foreign-workers/exemption-codes/canadian-interests-significant-benefit-general-guidelines-r205-c10.html.

172   Immigration, Refugees and Citizenship Canada, "Work Off Campus as an International Student."

173   This is possible with a post-graduation work permit, considered as part of the International Mobility Program. Immigration, Refugees and Citizenship Canada, "Work in Canada after You Graduate: About the Post-graduation Work Permit," last modified 15 April 2024, https://www.canada.ca/en/immigration-refugees-citizenship/services/study-canada/work/after-graduation/about.html.

permanent resident status – has come under scrutiny for how it fits into wider aspects of Canada's overall immigration program.[174] Unfortunately, international students represent a group that may be poorly captured in official statistics on the workforce, and hence effective evaluation of their impact is challenging.[175]

Estimates of visa overstayers in Canada range between a few hundred thousand to a million or more and are based on little more than guesswork. In the United States, undocumented immigration is a major public policy issue. Information on the numbers and their locations matters when public funds are allocated based on population. Hence, careful research to provide reliable estimates is carried out. A similar level of detail will presumably be generated in Canada if the issue becomes sufficiently controversial.

A Problematic Scenario: Restructure Then Quickly Expand

Changes over the past two decades have given a dramatically new look to Canadian immigration policy in its most central feature, the economic stream. New programs have shifted selection priorities for permanent settlement to addressing short-term labour market needs in specific occupational categories, and to preferring candidates with previous Canadian work experience and those who meet requirements set by provincial governments. The Express Entry applicant management system has provided the government with additional flexibility in implementing new selection criteria quickly. And since 2015, the already high numbers of both permanent and temporary immigrants have been increased substantially, basically doubling these numbers.

---

174 Sandra Schinnerl and Antje Ellermann, "The Education-Immigration Nexus: Situating Canadian Higher Education as Institutions of Immigrant Recruitment," *Journal of International Migration and Integration* 24, Supplement 3 (2003): 599–620, https://doi.org/10.1007/s12134-023-01043-7.
175 Skuterud, "Canada's Missing Workers."

There has been no comprehensive and systemic analysis on how these shifts have changed the characteristics of immigrants selected or addressed the problems of immigrant employment and skill underutilization, or more recently the concerns about "labour shortages," which they were intended to address. As far as we can tell based on available information, success in addressing these broader problems is far from assured. Nor have the changes helped struggling immigrants already in Canada.

The *Immigration and Refugee Protection Act 2001* requires the government to report annually to Parliament on the number of permanent residents and foreign nationals admitted each year.[176] It is also required to present prospective levels of permanent residents for the following year.[177] These are contained in the minister's annual report to Parliament. But there is no requirement for prior consultation on the levels, as was past practice.[178]

As a result, the rationale for new admissions criteria does not reflect extensive public discussion and debate. Hundreds of thousands of immigrants arrive annually as economic immigrants and temporary foreign workers. Their number and composition should be based on assessments of economic need, performance, and impact over subsequent years. Such analysis would also help to understand the "absorptive capacity" of the country, which is one of the least analysed aspects of immigration policy. The immigration system itself is dauntingly complex, and major components are poorly described or, in the case of Provincial Nomination Programs, not described at all.

Of additional concern, there is no annual reporting on the planned number of temporary workers under the Temporary Foreign Worker Program and the International Mobility Program. Given the dramatic rise in the number of temporary workers to Canada since the Liberals came to power in 2015, there is a clear need for a requirement to do so, in order to ensure greater public transparency. This need is especially pronounced post COVID-19,

---

176 *Immigration and Refugee Protection Act,* S.C. 2001, s. 94.
177 *Immigration and Refugee Protection Act,* S.C. 2001.
178 Provided for in the *Immigration Act, 1976,* S.C. 25-26 Elizabeth II, c. 52.

when the issue of rapidly rising housing costs and housing short-ages, especially in Toronto and Vancouver, has become a serious concern for Canadians.

A key feature of the new approach is a focus on short-term rather than on long-term needs. A job offer may ensure early employ-ment. However, when conditions change, and the job disappears, will immigrants have the same resilience as those selected more on general human capital factors that aim to reflect future potential?

The *Immigration and Refugee Protection Act 2001* adopted selec-tion criteria embedded in regulations, which had rejected selec-tion on specific occupational demand criteria in favour of criteria reflecting a more general capacity to adapt to a changing economic environment, such as higher levels of education. Changes to these criteria, including the focus on meeting short-term labour market needs, have been made through Ministerial Instructions without consultation with Parliament.

Research to date has thrown up more questions than answers. Existing assessments of programs under the economic stream and temporary foreign work stream are tentative and incom-plete. Evaluation studies have been conducted "in-house," and criteria of evaluation have often avoided key issues. We do not have complete answers to basic questions about the characteris-tics and employment outcomes for new immigrants. Evaluation by experts independent of government is rarely conducted, and sorely needed.

The policy changes in the past twenty years appear not to have not resulted in a reduction in the human capital charac-teristics of immigrants, judging from census data available for 2021. Education levels of arrivals have kept pace with those of the Canadian-born population. However, the emphasis on occu-pations that are in demand has made little or no evident differ-ence in their labour market success relative to Canadian-born workers beyond the likelihood that previous work experience in Canada gives immigrants something of a head start. Effective longitudinal studies, especially measuring the merits of occupa-tion-specific selection under Express Entry, will hopefully shed light in this area in the future.

Evidence also suggests that slightly higher employment rates and earnings among those in the Canada Experience Class – which apply mainly for a relatively small elite group – have been offset, to a degree, by the more negative trends for Provincial Nominees. Greater investment in studies with comparisons to Canadian-born workers is necessary to assess earnings trajectories over time, and whether the earnings gaps between immigrants and Canadian-born workers are likely to close.

The impacts of economic-stream selection policies may become evident only over significant periods of time, up to ten to twelve years or more, so policy development requires a longer-term view, and an incremental approach. Some selection criteria matter more for early employment success, such as initial knowledge of English or French, while the predictive power of levels of education is greater after longer periods of time.[179] Hence the significance of many changes in selection criteria can be known with confidence only after a decade or more. Under such circumstances, incremental rather than radical change in selection policies seems most advisable, and such incrementalism matters even more if numbers are to be increased.

Meanwhile, addressing labour market disadvantages of immigrants already in the country has seemed to fade as a public policy issue. Since 2013, education qualifications must meet the test of Canadian equivalence to be used in selection decisions, but employment disadvantages and disparities among racialized immigrant groups remain.[180] One of the objectives of the *Immigration and Refugee Protection Act 2001* was to work with provinces to improve recognition of foreign qualifications,[181] yet this issue is absent from the immigration department's annual reports to Parliament.

Employment and Social Development Canada has a Foreign Credential Recognition Program that works to develop common

---

179 Picot et al., *Which Immigration Selection Factors*; Bonikowska et al., *Which Human Capital Characteristics*.

180 Banerjee et al., "Evaluating Foreign Skills."

181 *Immigration and Refugee Protection Act*, S.C. 2001, s. 3(1)j.

standards and harmonizing processes among provinces and territories, but an evaluation published in 2020 states that the impact on immigrant employment is "unclear" because of a "lack of data."[182]

Increased reliance on temporary immigration is perhaps the most difficult to assess. The Temporary Foreign Worker Program has met with significant public criticism, and the government's commissioned research shows that increased reliance on temporary foreign workers undermines the position of low-wage Canadian workers, and that policy reforms introduced in the wake of public controversy have made little difference. Meanwhile, we have witnessed a rapid shift towards use of the International Mobility Program, under which work permits are exempt from requirements related to labour market impact.

Explanations for the objectives of the International Mobility Program are vague and incomplete. The many categories for which visas are provided are grouped under labels such as "Canadian interests" and "competitiveness and public policy" that are so broad as to convey little meaning. Some workers in this program come to Canada under international trade agreements, but there has been no attempt to explain why so many others are exempt from the Labour Market Impact Assessment, or why this stream of temporary workers has been expanding so quickly.

In addition, the very large increase in the numbers of international students adds to the uncertainty about the impact of foreign workers on the Canadian labour market and other institutions. Based on employment practices of Canadian students generally, that roughly half of them work, the numbers of international students could boost temporary foreign workers in the country in 2023 from 1.3 million to 1.8 million.

Accessing the data necessary for systematic reviews has become more difficult. It is not only the lack of transparency in the

---

182 Employment and Social Development Canada, *Evaluation of the Foreign Credential Recognition Program: Report* (Ottawa: Employment and Social Development Canada, 2020), https://www.canada.ca/content/dam/canada/employment -social-development/corporate/reports/evaluations/foreign-credential-recognition -program/evaluation-foreign-credential-recognition-program-EN.pdf.

temporary foreign worker program just described. Many official announcements are uninformative about the direction and impact of economic immigration. Canada's official data portal, Open Government, is difficult to navigate, particularly for the broader public seeking specific information.[183] Useful annual statistical summaries such as the "Facts and Figures" series were discontinued in 2016, and today much of the data on immigrant selection are posted in the form of computer spreadsheet Excel files, with no systematic listing of what files are available, and no clear definitions of data categories.

Reduced information means reduced public awareness and input into decision-making. Researchers must sift through long lists of files without useful search tools or other forms of guidance in seeking specific information. Some of the files turn out to be broken, and their data useless. Available help includes only discussion forums among users, rather than staff who respond to questions. Online reviews of Open Government reflect the frustration experienced by most users.

Canadian immigration policy has garnered substantial support among Canadians due to the perception that the program is effectively managed in the public interest. Sustaining this support remains crucial for upholding the notion of "Canadian exceptionalism," in which Canada has avoided the level of hostility towards immigrants observed in many other nations. The domestic popularity of Canada's multiculturalism has played a significant role in this regard.

Is Canada ready for the impact of the major expansion of immigration recently experienced? Will we be able to explain this expansion by pointing to evidence of the success of new immigration programs put in place recently? Current public support may be declining somewhat for record immigration levels given the housing shortage crisis among other concerns. It is essential to prevent any perception of the immigration program being out of control or of imposing more costs than benefits.

---

183 Treasury Board of Canada Secretariat and Treasury Board Secretariat of Canada Open Government, "Open Government," accessed 2 August 2023, http://open.canada.ca/en.

This has been known to lead to public backlash against immigrants in other countries. It is important to ensure that this does not happen in Canada. Fostering greater public engagement in policy setting and transparent systematic impact assessments are urgently needed. We recommend that a full public review of the policies governing the economic stream be undertaken with a particular focus on selection criteria including the relevance of human capital, previous Canadian work experience, designated occupational categories and the balance between permanent and temporary economic immigration. The aim should be that the economic stream fulfills the legislative mandate to provide "economic benefits" to the country, such as to improve gross domestic product per capita, while also ensuring "successful integration" as assessed by the employment success of immigrants admitted under this stream.

Family Sponsorship: Raising Requirements

"Family reunification through immigration is not only a matter of compassion; it is a fundamental pillar of Canadian society."[1] These were the words of Sean Fraser in May 2023 when he was Minister of Immigration. And family reunification has always been a part of Canadian immigration policy, so his words ring true to that extent. But the reality of the last twenty years speaks to a more qualified truth.

In this chapter, we look at how the rules governing family sponsorship have been transformed in the contemporary period. We examine the underlying assumptions and highlight some of the consequences of the changes. And we see how the basic definitions used in immigration policy do not reflect wider shifts in society about what constitutes a family. We also look at ways in which better data could help shape policy, especially by shedding new light on the costs and benefits of family sponsorship, the accessibility of family sponsorship to all Canadians and permanent residents, the role family plays in integration and the adequacy of settlement support.

Family members can immigrate to Canada in one of three ways. First, a person applying to be a permanent resident can include their spouse and eligible dependents. More than half of all immigrants

---

1 Immigration Canada Refugees and Citizenship, "Canada Is Reuniting Loved Ones through New Immigration Measures," News Release, 26 May 2023, https://www.canada.ca/en/immigration-refugees-citizenship/news/2023/05/canada-is-reuniting-loved-ones-through-new-immigration-measures-new-measures-also-address-labour-shortages-in-canada.html.

who enter Canada permanently under the economic stream are accompanying family members. Second, recognized refugees and some temporary residents can also apply for the admission of their dependents. The third route is the focus of this chapter: how Canadian citizens and/or permanent residents within Canada can sponsor eligible family members to join them.

Each year, tens of thousands of immigrants make their way to Canada as sponsored family members. Former immigrants make up the largest group of family sponsors. Surveys for the period 2007 to 2011 have shown that 75 per cent of sponsors themselves came to Canada as immigrants. One third of sponsors have come through the economic stream, and 25 per cent through the family stream.[2]

In the mid-1980s, family sponsorships comprised close to 50 per cent of annual immigrant admissions. This began to fall in the 1990s, reaching around 30 per cent at the end of the decade. Since then, arrivals through family sponsorship have averaged around 25 per cent.[3]

Over the last two decades, significant changes in the family sponsorship stream have tightened criteria for those who can be sponsored. They have increased the responsibilities placed on sponsors. Family reunification beyond partners and dependent children has been made more difficult. This appears to have had a disproportionate impact on Canadians and permanent residents with lower incomes. Most changes were introduced during the tenure of the Conservative government from 2006 to 2015. While certain stringent measures were later reversed by the Liberal government, many other restrictions on family sponsorship remain in place.

As with other areas of reform discussed in this book, we note where more research and analysis are needed. Assessments of family sponsorships frequently focus on the economic contributions of sponsored family members and not on how sponsored family

---

2 Citizenship and Immigration Canada, "Evaluation of the Family Reunification Program," February 2014, https://www.canada.ca/content/dam/ircc/migration/ircc/english/pdf/pub/e4-2013-frp.pdf.

3 Citizenship and Immigration Canada, *Canada Facts and Figures–Immigration Overview Permanent and Temporary Residents 2010* (Ottawa: Public Works and Government Services Canada, 2010), 6–10; Citizenship and Immigration Canada, *Annual Report to Parliament on Immigration 2010*, https://publications.gc.ca/site/eng/359079/publication.html.

members enhance the earning potential of other family members or facilitate the integration of the family unit. More comprehensive studies are required to provide a more holistic view. We also highlight where further reforms may align the practice of family sponsorship more closely with the ambitions expressed for it, as stated by the minister above and reflected in the *Immigration and Refugee Protection Act 2001*: "to see that families are reunited in Canada."[4]

Context

The admission of family members to Canada as permanent residents has a long tradition. From the early period of colonial settlements, immigrants were encouraged to bring over family members and establish roots in Canada. Inducements were used. In 1783, the British government provided free grants of land to United Empire Loyalists who settled in Canada, and additional acres for each member of their family.[5] In the late nineteenth and early twentieth centuries, Canadian immigration agents were sent to Great Britain, parts of Europe and the United States to promote Canada to individuals, families, and groups as a place to settle.

Men frequently arrived first. Family members then joined them, often with the assistance of immigration agents and officials.[6] There were schemes for the family settlement of farms and financial conditions for immigrants were waived for those who had relatives in Canada willing to provide support.[7]

The range of relations included in the family class has always shifted, often in response to prevailing economic conditions. It has ranged from spouses and dependent children to a broader set of family members, including parents, grandparents, aunts, uncles, nephews, and nieces.[8]

---

4 *Immigration and Refugee Protection Act*, S.C. 2001, c. 27, s. 3(1)d (Can).
5 Kelley and Trebilcock, *Making of the Mosaic*, 43.
6 Kelley and Trebilcock, *Making of the Mosaic*, 121.
7 Kelley and Trebilcock, *Making of the Mosaic*, 139.
8 Rell DeShaw, "The History of Family Reunification in Canada and Current Policy," *Canadian Issues* (2006): 9–14, https://acs-metropolis.ca/wp-content/uploads/2019/05/CITC-2006-Spring-Printemps-2.pdf.

As discussed in part 1, race-based selection criteria limited all immigration to Canada to those from "preferred countries" for most of the twentieth century. In the early 1960s, race-based selection criteria were eased but not eliminated. All Canadian citizens and permanent residents could sponsor immediate family members. However, the sponsorship of more extended family members was limited to individuals from preferred countries in the Americas, Europe, and the Middle East.[9]

In 1967, new regulations eliminated all explicit admission restrictions based on nationality, ethnicity, or racial identity, and a more uniform approach to family sponsorship was adopted. A wide array of family relationships was recognized for immigration purposes, which led to a steady increase in the proportion of the family stream in annual immigration totals. In 1976, the family stream comprised 62 per cent of annual immigrant arrivals.[10] The range of relatives that could be sponsored was narrowed in subsequent years and the proportion of family class immigrants steadily declined (see figure 3). Over time the priority shifted to selecting economic immigrants, making the economic stream dominant.

Relevant Legislative Provisions

Family reunification is among the core objectives of the *Immigration and Refugee Protection Act 2001* in keeping with previous legislation.[11] The act's definition of family includes a spouse, common-law partner, child, parent, or "other prescribed family member of a Canadian citizen or permanent resident."[12] Although the latter

---

9   Order in Council, P.C. 1962-86, 18 January 1962. Middle Eastern countries included Egypt, Israel, Lebanon, and Turkey.

10 Kelley and Trebilcock, *Making of the Mosaic*, 353. This is inclusive if immediate and more distant relatives are authorized under the act and regulations.

11 *Immigration and Refugee Protection Act*, S.C. 2001, s. 3(1)(d).

12 *Immigration and Refugee Protection Act*, S.C. 2001, s. 12(1).

category suggests a broad range of relatives, the regulations limit those who can qualify.

The family class sponsorship requirements differ, depending on the type of relative. The rules for spouses, common-law or conjugal partners, and dependents are more relaxed than those for parents and grandparents and more distant relatives. There is a right to appeal if applications are turned down. The sponsor may appeal the decision to the Immigration Appeal Division of the Immigration and Refugee Board,[13] and then has recourse to seek judicial review by the Federal Court.[14]

Requirements of Sponsors

Eligible Sponsors

Family sponsors must be eighteen years of age and need to establish that the relationship is genuine as well as within an admissible category. Other requirements are set out below.

Income Requirements

Income requirements vary, depending on which relatives are being sponsored and in what number. Generally, they do not apply for sponsorship of a spouse, common-law or conjugal partner, or dependent child.[15] In all other cases, the sponsor must meet the minimum income requirements for three consecutive years preceding their application, substantiated by documentation from the Canada Revenue Agency.

Except for Quebec, the minimum income requirements are the same across the country, regardless of where the sponsor lives. Some commentators have called for regional adjustments to reflect

---

13 *Immigration and Refugee Protection Act,* S.C. 2001, s. 63(1).
14 *Immigration and Refugee Protection Act,* S.C. 2001, s. 72(1).
15 Unless one of the family members being sponsored has a dependent child in which case the sponsor must meet the applicable low-income cut-off.

significant variations in the cost of living,[16] although that would mean a sponsor could apply from a low-cost area before moving to a higher cost one on being accepted.

Support Undertakings

In all cases, the sponsor must sign an agreement to support those they bring in for a specified length of time. This varies, depending on the relationship involved. Spouses, partners, and dependent children over twenty-two years of age must be supported for three years. A dependent child under twenty-two years old must be supported for ten years, or until the child reaches twenty-five years old.

All other relatives must also be supported for ten years, except for parents and grandparents, for whom support for twenty years is required.[17] During the period, the sponsor must provide financial support for their sponsored family member and repay any social assistance that person receives, aside from health care, which is covered by provincial systems.[18] The undertaking remains binding even if circumstances change, including loss of employment, medical disability, or any breakdown in relations between the sponsor and the relative, including divorce.

Bars to Sponsorship

There is a long list of factors that can render a person ineligible to sponsor a family member.

16　Canadian Bar Association, "Family Reunification – We're for It," 26 October 2016, https://www.cba.org/Our-Work/cbainfluence/Submissions/2016/November/Family-reunification. Others made similar arguments to the House of Commons Standing Committee on Citizenship and Immigration. See Borys Wrzesnewskyj, *Family Reunification: Report of the Standing Committee on Citizenship and Immigration* (Ottawa: House of Commons Canada, 2017), 24, https://www.ourcommons.ca/Content/Committee/421/CIMM/Reports/RP8810563/cimmrp08/cimmrp08-e.pdf.

17　Of note, the sponsorship requirements can vary for the Province of Quebec.

18　*Immigration and Refugee Protection Act*, S.C. 2001, s. 13.1.

Violence, Criminality, Indebtedness

The list includes individuals who have used or threatened violence against another family member. Financial issues barring candidates include persons in the process of bankruptcy and those who failed to meet the terms of a previous sponsorship agreement or failed to pay an immigration loan on time. Immigration loans are provided in exceptional cases, generally to sponsored refugees to assist them in getting required documents and pay fees associated with their resettlement.[19]

Misrepresentation

Those who apply for permanent residence in Canada are required to declare all their dependent relatives.[20] If they do not, and subsequently try to sponsor such a relative, the sponsorship will be denied. The applicant is banned for life from trying to sponsor the person again and cannot appeal the decision to the Immigration Appeal Division.[21]

This part of the regulation has been criticized as being harsh – especially in terms of the consequences – which come regardless of reasons for the omission, however compelling.[22] Critics point out that it is

---

19 Immigration, Refugees and Citizenship Canada Immigration, "Immigration Loans Program (ILP)," last updated 31 March 2016, https://www.canada.ca/en/immigration-refugees-citizenship/corporate/publications-manuals/operational-bulletins-manuals/service-delivery/immigration-loans-program.html. They are to help to defray costs associated with the immigration application such as obtaining travel documents, paying for transportation to Canada, and covering the cost of application fees.

20 *Immigration and Refugee Protection Regulations*, S.O.R./2002-227, s. 117(9)(d).

21 *Immigration and Refugee Protection Regulations*, S.O.R./2002-227, s. 117(9)(d).

22 Canadian Bar Association, "Family Reunification"; Canadian Council for Refugees, "Excluded Family Members: Brief on R. 117(9)(d)," May 2016, https://ccrweb.ca/sites/ccrweb.ca/files/excluded-family-members-brief-may-2016.pdf; McCuaig Desrochers, "117(9)(d) Failure to Disclose Family Members Results in Future Exclusion from the Family Class," 21 July 2015, https://www.mccuaig.com/1179d-failure-disclose-family-members-results-future-exclusion-family-class/.

also inconsistent with other comparable aspects of the act, with other kinds of misrepresentation leading only to a five-year ban.[23]

In 2015, a study of 105 refusals showed that, in 92 per cent of the cases, the misrepresentations were unintentional.[24] The ban has applied when family members were separated at the time of the application[25] and where the sponsor was unaware of the existence or whereabouts of an undeclared dependent.[26] There have also been identified cases where a woman has failed to initially disclose a child born out of wedlock – including as a result of rape – out of fear of being ostracized by her family or community.

A barred applicant can seek to have the person admitted as a permanent resident for humanitarian and compassionate reasons. However, advocates point to the fact that applications are expensive to file and cases can be protracted. They also claim that decisions from immigration officers often seem arbitrary and that the best interests of any children concerned are not properly or systematically considered.[27]

In 2019, the government recognized the "disproportionate impact" of the lifetime bar, particularly on children. It implemented a pilot policy to lift the provision for certain types of sponsors and family applicants. Exempted from the ban is a sponsor who obtained permanent residence as a refugee, protected person, or as part of a family sponsorship and is sponsoring a spouse, a common-law or conjugal partner, or a dependent child.[28]

---

23 Canadian Council for Refugees, "Families Never to Be United: Excluded Family Members," Background Paper, January 2007, https://ccrweb.ca/files/excluded-fammembers.pdf; Megan Gaucher, *A Family Matter: Citizenship, Conjugal Relationships, and Canadian Immigration Policy* (Vancouver: UBC Press, 2018), 5.

24 Canadian Council for Refugees, "Excluded Family Members," 3.

25 Such as spouses who separated but then reconciled.

26 Not uncommon in refugee situations where the applicant has assumed his/her relatives have died or does not know their whereabouts.

27 In its investigation, the Canadian Council for Refugees found that 55 per cent of the sponsorships refused based on failure to disclose involved children. Canadian Council for Refugees, "Excluded Family Members," 9.

28 The pilot policy was extended to 23 September 2023. Immigration, Refugees and Citizenship Canada, "Pilot Program to Exempt Permanent Residence Applicants

There seems no reason why the government should not make this policy permanent and eliminate the lifetime ban for others where there are compelling reasons. This was also among the recommendations from the House of Commons Standing Committee on Citizenship and Immigration that studied family reunification in 2016 and issued its report in 2017.

The Standing Committee heard from fifty-one witnesses and received many written submissions. On the issue of misrepresentation, it suggested that visa officers be required to consider all the facts of the case, including intention and any mitigating circumstances. If an exclusion is imposed, the committee recommended that it should not exceed five years, in accordance with the penalties for misrepresentation elsewhere in the act.[29]

Social Assistance

Sponsors who are receiving social assistance are likewise prohibited from sponsoring a family member, even an immediate family member. This policy has attracted criticism for being excessively stringent and potentially counterproductive. For example, an individual who is a single parent and reliant on social assistance is prevented from sponsoring their partner, even when the partner's presence could be the most viable route away from public support. Reforms should be considered that provide an exception in such cases.

Eligible Family Members

Current immigration policy sets a preference for immediate family members such as intimate partners and dependent children. Quotas

---

in the Family Class or the Spouse or Common-Law Partner in Canada (SCLPC) Class from Paragraph R117(9)(d) or R125(1)(d) Exclusion," 30 October 2023, https://www.canada.ca/en/immigration-refugees-citizenship/corporate /publications-manuals/operational-bulletins-manuals/permanent-residence /non-economic-classes/family-class-spouse/pilot-exempt-r117-r125.html.

29 Wrzesnewskyj, *Family Reunification: Report*, 55.

and other restrictions apply to parents and grandparents, while other relatives are admitted only under narrow circumstances.

All sponsored relatives must meet the general admissibility requirements discussed earlier in part 2, with the exception of sponsored spouses, common-law partners, and dependent children who cannot be denied admission to Canada on health grounds.[30]

Spouses and Partners

Three kinds of intimate partners are recognized under the act for the purposes of family admissions: spouses, common-law partners, and conjugal partners, including same-sex partners. These are explained more fully below.

Spouses must be legally married. A foreign marriage must be legally recognized in the country where it took place and in Canada. Common-law partners must show they have lived together for at least one year in a continuous, uninterrupted relationship. Conjugal partners are those who have not been able to marry or live together for reasons beyond their control.[31] This can include couples who are separated because of war, or same-sex partners who are prohibited by law to marry and face criminal prosecution if their relationship is revealed.

As part of its comprehensive reform of immigration policy, in 2011, the Conservative government looked at what it argued were elevated instances of marriage fraud. Statistics validating this view were lacking.[32] But the government's communications initiatives

---

30 These are set out in sections 33–43 of the *Immigration and Refugee Protection Act,* S.C. 2001. In addition to the health grounds are those that relate to criminality, security, human or international rights violations, and non-compliance with the act.

31 For example, same-sex partners whose relations are unlawful in their country. For more on this amendment, see Gaucher, *A Family Matter,* 64.

32 The Minister of Public Safety acknowledged this in 2007, as the system only recorded the number of decisions made on the basis "misrepresentation" and not on the precise misrepresentation. The anecdotal nature of the assessment of marriage fraud cases did not improve in subsequent years with both the Immigration, Refugees and Citizenship Canada and the Canadian Border Service Agency reporting statistics that were not comparable. Moreover, the reported number of cases did not reveal the number substantiated. Gaucher, *A Family Matter,* 137–9.

consistently conveyed the perception that marriage fraud posed a substantial threat to the credibility of the immigration system. Its anti-marriage fraud campaign encompassed information circulars, public surveys, and specialized training for immigration officers – all of which contributed to the impression that marriage fraud was widespread.[33]

New restrictions were imposed, including a requirement that a sponsored common-law partner initially receive a conditional permanent landing certificate. This would only become permanent after two years of cohabitation. The rule was widely criticized as it left partners in abusive situations highly vulnerable. The provision was repealed by the Liberal government in 2017.

The Liberals also amended the law to permit the sponsorship of spouses, common-law partners, and conjugal partners already living in Canada. Previously, only those living abroad could be sponsored. Advocates had long sought this change and applauded the amendment. But they remain critical of the fact that a rejected sponsorship application in this category cannot be appealed to the Immigration Appeal Board. This creates an anomaly that the advocates argue is unjustifiable, where sponsors of applicants within Canada have fewer rights for a review of a rejected sponsorship application than sponsors of applicants who are applicants abroad.[34]

One remaining restriction concerns the assessment of the authenticity of a relationship. Previously, the emphasis was on the primary intention underlying the partnership, requiring the sponsor to demonstrate a genuine intent to establish a permanent life together. For instance, if a marriage was initially contracted for immigration purposes – but also involved a sincere intention

---

The absence of reliable data was also a finding of the 2014 government evaluation of the family program. Citizenship and Immigration Canada, "Evaluation of the Family Reunification Program," vii, xii.

33 For a comprehensive review of the various prongs to its campaign see Gaucher, *A Family Matter*.

34 As observed by immigration law specialist Robin Seligman of Seligman Law. Robin Seligman, interview with author, Toronto, September 2023.

of permanence or evolved into a genuine relationship – it could be approved for sponsorship.[35] The law has since been altered to assume "bad faith" if immigrating into or remaining in Canada was one of the motivations for entering into the marriage.

According to the regulations, a relationship will be deemed to lack authenticity if it is "primarily established to gain any status or privilege under the [Immigration] Act."[36] The guidance provided by Immigration Refugees Citizenship Canada to visa officers is more explicit: "A spousal relationship or common-law partnership that is not genuine *or* that was entered into primarily for the purpose of acquiring any status or privilege will be refused" (emphasis added).[37]

This has proved problematic for persons whose marriages are arranged and when the sponsor being a permanent resident or citizen of Canada is considered a desirable quality for the match. Regardless of the intention to live together permanently, evidence of an "immigration factor" can lead to a rejection of the application.

The same is true of a sponsor who marries a partner in Canada when the partner is neither a permanent resident nor a Canadian citizen. The desire to secure the partner's ability to remain in Canada can lead to a rejection of the application, regardless of the love and affection between the couple and their intention to live together permanently.[38] We endorse the 2017 recommendation of the Standing Committee that a "finding of bad faith should

---

35 Immigration and Refugee Protection Act Regulations, S.O.R./2004-167, s. 3(E): "For the purposes of these Regulations, a foreign national shall not be considered a spouse, a common-law partner, a conjugal partner or an adopted child of a person if the marriage, common-law partnership, conjugal partnership or adoption is not genuine AND was entered into primarily for the purpose of acquiring any status or privilege under the Act" (emphasis added).

36 *Immigration and Refugee Protection Regulations*, S.O.R./2002-227 s. 4(1)(a).

37 Immigration, Refugees and Citizenship Canada, "Assessing the Relationship between Spouses or Common-Law Partners," 12 March 2018, https://www.canada.ca/en/immigration-refugees-citizenship/corporate/publications-manuals/operational-bulletins-manuals/permanent-residence/non-economic-classes/family-class-determining-spouse/assessing-relationship.html.

38 Also discussed in Gaucher, *A Family Matter*, 123–4.

require both that the relationship is not genuine at the time of consideration and that its primary purpose is to acquire immigration benefits." In other words, an immigration motive alone should not be reason to assume bad faith if the relationship is shown to be genuine.[39]

The Standing Committee also recommended cultural sensitivity training for immigration officers. This was in response to concerns that immigration officers apply their own subjective criteria in assessing the genuineness of the union. For example, immigration officers have found that differences in age, education, or interests between the couple show a lack of compatibility and demonstrate bad faith.[40]

Immigration officers could benefit from training in cross-cultural awareness provided by experts, including experts on family life in Canada. Greater clarity should be introduced in immigration guidelines and training resources to convey that a marriage can be authentic even if immigration to Canada was one of the motivating factors. The materials should also offer more precise directives to eliminate the subjective consideration of "compatibility" as a relevant determinant in the final assessment.[41]

Dependent Children

Dependent children include biological and adopted children. A dependent child must be under twenty-two years of age and not have a spouse or common-law partner. Older children can qualify if they have depended on their parents since before the age of twenty-two, and they are unable to financially support themselves due to a physical or mental condition.

---

39 Wrzesnewskyj, *Family Reunification: Report*, 56.
40 Gaucher, *A Family Matter*, 125–6.
41 The Standing Committee similarly recommended, "That Immigration, Refugees and Citizenship Canada mainstream training provide country-specific cultural awareness including awareness of different classes and how intimacy is discussed, so that bone fide relationships are not penalized." See Wrzesnewskyj, *Family Reunification: Report*, 56.

Initially, the age cap on dependent children was eighteen. This was subject to considerable controversy, with critics pointing out that, in Canada, 50 per cent of children between twenty and twenty-four years of age live with their parents. They also noted that the eighteen-year age limit was a disincentive for families who wished to immigrate but not by leaving their young adult members behind and possibly at risk.[42] The age limit was raised to twenty-two by the Liberal government in 2017.

Applicants must establish that the parent-child relationship is genuine. Supporting documents include birth certificates and DNA tests for biological children. As with marriages, adoptions must be legally valid in the country where they took place and in Canada.

DNA Tests

Canada is among more than twenty-one countries using DNA testing within immigration procedures. Across Europe and North America, there is a substantial body of literature examining the ramifications of incorporating DNA tests in family class applications.[43] Analysts acknowledge several advantages. They include the confirmation of a biological relationship in instances without dependable documentary evidence, the prevention of fraudulent activities, the reduction of subjectivity inherent in immigration officer evaluations, and the facilitation of timely application processing.[44]

However, many analysts also emphasize the drawbacks of heavy reliance on DNA testing and advocate prudence,

---

42 Beth Martin, "Immigrants are Family Members Too," in *Putting Family First: Migration and Integration in Canada*, ed. Harald Bauder (Vancouver: UBC Press, 2019), 27.

43 Palmira Granados Moreno, Ida Ngueng Feze, and Yann Joly, "Does the End Justify the Means? A Comparative Study of the Use of DNA Testing in the Context of Family Reunification," *Journal of Law and the Biosciences* 4, no. 2 (2017): 251, https://doi.org/10.1093/jlb/lsx012. This became more widespread during the 1990s.

44 Moreno, Feze, and Joly, "Does the End Justify the Means?," 265.

particularly concerning its implementation in family class applications. The prevailing concern is that its use reinforces a restricted interpretation of family – defined by blood or adoption – as in Canadian immigration law. As noted by one observer, the emphasis on biological linkage perpetuates the view that "shared genes are the principal means of identifying human relationships and that one should be entitled to legal benefits solely on this basis."[45]

There are other drawbacks. In Canada, the provisions for using DNA tests in assessing family class applications are set out in guidance materials that the government provides to immigration officers. DNA is to be relied on "only as a last resort," where there are doubts concerning a parent-child relationship or where it is not possible to obtain satisfactory documentary proof.[46]

Studies have shown that adherence to the guidance is not uniform. More frequent requests for DNA tests are made for applicants from certain countries, irrespective of documentary evidence they provide to substantiate claims.[47] Additionally, concerns have been raised over the apparent lack of consideration for the potential harm such requests can cause. There have been cases where a child's conception has resulted from rape, which the mother has kept from disclosing for religious, cultural, or other reasons that could place her or the child at risk.[48] Commentators also highlight that DNA tests are frequently expensive, enough to prohibit some

---

45 Janice D. Villiers, "Brave New World: The Use and Potential Misuse of DNA Technology in Immigration Law," *Boston College Third World Law Journal* 30, no. 2 (2010): 239. See also Moreno, Feze, and Joly, "Does the End Justify the Means?," 273–4; Iseult Honohan, "Reconsidering the Claim to Family Reunification in Migration," *Political Studies* 57, no. 4 (2009): 775, https://doi.org/10.1111/j.1467-9248.2008.00761.x.

46 Refugees and Citizenship Canada Immigration, "DNA Testing," 13 February 2017, https://www.canada.ca/en/immigration-refugees-citizenship/corporate/publications-manuals/operational-bulletins-manuals/standard-requirements/dna-testing.html.

47 Yann Joly et al., "DNA Testing for Family Reunification in Canada: Points to Consider," *Journal of International Migration and Integration* 18, no. 2 (2017): 395, https://doi.org/10.1007/s12134-016-0496-7. The studies are cited in this article.

48 Joly et al., "DNA Testing," 396.

applications.[49] This disproportionately affects immigrants with limited financial resources.

Immigration officers have the discretion to approve family class applications based on humanitarian and compassionate considerations, even in the presence of unfavourable DNA test results. However, there is little guidance provided on how this should be exercised and there are no accessible data regarding the frequency and conditions under which this discretion is exercised.[50]

Short of revising the definition of family within the *Immigration and Refugee Protection Act 2001*, there are other measures available to improve evidentiary requirements. One viable approach involves issuing more specific and transparent directives concerning when to require DNA tests, along with the factors to be considered when they produce an unfavourable outcome. This guidance should be complemented by comprehensive training for immigration officers. Additionally, applicants could be afforded more time to compile supplementary evidence, and to include diverse forms of verification such as attestations, photographs, financial support records, and communications.[51]

Achieving transparency also depends on providing accessible data that shows the extent to which DNA evidence is relied upon by an applicant's country of origin, along with the associated costs and processing times.[52]

Adoption Criteria

Canadian citizens and permanent residents can sponsor their adopted children for admission to Canada. Adoption can take

---

49   Moreno, Feze, and Joly, "Does the End Justify the Means?," 262–3, 269. These authors note that the test can be requested of more than one family member and each test can range from US$230 to US$1,250 per test.

50   Discussed more fully in Moreno, Feze, and Joly, "Does the End Justify the Means?," 270–3; Ida Ngueng Feze et al., "Flying under the Radar: Two Decades of DNA Testing at IRCC," *Canadian Journal of Law and Technology* 17, no. 2 (2019): 226–75, https://digitalcommons.schulichlaw.dal.ca/cgi/viewcontent.cgi?article =1257&context=cjlt.

51   Joly et al., "DNA Testing," 398.

52   Joly et al., "DNA Testing," 400.

place abroad or within Canada. The process is thorough – but also complicated and expensive.

Canada uses the *Hague Adoption Convention*,[53] which sets out internationally recognized criteria regarding Inter-country adoptions. Among them is a requirement that the adoption creates a legal relationship between parent and child and extinguishes previous parental-child legal bonds. Sponsors seeking to bring in their children adopted abroad can run into difficulties if the adoption took place in a country where, for religious or cultural reasons, adoption must not sever the bonds between the birth parent and the child. Adoptions within those countries are not recognized in Canada, although other jurisdictions permit them.[54]

International adoptions within Canada must be conducted through agencies that are approved by the province or territory where the sponsor lives. This is designed to ensure that adoptions are conducted in a legitimate manner and with the best interests of the child in mind. However, approved adoption agencies from Canadian provinces or territories do not operate in many of the immigrant source countries. This poses an insurmountable hurdle for families who wish to adopt children from these countries.

One suggestion is to consider the application of humanitarian and compassionate considerations when there are obstacles preventing the reunification of a genuine parent-adopted child relationship.[55] This recommendation was also endorsed by the Standing Committee, which called for greater flexibility and accommodation in the sponsorship of adopted children and improved coordination with provincial authorities.[56]

---

53 Hague Conference on Private International Law, "Convention of Protection of Children and Co-operation in Respect of Intercountry Adoption," 29 May 1993, https://assets.hcch.net/docs/77e12f23-d3dc-4851-8f0b-050f71a16947.pdf.

54 Melissa Redmond and Beth Martin, "All in the (Definition of) Family: Transnational Parent–Child Relationships, Rights to Family Life, and Canadian Immigration Law," *Journal of Family Issues* 44, no. 3 (2021), https://doi.org/10.1177/0192513X211054461. Other jurisdictions include the United Kingdom and the United States.

55 Canadian Bar Association, "Family Reunification."

56 Wrzesnewskyj, *Family Reunification: Report,* 57–8.

Parents and Grandparents

In 2011, the government imposed a moratorium on new family class applications for parents and grandparents. It was justified on two grounds. One was the huge backlog of cases that were tying up the system, with over 165,000 pending applications and processing times reaching over seven years.[57] The other was that parents and grandparents imposed more social costs than economic gains, especially when sponsorship undertakings were not honoured, and sponsored applicants relied on public assistance.

The suspension was lifted in 2013, and new criteria introduced, aimed at limiting the number of applications and alleviating the "burden" parents and grandparents allegedly place on the health care system and other social resources. The Minister of Immigration, Jason Kenny, stated they were necessary to end "abuse of Canadian generosity."[58]

As with the similar justification for changes to spousal and partner sponsorships, the government's rationale for the restrictions on parents and grandparents was also criticized as lacking a sound evidentiary foundation.[59]

---

57 Naomi Alboim and Karen Cohl, *Shaping the Future: Canada's Rapidly Changing Immigration Policies* (Toronto: The Maytree Foundation, 2012), 28, https://maytree.com/wp-content/uploads/shaping-the-future.pdf; Citizenship and Immigration Canada, "Government of Canada to Cut Backlog and Wait Times for Family Reunification–Phase I of Action Plan for Faster Family Reunification," 4 November 2011, https://www.canada.ca/en/news/archive/2011/11/government-canada-cut-backlog-wait-times-family-reunification-phase-action-plan-faster-family-reunification.html. The conditions for the delays and the backlogs began during the previous government when restrictions were placed on the number of annual sponsorships of parents and grandparents and processing times were intentionally extended. Xiaobei Chen and Sherry Xiaohan Thorpe, "Temporary Families? The Parent and Grandparent Sponsorship Program and the Neoliberal Regime of Immigration Governance in Canada," *Migration, Mobility, & Displacement* 1, no. 1 (2015): 87–8, https://doi.org/10.18357/mmd11201513308.

58 Meagan Fitzpatrick, "Don't Bring Parents Here for Welfare, Kenney Says," *CBC News*, 10 May 2013, https://www.cbc.ca/news/politics/don-t-bring-parents-here-for-welfare-kenney-says-1.1351002.

59 Canadian Bar Association, "Family Reunification."

A government evaluation of the family class stream in 2014 painted a more nuanced picture, as did evidence before the Standing Committee in 2016.[60] Evidence showed that parents and grandparents had the lowest earnings of all immigrants, yet they contributed to faster integration, emotional stability, and overall economic well-being of the family unit. Their economic contributions included the personal wealth they bring with them and the childcare they provide, which enables other members of the family to work or take additional job or skills training.

As for social assistance, evidence before the Standing Committee showed that "the incidence of social assistance to parent and grandparents and dependent children is almost half the national average." Moreover, the evaluation reported a decrease in costs resulting from sponsorship defaults.[61]

The new rules, implemented in 2013, increased the minimum income requirement for sponsors by 30 per cent and extended the sponsorship commitment from ten to twenty years.[62] Emphasizing the need for these changes to safeguard Canadian taxpayers, Minister Kenny reiterated that "we are not looking for more people

---

60 Citizenship and Immigration Canada, "Evaluation of the Family Reunification Program," 55–65; Wrzesnewskyj, *Family Reunification: Report*, 11–17. This report of Citizenship and Immigration Canada presents the results of the evaluation of its Family Reunification Program that was carried out from December 2012 to September 2013. The evaluation covers the period from 2007 to 2011 and was conducted in fulfilment of requirements under the Treasury Board Secretariat's policy on evaluation.

61 Citizenship and Immigration Canada, "Evaluation of the Family Reunification Program," 79. According to the evaluation, "A comparison of the period of the evaluation (2007-2011) with the previous five-year period (2002-2006) demonstrated a reduction in the total costs associated with sponsorship default. More recently selected immigrants are less likely to rely on social assistance than their counterparts who landed in earlier years. This finding, together with the active enforcement and debt recovery programs implemented in some provinces, has resulted in a reduction in the total amount of unpaid sponsorship debt over the last few years."

62 Immigration, Refugees and Citizenship Canada, "Applications under Family Classes: Assessing the Sponsor," 12 March 2018, https://www.canada.ca/en/immigration-refugees-citizenship/corporate/publications-manuals/operational-bulletins-manuals/permanent-residence/non-economic-classes

on welfare, we're not looking to add people as a social burden to Canada."[63]

While acknowledging the valuable family support parents and grandparents can provide, the Liberal government did not relax the restrictions on applications to sponsor parents and grandparents for permanent residency.

The application process is also different for parents and grandparents. While other family class sponsorships are initiated through an application by the sponsor, for a parent or grandparent the sponsor must first submit an "interest to sponsor" form and then wait for the government to send an "invitation to sponsor."[64] And there are only specific and narrow time periods when an expression of interest can be made. In 2020 and 2021, this window was for three and two weeks, respectively.

From these expressions of interest, the government randomly selects prospective sponsors to submit a complete application, up to a certain threshold number.[65] The applications are long and must be accompanied by specific documentation. Evidence also points to a cumbersome application process. Minor mistakes can lead to a rejection of an otherwise sound application.

In 2020–1, the government sent out close to 50,000 invitations to apply. Just under 12,000 approved sponsored parents and grandparents came as permanent residents in 2021.[66] This number rose considerably in 2022 to over 27,000.[67]

/family-class-assessing-sponsor.html. This 30 per cent hike was not applied for the 2020 and 2021 taxation years in lieu of the fact that the COVID-19 pandemic had impacted family incomes. The required level of income is calculated by applying the low minimum income requirement "plus 30% for each of the 3 taxation years immediately preceding the date of the application."

63 Fitzpatrick, "Don't Bring Parents Here for Welfare."
64 Immigration, Refugees and Citizenship Canada, "Sponsor Your Parents and Grandparents: Find out If You're Invited to Apply," 8 May 2017, https://www .canada.ca/en/immigration-refugees-citizenship/services/immigrate-canada /family-sponsorship/sponsor-parents-grandparents/selected.html.
65 Immigration, Refugees and Citizenship Canada, "Sponsor Your Parents and Grandparents."
66 Fraser, *2022 Annual Report to Parliament on Immigration*, 30.
67 Miller, *2023 Annual Report to Parliament on Immigration*, 61.

Since 2017, the annual number of applications awaiting processing has consistently surpassed admissions, with over 70,000 applications pending in 2022. While processing times have seen some improvement from nearly six years in 2017 to just over eighteen months in 2022, they have begun to lengthen again, exceeding two years by 2024.[68]

While processing times are relatively better than in 2017, the waiting periods for being able to sponsor a parent or grandparent remain indeterminate and, at best, take several years. As critics have pointed out, a sponsor must now wait for an opportunity to express an interest to sponsor; then wait to be selected through the lottery process to apply; and then wait for an approval of their application.[69]

Others have noted that the restrictions on parent and grandparent sponsorship are most keenly felt by women, who take on the additional responsibilities of childcare, impacting on their social and professional lives.[70] Studies also reflect the costs to children of being separated from grandparents who, alongside home help, also provide stability and security for children adapting to life in Canada.[71]

---

68 And up to fifty-one months for applicants from Quebec. Immigration, Refugees and Citizenship Canada, "Check Processing Times," last updated 11 July 2024, https://www.canada.ca/en/immigration-refugees-citizenship/services/application/check-processing-times.html. Quebec has also put a cap on how many immediate family members it will permit to immigrate to the province which has meant that spouses and dependent children can also wait for relatively long periods before being reunited in Canada. This has raised tensions between the federal and provincial government, with the former finding the delays unacceptable and the Minister of Immigration saying that it will by-pass the Quebec cap if the province does not take action to remedy the delays. Sabrina Jonas, "Ottawa Says It Will Bypass Quebec's Immigration Cap to Speed Up Family Reunification," *CBC News*, 4 March 2024, https://www.cbc.ca/news/canada/montreal/family-reunification-federal-minister-quebec-1.7132823.

69 Danièle Bélanger and Guillermo Candiz, "The Politics of 'Waiting' for Care: Immigration Policy and Family Reunification in Canada," *Journal of Ethnic and Migration Studies* 46, no. 16 (2019): 3478.

70 Bronwyn Bragg and Lloyd L. Wong, "'Cancelled Dreams': Family Reunification and Shifting Canadian Immigration Policy," *Journal of Immigrant & Refugee Studies* 14, no. 1 (2016): 53, https://doi.org/10.1080/15562948.2015.1011364.

71 Bragg and Wong, "'Cancelled Dreams,'" 57.

Financial undertakings to sponsor parents and grandparents can be onerous for those who need this kind of support the most to improve their economic well-being: low-income families. Considering this, the Standing Committee has recommended a more flexible approach over demonstrating the minimum income required to sponsor parents and grandparents. This can include allowing siblings to co-sponsor an application, reducing the number of years required of proof of income, from three years to one, and shortening the undertaking period to ten years for parents and grandparents under sixty years of age.[72]

Temporary Visa Program

In 2011, the government introduced a super-visa program as an alternative and more temporary route for parents and grandparents to be reunited with their families in Canada. It permits parents and grandparents to come to Canada multiple times over a period of ten years. While in Canada, they are not permitted to work or access social services, including health care funded by provinces and territories. The resident child or grandchild must meet a certain income threshold. The applicants must pass a medical exam and provide proof of private health insurance.

Within a few years of its implementation, critics pointed to higher approval rates for those from Europe and United States and substantially lower ones for applicants from Africa, Asia, and the Middle East.[73]

Initially, the regulations enabled those with a super visa to remain in Canada continually for up to two years, whereupon they had to leave and be readmitted under their ten-year super visa. This cap was raised by the Liberal government to five years in 2022. In explaining the change, Minister Sean Fraser extolled the virtues of easing the entry of parents and grandparents. Allowing them "to reunite for longer in Canada," he explained, "helps everyday Canadian citizens and permanent residents succeed and

---

72 Wrzesnewskyj, *Family Reunification: Report*, 58–9.
73 Chen and Thorpe, "Temporary Families?," 92.

contribute to society."[74] Earlier the Liberal government had raised the number of annual super visas to 20,000 in 2017, from the 5,000 imposed by the previous government. Figures for 2022 show that close to 49,000 super visas were issued.[75]

The Liberal government also attempted to reduce processing times, but these had mixed results. At the start of 2023, the government reported that most applications for a super visa were being processed "within a few weeks or less." To get a better sense of how this statistic is calculated, it is necessary to run a data query by country of application. A random search from centres across all continents revealed that processing times varied – from seven months to close to one year.[76]

Sponsors and applicants are required to have Canadian medical insurance. For those with limited financial resources, this has become a notably burdensome administrative requirement. Parents and grandparents who apply for a super visa are obligated to provide proof of private medical insurance sourced from a Canadian insurance provider. The proof must include payment documentation, validity for a minimum of one-year, minimum emergency coverage of $100,000 and coverage for health care, hospitalization, and repatriation expenses.[77]

Critics argue that this requirement often exceeds the financial capabilities of many applicants. In this context, it would be prudent for the government to explore alternatives, such as identifying sound insurance providers situated outside of Canada as potential options.[78]

---

74 Daniel Otis, "'Super Visa' Allows Some People to Stay in Canada for up to 7 Years, Here's Who Is Eligible to Apply," *CTV News*, 7 June 2022, https://www. ctvnews.ca/canada/super-visa-allows-some-people-to-stay-in-canada-for-up-to -7-years-here-s-who-is-eligible-to-apply-1.5936961.

75 Miller, 2023 *Annual Report to Parliament on Immigration*, 30.

76 Immigration, Refugees and Citizenship Canada, "Check Processing Times," https://www.canada.ca/en/immigration-refugees-citizenship/services /application/check-processing-times.html.

77 Immigration, Refugees and Citizenship Canada, "Super Visa (for Parents and Grandparents): Who Can Apply," 5 October 2023, https://www.canada.ca/en /immigration-refugees-citizenship/services/visit-canada/parent-grandparent- super-visa/eligibility.html.

78 Wrzesnewskyj, *Family Reunification: Report*, 46, 59. Less expensive options were presented to the Standing Committee on Citizenship and Immigration.

Other Relatives

Orphaned siblings, grandchildren, nieces, and nephews can only be sponsored in limited circumstances. These include situations where they are under eighteen years of age, their parents have passed away, and they are single.[79] Other relatives can only be sponsored in exceptional circumstances. Individuals may be allowed to sponsor certain extended family if the sponsor has no immediate family members in Canada nor living abroad to sponsor.[80]

In 2023, the government launched a special program for the permanent immigration of up to 3,250 Sudanese extended family members of Canadian citizens or permanent residents. It applies to those who resided in Sudan when hostilities began in April 2023.[81] The following year, it opened a temporary resident pathway for up to 1,000 extended family members in Gaza of Canadian citizens or permanent residents.[82]

Family: A Cornerstone of Effective Integration

Critics claim that the more restrictive provisions on family sponsorship come from unsubstantiated claims concerning the net costs

---

79 Immigration, Refugees and Citizenship Canada, "Sponsor Your Relatives: Who You Can Sponsor," 4 August 2023, https://www.canada.ca/en/immigration -refugees-citizenship/services/immigrate-canada/family-sponsorship/other -relatives/who-you-can-sponsor.html.
80 Immigration, Refugees and Citizenship Canada, "Sponsor Your Relatives." The relatives must have no spouse, common-law or conjugal partner and no child, parent, or grandparent who is a Canadian citizen or permanent resident.
81 Refugees and Citizenship Canada Immigration, "Family-Based Permanent Residence Pathway for People Affected by the Conflict in Sudan," 23 February 2024, https://www.canada.ca/en/immigration-refugees-citizenship/services /sudan2023/pr-pathway.html.
82 Refugees and Citizenship Canada Immigration, "Temporary Resident Pathway Opens for Palestinian Extended Family in Gaza," News Release, 9 January 2024, https://www.canada.ca/en/immigration-refugees-citizenship/news/2024/01 /temporary-resident-pathway-opens-for-palestinian-extended-family-in-gaza. html.

of family immigration. They say that the changes fail to account for the benefits of facilitating the immigration of relatives beyond immediate family members.

More commonly, the economic gains from family class immigration are evaluated predominantly through the employment earnings of newcomers and weighed against social assistance used.[83] However, these assessments do not provide a more holistic view of how the sponsored family members affect the earning potential of the sponsors or other family members.

As noted, family income can be enhanced where parents and grandparents work, or where they take care of children, enabling other family members to work or upgrade skills. Relatives have been shown to assist in family businesses and provide emotional, educational, and housekeeping support, all of which contributes positively to the integration of the family unit.[84] These benefits can be particularly important to immigrants and refugees as they establish themselves in a new country.[85] Conversely, family separation can contribute to difficulties in adjusting.[86] And family reunification plays a pivotal role in anchoring immigrant settlement in Canada, both nationally and regionally.[87]

---

83 Citizenship and Immigration Canada, "Evaluation of the Family Reunification Program."

84 Bélanger and Candiz, "Politics of 'Waiting' for Care." Researchers also point out that women family members often take on low-paying jobs, often below their skills, in support of husbands who look for better work or training to improve their skills. Staying home to care for children, working part-time, or working in low-paying jobs can reflect unfavourably in comparison to Canadian-born women, yet this comparison does not account for the way they are contributing to the economic and social integration of the family as a whole. Mehrunnisa Ahmad Ali and Assel Baitubayeva, "Immigrant Women's Roles in Family Settlement," in *Putting Family First: Migration and Integration in Canada*, ed. Harald Bauder (Vancouver: UBC Press, 2019), 177–97.

85 Mehrunnisa Ahmad Ali, Marc Yvan Valade, and Tania Dargy, "How Families Shape Settlement Trajectories," in *Putting Family First: Migration and Integration Canada*, ed. Harald Bauder (Vancouver: UBCPress, 2019), 158–73.

86 References to literature elaborating on the importance of family to immigrant settlement can be found in Redmond and Martin, "(Definition of) Family," 770; Moreno, Feze, and Joly, "Does the End Justify the Means?" 253–4, 273.

87 Madine VanderPlaat, Yoko Yoshida, and Howard Ramos, "The Role of Spouses and Children in the Decision to Settle or Not to Settle into a Certain Community:

Studies have shown that the inability to sponsor parents and grandparents negatively affects the sense of belonging immigrants have, and their sponsors' sense of belonging and status as Canadians.[88] Moreover, critics claim that the stringent rules have had a disproportionate impact on racialized immigrant woman working in low paid jobs who would benefit significantly from the support parents, grandparents and other close relatives could provide.[89]

Some critics also suggest that by making it more difficult to sponsor parents, grandparents, and other close relatives, Canada may become less competitive in attracting the best and brightest economic immigrants. Prospective immigrants may consider the ability to be reunited with their families in their immigration decisions.[90] Further study would help reveal whether widening family eligibility would also enhance immigrant retention in Canada.

Census data seems to support some of these claims, showing that family class immigrants remain in Canada longer than immigrants admitted through the economic stream.[91] This implies that the opportunity for family reunification in Canada plays a significant role in the integration process and contributes to the intended goal of ensuring that immigrants establish permanent residence in the country.

A Focus on Cities Outside of Montréal, Toronto, and Vancouver," Research Brief, Research and Evaluation, Citizenship and Immigration Canada, 2013, https://www.canada.ca/content/dam/ircc/migration/ircc/english/resources/research/documents/pdf/r2-2012-role.pdf.

88 Employment and Social Development Canada, "Government of Canada to Cut Backlog and Wait Times for Family Reunification – Phase I of Action Plan for Faster Family Reunification," News Release, 4 November 2011, https://www.canada.ca/en/news/archive/2011/11/government-canada-cut-backlog-wait-times-family-reunification-phase-action-plan-faster-family-reunification.html.

89 Ali, Valade, and Dargy, "How Families Shape Settlement Trajectories," 15.

90 Alboim and Cohl, *Shaping the Future*, 29.

91 Abdurrahman Aydemir and Chris Robinson, *Return and Onward Migration among Working Age Men* (Ottawa: Statistics Canada, 2006), https://www150.statcan.gc.ca/n1/en/pub/11f0019m/11f0019m2006273-eng.pdf?st=XjWll5up. The 2021 census data seem to confirm that this tendency persists. While family class immigrants have remained a constant 25 per cent of all immigrants over the period 2001 to 2022, census data for 2021 show that among immigrants still in the country, those from the earlier decade are significantly more likely to have entered

Emigration rates from Canada are high. Recent reports suggests that the number of immigrants who do not remain in Canada has risen steadily since the 1980s with the rate of immigrants leaving Canada being the highest in two decades.[92] Canada allocates considerable resources to the selection, administration, and settlement services for newcomers. The corresponding benefits of their enduring presence cannot be realized if they leave.

Scholars point out that there are numerous studies across various countries that underscore the many factors – including family – that underpin positive immigration outcomes.[93] For Canada, there are various studies that underscore the importance of family relations in immigrant settlement, but these tend to focus on specific cities and immigrant groups. There are few more wide-ranging studies on the links between immigrant integration and family reunification. Moreover, the role that family plays in immigrant economic performance is largely unexplored.[94]

Economic assessments tend to focus on the individual principal applicant. That means they cannot account for the constellation of factors that contribute to those outcomes for the individuals concerned. For example, an evaluation for the years between

---

the country in the family class. See Statistics Canada, "Admission Category by Period of Immigration and Pre-Admission Experience," Table: 98-10-0318-01, accessed 30 August 2024, https://www150.statcan.gc.ca/t1/tbl1/en /tv.action?pid=9810031801.

92 Dennler, *The Leaky Bucket*; Lone "Canada's Surging Cost of Living Fuels Reverse Immigration"; Bérard-Chagnon et al., *Emigration of Immigrants*.

93 The research across various contexts points to the variety of factors that help new immigrants build skills, forge networks and improve their labour mobility. Diane Dyson, Ezekiel Roos-Walker, and Charity-Ann Hannan, "A Systems Approach to Immigrant Families and the Labour Market," in *Putting Family First: Migration and Integration in Canada*, ed. Harald Bauder (Vancouver: UBC Press, 2019), 95. In 2013, the European Union published the results of a study that examined the effects of family reunification on integration. Noting that it was difficult to isolate and measure the impact of various factors, the authors concluded that there was evidence to demonstrate the restrictions imposed across Europe did not further integration and in many cases hindered it. Tineke Strik, Betty de Hart, and Ellen Nissen, *Family Reunification: A Barrier or Facilitator of Integration? A Comparative Study* (Brussels: European Commission, 2013), 110–11, https://emnbelgium.be /sites/default/files/publications/familyreunification-web.pdf.

94 Dyson, Roos-Walker, and Hannan, "Systems Approach to Immigrant Families."

2002 and 2009 showed that sponsored spouses and partners – who accounted for most of the family sponsorships – had higher rates of employment earnings within the first five years than did the accompanying spouses of economic immigrants.[95]

The evaluation also found that among those surveyed, the economic outcomes of parents and grandparents were below the average of all immigrants. As a group they had low average earnings and increased employment insurance use. However, the evaluation also noted that most parents and grandparents contribute to the economic well-being of the family unit through direct and indirect economic contributions, including the provision of childcare.[96]

These findings highlight the need to gain a deeper understanding of how family, community, formal, and informal support systems impact individual performance.[97] More study is also required to assess how family reunification influences the economic well-being of the family unit and contributes to both immigrant recruitment and retention in Canada. Such research would help to inform future admissions policy, as well as settlement services. Researchers who have examined the efficacy of Canadian settlement services point out that while settlement workers recognize the importance of family in settlement outcomes, their funding is largely provided to work with the principal applicant.

A more holistic approach that works with the family could help ensure that secondary earners – and non-earning members of the family – are best equipped to advance the settlement of the family. For instance, this could involve offering guidance to families on accessing language training, enrolling children in schools, navigating medical services, and understanding landlord and tenant rights. Extending this approach over the longer term could

---

95 Citizenship and Immigration Canada, "Evaluation of the Family Reunification Program," 57.

96 Citizenship and Immigration Canada, "Evaluation of the Family Reunification Program," x, 66, 78.

97 Dyson, Roos-Walker, and Hannan, "Systems Approach to Immigrant Families," 103.

encompass providing advice on job prospects, professional qualification programs, and the intricacies of establishing a business.[98]

While recognizing that an expansion of settlement services would require additional investments, advocates claim that it is likely to have significant long-term benefits and should be a high priority for Canada. Such investments should be accompanied and supported by more research into the impact of settlement services on income and employment for the household or family unit.[99]

Family Redefined

A related issue is whether the current definition of family in the *Immigration and Refugee Protection Act 2001* should be broadened, taking it closer to alignment with international and other domestic legal norms. These recognize that vital family relationships extend beyond parents and their dependent biological and adopted children.

International and Regional Norms

The right to family is among the core principles of the 1948 *Universal Declaration of Human Rights*.[100] This protected right and the right to family unity is also found in other international human

---

98 Ali, Valade, and Dargy, "How Families Shape Settlement Trajectories," 173.

99 As Reitz previously noted, "An IRCC evaluation over the period 2011–2016 focused on such issues as continuing need, number of clients, and perceptions of outcomes and costs but did not analyze the impact of specific settlement programs on clients." See Reitz, "Canada: Continuity and Change in Immigration for Nation-Building," 138. Additionally, some have suggested seeking ways to ensure effective coordination between federal, provincial, and municipal services. For a review of various services available and gaps, see Shuguang Wang and Skylar Maharaj, "Community Support for Immigrants and their Families," in *Putting Family First: Migration and Integration in Canada*, ed. Harald Bauder (Vancouver: UBC Press, 2019), 67–91.

100 UN General Assembly, Resolution 217A, *Universal Declaration of Human Rights* (Dec. 10, 1948), Article 16(3), https://www.un.org/en/about-us /universal-declaration-of-human-rights.

rights conventions, and specific international conventions relating to children, refugees, and migrant workers.[101] Although there is no universal definition of family, legal scholars and United Nations bodies have stressed the importance of interpreting human rights treaties in consideration of subsequent developments in international and domestic law. Over the years, conceptions of what constitutes a family have evolved.

International human rights bodies have urged a flexible approach to determining who counts as a member of a family. The United Nations Human Rights Committee recognizes that the definition of family differs from country to country, making a universal definition impossible. However, it emphasizes that the states should apply their interpretation consistently across all aspects of their domestic law and practice.[102]

The United Nations Committee on the Rights of the Child has provided further guidance. The *Convention on the Rights of the Child*

---

101   UN General Assembly, Resolution 2200A (XXI), *International Covenant on Economic, Social and Cultural Rights* (Dec. 16, 1966), Article 10, https://www .ohchr.org/en/instruments-mechanisms/instruments/international -covenant-economic-social-and-cultural-rights; UN General Assembly, Resolution 2200A (XXI), *International Covenant on Civil and Political Rights* (Dec. 16, 1966), Article 23(1), https://www.ohchr.org/en/instruments-mechanisms /instruments/international-covenant-civil-and-political-rights; UN General Assembly, Resolution 44/25, *Convention on the Rights of the Child* (Nov. 20, 1989), preamble, https://www.ohchr.org/en/instruments-mechanisms/instruments /convention-rights-child; UN General Assembly, Resolution 45/158, *International Convention on the Protection of the Rights of All Migrant Workers and Members of Their Families* (Dec. 18, 1990), Article 44(1), https://www.ohchr.org/en /instruments-mechanisms/instruments/international-convention-protection -rights-all-migrant-workers; UN General Assembly, A/RES/61/106, *Convention on the Rights of Persons with Disabilities* (Dec. 12, 2006), preamble, https://www .ohchr.org/en/instruments-mechanisms/instruments/convention-rights -persons-disabilities.
102   UN Human Rights Committee, "CCPR General Comment No. 16: Article 17 (Right to Privacy) The Right to Respect of Privacy, Family, Home and Correspondence, and Protection of Honour and Reputation" (8 April 1988), para. 5, http://www.refworld.org/docid/453883f922.html; UN Human Rights Committee, "CCPR General Comment No. 19: Article 23 (The Family) Protection of the Family, the Right to Marriage and Equality of the Spouses" (27 July 1990), para. 2, http://www.refworld.org/docid/45139bd74.html.

obligates states parties to ensure that children are not separated from parents, except in accordance with law and where necessary in the child's best interests.[103] It also urges decision-makers to ensure that children are not separated from family and other persons with whom the child has had strong personal relationships, unless it is in the child's best interests.[104]

The 1990 *International Convention on the Protection of the Rights of All Migrant Workers and Members of Their Families* also adopts a broad view of family. It defines family as including spouses, conjugal partners, dependent children, and other dependents that are "recognized as members of the family by applicable legislation or applicable bilateral or multilateral agreements between the states concerned."[105]

Regional human rights bodies in Europe and the Americas have taken a similar approach and the rights of extended family members are recognized in regional jurisprudence. Several states also adopt a broad view of family – one that embraces biological ties – but also social customs and factors, including psychological, emotional, and economic dependency.[106] This is evident in child

---

103 UN General Assembly, *Convention on the Rights of the Child*, Article 9.

104 UN Committee on the Rights of the Child, "General Comment No. 14 (2013) on the Right of the Child to Have His or Her Best Interests Taken as a Primary Consideration (Art. 3, para. 1)" (29 May 2013), paras. 60, 65, https://www2 .ohchr.org/english/bodies/crc/docs/gc/crc_c_gc_14_eng.pdf. UN interpretative guidance has long stressed that the best interests of the child should be paramount in all judicial and administrative practices related to children. For detailed sources, see Magdalena Sepúlveda Carmona, *A Contemporary View of 'Family' in International Human Rights Law and Implications for the Sustainable Development Goals (SDGs)* (New York: UN Women, 2017), 22, https://www .unwomen.org/sites/default/files/Headquarters/Attachments/Sections /Library/Publications/2017/Discussion-paper-A-contemporary-view-of-family -in-international-human-rights-law-en.pdf.

105 UN General Assembly, *Protection of the Rights of All Migrant Workers*, Article 4.

106 For a review of the relevant European Directives, the European Court of Human Rights and the Inter-American Court of Human Rights, and national courts, see Frances Nicholson, *The Right to Family Life and Family Unity of Refugees and Others in Need of International Protection and the Family Definition Applied*, 2nd ed. (New York: UNHCR, 2018), https://www.unhcr.org/dach/wp-content /uploads/sites/27/2018/03/CH_Essential-right-to-family-unity_Frances -Nicholson_2018.pdf.

custody arrangements where custodial rights can extend beyond the biological parents whenever that is in the child's best interest.

And yet Canadian immigration law focuses on the immediate nuclear family, with a reliance on DNA testing to establish the parent-child relationship. It deprioritizes the role of parents and grandparents of the principal applicant, and largely excludes relatives regardless of the impact that family separation has on them or the applicant. In these respects, it is out of step with international principles. It is also inconsistent with domestic law.

Domestic Law

Several provinces recognize the rights of adult friends to co-parent for the benefit of children. In Ontario for example, legislation provides that in child custody matters, a court shall only consider the best interests of the child. This is determined by considering several factors, including "the nature and strength of the child's relationship with each parent, each of the child's siblings and grandparents and any other person who plays an important role in the child's life."[107]

While domestic policy has changed to recognize shifting social norms around family, Canadian immigration policy has not. Critics point to the perverse results that can arise from inconsistent approaches. This includes situations where a family relationship is recognized by provincial courts but the child's application for family reunification is denied because the relationship is not recognized under immigration law.[108] Such inconsistencies, critics point out, deny "immigrants the benefits of the very same customs and values of the society into which they are expected to integrate."[109]

The historically narrow breadth of family sponsorship reflected in current Canadian immigration law does not recognize the potential role that extended family members can play in the successful integration of the sponsor. Advocates also note that it does

---

107   *Children's Law Reform Act*, R.S.O. 1990, c. C. 12, s. 24(3)(b).
108   Feze et al., "Flying under the Radar," 255–6.
109   Moreno, Feze, and Joly, "Does the End Justify the Means?," 269.

not recognize the practice of diverse cultures represented in Canadian communities.[110]

This could be remedied by expanding the scope of eligible family members for sponsorship to encompass a broader network of biological relatives, provided they meet the stipulated security, medical, and financial prerequisites. Another approach would be to permit the sponsor to include individuals they deem integral to their family unit. This would necessitate furnishing evidence of the genuineness of the relationship, akin to the requirements imposed on spouses and partners, in addition to adhering to the established security, medical, and income criteria.

At the very least, a public and transparent discussion is needed around how to adjust the current system to foster integration and align it with domestic and international norms.

Future Priorities

Since the enactment of the *Immigration and Refugee Protection Act 2001*, the family sponsorship stream has been significantly adjusted. Canadian citizens and permanent residents can sponsor spouses, common-law partners, conjugal partners, and dependent biological children relatively easily. Efforts have been made to improve processing times for these close relatives. At the same time, some barriers continue to exist that are worthy of further review. They include the way in which the genuineness of a marriage or partnership is assessed, and the obstacles faced in various adoption situations.

Beyond the most immediate family members, the ability of Canadian citizens and permanent residents to sponsor their close relatives has been restricted. Among the most notable issues is the imposition of higher barriers to the sponsorship of parents and grandparents. The changes have been justified with reference to

---

110 This was a point raised by several witnesses before the Standing Committee on Citizenship and Immigration in 2017. Wrzesnewskyj, *Family Reunification: Report*, 19–20.

Canadian taxpayers and the burdens they face. But assumptions of the public financial impact have not been based on rigorous study or analysis. Like many aspects of Canadian immigration policy, the family class stream has been largely understudied from a longitudinal impact assessment.

Given the importance of family reunification, alongside these important policy areas which require attention, there are administrative obstacles that also need to be addressed. Immigration officer assessments of family sponsorship applications should be reviewed, with an emphasis on ensuring culturally sensitive assessments and enhancing transparency. This should include the assessment criteria employed to ascertain the authenticity of a marriage and to confirm the parent-child relationship.

Scholars and advocates contend that the fees associated with family class sponsorships disproportionately negatively impact individuals with more modest financial resources – those who might stand to benefit the most from family reunification. Critics also claim that processing times and evidentiary prerequisites seemingly exhibit a bias towards applicants from higher-income nations. They argue that individuals from middle- and low-income countries often contend with extended waiting periods and more demanding requests for supplementary corroborative documentation. We are not able to assess this claim, but if the government made more disaggregated data easily available, it would bring clarity to whether these allegations are substantiated.

In 2017, the Standing Committee noted the absence of available comprehensive and longitudinal data relevant to family reunification policies. It recommended greater study into the accessibility of family sponsorship to all permanent residents and Canadian citizens, more detailed information on the costs and benefits of family sponsorship and the adequacy of settlement support.[111]

---

111 Specifically, it called for better data to track the impact of sponsored parents and grandparents on Canada's health care and social welfare system, disaggregated by age and place of residence; the provincial retention rates of family class applicants; and the economic and other contributions to the family unit of the sponsored family members. Wrzesnewskyj, *Family Reunification: Report*, 59–60.

We support the Standing Committee's recommendation for the government to reduce its reliance on qualitative and anecdotal evidence and instead invest in collaborative data gathering and analysis of the family sponsorship program with the provinces. This effort should focus on tracking quantifiable information to provide a more solid foundation for making well-informed policy decisions.

Assessments of the economic value of the family class must review more than the employment earnings of the principal applicant. A holistic approach is needed, one which examines how family reunification contributes to the economic welfare of the family unit and its impact on immigrant retention.

Canada welcomed immigrants from its very inception, and family reunification has remained a central policy objective. It is crucial for the government to ensure a transparent, systematic review of this immigration stream given the vital role it plays in the immigrant experience, the widespread public support for it, and the challenges posed by several recent restrictions on family reunification.[112]

---

112 Between 2016 and 2020, the number of survey respondents saying family members of people already in Canada should be the top priority increased from 30 to 36 per cent. Shelby Thevenot, "Canadians See Family Reunification as Biggest Priority in 2020," *Canada Immigration News*, 1 September 2020, https://www.cicnews.com/2020/09/canadians-see-family-reunification-as-biggest-priority-in-2020-0915631.html.

Refugees: Greater Selectivity and Barriers to Asylum

Currently, over 120 million people worldwide have been forcibly displaced from their homes. Two-thirds of them are in low- and middle-income countries. Canada is geographically distant from the crises that have created this global population of forced migrants, the majority of whom fled within their own countries, becoming internally displaced. Those crossing national borders become refugees. They now number over 43 million.[1]

The history of refugee admissions in Canada is complicated. Canada maintained a selective and highly restrictive policy for most of the nation's history, including during the unprecedented displacement crisis provoked by the Second World War. In the 1960s Canada's responses to refugees took a more progressive turn, along with other immigration liberalization policies. And in 1976, fulfilling Canada's international obligations to refugees became an objective of the *Immigration Act*. It has remained so for nearly half a century.

In this chapter, we examine how Canada's approach to refugees has shifted since the implementation of the *Immigration and Refugee*

---

1 UNHCR, "Global Trends Report 2023," 2, https://www.unhcr.org/global-trends -report-2023. Host countries with the largest refugee populations are the Islamic Republic of Iran with 3.4 million, Turkey with 3.4 million, Germany with 2.5 million, Colombia with 2.5 million, and Pakistan with 2.1 million. In April 2024 these figures were updated by UNHCR and can be found on the Global Trends website at https://www.unhcr.org/global-trends.

Protection Act 2001. Over the past two decades, Canada has consistently remained a top donor to international humanitarian refugee relief efforts. In parallel, the annual number of refugees that Canada selects has increased, alongside larger annual immigration levels (see figure 3). This speaks of progressive trends. However, the country has also taken many steps to reduce the number of refugees eligible to seek asylum from within Canada or at its borders. It has also reduced appeal rights for certain refugee claimants.These measures have been put in place through legislative changes and by special agreement with the United States.

Context

The character of Canada's refugee policies over time have largely resembled its approach to other immigrant admissions. Both are canvassed in part 1 where the history of Canada's immigration policy is summarized. However, to appreciate some of the nuances in contemporary policy, it is helpful to recall several salient characteristics and developments of the past.

First, for most of its history, Canada was reluctant to accept refugees unless they met general immigration criteria. The criteria discriminated against those who were deemed unsuitable from a racial, ethnic, cultural, or political perspective.

The rigidity of Canada's approach meant that it largely closed its doors to Armenian and Jewish refugees fleeing genocide during the First World War and the Second World War, respectively. One of the reasons the country did not sign the 1951 international *Convention Relating to the Status of Refugees* (1951 Convention)[2]

---

2 UN General Assembly, *Convention Relating to the Status of Refugees*, 28 July 1951, United Nations, Treaty Series, vol. 189, p. 137; UN General Assembly, *Protocol Relating to the Status of Refugees*, 31 January 1967, United Nations, Treaty Series, vol. 606, p. 267. The 1951 Convention had temporal and geographic limitations that were lifted with the 1967 Protocol. For our purposes, reference to the 1951 Convention's definition includes the Protocol.

until 1969 was due to concerns that it would limit its ability to reject or deport refugees with communist sympathies. Cold-war politics also influenced the refugees that were admitted in special programs as illustrated in Canada's ready response to Hungarian refugees in 1956, Czech refugees in 1969, and Indo-Chinese refugees in the 1970s and 1980s.

Second, it was not until 1976 that refugee policy was formally incorporated into Canadian legislation with the *Immigration Act, 1976*. One of its objectives was to fulfil "Canada's international legal obligations over refugees and to uphold its humanitarian tradition with respect to the displaced and the persecuted." The act and regulations contained rules for admitting refugees from abroad through resettlement and for refugee claims to be determined from within Canada or at its ports of entry. For the first time, the government included refugee admissions in its detailed planning. It established dedicated overseas resettlement processes and inland refugee determination procedures. And in 1989, the government established the Immigration and Refugee Board, an independent administrative tribunal responsible for reviewing immigration decisions and determining refugee claims.

Third, over time, Canadian resettlement efforts would be broadened to reflect humanitarian needs. While geopolitical concerns would remain relevant, refugee selection would become more diverse, and came to better represent the global displacement priorities established in consultation with the United Nations and other stakeholders.[3]

The annual number of refugees who have resettled in Canada has risen and fallen in line with fluctuations in overall immigration levels. Refugee resettlement has consistently represented between 5 and 7 per cent of total annual permanent resident admissions, rising to 10 per cent in the 2021–2 period.[4] In more recent years,

---

3 Since 1995, Canada has participated in the Annual Tripartite Consultations on Resettlement (ATCR), a global policy group of the UNHCR, governments, and civil society to coordinate refugee strategies, criteria, and priorities.

4 Immigration, Refugees, and Citizenship Canada, *Annual Report to Parliament on Immigration* (Ottawa: 2020–2022). Annual Reports can be found on the Government of Canada website by year, https://www.canada.ca/en/immigration-refugees-citizenship/corporate/publications-manuals/annual-reports-parliament-immigration.html.

there has been greater reliance on private groups to assume the settlement costs and obligations associated with refugee resettlement as discussed more fully in this chapter.

Fourth, the refugee determination process has changed frequently, often in reaction to specific arrivals, growing backlogs, and in response to judicial decisions.

The adoption of the *Canadian Charter of Rights and Freedoms* (the *Charter*) in 1982 led to a transformational change in refugee determinations: from a process determined through written submissions to one requiring an oral hearing. As described earlier in part 1, however, instances of a surge in annual refugee claims, or unconventional arrivals by sea, have frequently led to a tightening of procedures and a narrowing of admissibility requirements.

Two examples were harbingers of responses in the contemporary period. In 1987, the arrival of 173 East Asian refugee claimants off the coast of Nova Scotia prompted significant legislative changes to discourage such arrivals. Admissibility criteria were tightened and border security fortified. Fines and jail terms were raised for those responsible for bringing individuals to Canada without the necessary prior authorization. These deterrents remain in place. In 1999, while a new immigration act was under discussion, the arrival of 600 Chinese migrants by sea brought additional scrutiny to the refugee determination procedure. The *Immigration and Refugee Protection Act 2001* ushered in a series of amendments to further tighten processes.

Relevant Legislative Provisions

The *Immigration and Refugee Protection Act 2001* introduced multiple objectives pertaining to refugees, replacing the single objective present in previous acts. These include upholding Canada's international legal responsibilities concerning refugees and affirming Canada's commitment to international refugee resettlement efforts.[5] The act also expanded Canada's protection obligations to include those who

---

5 *Immigration and Refugee Protection Act*, S.C. 2001, c. 27 s. 3(2).

met the 1951 Convention's definition of refugee,[6] as well to others at risk of torture or cruel and unusual treatment or punishment.[7]

Other specific refugee-related objectives in the act are to establish fair and efficient refugee determination procedures and to support the self-sufficiency and the social and economic well-being of refugees by facilitating family reunification. Significantly, the refugee-related objectives of the act also include protecting the health, safety, and security of Canadian society and denying access to persons who are security risks or serious criminals. These reflect the public safety concerns that have gained greater prominence after the 11 September 2001 terrorist attacks in the United States.

In the early 2000s, approximately 10,000 refugees were admitted annually through the overseas resettlement program.[8] In the following decade, annual resettlement numbers grew, close to doubling by 2015 and further rising to over 51,000 refugees in 2023.[9] (See figure 8.) The proportion of resettled refugees compared to the total number of permanent residents admitted annually has risen from 5 per cent in the first decade of the twenty-first century to between 7 and 10 per cent in more recent years.[10]

For refugee claims made at the border, or from within Canada, between 2001 and 2016 the country received some 26,000 refugee claims each year. Beginning in 2017, asylum claims shot up to over

---

6 A refugee is defined as a person with a well-founded fear of persecution based on race, religion, nationality, political opinion, or membership in a particular social group.

7 In line with the *Convention Against Torture and Other Cruel, Inhuman or Degrading Treatment or Punishment*, 10 December 1984, United Nations, Treaty Series, vol. 1465, p. 85.

8 Citizenship and Immigration Canada, "Canada Facts and Figures–Immigration Overview Permanent and Temporary Residents 2010," 6.

9 Immigration, Refugees, and Citizenship Canada, *Annual Report to Parliament on Immigration* (Ottawa: 2011-2023). Citizenship and Immigration Canada, *Facts and Figures 2016: Immigration Overview–Permanent Residents* (Ottawa: Citizenship and Immigration Canada, 2016), 5.

10 Immigration, Refugees, and Citizenship Canada, *Annual Report to Parliament on Immigration* (Ottawa: 2011-2023). Between 2016 and 2019 resettlement averaged around 10 per cent, falling again to 5 per cent in the following two years, but rising again in 2022.

50,000. In 2022, they continued to rise, more than doubling in 2023 to over 143,000.[11] (See figure 9.) Over the past decade, over 65 per cent of refugee determinations resulted in a positive decision (see figure 10).

Several factors have contributed to the increase in the annual number of refugee claims. Growing global levels of forced displacement is one. The lifting of COVID-19 travel restrictions also meant that those waiting to come to Canada joined other annual arrivals. Other factors include restrictive and protracted US polices that render Canada a more attractive place to make a claim, and the 2023 relaxation of visa requirements that contributed to making it easier for individuals to get to Canada in order to make a refugee claim.[12] Additionally, the country saw a surge in asylum claims by international students whose numbers have increased significantly in recent years.[13]

As noted in the discussion that follows, in some respects, Canadian refugee policy over the past two decades is consistent with the government's legislative objectives. Canada has maintained its humanitarian donations to international relief efforts. The number of refugees sponsored abroad has increased. Nevertheless, Canada's reception of refugees who seek asylum at the border, or within the country, has not consistently matched the

---

11 Immigration, Refugees and Citizenship Canada, "Asylum Claims by Year – 2023," last updated 2 July 2024, https://www.canada.ca/en/immigration-refugees-citizenship/services/refugees/asylum-claims/asylum-claims-2023.html.

12 Immigration, Refugees and Citizenship Canada, "Temporary Public Policy to Facilitate the Processing of Temporary Resident Visa Applications in Inventory," 29 June 2023, https://www.canada.ca/en/immigration-refugees-citizenship/corporate/mandate/policies-operational-instructions-agreements/public-policies/processing-trv-apps-inventory.html. Anna Mehler Paperny and Ted Hesson, "Insight: Canada Immigration: Why Asylum Seekers Are Crossing the Border," *Reuters*, 14 March 2023, https://www.reuters.com/world/americas/canada-immigration-why-record-asylum-seekers-are-crossing-us-border-2023-03-11/; Matt Lundy, "Asylum Claims Jump at Canadian Airports after Ottawa Eases Some Visitor Visa Requirements," *Globe and Mail*, 23 October 2023, https://www.theglobeandmail.com/business/article-canada-airports-asylum-claims/.

13 Marie Woolf, "Spike in International Student Asylum Claims an Abuse of Study Permits, Experts Warn," *Globe and Mail*, 22 April 2024.

act's international protection and burden sharing objectives. Priority has instead been given to other considerations, such as deterring refugee arrivals and/or rising administrative backlogs for determining applications.

Our analysis starts with Canadian overseas refugee selection since the *Immigration and Refugee Protection Act 2001*, followed by an examination of the country's inland refugee determination process.

Overseas Selection

Refugee Resettlement

Refugee resettlement applies to those who are outside their country of origin and who meet the 1951 Convention refugee definition or who are personally affected by civil war, armed conflict, or massive human rights violations.[14] Refugees who come through the resettlement program are referred to Canadian visa offices by the United Nations High Commissioner for Refugees (UNHCR), private sponsors, or other organizations with whom the government has an agreement.

Applicants are first assessed by a Canadian visa officer to confirm their refugee or protected status. Once this is established, they are screened based on medical, criminal, and security considerations. Quebec has a special agreement that enables it to undertake the selection of refugees destined for the province.[15]

---

14   This is known as the "country of asylum class." *Immigration and Refugee Protection Regulations* (S.O.R./2002-227), 147.

15   Immigration, Refugees and Citizenship Canada, "Canada–Québec Accord Relating to Immigration and Temporary Admission of Aliens," 5 February 1991, https://www.canada.ca/en/immigration-refugees-citizenship/corporate /mandate/policies-operational-instructions-agreements/agreements/federal -provincial-territorial/quebec/canada-quebec-accord-relating-immigration-tem-porary-admission-aliens.html. The aim is "to ensure the integration of immigrants in Québec in a manner that respects the distinct identity of Québec."

The ability to successfully establish in Canada has long been a criterion in selecting refugees for resettlement. In the past, failure to meet it meant the person was rejected. Then, the *Immigration and Refugee Protection Act 2001* and its regulations provided an exception for those who are vulnerable or in urgent need of protection.[16] The government background policy circular notes that "as the protection need becomes greater, lesser weight should be placed on the integration potential of the applicant."[17]

To be resettled, refugees must be sponsored. There are three sponsorship programs: government sponsorship, private sponsorship, and the blended program (joint government and private sponsorship).

Until recently, *government sponsorship* was the dominant resettlement pathway. UNHCR has traditionally been the main referral agency for government-sponsored refugees. Because the global number of resettlement places is so small compared to the overall number of refugees – less than 1 per cent – UNHCR prioritizes those who are most at risk and those who have specific vulnerabilities that place their well-being in jeopardy where they are.

This can include survivors of torture, single mothers with young children, and individuals with disabilities or medical conditions that cannot be treated in the country of residence.[18] For many years, Canada has prioritized women at risk and, in more recent times, has also prioritized LGBTQ2 refugees.[19] It has also created special programs for certain groups such as global human rights

---

16 *Immigration and Refugee Protection Act Regulations*, s. 139(2).

17 Immigration, Refugees and Citizenship Canada, "Policy Background: Ability to Establish in Canada," 26 February 2021, https://www.canada.ca/en /immigration-refugees-citizenship/corporate/publications-manuals /operational-bulletins-manuals/refugee-protection/resettlement/eligibility /ability-establish-background.html. For more on the evolution of this policy, see Shauna Labman and Adèle Garnier, "A Necessary Re-assertion of Government Resettlement," in *Canada and the Global Refugee Regime: Continuity, Change, Challenges and Critiques*, ed. Nathan Benson, James Milner, and Delphine Nakache (Montreal: McGill-Queen's University Press, forthcoming).

18 UNHCR, *UNHCR Resettlement Handbook*, accessed 16 July 2024, https://www .unhcr.org/resettlement-handbook/.

19 Lesbian, gay, bisexual, transgendered, queer, and two spirited people.

defenders, Yazidi refugees, and other survivors of the Islamic State in Iraq and Syria ("Daesh").[20]

Refugees accepted for government sponsorship are entitled to up to one year of financial support to help establish themselves in Canada. They are also supported with settlement services, including assistance in finding accommodation, guidance on financial matters, and language training.

Over the last two decades, the annual admission of refugees under government sponsorship has typically fluctuated within the range of 7,000 to 9,000 individuals. In 2016, total resettlement arrivals more than doubled, as a result of a mission called "Operation Syrian Refugees," which expedited the admission of 40,000 Syrian refugees. In that year, government-sponsored refugees surged to nearly 24,000.

Private groups have a long history of supporting refugees to resettle in Canada, dating back over 100 years.[21] This became more systematic with the *Immigration Act, 1976*, which authorized the minister to pass regulations for the private sponsorship of refugees.[22] A group of five individuals, or a community organization, can apply to sponsor a refugee, provided the person has been

---

20 The Yazidis are a Kurdish-speaking religious minority brutally targeted by the Islamic State in Iraq and Syria. For more on these special programs, see Immigration, Refugees and Citizenship Canada, "Canada Expands Efforts to Welcome More Yazidi Refugees and Other Survivors of Daesh," 30 March 2021, https://www.canada.ca/en/immigration-refugees-citizenship/news/2021/03 /canada-expands-efforts-to-welcome-more-yazidi-refugees-and-other-survivors -of-daesh.html; Immigration, Refugees and Citizenship Canada, "Resettlement: Cases for Priority or Special Processing (REF-OVS-13)," 5 October 2020, https://www.canada.ca/en/immigration-refugees-citizenship/corporate /publications-manuals/operational-bulletins-manuals/refugee-protection /resettlement/priority-special.html.

21 Kelley and Trebilcock, *Making of the Mosaic*. Refugee groups who arrived in the late nineteenth and early twentieth centuries were often assisted by members of their own ethnic, national, or confessional communities in Canada. During the interwar period in the early twentieth century, private groups petitioned the government to permit refugees to enter Canada with promises of support.

22 *Immigration Act, 1976*, SC 25-26 Elizabeth II, c. 52, ss. 115(1)(d) and (k.1). Private sponsorship gained momentum during the Indo-Chinese boat people crisis. Kelley and Trebilcock, *Making of the Mosaic*, 398.

recognized as a refugee by UNHCR or a foreign state.[23] As well, groups that have an agreement with the immigration department can sponsor persons who have not yet been formally recognized.[24]

While government-sponsored refugees are selected based on vulnerability, privately sponsored refugees are often those who have links to Canadian citizens or to permanent residents such as family and friends. Private sponsors of refugees include a settlement plan in their applications and undertake to provide financial assistance and help with settlement for up to one year. They must demonstrate the financial means to do so.

Private sponsorship has grown substantially over the past two decades. From 2007 to 2014, approximately 4,700 refugees were privately sponsored annually. This figure nearly doubled in 2015, surging to over 18,000 in the subsequent year.[25] (See figure 8.) Between 2017 and 2021, the number of privately sponsored refugees surpassed the number of refugees resettled by the government, and for several of those years by more than 50 per cent. Within that period, some 69,200 refugees were admitted under private sponsorship compared to 41,300 under government sponsorship. In 2023, the total number of refugees resettled rose to over 51,000 persons, with private and government totals comprising 46 and 54 per cent, respectively.[26]

The *blended visa office referral program* began in 2013. It is a small program. It matches refugees referred to the government by UNHCR or other approved organizations with private sponsors. The financial costs are shared between the government and the private group. The private sponsors provide settlement support.

---

23 *Immigration and Refugee Protection Act Regulations*, s. 153(1)(b).
24 Sponsoring groups can be a group of five individuals, an organization, or a sponsorship agreement holder. The first two must demonstrate they have the human resources and financial capacity to be sponsored. The third group is an incorporated organization that has an agreement with the Minister of Immigration, Refugees and Citizenship.
25 Citizenship and Immigration Canada, "Canada Facts and Figures," 8.
26 Immigration, Refugees and Citizenship Canada, *Annual Report to Parliament on Immigration* (Ottawa: 2018–2023).

The number of refugees resettled to Canada in this manner has tended to range from less than 100 annually to just over 1,000 annually between 2014 and 2023.[27] The one exception was in 2016 during Operation Syrian Refugees, when over 4,000 refugees were sponsored through the blended program (see figure 8).

Government vs. Private Sponsorship

The private sponsorship model's considerable growth has followed enthusiastic promotion from the government and the organizations involved. They were behind a major initiative, introduced in 2016, to encourage private sponsorship in other countries. Launched by Canada, UNHCR, and the Open Society Foundation, the Global Refugee Sponsorship Initiative and its advocates claim that the private sponsorship model is a means to improve refugee integration outcomes, broaden awareness of the refugee experience, and create more welcoming communities.[28]

A government-commissioned study, published in 2020, examined the economic performance of privately sponsored refugees between twenty and fifty-four years of age compared with those sponsored by the government between 1980 and 2009. It took varying levels of education and skills into account and found that privately sponsored refugees initially had higher employment rates and earnings than government-sponsored refugees. But these differences diminished over time.[29]

Advocates of maintaining a robust government refugee sponsorship program point to the different communities it serves. Selection

27 Immigration, Refugees and Citizenship Canada, *Annual Report to Parliament on Immigration* (Ottawa: 2011–2023).

28 Global Refugee Sponsorship Initiative, "About the Global Refugee Sponsorship Initiative," accessed 16 July 2024, https://refugeesponsorship.org/about -the-global-refugee-sponsorship-initiative/.

29 Lisa Kaida, Max Stick, and Feng Hou, *The Long-Term Economic Outcomes of Refugee Private Sponsorship* (Ottawa: Statistics Canada, 2020), https://www150.statcan. gc.ca/n1/pub/11f0019m/11f0019m2019021-eng.htm. These authors also provide a review of other relevant literature.

for government sponsorship is primarily based on vulnerability and urgent need. Refugees selected through private sponsorship are often identified based on links to Canadians or permanent residents and may not be among those most in need of resettlement. In this important respect, private sponsorship cannot be easily compared to government sponsorship, or used to replace it.

A study examining Syrian refugees who resettled in Canada between 2016 and 2017 has highlighted the differences between government and private sponsorship. It noted that most privately sponsored refugees had family members in Canada. Two-thirds were Christians who were mostly sponsored by faith-based groups. In contrast, government-sponsored refugees were primarily Muslim, and did not have pre-existing family or social connections in Canada. And they had been displaced for twice as long, "suggesting longer exposure to the psychological and physical hardships of asylum."[30]

Persons covered by the government scheme were chosen based on their vulnerability, with priority given to single mothers with small children or refugees with severe medical conditions or disabilities. These differences are significant enough to make the outcomes of government-sponsored, and privately sponsored refugees problematic for direct comparison.[31]

A study published in 2024 examined the short-term economic outcomes of refugees resettled through the blended visa officer program compared to those sponsored exclusively by the government or by private sponsors. It examined the extent to which socio-economic factors could make a difference.

The study revealed that those sponsored through the blended program initially had less employment earnings than privately sponsored refugees, although after five years their employment

---

30 Michaela Hynie et al., "What Role Does Type of Sponsorship Play in Early Integration Outcomes? Syrian Refugees Resettled in Six Canadian Cities," *Refuge: Canada's Journal on Refugees* 35, no. 2 (2019): 47, https://refuge.journals.yorku.ca /index.php/refuge/article/view/40600.
31 See Labman and Garnier, "A Necessary Re-assertion."

earnings were similar. And while sharing the same human capital characteristics as government-sponsored refugees, they initially faired comparatively better in terms of employment earnings, which could be attributed to the support received from the private groups that partnered in their resettlement. The study also found that, over time, government-sponsored refugees and those who came through the blended program, experienced more growth in earnings than privately sponsored refugees.[32]

Refugee resettlement is a small but significant solution to forced displacement. UNHCR has for years tried to encourage states to select refugees based on their acute needs. In the 1990s, Canada adopted a needs-based selection system for government-sponsored refugees, who constituted the majority of those being resettled until 2016.[33] Since then, private sponsorship has generally accounted for most refugees resettled in Canada. This raises questions about whether the prioritization of cases based on severe vulnerability may be in jeopardy.

The question for the future is whether Canada will ensure that the number of refugees the government sponsors each year rises in proportion to increasing annual immigration targets, and/or whether increased commitments to refugee resettlement will continue to depend mostly on the private sector. The government's specific ambitions for 2023 to 2025 provide some indication.

By the end of the period, it planned a significant increase in annual permanent residents, to half a million a year. It set annual targets for resettled refugees at between 10 and 11 per cent of total permanent resident arrivals to Canada, an increase over previous years.[34] However, the proportion of government-sponsored refugees is planned to fall to 35 per cent, the lowest in recent decades.

---

32 Yasmine Gure and Feng Hue, *The Short-Term Labour Market Outcomes of Blended Visa Office-Referred Refugees* (Ottawa: Statistics Canada, 2024), https://www150.statcan.gc.ca/n1/pub/36-28-0001/2024001/article/00003-eng.htm.

33 Labman and Garnier "A Necessary Re-assertion."

34 The government planned for 53,000 refugees to be resettled in 2023, and for 49,000 and 43,000 for 2024 and 2025. Immigration, Refugees and Citizenship Canada, "Notice – Supplementary Information for the 2023-2025 Immigration Levels Plan," 1 November 2022, https://www.canada.ca/en/immigration-refugees-citizenship

It is also not clear whether the increase in resettlement numbers can be achieved. Experience with the Afghan program casts doubt on the government's willingness and capacity to manage increased caseloads of refugees sponsored by either the government or private groups. In the months leading up to the fall of Kabul to the Taliban in August 2021, Canada announced a unique immigration program for local embassy staff or other Afghan nationals employed by the Government of Canada during the Canadian Armed Forces mission between 2001 and 2014. The details were unclear, although it eventually emerged that Canada had imposed an initial cap of 2,500, which it raised to 18,000 in the following year.[35]

The movement was slow to get off the ground. The government was criticized in Parliament and the press for not doing more. Eventually, two additional avenues were added for the immigration of 40,000 Afghan refugees and vulnerable Afghans by the end of 2023: a special residence pathway for extended family members of former interpreters residing in Canada and a humanitarian resettlement program through government and private sponsorship. Eighteen months after the initial announcement, some 26,000 Afghans had arrived in Canada, just over half the overall commitment. These numbers picked up in 2023, with the government reporting it had met its target.[36]

Meanwhile, over 100,000 Ukrainians affected by the Russian invasion of Ukraine arrived in Canada within ten months in 2022, under temporary permits. By October 2023, close to 923,000 applications

---

/news/notices/supplementary-immigration-levels-2023-2025.html. These levels might increase slightly as a result of the unanimous resolution by Parliament to resettle over 10,000 Uighurs over two years, on top of existing levels. Parliament of Canada, "M-62 Uyghurs and Other Turkic Muslims," 44th Parliament, 1st Session –House of Commons of Canada, 1 February 2023, https://www.ourcommons.ca /members/en/54157/motions/11892002.

35 Marsha MacLeod, "Ottawa Capped Immigration Program for Afghans Who Worked with Canada since Its Launch," *Globe and Mail*, 14 December 2022, https:// www.theglobeandmail.com/politics/article-canada-afghan-resettlement/.

36 Immigration, Refugees and Citizenship Canada, "#WelcomeAfghans: Key Figures," last updated 3 July 2024, https://www.canada.ca/en/immigration -refugees-citizenship/services/refugees/afghanistan/key-figures.html.

were approved and over 198,000 Ukrainians arrived.[37] The relatively quick processing followed the elimination of regular visa requirements and the relaxation of other immigration screening requirements. Ukrainians are authorized to remain in Canada for up to three years. There are no caps on the numbers that can come.[38]

Advocates applaud the program for Ukraine, but also point to the contrast between the swift government action to set it up and the slow response to the urgent needs of Afghans. The government claims that the programs are not comparable: the Ukrainian movement is temporary, and many Afghans are trapped within Afghanistan where the government has no consular services.[39] Yet, even for those outside Afghanistan, the wait is long due the government's protracted processes, and they are only relaxed in relatively limited circumstances.[40]

---

37 Government of Canada, "Canada-Ukraine Authorization for Emergency Travel: Key Figures," 14 October 2023, https://www.canada.ca/en/immigration-refugees -citizenship/services/immigrate-canada/ukraine-measures/key-figures.html.

38 Immigration, Refugees and Citizenship Canada, "Canada to Welcome Those Fleeing the War in Ukraine," 3 March 2022, https://www.canada.ca/en /immigration-refugees-citizenship/news/2022/03/canada-to-welcome-those- fleeing-the-war-in-ukraine.html; Immigration, Refugees and Citizenship Canada, "Canada-Ukraine Authorization for Emergency Travel," 17 March 2022, https://www.canada.ca/en/immigration-refugees-citizenship/news/2022/03 /canada-ukraine-authorization-for-emergency-travel.html. On 22 March 2022, the deadline to apply for the special visa was extended to July 2023. Immigration, Refugees and Citizenship Canada, "Canada Extends Support for Those Fleeing Russia's Illegal and Unjustifiable Invasion of Ukraine," 22 March 2023, https://www.canada.ca/en/immigration-refugees-citizenship/news/2023/03 /canada-extends-support-for-those-fleeing-russias-illegal-and-unjustifiable -invasion-of-ukraine.html.

39 CBC Radio, "Immigration Minister Responds to Criticism over Afghan Resettlement Numbers," *As It Happens*, 16 August 2022, https://www.cbc.ca/radio /asithappens/as-it-happens-monday-edition-1.6551438/immigration-minister -responds-to-criticism-over-afghan-resettlement-numbers-1.6552003.

40 The one exception was its waiving the requirement that refugees sponsored by groups of five individuals and community organizations had to first have recognized refugee status. This, however, was short lived and lifted once the government received 3,000 applications under the waiver. For an example of the hardships see Janice Dickson, "Stranded in Pakistani Hotels for Months, Afghan Refugees Struggle with Hopelessness While Awaiting Word from Canada," *Globe and Mail*, 14 December 2022, https://www.theglobeandmail.com/politics /article-afghan-refugees-waiting-canada-pakistan/.

There are other precedents for doing more, including waiving regular requirements for Syrian refugees in 2016 and permitting group resettlement of certain refugees based on their prima facie refugee status, rather than on individual determinations.[41]

A 2023 Auditor General's report also highlighted inefficiencies in the system that had contributed to refugee resettlement applicants waiting three years on average for a decision. At the end of 2022, there were 99,000 refugee applications still waiting to be processed. The Auditor General acknowledged that the department's ability to reduce the backlog was constrained by the annual number of resettlement places. However, she also found that there was considerable room to improve processing, noting that some offices with large caseloads were chronically understaffed compared with other offices with a lower volume of cases.[42]

If government refugee targets are to be met in the coming years, processes must be streamlined. Official commitment to the critical role that government sponsorship plays should be renewed considering the objectives in the *Immigration and Refugee Protection Act 2001*: to save lives, offer protection, and honour Canada's commitment to assistance for those in need of resettlement.[43] The government-sponsorship program helps ensure that among the many millions of refugees who could benefit from resettlement, Canada prioritizes those most in need. For this to continue, government resettlement efforts should not be diminished, especially in a period of unprecedented immigration.

In 2022, the US government launched a new multilateral initiative, the Refugee Diplomacy Network. Its stated aim is "to drive high-level strategic and diplomatic engagement aimed at strengthening and expanding global resettlement and other pathways to

---

41 These include Sudanese and Somali refugees in Kenya (2004–5); Bhutanese refugees in Nepal and various other countries (2006–15); and Burmese refugees in Thailand (2006). References to these movements and other sources on them can be found in Labman and Garnier, "A Necessary Re-assertion."

42 Auditor General of Canada, "Report 9."

43 *Immigration and Refugee Protection Act*, S.C. 2001, ss. 3(2) (a) and (b).

protection." Canada is among the participants.[44] Chaired by the US, it held its first Ministerial Meeting in September 2023.[45] It remains unclear how this new network will operate, and whether it will seek to pursue state-led resettlement priorities driven by geopolitical concerns over the vulnerability-based priorities long advocated by the United Nations.

Complementary Pathways

In theory, refugees should also be able to access other non-refugee specific immigration pathways, including the economic stream. But they face significant barriers. These include a lack of awareness of the often-complicated visa processes, an absence of required documentation and/or evidence demonstrating that the person will not become dependent on public funds, as well as insufficient funds to pay processing fees.

In recent years, states have formally recognized the value of making other immigration streams – known as "complementary pathways" – accessible to refugees, in addition to UNHCR-referred resettlement programs and state asylum programs. They include family reunification, work, education, and humanitarian and private sponsorship programs.[46]

In 2016, United Nations General Assembly members committed to a range of measures to improve protection and solutions for refugees and migrants, including expanding complementary pathways. This was later carried forward in two multilateral compacts: the 2018 Global Compact on Refugees, and the Global Compact for

---

44 Others include Australia, Italy, New Zealand, Spain, the United Kingdom, and the European Commission.

45 United States Department of State , "Resettlement Diplomacy Network Senior Officials Meeting," 22 June 2023, https://www.state.gov /resettlement-diplomacy-network-senior-officials-meeting/.

46 United Nations High Commissioner for Refugees, "Complementary Pathways for Admission to Third Countries," accessed 16 July 2024, https://www.unhcr .org/complementary-pathways.html.

Safe, Orderly, and Regular Migration (GCM).[47] But progress has been slow.[48]

Canada, however, has taken steps to advance its commitment. The expansion of private sponsorships is an example, although whether this is an added benefit depends on a similarly robust government sponsorship regime remaining. It has also taken initial steps to facilitate refugee immigration through employment streams.

For example, in 2018, the government launched the Economic Mobility Pathways Pilot, which identified ten to fifteen people in the Middle East and East Africa who qualified for economic immigration programs.[49] The first stage of the pilot identified obstacles that needed to be overcome for the project to be scaled up. These included criteria and expenses that refugees could not meet, cumbersome processes, lack of awareness of the program, and problems connecting with prospective employers.[50] The second phase introduced adjustments and increased the admission target to 500 refugees and their families.[51]

47 New York Declaration for Refugees and Migrants, UN Doc. A/RES/71/1 (Sept. 19, 2016); Global Compact on Refugees, UN Doc. A/73/12 (2018); Global Compact for Safe, Orderly and Regular Migration, UN Doc. A/RES/73/195 (Dec. 19, 2018), UNGA Res. 73/195; Global Compact for Safe, Orderly and Regular Migration (19 December 2018), UN Doc A/RES/73/195, Objective 5.

48 Kelley, *People Forced to Flee*.

49 Immigration, Refugees and Citizenship Canada, "The Economic Mobility Pathways Pilot: Exploring Labour Mobility as a Complementary Pathway for Refugees," 14 October 2020, https://www.canada.ca/en/immigration-refugees -citizenship/corporate/publications-manuals/economic-mobility-pathways -project-labour-mobility.html.

50 Brittany Trafford, "Update on the Economic Mobility Program for Refugees (Phase 2): The Economic Mobility Pathways Project ('EMPP)," in *Beyond the Border: Immigration Update July 2022* (Halifax: Stewart McKelvey, 2022), 12–13, https://www.stewartmckelvey.com/thought-leadership/update-on-the-eco- nomic-mobility-program-for-refugees-phase-2-the-economic-mobility-pathways -project-empp/.

51 These include permitting applicants to apply for a loan through the Immigrant Loan Program to help meet financial requirements; exempting them from certain documentation requirements in lieu of alternative forms of proof; and extending the period of relevant work experience. Trafford, "Update on the Economic Mobility Program."

At the end of its first year, the federal government announced $6.2 million in new funding for the Economic Mobility Pathways Project. The aim was to bring 2,000 skilled refugees to Canada over several years to serve in high-demand sectors, such as healthcare, skilled trades, and information technology.[52] By mid-2024, just 257 forcibly displaced persons and their dependents had been admitted under the program.[53]

While still a small program, the government has indicated the potential for further scaling up, while supporting a global effort to make opportunities more widely available. In 2022, Canada was one of the founding members and the first chair of the Global Task Force on Refugee Labour Mobility.[54] The Task Force has aimed to expand the availability of labour market complementary pathways globally by engaging with relevant stakeholders, undertaking relevant research, and providing technical advice and support.[55]

There are other areas where Canada could act. It could make it easier for refugees to bring family members into Canada through the family sponsorship program. This would require broadening eligibility criteria beyond immediate family members, waiving processing

---

52 Javier Ortega-Araiza, "Canada Invests $6.2M to Help Skilled Refugees Find Jobs," *New Canadian Media*, 22 December 2022, https://newcanadianmedia.ca/canada-invests-6-2m-to-help-skilled-refugees-find-jobs/.

53 Marie Woolf, "Federal Program Matching Refugees with Jobs set to be Made Permanent," *Globe and Mail*, 7 May 2024. More than half that total were admitted between then and the end of 2022 when the government reported that 116 people (forty-three principal applicants and seventy-three dependents) were admitted under the program. Immigration, Refugees and Citizenship Canada, *2023 Annual Report to Parliament on Immigration* (Ottawa: 2023), 27.

54 Other founding members were the UNHCR, Australia, the International Chamber of Commerce, the International Organization for Migration, and the NGOs Frangomen, RefugeePoint, and Talent Beyond Borders. Immigration, Refugees and Citizenship Canada, "The Global Task Force on Refugee Labour Mobility," 6 April 2022, https://www.canada.ca/en/immigration-refugees-citizenship/corporate/mandate/corporate-initiatives/global-task-force-refugee-labour-mobility.html.

55 The Task Force has emphasized that the pathways must be additional to government resettlement commitments, provide an avenue to permanent protection and settlement of refugees and their families, and meet labour market needs to increase their scalability and longevity.

fees and easing some financial requirements that resident family members must demonstrate to show they can support applicants.

Widening access to education pathways is another option. Currently Canada has one long-standing program coordinated by the World University Services of Canada. Within this program, some 150 refugees gain admission yearly and receive support from participating colleges, universities, and students to complete their studies and remain in Canada. Over 2,200 refugees have been admitted to Canada in this program since its inception in 1978.[56] Given Canada's need for more skilled workers – and its immigration targets for the coming years – there would seem to be ample justification for supporting this complementary pathway and scaling it up.

Inland Refugee Determination

The *Immigration and Refugee Protection Act 2001* made significant changes to Canada's refugee determination process. As noted, it extended protection – taking it beyond those who met the 1951 Convention refugee definition – to those who would be at risk of torture, death, or cruel and unusual treatment if returned to their country of nationality.[57]

In a legislative first, it also provided for the right to appeal a refugee decision to an independent specialized Refugee Appeal Division of the Immigration and Refugee Board. However, it was not until 2012 that the Appeal Division was established and whose members would be appointed by the federal Cabinet.

Expanding who qualified for Canadian protection and establishing a specialized Refugee Appeal Division were progressive changes introduced in the act. However, over the years, the act has been amended in a manner that has narrowed access to Canada's

---

56 World University Services of Canada, "Student Refugee Program–Finding Hope in Higher Education," accessed 16 July 2024, https://srp.wusc.ca/.

57 *Immigration and Refugee Protection Act*, S.C. 2001, s. 97. This extended definition was intended to give effect to Canada's obligations under the 1984 *Convention Against Torture and Other Cruel, Inhuman or Degrading Treatment or Punishment*.

refugee determination system, broadened powers to detain certain refugee claimants, and restricted rights to appeal. Many of the restrictive changes were introduced between 2009 and 2010 following the arrival of over 550 Tamil refugee claimants from Sri Lanka in two boats off the West Coast. As noted, boat arrivals have a long history of causing alarm in Canada and leading to legislative changes. The Tamil episode was no different.

The Tamil refugees arrived at the conclusion of the twenty-six-year armed conflict in their homeland and during a period of a sustained offensive of the Sri Lankan army against Tamil insurgents. Over a quarter of a million people were forcibly displaced. Human rights organizations decried grave abuses perpetrated by both sides of the conflict.[58]

Tamil arrivals received largely negative coverage in the press. They were characterized by Immigration Minister Jason Kenny as queue jumpers and possible terrorists.[59] He promised to introduce more restrictive measures to limit access to Canada's refugee determination system. His spokesperson said at the time: "We won't allow Canada to become a place of refuge for terrorists, thugs, snakeheads and other violent foreign criminals."[60] What followed was a raft of measures to deter refugee arrivals.

Among these measures, the government introduced two pieces of legislation expanding ministerial discretion and limiting refugee procedural protections. The bills were highly controversial, with many critics claiming they were overly broad and based on

---

58 Human Rights Watch, "Sri Lanka: Events of 2009," in *World Report 2010*, https://www.hrw.org/world-report/2010/country-chapters/sri-lanka.

59 For a review of the coverage, see Ashley Bradimore and Harald Bauder, "Mystery Ships and Risky Boat People: Tamil Refugee Migration in the Newsprint Media," *Canadian Journal of Communication* 36, no. 4 (2012): 637–61, https://doi.org/10.22230/cjc.2011v36n4a2466; Canadian Council for Refugees, "Sun Sea: Five Years Later," August 2015, https://www.ccrweb.ca/en/sun-sea-five-years-later; Stelian Medianu, Alina Sutter, and Victoria Esses, "The Portrayal of Refugees in Canadian Newspapers: The Impact of the Arrival of Tamil Refugees by Sea in 2010," *Idées d'Amériques*, no. 6 (2015), https://doi.org/10.4000/ideas.1199.

60 Stewart Bell, "Passenger Wanted in Sri Lanka," *National Post*, 22 October 2009, https://immigrationwatchcanada.org/2009/10/22/passenger-wanted-in-sri-lanka/.

unfounded claims that the refugee system was overrun with abuse and gamed by "bogus" refugees.[61] One of the bills was enacted but not implemented, and the other was not enacted before Parliament adjourned in 2010.[62]

However, in 2012, new legislation was passed that brought forward many of the previously proposed changes. The *Protecting Canada's Immigration System Act* introduced various amendments to the *Immigration and Refugee Protection Act 2001* as well as related legislation.[63] The changes expanded the grounds on which a person could be found ineligible to make a refugee claim, broadened the basis for detaining refugee claimants, and imposed additional limits on rights of review. These shifts are discussed below.

Process

Eligibility

A person who seeks refugee status in Canada must first be determined as eligible to make a claim. The Canadian Border Services Agency determines eligibility at ports of entry. Within Canada, this is determined by officers of either the Canadian Border Services Agency or Immigration, Refugees and Citizenship Canada.

Referral to the Refugee Protection Division

If found to be eligible, the person's refugee claim is referred to the Refugee Protection Division of the Immigration and Refugee

---

61 Ontario Public Service Employees Union, "Legal Community Decries Proposed Refugee Reform Bill," 12 March 2014, https://opseu.org/information/general/legal-community-decries-proposed-refugee-reform-bill/9761/.

62 The *Balanced Refugee Reform Act* was passed in 2010 but not implemented. Its companion legislation, the *Preventing Human Smugglers from Abusing Canada's Immigration System Act*, was not enacted before Parliament was prorogued in 2010.

63 The legislation protected Canada's *Immigration System Act*, S.C. 2012, c. 17. It amended the *Balanced Refugee Reform Act*, the *Marine Transportation Security Act*, and the *Department of Citizenship and Immigration Act*, in addition to the *Immigration and Refugee Protection Act 2001*.

Board for a hearing. If found ineligible to make a claim, the person can be refused entry or ordered to be removed from Canada.

Refugee claims continue to be determined in a quasi-judicial hearing. The *Immigration and Refugee Protection Act 2001* requires only one decision-maker to hear a refugee claim in place of the previous two.[64] In 2012, the membership of the Refugee Protection Division was changed from Cabinet appointees to public servants.

Acceptance rates since 2013 have averaged around 67 per cent per year.[65] (See figure 10.)

Appeal and Judicial Review

Decisions of the Refugee Protection Division can be appealed to the Immigration Appeal Division, subject to various exceptions. Among those denied this opportunity are persons whose refugee claim is determined to be "manifestly unfounded" (clearly fraudulent) or having no "credible basis" (a lack of trustworthy evidence to support the claim).[66]

The Refugee Appeal Division has broad powers of review. The Appeal Division can uphold the Refugee Protection Division's decision, reverse it, or make its own decision.[67] If a hearing is required, the Appeal Division can conduct a hearing in exceptional cases

---

64 Under the previous legislation, however, a claimant could consent to a hearing by one decision-maker.

65 Immigration and Refugee Board of Canada, "Refugee Protection Claims (New System) Statistics," last updated 1 December 2021, https://irb.gc.ca:443/en/statistics/protection/Pages/RPDStat.aspx.

66 *Immigration and Refugee Protection Act*, S.C. 2001, ss. 107.1 and 107.2. Limited rights of review for claims with no credible basis has existed since 1989. The extension to manifestly unfounded claims came in 2002.

67 Initially the Refugee Appeal Division would only interfere with a decision of the Refugee Protection Division if it found the decision to be unreasonable. This was overturned by the Federal Court on the grounds that the act gave the Appeal Division full authority to reverse decisions of the Refugee Protection Division whenever it disagreed with its decisions. *Huruglica v. Canada (Citizenship and Immigration)*, 2016 FCA 93.

or send the case back for a new determination.[68] Introducing new evidence during an appeal is allowed only in specific situations.[69]

Further review by the Federal Court of Canada requires leave of the court. This is not automatic and depends on the applicant establishing that there is clear error, or the case raises a significant legal issue warranting further consideration.

The *Immigration and Refugee Protection Act 2001* provides two additional mechanisms to apply to remain in Canada for persons ordered removed: the Pre-Removal Risk Assessment and an application based on humanitarian and compassionate grounds.

Pre-Removal Risk Assessment

A refugee claimant who has been ordered removed from Canada can make a written submission for a Pre-Removal Risk Assessment, except those for whom the Safe Third Country agreement applies. A removal order is stayed pending a decision. In making the assessment, Immigration Refugees and Citizenship Canada looks at factors such as risks to life, risks of torture, persecution, or cruel and unusual treatment or punishment. A hearing is only permitted in limited circumstances.[70]

---

68 An independent review of the Immigration and Refugee Board recommended that the act be amended so that cases were not returned to the Refugee Protection Division noting that oral hearings before the Immigration Appeal Board took less time than paper reviews and sending cases back to the Division could be cumbersome. Neil Yeates, "Report of the Independent Review of the Immigration and Refugee Board," 10 April 2018, https://www.canada.ca/en/immigration-refugees-citizenship/corporate/publications-manuals/report-independent-review-immigration-and-refugee-board.html#foreword.

69 *Immigration and Refugee Protection Act*, S.C. 2001, s. 110(4). Refugee claimants could present evidence that only arose after the Refugee Protection Division rejected their claim or that was not reasonably available, or evidence that they could not reasonably have been expected to have been presented in the circumstances, at the time of the rejection.

70 *Immigration and Refugee Protection Act Regulations*, s. 167. Specifically in situations where there exists pivotal evidence concerning the credibility of the applicant, crucial to determining their eligibility for protection, and that could substantiate the grounds for approving the protection.

For failed refugee claimants, a Pre-Removal Risk Assessment can only take place after twelve months from the date the refugee claim was rejected. Acceptance rates vary. It is rarely exercised in favour of those who have had a hearing on their claim and an opportunity to appeal a negative decision. For those who have been found ineligible to make a claim, approval rates are higher – close to 30 per cent.[71]

Humanitarian and Compassionate Application

Another mechanism to apply to remain in Canada is through an online application for permanent residence status, based on humanitarian and compassionate grounds.[72] The applicant must set out all the reasons why they would face disproportionate hardship if removed. Unless the person falls within limited exceptions, a failed refugee claimant can only make the application one year after their claim has been rejected by the Refugee Protection Division or the Refugee Appeal Board.[73] Unlike the Pre-Removal Risk Assessment, a removal order is not stayed pending the decision.

Relevant considerations include how well the person has become established in Canada, the impact of removal on the remaining family members, the effect on the applicant's health, the best interests of dependent children, and conditions in the country of origin unrelated to risk of persecution. The decision is made by an immigration officer.

---

71 Evaluation Division of Immigration, Refugees and Citizenship Canada, "Evaluation of the Pre-Removal Risk Assessment Program," 2 August 2016, https://www.canada.ca/en/immigration-refugees-citizenship/corporate /reports-statistics/evaluations/removal-risk-assessment-program/prra.html; Jean-Nicolas Beuze, "UNHCR's Statement to the Committee on Citizenship and Immigration," 7 May 2019, https://www.unhcr.ca/news/unhcrs-statement-to -the-committee-on-citizenship-and-immigration-7-may-2019/.

72 *Immigration and Refugee Protection Act*, S.C. 2001, s. 25.

73 Exceptions to the twelve-month waiting period are for those whose lives would be at risk if removed because of inadequate health medical care in the destination country or where their removal would not be in best interests of an affected child. *Immigration and Refugee Protection Act*, S.C. 2001, ss. 25(1.21).

Information is not readily available on the percentage of failed refugee claimants that apply and receive a favourable humanitarian and compassionate decision.

Ineligibility Grounds

There are various reasons why a person may not be eligible to have their claim determined by the Refugee Protection Division.

Previous Claims

A person who has made a previous refugee claim that they abandoned or withdrew is not eligible. So too are those whose claims were previously rejected, as well as those whose protected status was removed.[74] They are ineligible even if the situation in the country where they feared persecution has changed substantially, or if new evidence has come to light that would make their fears well-founded. Additionally, individuals who have received protection in another country are ineligible.

In 2019, the Liberal government added another ineligibility provision. It applies to refugee claimants who, before making their claim in Canada, made a refugee claim in a country with which Canada has an information-sharing agreement.[75] Currently, those countries are Australia, New Zealand, the United Kingdom, and the United States. Together with Canada, they are known as the "Five Eyes" countries.

Inadmissibility Grounds

As explained in the introduction to part 2, foreign nationals and permanent residents can be denied entry and removed from Canada if they are found to be inadmissible. If a refugee claimant is found to be inadmissible for reasons of serious criminality,

---

74 *Immigration and Refugee Protection Act*, S.C. 2001, ss. 101(1)(b) and (c).

75 *Immigration and Refugee Protection Act*, S.C. 2001, s. 101(1)(c.1).

security risks or human or international rights violations, their claim will not be referred to the Refugee Protection Division. If these grounds of inadmissibility subsequently come to light following a referral, they can be used to exclude the refugee from international protection.

International law recognizes that certain offences are so severe that they become grounds for exclusion from international refugee protection. People reasonably suspected of committing grave international and serious non-political crimes are excluded from international protection under Article 1F of the 1951 Convention.[76] This ensures that those guilty of "heinous acts, and serious common crimes" do not abuse the institution of refuge to avoid being held accountable for their acts.[77]

Because the consequence of exclusion is so severe, the United Nations High Commissioner for Refugees (UNHCR) has consistently advocated that it should not bar an individual from having their refugee claim determined. Rather, the issue of exclusion should be considered in the refugee determination hearing. Exclusion should only be applied with great caution, in a restricted manner, and following a full assessment of the individual case. Specifically, UNHCR urges that the refugee determination hearing first consider the basis for the refugee claim before deciding whether the person should be excluded from international protection.

Canada has not followed this guidance. Individuals have been found ineligible to make a refugee claim and/or excluded from international protection for reasons far less serious than envisioned under Article 1F. For example, a person can be found inadmissible on grounds of serious criminality for having been convicted of a crime with a possible sentence of ten years or more, or one where

---

76 UN General Assembly, *Convention Relating to the Status of Refugees*. This includes a crime against peace, a war crime, or a crime against humanity; a serious non-political crime outside the country of refuge; or is guilty of acts contrary to the purposes and principles of the United Nations.

77 UNHCR, "Guidelines on International Protection No. 5: Application of the Exclusion Clauses: Article 1F of the 1951 Convention Relating to the Status of Refugees," https://www.refworld.org/docid/3f5857684.html.

the person was sentenced to more than six months in prison.[78] The provision includes a vast array of crimes within the definition, including relatively minor offences, alongside some egregious ones.[79]

Serious criminality extends to criminal activity outside Canada. It covers people convicted of crimes that would carry a sentence of ten years or more in Canada and those believed to have done so. An actual conviction is not necessary; it merely has to be a reasonable belief that the person has committed a serious crime.

The act's provisions regarding security also cast a broad net. They apply to persons engaging in acts of violence that would or might endanger the lives or safety of persons in Canada. The provisions also extend to spies, subversives, terrorists, and members of organizations reasonably suspected of such activity, or associating with those who do.[80]

Several Supreme Court decisions have considered how the security provisions should be applied in refugee situations. In 2023, the Court held that the security inadmissibility provisions of the act must be interpreted in compliance with Canada's obligation under the *International Refugee Convention* not to return refugees to a country where their life or freedom would be threatened (*non-refoulement* principle). Moreover, inadmissibility for engaging in acts of violence "requires a nexus to national security or the security of Canada."[81] In other words, not all violent acts fall within the security provisions, only those that endanger national security.

In 2013, the Supreme Court considered the inadmissibility provisions applicable to individuals believed to be members of a terrorist organization. As worded in the act, the prohibition could be applied against an individual who may not have known the organization was engaged in terrorist activities or was not a member at

---

78 *Immigration and Refugee Protection Act*, S.C. 2001, s. 36.
79 Discussed further in chapter 3.1, "Deportation: Disproportionate Response."
80 *Immigration and Refugee Protection Act*, S.C. 2001, s. 34.
81 *Mason v. Canada (Citizenship and Immigration)*, 2023 SCC 21.

the time the organization engaged in prohibited acts.[82] The Court clarified that a person should not be excluded from refugee protection based on guilt by association. At a minimum, "complicity under international criminal law requires an individual to knowingly (or, at the very least, recklessly) contribute in a significant way to the crime or criminal purpose of a group."[83]

In the following year, the Supreme Court scrutinized the provisions related to criminal inadmissibility that had been employed to bar a refugee from international protection.[84] The Court ruled that the legislation should be interpreted to withhold refugee protection from individuals who have committed significantly grave acts.

It agreed with UNHCR that offences such as homicide, rape, child molestation, assault causing bodily harm, arson, drug trafficking, and armed robbery are examples of crimes of sufficient severity to warrant an individual's exclusion from refugee status. While crimes carrying a maximum sentence of ten years or more in Canada are generally considered serious enough to justify exclusion, it emphasized that this determination should not be applied automatically. Refugee claimants must have the opportunity to respond and refute such findings.[85]

The Supreme Court's direction has not been consistently followed, according to an exhaustive review of exclusion decisions of the Refugee Protection Division over subsequent years. Refugee claimants have been excluded for crimes that fell well below

---

82 Molly Joeck, "Canadian Exclusion Jurisprudence Post-Febles," *International Journal of Refugee Law* 33, no. 1 (2021): 88.

83 *Ezokola v. Canada (Citizenship and Immigration)*, 2013 SCC 40 at para. 68.

84 *Febles v. Canada (Citizenship and Immigration)*, 2014 SCC 68. The case involved a refugee claimant from Cuba who had two convictions in the United States for assault with a deadly weapon. The Refugee Division applied Article 1F, finding that Febles was excluded from refugee protection.

85 *Febles v. Canada (Citizenship and Immigration)*, para. 62. As for Febles, the Supreme Court found his crimes were serious enough to bring him within the exclusion provisions and the board was correct in finding him ineligible for refugee protection in Canada. It further noted that he had recourse to other legal means to stay his removal should his removal to Cuba place him at risk of death, torture, or cruel and unusual treatment or punishment.

the seriousness suggested by UNHCR and endorsed by the Court, including bribery, falsifying business documents, impaired driving, and possessing less than one gram of cocaine.[86]

The Federal Court has overturned some such cases, but advocates note that few cases reach that stage of review. Advocates have urged the Immigration and Refugee Board to ensure that the Refugee Protection Division has more explicit guidelines for determining which individuals are to be excluded from international protection, so the law is applied consistently.[87]

The government has recently announced it intends to examine the *Immigration and Refugee Protection Act 2001* and assess the need for reform.[88] This should include amending the inadmissibility and exclusion provisions relating to refugees. The aim should be to ensure they are consistent with international obligations – by narrowing their application to egregious acts and ensuring that a consideration of such behaviour is considered within the context of a refugee determination hearing and not before.

Safe Third Country

Another controversial ineligibility provision denies access to the refugee process to persons who have arrived in Canada from another country that is designated as a "safe third country." The act provides that countries must only be designated as safe if they comply with their international protection obligations.[89] This includes abiding by the *non-refoulement* principle, which prohibits returning a person directly or indirectly to a place where their life or security of the person is at risk.

---

86 Joeck, "Canadian Exclusion Jurisprudence," 56.

87 Joeck, "Canadian Exclusion Jurisprudence," 85. Joeck's article also provides a review of the Federal Court decisions.

88 Immigration, Refugees and Citizenship Canada, "An Immigration System for Canada's Future: Strengthening Our Communities," 23 February 2023, https://www.canada.ca/en/immigration-refugees-citizenship/campaigns/canada-future-immigration-system.html.

89 *Immigration and Refugee Protection Act*, S.C. 2001, s. 102(1)(a).

The act lists the factors for the Cabinet to consider in designating a country as safe. It also obliges Cabinet to ensure the continuing review of those factors with respect to each designated country. The United States is the only country yet to be designated as "safe."[90]

The Canada-United States Safe Third Country Agreement was signed on 5 December 2002 and came into effect in 2004.[91] In essence, it means that refugee claimants must seek protection in whichever of the two countries they arrive in first. Before more recent amendments, it applied to only official land border crossings, requiring refugee claimants arriving at Canadian official land border crossings from the United States first to seek refugee protection in the United States.

There are a few exceptions, including having a family member with legal status in Canada, being an unaccompanied minor, having a valid Canadian immigration document, or being subject to the death penalty in the United States.[92]

The agreement led to an initial drop in refugee claims at official Canada-US border land ports of entry. This, however, was short lived as more individuals began to come to Canada through unofficial border crossing points. Following the 2022 surge in refugee claims – to over 90,000[93] – the agreement was amended to extend along the entire length of the US-Canada land border.[94]

---

90 *Immigration and Refugee Protection Act Regulations*, s. 159.3. The safe third country provisions were first introduced in 1989.

91 Immigration, Refugees and Citizenship Canada, "Safe Third Country Agreement between Canada and the United States," last updated 27 March 2023, https://www.canada.ca/en/immigration-refugees-citizenship/corporate/mandate/policies-operational-instructions-agreements/agreements/safe-third-country-agreement.html.

92 *Immigration and Refugee Protection Act Regulations*, s 159.6, provide that the safe third country does not apply in situations where the claimant is charged or convicted in the United States of an offence that is punishable with the death penalty there. Note, however, that a person could be found ineligible on other grounds.

93 Immigration, Refugees and Citizenship Canada, "Asylum Claims by Year – 2023."

94 Immigration, Refugees and Citizenship Canada, "Additional Protocol to the Safe Third Country Agreement," last updated 24 March 2023, https://www.canada.ca/en/immigration-refugees-citizenship/corporate/mandate/policies-operational-instructions-agreements/agreements/safe-third-country-agreement/additional-protocol.html.

The designation of the United States as a safe country is of concern to critics for several reasons. They note that asylum claimants in the United States are systematically detained often under harsh conditions, without an automatic review and in a manner that limits their ability to find legal counsel and pursue their asylum claims.[95]

Another concern is that asylum seekers in the United States must make their claim within one year, with few exceptions. Failing to do so means they are barred from the asylum process and can be removed unless they show they are *more likely than not* to be persecuted or tortured if returned to their country of origin: a much higher standard than applicable to other asylum claims.

A further concern is that American jurisprudence does not recognize certain types of claims that are recognized in Canada. This includes various gender-based claims and flight from gang violence. This means that persons who could be recognized as refugees in Canada could have their claims denied in the United States and returned to the country of origin where they would be a risk.

The Supreme Court of Canada considered the matter in 2023.[96] Several arguments were made in the case, including that the provisions were unconstitutional, for failing to respect rights enshrined in the *Charter*. For example, refugee claimants who are returned to the United States are subject to mandatory and prolonged detention. It was argued that this triggered their section 7 *Charter* right not to be deprived of liberty and security of the person except in accordance with fundamental justice. While agreeing that this right was engaged, the Court said that the legislative scheme was neither overly broad nor disproportionate and, as result, no principles of fundamental justice were violated.

Of relevance to the Supreme Court's analysis was that there are mechanisms in the United States to provide opportunities

---

95 Lloyd Axworthy and Allan Rock, "The Safe Third Country Agreement Is Unsafe – and Unconstitutional," *Globe and Mail*, 11 October 2022, https://www.theglobeandmail.com/opinion/article-the-safe-third-country -agreement-is-unsafe-and-unconstitutional/.

96 *Canadian Council for Refugees v. Canada (Citizenship and Immigration)*, 2023 SCC 17.

for release from detention. Additionally, it cited provisions in the Canadian regulations to enable the person to remain in Canada such as administrative deferrals of removal, temporary admission, humanitarian and compassionate exemptions, and public policy exemptions. The Court concluded that these safety valves "properly interpreted and applied – are sufficient to ensure that no deprivations contrary to the principles of fundamental justice occur." This was a controversial finding. Many critics and human rights agencies noted that these mechanisms were not accessible to refugee claimants facing return to the United States.[97]

The Supreme Court also found that the safe third country provisions could violate the *Charter* right in section 15 to equal protection of the law without discrimination based on race, national or ethnic origin, colour, religion, sex, age, or mental or physical disability. Equality rights, for example, could be infringed for a person who made a gender-based claim that would be recognized in Canada but not in the United States. The Court referred this issue back to the Federal Court to determine. In this respect, the constitutionality of the safe third country agreement awaits further consideration in the courts.

UNHCR advises states that the designation of a safe third country must be transparent, and based on reliable, objective, and up-to-date information from various sources. It also recommends that procedural safeguards enable an individualized assessment of the specific profile and circumstances of the case.[98]

---

97 Canadian Civil Liberties Association, "CCLA Reacts to SCC Decision on Safe Third Country Agreement," 16 June 2023, https://ccla.org/equality/ccla-reacts -to-scc-decision-on-safe-third-country-agreement/; Cory Ruf, "Supreme Court Decision on Safe Third Country Agreement Ultimately Fails Refugees," Amnesty International Canada, 16 June 2023, https://amnesty.ca/human-rights-news /safe-third-country-agreement-ruling/.

98 UNHCR, "Legal Considerations Regarding Access to Protection and a Connection between the Refugee and the Third Country in the Context of Return or Transfer to Safe Third Countries," April 2018, https://www.refworld.org /docid/5acb33ad4.html; UNHCR, "Guidance on Responding to Irregular Onward Movement of Refugees and Asylum-Seekers," September 2019, https://www.refworld.org/docid/5d8a255d4.html.

While the act requires that the Cabinet "must ensure the continuing review" of the reasons for the designation of each designated country, it does not require the government to provide reasons for the safe third country designation. It also does not provide a meaningful opportunity for refugee claimants to establish why the United States is unsafe for them. The act is applied on the basis that a person could have claimed refugee status in the United States and not on whether it is reasonable for them to do so based on their links or connections there. To bring the act into line with UNHCR guidance, it should – at a minimum – include safeguards to enable a claimant in a fair process to show why the return to a designated safe country may not be reasonable in their case. This must be part of the assessment process.

The various ineligibility screens are time consuming. Since the creation of the Immigration and Refugee Board in 1989, Canada has added screening criteria to limit access to the refugee determination process. These have often proved to be cumbersome, leading to further rationalization.

A review of the *Immigration and Refugee Protection Act 2001* should consider a more streamlined process. The Refugee Protection Division was established as an expert tribunal to determine refugee claims. Its jurisdiction has been unnecessarily limited by eligibility screens that prevent certain claims from being referred to it. Properly staffed and resourced, the Refugee Protection Division should have jurisdiction to consider the eligibility grounds within the context of the refugee determination hearing. This would help to ensure fair and efficient procedures in line with the act's commitments to refugee protection and international burden sharing.

Backlogs

Since the creation of the Immigration and Refugee Board in 1989, ensuring that decisions are made promptly has been a frequent concern of successive governments. In the late 1990s, in response to the observations made in a federal audit, the government took measures to ensure that the number of board members was sufficient to manage the annual number of refugee claims referred to it.[99] This helped to reduce the size of the backlog.

The approach shifted with the election of the Conservative government in 2006. The Immigration and Refugee Board faced a substantial decrease in decision-makers, just as the number of refugee claims started to rise. By 2009, the Auditor General reported a 23 per cent vacancy rate, leading to an exceptionally high level of unresolved cases. The Auditor General characterized the government's performance as "unsatisfactory."[100]

By 2010, there were 59,000 pending refugee claims with an average processing time of nineteen months.[101] Refugee advocates accused the government of deliberately creating the backlog to justify introducing more restrictive policies.[102] For its part, the government claimed that backlogs were caused by increased claims made by persons who did not need international protection and were abusing the system.

The restrictive measures introduced in 2012 included mandating a refugee determination hearing within sixty days of a refugee claim being referred to the board. Even faster time periods were applied to claims from designated countries.[103]

With the introduction of these new time frames, 32,000 claims, made prior to 2012, were deprioritized. That further delayed their determinations. Five years later, the Immigration and Refugee

---

99   Auditor General of Canada, "Chapter 2 – The Governor in Council Appointment Process," *2009 March Status Report of the Auditor General of Canada* (Ottawa: Office of the Auditor General of Canada, 2009), https://www.muskratfallsinquiry.ca /files/P-01777.pdf.

100   Auditor General, "Chapter 2 – The Governor in Council," 4.

101   Auditor General of Canada, "Report 2 – Processing of Asylum Claims," *Report of the Auditor General of Canada* (Ottawa: Office of the Auditor General of Canada, 2019), para 2.15, https://www.oag-bvg.gc.ca/internet/English/parl _oag_201905_02_e_43339.html.

102   David McKie, "Backlog of Refugee Claims Has Grown under Conservatives," *CBC News*, 4 December 2009, https://www.cbc.ca/news/politics /backlog-of-refugee-claims-has-grown-under-conservatives-1.863218.

103   *Immigration and Refugee Protection Regulations*, s. 159.1.

Board created a special Legacy Task Force to deal with these cases. It took until 2019 for the legacy backlog to be cleared.[104]

Meanwhile, a more extensive backlog began to accumulate almost immediately. Funding for processing claims remained fixed, resulting in inadequate resources to handle the increasing number of claims received by Canada. This issue persisted after the Liberal government came to power in 2015. By 2017, the backlog had surpassed 71,000 claims, with fewer than 20 per cent of claims being heard within the sixty-day timeframe.[105]

In 2019, the Auditor General attributed prolonged processing delays to insufficient financial resources to support the additional capacity needed for increased annual refugee claims and inefficiencies in the system. Contributing factors included a failure to expedite cases eligible for faster processing, frequent postponements due to issues within the government's control, and a lack of efficient information sharing among relevant government agencies.

Immigration, Refugees and Citizenship Canada, the Canada Border Services Agency, and the Immigration and Refugee Board of Canada lacked interoperable information systems and primarily relied on the exchange of paper files. Subsequent measures to address these problems helped to reduce the backlog by 40 per cent by February 2022.[106] However, backlogs have again risen, corresponding to the surge in refugee claims throughout 2022 and 2023. Currently, there are over 174,000 claims pending.[107]

One response from the government has been to terminate a program initiated in 2023 that relaxed requirements for many

---

104 Teressa Wright, "Canada's Backlog of 'Legacy' Refugee Claims Soon to Be Cleared – but a New List Is Growing," *Global News*, 30 April 2019, https://globalnews.ca/news/5220024/refugee-legacy-claims-cleared/.

105 Auditor General, "Report 2 – Processing of Asylum Claims," para. 2.25. By 2020, the backlog had grown to over 101,000 pending claims, partly due to reduced productivity during the COVID-19 pandemic.

106 UNHCR, "Effective Processing of Asylum Applications: Practical Considerations and Practices," March 2022, https://www.refworld.org/docid/6241b39b4.html. This publication documents some of the practices.

107 Immigration and Refugee Board of Canada, "Recent Trends," September 2023, https://irb.gc.ca:443/en/statistics/Pages/volume-reports.aspx.

foreigners applying for temporary visas to Canada.[108] This policy was initially introduced to address the significant backlog in processing visa applications, delays which were highlighted in the Auditor General's report of 2023.[109]

Following the relaxation of visa requirements, Canada experienced an increase in the volume of asylum claims filed by those who benefited from the temporary program. The total number of asylum claims grew from 91,000 in 2022 to over 143,000 in 2023.[110] However, nationals from the countries that enjoyed easier visa requirements constituted only 19,400 of the total asylum claims in 2023.[111]

Asylum claims from Mexicans rose substantially between 1922 and 1923: from 230 to 25, 236.[112] They accounted for some 17 per cent of the total number of claims in 2023.[113] But they too could not account for the overall surge in numbers. Nevertheless, despite this, and the fact that the Immigration and Refugee Board accepted 54 per cent of Mexican claims heard in 2023,[114] alleged abuse of the system was used to justify tightening visa requirements for Mexicans in February 2024.[115]

---

108 Refugees and Citizenship Canada Immigration, "Temporary Public Policy to Facilitate the Processing of Temporary Resident Visa Applications in Inventory," 29 June 2023, https://www.canada.ca/en/immigration-refugees-citizenship/corporate/mandate/policies-operational-instructions-agreements/public-policies/processing-trv-apps-inventory.html.

109 The report, discussed in the introduction, looked at Immigration, Refugees and Citizenship Canada's processing of permanent resident applications following the release of figures showing that the department had an inventory of over 2 million pending permanent, temporary and citizenship applications. Auditor General of Canada, "Report 9."

110 Immigration, Refugees and Citizenship Canada, "Asylum Claims by Year – 2021," 22 February 2021, https://www.canada.ca/en/immigration-refugees-citizenship/services/refugees/asylum-claims/asylum-claims-2021.html.

111 Immigration, Refugees and Citizenship Canada, "Revoking the Temporary Public Policy to Facilitate Processing of Temporary Resident Visas (Visitors Only) in the Inventory," Memorandum to the Minister. Obtained through an Access to Information request by Steven Meurrens, @smeurrens, X/Formerly Twitter, 1 March 2024, https://x.com/smeurrens/status/1770947087183606201/photo.

112 Immigration, Refugees and Citizenship Canada, "Asylum Claims by Year – 2021."

113 As noted by the minister. See Darren Major, Louis Blouin, and Romain Schué, "Canada Bringing Back Visa Requirements for Mexican Nationals to Curb Asylum Seekers," *CBC News*, 28 February 2024, https://www.cbc.ca/news/politics/mexico-canada-visas-asylum-1.7128408.

114 Statistics compiled by UNHCR using Immigration and Refugee Board data base.

115 Major, Blouin, and Schué, "Canada Bringing Back Visa Requirements."

Enhancing the refugee determination system does not lie in the imposition of visas. A blueprint for reform was presented to the government in 2018, aiming to streamline processing in a fair and efficient manner.[116] While the government has indicated that reforms are underway, it has not committed to a comprehensive and transparent review, which we believe is necessary given the vital role refugee determination plays in saving lives and meeting our international obligations.

Cessation of Refugee Status

The 1951 Refugee Convention recognizes that refugee status can end under certain conditions, such as when the refugee re-establishes in the country of origin or when there is a fundamental change of circumstances there. These grounds have been incorporated into Canadian immigration legislation. Historically, the application of cessation was rare in Canada. This was because recognized refugees were granted permanent residence status and cessation did not affect that status. This changed in 2012 when the *Immigration and Refugee Protection Act 2001* was amended to enable cessation to be applied against recognized refugees who are permanent residents.

If cessation is applied, the refugee loses refugee status as well as permanent residency status and can be removed from Canada.[117] This can be invoked against long-time permanent residents, including those with significant economic, social and family links in Canada. And like any rejected refugee claimant, they are barred from having a Pre-Removal Risk Assessment or seeking humanitarian and compassionate consideration for twelve months. There is also no right to appeal a cessation decision to the Refugee Appeal Division.[118]

---

116 Yeates, "Report of the Independent Review."

117 *Immigration and Refugee Protection Act*, S.C. 2001, s. 108(2). The grounds include the person having voluntarily re-availed themselves of the protection of their country of nationality; voluntarily reacquired their nationality; acquired a new nationality and enjoys the protection of the country of that new nationality; has voluntarily become re-established.

118 *Immigration and Refugee Protection Act*, S.C. 2001, s. 110(2)(e).

Applications for cessation are made to the Refugee Protection Division on behalf of the Minister of Citizenship and Immigration. The most common ground for invoking cessation is where a person has applied for a passport from the country of origin or made a return trip there.[119]

The number of cessation applications allowed has risen substantially since 2013: from just 46 to 307 in 2023, with an additional 331 applications pending a decision.[120] Acceptance rates are high, over 85 per cent.

In 2022, the Federal Court of Appeal ruled the board should not apply the provisions of the act in a "mechanistic or rote manner." It noted that the focus must be on whether the refugee's conduct can "reliably indicate that the refugee intended to waive the protection of the country of asylum." The court provided detailed guidance on relevant considerations. These include the severity of the consequences; the age, education, and sophistication of the person; and knowledge of the cessation provisions. Other important considerations include the source of persecution (state or non-state agent), the purpose and frequency of travel to the country of origin, and whether the persons took security precautions while in the country.[121]

It remains to be seen whether the Refugee Protection Division will systematically consider these factors and result in a reduction in the approval rate of cessation applications. Meanwhile the Federal Court is currently considering another challenge of the cessation provisions on the grounds that they contravene the *Charter*.[122]

---

119 In 2014 the Canadian Boarder Services Agency issued a bulletin announcing that it referred over 800 cases a year to the Immigration and Protection Division to vacate (for misrepresentation) or invoke cessation. CBSA Operational Bulletin PRG-2013-59, 19 September 2013. See also Canadian Council for Refugees, "Cessation: Stripping Refugees of their Status," May 2014, https://ccrweb.ca/files/cessation-report-2014.pdf.

120 Immigration and Refugee Board of Canada, "Applications to Cease or Vacate Refugee Protection," last updated 15 May 2024, https://irb.gc.ca:443/en/statistics/protection/Pages/RPDVacStat.aspx.

121 *Canada (Citizenship and Immigration) v. Galindo Camayo*, 2022 FCA 50, paras. 83-4.

122 *Gnanapragasam v. MCI* has been filed with the Federal Court. *The case has yet to be fully argued before the court but a* summary of procedural orders made up to June 2024 can be found at the Federal Court's website, https://www.fct-cf.gc.ca/en/court-files-and-decisions/court-files.

Future Priorities

The refugee objectives of the *Immigration and Refugee Protection Act 2001* are broad. The act recognizes that the refugee program is "in the first instance about saving lives and offering protection to the displaced and persecuted." It aims to fulfil Canada's international legal obligations towards refugees. It seeks to affirm Canada's commitment to refugee resettlement, and "establish fair and efficient procedures that will maintain the integrity of the Canadian refugee protection system, while upholding Canada's respect for the human rights and fundamental freedoms of all human beings."

The refugee program also seeks to support the self-sufficiency of refugees – and their social and economic well-being – by facilitating family reunification. It intends to "protect the health, safety and security of Canadians" – and to promote international justice – by "denying access to Canadian territory to persons, including refugee claimants, who are security risks or serious criminals."

These objectives provide an appropriate means to evaluate Canada's refugee policy over the past twenty years. The results are mixed. Compared to many high-income countries, Canada's refugee resettlement program has fared well. It remains one of the leading resettlement countries in the world among immigrant-receiving states.

As Canada has increased its annual immigration levels, it has also anticipated higher levels of resettled refugees. But most of this increase is expected to come from the private sector. The proportion of government-sponsored refugees – which selects the neediest refugees – has seen a decline. This is a concern, and should it continue, it will erode the country's commitment to offering protection to the most vulnerable.

Canada's inland refugee determination process has been the focus of constant change and adjustment since it was first implemented in 1978. History reveals that in some cases cumbersome procedures stood in the way of fair and efficient determinations. At other times, governments used increased refugee arrivals to rally support for policies restricting people from making refugee claims, both at border crossings and from within Canada. This has been true again in the recent past.

The Refugee Appeal Division was established after years of advocacy and a decade after the *Immigration and Refugee Protection Act 2001* authorized it. Its effectiveness over the years has been somewhat constrained by a lack of capacity to meet the volume of appeals. In 2018 an independent review of the Immigration and Refugee Board made many recommendations to improve the quality and efficiency of the refugee determination process.[123]

Subsequent reports from the Immigration and Refugee Board speak to measures the board is taking to improve the decision-making of the Refugee Protection Division.[124] Advocates have noted the ways in which improved training, more streamlined case management, and the hiring of qualified decision-makers have helped to improve performance.

Long-standing preoccupations over misuse of the refugee determination stream have continued. Some restrictive eligibility provisions carried over from the previous *Immigration Act* and other measures have been added. These have broadened the grounds for finding a person ineligible to make a refugee protection claim. They have limited rights of review for certain groups and facilitated their removal without a meaningful risk assessment. The increased use of cessation to remove recognized refugees is at odds with the act's objectives of protecting refugees and ensuring their integration.

These changes were all instituted in the name of fairness, efficiency, and ensuring the integrity of the refugee program. As this

---

123 Yeates, "Report of the Independent Review." These include harmonized country of origin information, triaging of cases according to complexity, decision-maker guides and templates, early identification of the main issues to focus on in a hearing, resorting to oral decisions for decisions in favour of the claimant and foregoing hearings where a positive decision can be made on a paper review. Some of the suggestions were surprising since the board used them in previous periods, notably in the 1990s.

124 Immigration and Refugee Board of Canada, "Management Response and Action Plan: Assessment of Decision-Making Quality in the Refugee Protection Division (2019–2020)," 2 June 2021, https://irb.gc.ca:443/en/transparency/reviews-audit-evaluations/Pages/rpd-qmi-1920-mrap.aspx.

chapter reveals, however, they have not necessarily met those objectives. They must be reconsidered in the context of a broad and much needed review of Canada's refugee program.

There is considerable agreement for greater study on the impact of settlement services on refugee integration. In the meantime, some specific change is needed. The focus of settlement support should be broadened to include the family of the principal applicant. Information on the settlement services available should be more widely disseminated to refugees.

Studies have shown that government-sponsored refugees are better informed in this area. A common theme among settlement providers is they lack capacity, leading to delays and gaps in service.[125] Increased investment is needed – alongside impact evaluations – to ensure the appropriate level and means of support that is required for the integration of refugees into Canada.

---

125 Lori Wilkinson and Joseph Garcea, *The Economic Integration of Refugees in Canada: A Mixed Record?* (Washington, DC: Migration Policy Institute, 2017), https://www.migrationpolicy.org/research/economic-integration -refugees-canada-mixed-record.

PART 3

Membership and Belonging: Precarious Status

Overview

Canada admits immigrants to contribute to and enrich the economic, social, and cultural characteristics of society. Immigration policy aims to support a strong economy, facilitate family reunification, and provide protection to displaced and persecuted persons. Immigration policy is also about fostering a sense of membership and belonging within the country. The selection process for immigrants is carefully curated and considers their potential to make contributions to society. It is complemented by other processes aimed to promote integration and evolution, from permanent residency to full citizenship.

In part 2, we examined admissions policy. In part 3, we look at three aspects of immigration policy that have a bearing on membership and belonging: deportation, integration, and citizenship. Detention and deportation are part of the broader enforcement powers that Canada uses to maintain the integrity of the system. The focus of immigration policy is on the removal of those who have fraudulently gained entry or otherwise violated the conditions of their admission. This aspect has always been a central pillar of immigration enforcement.

Chapter 3.1, "Deportation: A Disproportionate Response," tracks the trajectory of deportation practices. Broadly speaking there have been three stages. The first spanned nearly a hundred years. During this phase, the Cabinet exercised extensive deportation powers. The grounds for removal were broad and reflected the social, political, and racial biases of the day. A person who was ordered deported had very little chance of contesting the order, even where it meant being removed to a place where they were at risk.

The second stage commenced in the 1960s with reforms that limited the grounds for removal, targeting serious criminal behaviour, security risks, and those who had misrepresented themselves in gaining admission to Canada. An independent appeal mechanism was also established with the authority to overturn a deportation order for legal and factual errors as well as for humanitarian and compassionate reasons.

The third stage spans the contemporary period under the *Immigration and Refugee Protection Act 2001*.[1] The last two decades have seen a significant expansion in the criteria leading to the loss of permanent resident status and subsequent removal from Canada. Simultaneously, the ability to appeal a removal order on various grounds has been significantly reduced. This shift indicates a regression in deportation policy. It has the potential to lead to the kinds of disproportionate responses typical of earlier periods.

Since 1976, one of the explicit objectives of Canadian immigration policy has been to facilitate the successful integration of immigrants into Canadian society. This took on broader significance in the 1980s. A national commitment to multiculturalism was enshrined in the 1982 *Canadian Charter of Rights and Freedoms*[2] and the *Multiculturalism Act* of 1988.[3] These constitutional and legislative measures aim to promote the full and equitable participation of individuals from diverse backgrounds in Canadian society.

In contrast to earlier periods of Canadian history, a substantial majority of Canadians support a broadly inclusive multiculturalism policy. It is widely perceived as a defining and cherished aspect of Canadian identity. This has resulted in a largely non-partisan contemporary political consensus surrounding the fundamental principles of existing immigration policy.

The high ideals of multiculturalism and immigrant integration, however, are not fully matched by outcomes. Some efforts are not fully effective, including measures to ensure that immigrants are welcomed in society and assisted in finding accommodation and health care. Their skills and qualifications are often not sufficiently recognized in the workforce. A recent study revealed that the already high emigration rates of permanent residents from Canada have surged in recent years.[4] This underscores the existing gap between integration goals and the reality on the ground.

---

1   *Immigration and Refugee Protection Act*, S.C. 2001, c. 27.
2   *Canadian Charter of Rights and Freedoms*, s. 7, Part 1 of the *Constitution Act, 1982*.
3   *Canadian Multiculturalism Act*, R.S.C., 1985, c. 24 (4th Supp.).
4   Bérard-Chagnon et al., *Emigration of Immigrants*. The study found that 0.1 per cent of immigrants admitted between 1982 and 2017 emigrated within five years of

Chapter 3:2, "Integration: Short-Term Programs, Long Term Benefits," examines various measures Canada has relied upon to promote immigrant integration. They range from supporting initial settlement services, promoting language instruction, enhancing skills recognition, and combatting racism and discrimination.

Integration support is provided by the federal, provincial, and municipal governments as well as by many non-governmental agencies. The decentralized process poses significant challenges in evaluating the effectiveness of these programs. Moreover, funding is not provided on a multi-year basis. Longitudinal studies on immigrant integration are sparse and impact evaluations are rare.

Chapter 3:3, "Citizenship: Raising the Bar," closes by evaluating citizenship policies in the context of membership and belonging.

Citizenship represents the culmination of a long journey for many immigrants, signifying full membership in Canadian society along with the associated rights and privileges. It is central to a successful immigration policy. Comparative evidence suggests that faster access to citizenship improves economic, educational, political, and social integration of immigrants.

For most of Canada's history, British subject status was the highest available status in Canada. Non-British immigrants acquired it through naturalization, a power exercised by the Cabinet in a highly partial manner. Races and classes of people deemed unsuitable for inclusion were frequently denied naturalization.

In 1946, Canada passed the *Canadian Citizenship Act*, which for the first time recognized a distinct Canadian citizenship status.[5] The path to Canadian citizenship through naturalization was accessible to all meeting the act's criteria. Executive discretion was curtailed, promoting a transparent and less arbitrary process. Since then, the rules for obtaining Canadian citizenship have frequently been adjusted. Significant changes have

---

landing. Within twenty years this rate rose to over 17 per cent. It also found that immigrants with higher levels of skills and education are more likely to leave than others (25). See also Kathryn Dennler, *The Leaky Bucket: A Study of Immigrant Retention Trends in Canada* (Ottawa: The Conference Board of Canada, 2023).

5 *An Act respecting Citizenship, Nationality, Naturalization and Status of Aliens, 1946,* S.C. 10 George VI, Chapter 15.

occurred in the contemporary period reflecting progressive and regressive shifts.

On a positive note, Canadian citizenship was granted to numerous individuals who found themselves without legal status due to shifts in citizenship legislation over time. Yet despite this progressive step, other changes imposed more stringent language proficiency requirements and citizenship tests and raised fees for naturalization. The once-high percentage of immigrants becoming naturalized has fallen dramatically. This is a disturbing trend, given that high and rapid naturalization rates appear strongly associated with successful integration.

We examine policy shifts around citizenship in the twenty-first century and their underlying rationale, alongside some of the possible implications of the changes. We also point out areas where more information is needed for a proper assessment of the impact of these policy shifts.

Deportation: Disproportionate Response

Permanent residents enjoy a broad range of rights. They can live anywhere and move throughout Canada. They can study and are entitled to access social services, including provincial health insurance. They are protected under the *Charter*. But unlike full citizens, they are unable to vote, run for political office, or hold certain high-level jobs requiring security clearance. They also do not have an unqualified right to remain or to return to Canada once they have left.

Permanent residents can retain their status as long as they comply with the requirements of the *Immigration and Refugee Protection Act 2001*.[1] If they do not, they become inadmissible to remain. They can be ordered to leave the country for failing to meet residency obligations, or for reasons relating to security, criminality, and misrepresentation. Despite the name, their residency is not necessarily permanent.

In this chapter, we focus on the grounds and processes used to detain and deport permanent residents. We start by putting the current statutory scheme into an historical context, with a look at how Canada's deportation laws have evolved over time. We then examine the changes that have been introduced under the *Immigration and Refugee Protection Act 2001* and their consequences. The rights of certain individuals to appeal their removal orders have been limited. These changes have attracted the most critical commentary because of the significant negative impact on the persons affected.

---

1 Statutes of Canada, 2001, c. 27.

Deportation and associated measures are all part of the enforcement provision of the act. The Canadian Border Services Agency is the leading government agency responsible for the enforcement. It works closely with Immigration, Refugees and Citizenship Canada in the process. Each year, thousands of foreign nationals and permanent residents receive removal orders. Some become immediately enforceable. Others may only become enforceable once the person has waived or exhausted all legal remedies to remain. Annual deportation figures are not easy to find, and once located, they do not provide a breakdown in terms of how many permanent residents were ordered removed, the reasons for the removal, or whether their departure was voluntary.

Cumulative statistics indicate that annual removals between 2006 and 2014 ranged from 10,000 to 14,000 persons.[2] Approximately 8,700 persons were removed each year from 2016 to 2019,[3] reportedly rising to over 10,000 annually through 2023.

Context

Canada has consistently retained broad grounds for removing non-citizens, including permanent residents.[4] For most of Canadian history, the government could order immigrants to be removed within several years of their arrival for wide-ranging reasons.[5] After they acquired domicile by living in Canada for a defined number of years, they could only be removed on very limited grounds, such as treason.

---

2 Never Home, "'Back to Where You Came From': Canada Deports 35 People Daily," Neverhome.ca, accessed 30 August 2022, http://www.neverhome.ca/deportation/.

3 Auditor General of Canada, "Report 1 – Immigration Removals," *Report of the Auditor General of Canada* (Ottawa: Office of the Auditor General of Canada, 2020), https://www.oag-bvg.gc.ca/internet/english/parl_oag_202007_01_e_43572.html.

4 For more on the history of deportation, see Kelley and Trebilcock, *Making of the Mosaic*; Dennis G. Molinaro, *Deportation from Canada*, Immigration and Ethnicity in Canada Series, Booklet No. 36 (Ottawa: Canadian Historical Association, 2018).

5 Domicile was three years under the *Immigration Act, 1910* and raised to five years in 1914.

The grounds for deportation proceedings reflected political, social, and cultural biases of the day. Early legislation provided for the removal of immigrants who had received social support, had been convicted of a crime, or had required hospital care. There was also a wide array of medical ailments that could initiate removal proceedings. Conduct that fell within the realm of "moral turpitude" could trigger removal as could being considered "feeble-minded" or an "idiot."[6]

Deportation grounds were expanded during periods of labour and social activism, notably leading up to First World War and spanning the 1920s and 1930s. Grounds for removal extended to persons advocating the overthrow of governments by force, attempting to create a riot or public disorder, and being affiliated with any organization advocating against organized government.

During wartime, immigrants from enemy countries could be deported. And as explained in the introduction, during the Second World War, this even included the deportation of Canadian citizens – those of Japanese descent.

Persons with deportation orders had few due-process protections. Boards of inquiry reviewed the orders, whose members were appointed by the minister. There was no right to an oral hearing nor opportunity to challenge the minister's evidence.[7] The boards of inquiry could consider any evidence they thought trustworthy. Most decisions could be appealed to the minister, but only on narrow grounds. They were rarely successful. Judicial review was confined to the examination of legal errors. This absence of fair process could lead to great hardship. It was at its worst for those whose lives were at risk upon removal, for spouses and children who were also removed, and for individuals who arrived in Canada at a young age, and so had no connection to their country of nationality.

These features – alongside the other tortuous and often unedifying aspects of Canadian deportation history – began to be

---

6 *Immigration Act, 1910*, S.C., c. 27, s. 3.
7 Molinaro, *Deportation from Canada*, 5.

addressed in the 1960s.[8] With the liberalization of immigration policy then and into the 1970s, the grounds for deportation became more clearly defined in legislation. This was accompanied by making removal order procedures fairer, providing those ordered to be removed more opportunity to know the case against them, and the ability to contest the removal order.

However, the protection that acquiring domicile used to provide from deportation was removed in the *Immigration Act, 1976*.[9] Consequently, a permanent resident could be removed from Canada if they contravened the provisions of it, irrespective of how long they had lived in country. The grounds for deportation focused on serious criminal behaviour, security risks, and misrepresentation.

In 1967, the Immigration Appeal Board was established. It was an independent tribunal with jurisdiction to hear appeals from persons issued with a deportation order, as well as from Canadians whose family sponsorships had been denied. It could overturn previous decisions if there were errors of fact or law, or if there were hardship factors and/or humanitarian and compassionate grounds to do so. This was an important development as it enabled the board to weigh the risk the individual posed to society against the harm the person or members of their family would suffer if removed.

An initial constraint on the Immigration Appeal Board's jurisdiction stopped it from considering humanitarian and compassionate grounds where a security certificate had been issued against the person. The government can issue a security certificate where the information supporting the removal order cannot be disclosed without endangering the safety of a person or risking national security. It has the effect of limiting a person's appeal rights. The limitation has since been expanded to apply to any permanent

---

8 In 1952, Special Inquiry Officers were established to investigate whether a person should be deported. Appeals were permitted to a three-person Immigration Appeal Board appointed by the minister. The minister retained the final decision. Molinaro, *Deportation from Canada*, 19.

9 Warren Black, "Novel Features of the Immigration Act, 1976," *Canadian Bar Review* 56, no. 4 (1978): 561–78, esp. 569 regarding criminal inadmissibility.

resident or refugee found inadmissible due to concerns related to national security, serious criminality, violations of human or international rights, or involvement in organized crime.[10]

The *Immigration Act, 1976* also set up three types of removal orders that remain in effect today: deportation, exclusion, and departure orders.

A deportation order prevents a person from returning to Canada without prior authorization. An exclusion order prevents return for a period of one year, unless otherwise authorized. A departure order means a person must leave Canada within a specified period, but they can return to the country provided they have complied with the order and otherwise qualify for admission.

In 1986, the Immigration Appeal Board ended, to be replaced by the Immigration and Refugee Board. It remains operational to this day. Within the board, the Immigration Appeal Division is responsible for addressing appeals connected to removal orders and rejected family sponsorship applications.[11] In 1993, an Adjudication Division was added to the board. It conducts admissibility hearings and detention reviews for foreign nationals and permanent residents suspected of being either inadmissible to Canada or removable from the country.[12]

In 1992, the Supreme Court of Canada issued a ruling that was to have profound influence on the ability of permanent residents to challenge the constitutionality of a removal order. The ruling in the case of *Chiarelli*[13] related to a man convicted of two criminal offences, receiving a suspended sentence for one, and six-month sentence for the other. He had been living in Canada for ten years, arriving at the age of fifteen. Because the maximum term of

10 Discussed more fully later in this chapter. Previously, a security certificate was issued upon the recommendation of the Minister of Manpower and Immigration and the Solicitor General. Under the *Immigration and Refugee Protection Act, 2001*, it is the Minister of Immigration and Citizenship and the Minister of Public Safety.

11 Refugee Determination Division and the Immigration Appeal Division.

12 Its members are from the Canadian civil service. Vinokur, "30 Years of Changes at the Immigration and Refugee Board of Canada," 8.

13 *Canada (Minister of Employment and Immigration) v. Chiarelli*, 1992 CanLII 87 (SCC), [1992] 1 SCR 711.

imprisonment for both offences was over five years, Chiarelli fell within the provision for serious criminality under the *Immigration Act, 1976* and a deportation order was issued.

The Solicitor General and the Minister of Immigration subsequently issued a security certificate against him on the grounds that he was likely to participate in organized crime. Chiarelli's right of appeal was therefore limited to questions of fact or law and did not include humanitarian and compassionate considerations. Chiarelli argued that this violated his right under the *Charter* not to be deprived of life, liberty, and security of the person except in accordance with the principles of fundamental justice.

The Supreme Court ruled against Chiarelli, and in its decision, it made several findings. First, it said it need not consider whether deportation amounts to a deprivation of life, liberty, or security of the person because there was no breach of fundamental justice. According to the Court, the content of fundamental justice depends on context, and specifically in this case, on the principles and policies underlying immigration law.

The Court elaborated by stating that an underlying principle of the *Immigration Act, 1976* was that non-citizens do not have an unqualified right to enter or remain in the country. Parliament, it said, has the right to establish the conditions upon which a person can be removed, and deportation is the only way to give those conditions practical effect.[14]

Considering this finding, the Court determined that the appeal rights in the act provided ample protection from an erroneous decision. The principles of fundamental justice did not require a consideration of Chiarelli's personal circumstances, any mitigating factors, or the harm he might face if removed.[15]

It was a noteworthy decision because the Court was willing to consider what fundamental justice required without considering if Chiarelli's life or liberty were at stake. It also narrowly defined the underlying principle of the *Immigration Act, 1976* – as enforcement – and used this to determine the content of the *Charter* right. It did not use the *Charter* as the benchmark to determine the

---

14 *Canada (Minister of Employment and Immigration) v. Chiarelli*, 733.
15 *Canada (Minister of Employment and Immigration) v. Chiarelli*, 734.

constitutionality of the act. In effect, this denied supremacy to the *Charter*. There was also no requirement that the government justify its actions as proportionate under section 1 of the *Charter*.

Ten years after *Chiarelli*, the Supreme Court of Canada considered the constitutionality of legislative provisions again – this time over the deportation of a suspected terrorist from Canada. The case of *Suresh* involved a refugee who had fled to Canada from Sri Lanka in 1990 and was recognized as a refugee the following year.[16] He had been detained and ordered removed following the issuing of a security certificate. The proceedings were based on allegations that he was a member of the Liberation Tigers of Eelam (LTTE), an alleged terrorist organization. Suresh was not provided the information that formed the basis of the removal order nor was he provided an opportunity to respond to it.

Suresh argued that if he returned to Sri Lanka he would face torture. Given this threat to his life and security of person he required a higher level of procedural fairness than was provided to him. The Court acknowledged that international law generally rejects deportation to torture, even where national security interests are at stake. However, it left open the possibility that deportation to torture could be constitutional in exceptional cases.

Where deportation to torture was under consideration, the Court held that the person must be informed of the case to be met, subject to privilege and other valid reasons for limited disclosure. The person must also be provided with an opportunity to respond in writing to the case, and to challenge the minister's information.

The Court placed the onus on the person named in the security certificate to establish a *prima facie* case of the risk of torture, noting that the minister had the discretion to determine whether that threshold was met. The Court made it clear that the minister's decision was entitled to deference and that courts should not interfere with the decision if the evidence reasonably supported a finding of danger to the security of Canada.[17]

---

16 *Suresh v. Canada (Minister of Citizenship and Immigration)* [2002] 1 S.C.R. 3.
17 *Suresh v. Canada (Minister of Citizenship and Immigration)*, 28–9, 64.

Both the *Chiarelli* and *Suresh* decisions limited the applicability of the *Charter* in deportation decisions and, as we shall see, that includes those decisions made under the authority of the *Immigration and Refugee Protection Act 2001*.

Relevant Legislative Provisions

The *Immigration and Refugee Protection Act, 2001* retained the basic deportation framework of previous legislation while expanding the grounds for which a permanent resident could be removed and limiting procedural protections for some.

Grounds

Permanent residents can be removed from Canada if they become inadmissible as defined by the act. There are several grounds of inadmissibility, as outlined in the beginning of part 2. The most used grounds relate to serious criminality, security, non-compliance with the act, and misrepresentation.

Removal order decisions can be appealed to the Immigration Appeal Division, apart from those based on violations relating to serious criminality, organized crime, security, and human or international rights. Judicial review by the Federal Court of Canada is only permissible if one of its judges certifies that a serious question of general importance is involved.[18]

Serious Criminality and Organized Criminality

A permanent resident can be ordered removed from Canada for having been convicted of a serious criminal offence punishable by at least ten years imprisonment or where a term of imprisonment of more than six months has been imposed.[19]

---

18 *Immigration and Refugee Protection Act*, S.C. 2001, s. 74(d).
19 *Immigration and Refugee Protection Act*, S.C. 2001, s. 36(1)(a) (b).

Amendments in 2013 also widened grounds for removal to cover crimes and potential offences committed beyond Canada's borders. Permanent residents can be ordered removed if they have been convicted of an offence that in Canada would qualify for a sentence of ten years or more, or if there are reasonable grounds to believe they have committed such an offence.[20] An actual conviction therefore is not necessary.

Being a member of an organization believed to be engaged in serious criminal activity can also be a basis for removal proceedings.[21]

Initially, serious criminality was defined as a conviction with a possible sentence of ten years or more, or one where the person was sentenced to more than two years in prison. In 2013, the Conservative government lowered the bar, to sentences of six months or more.[22] In 2017, the Supreme Court of Canada clarified that these provisions did not apply to individuals with a conditional sentence of more than six months.[23]

The change brought a vast array of crimes – from egregious offences to the relatively minor – within the definition of serious criminality, potentially triggering removal orders that could not be reviewed by the Immigration Appeal Division. It meant serious criminality now encompassed acts of violence, offences linked to drugs, convictions for driving under the influence, and a spectrum of theft and fraud transgressions exceeding $5,000 dollars.[24]

While most commentators acknowledge that serious criminality may be a justified ground for deportation, the low threshold of qualifying offences has attracted extensive criticism. So too has the removal of appeal rights. Many argue that deportation should be for the most serious offences and with due regard to other

---

20 *Immigration and Refugee Protection Act,* S.C. 2001, s. 36(1)(c).

21 *Immigration and Refugee Protection Act,* S.C. 2001, s. 37.

22 *Faster Removal of Foreign Criminals Act,* S.C. 2013, c. 16.

23 *Tran v. Canada (Public Safety and Emergency Preparedness),* 2017 SCC 50. Because the Supreme Court decided that sentence of imprisonment covered "prison" sentences, it did not apply to persons with a conditional sentence.

24 Foreign Worker Canada, "Crimes That Make You Inadmissible to Canada," accessed 18 July 2024, https://www.duicanadaentry.com/crimes-that-make-you -inadmissible-to-canada/.

mitigating and relevant factors, which the removal of the Immigration Appeal Division's jurisdiction denies.[25]

Some legal advocates argue that deporting permanent residents convicted of a criminal offence amounts to a form of double jeopardy. Having already been convicted and served their sentence, they face further punishment through deportation.[26] Eliminating their right to appeal to the Immigration Appeal Board over the deportation process exacerbates the harm.

Security

Scholars and advocates were very critical of the increased use of security certificates following the 11 September 2001 terrorist attacks in the United States. They were seen as a way of limiting fair process and expediting removals. The certificate process proved unwieldly and exceedingly complex. It is now rarely used, although it has not been repealed. Instead, the legislation was changed to broaden the grounds of removal, limit rights of appeal, and provide for expedited removals on security grounds. As with security certificates, disclosure of evidence leading to the removal order can be limited. And there is no right of appeal to the Immigration Appeal Division.[27]

Acts that fall within the security grounds include engaging in an act of espionage against Canada or Canadian interests; subversion by force of any government; and subversion of any kind against a democratic government, institution, or process. Security grounds also include engaging in terrorism; being a danger to the security of Canada or to the lives and safety of persons in Canada. Being a member of an organization that there are reasonable grounds

---

25 Canadian Bar Association, "Bill C-43, Faster Removal of Foreign Criminals Act," accessed 18 July 2024, https://carl-acaadr.ca/bill-c-43-the-faster-removals-of -foreign-criminals-act/.

26 Souheil Benslimane and David Moffette, "The Double Punishment of Criminal Inadmissibility for Immigrants," *Journal of Prisoners on Prisons* 28, no. 1 (2019): 44–65, https://doi.org/10.18192/jpp.v28i1.4351.

27 *Immigration and Refugee Protection Act*, S.C. 2001, ss. 64(1), 86.

to believe engages in espionage, subversion, or terrorism is also grounds for removal.[28]

The membership provisions have been criticized as overly harsh because they can include individuals who may not be aware of the criminal activities of the group. They may have become members because of cultural, social, or humanitarian activities.

Commentators have pointed out that the wording in the *Immigration and Refugee Protection Act 2001* regarding terrorism is far vaguer than in the *Criminal Code*. The *Criminal Code* defines terrorism, requires criminal misconduct, and excludes activities that are not intended to harm such as advocacy, protest, and other forms of dissent. The act's legislation does not.[29] The provisions of the act cast a wider net and can be used against individuals who join associations that are subsequently declared to be terrorist organizations, or who are not associated with violent activity, or were even unaware of it.

Human or International Rights Violations

Inadmissibility also applies to persons who have held office or participated in governments that have been involved in systematic or severe human rights violations, genocide, war crimes, or crimes against humanity.[30]

Non-Compliance with the Act and Misrepresentation

Permanent residents are required to live in Canada for two out of five years. Those who fail to meet this requirement can be found inadmissible and removed. Additionally, those who provided false or misleading information during the immigration process can have their status revoked and be ordered removed.[31]

---

28 *Immigration and Refugee Protection Act,* S.C. 2001, s. 34(1).
29 Barbara Jackman, "Charter Rights to Privacy and Security: The Impact of International Terrorism and Globalization: Impact on Charter Rights in Immigration Law," *National Journal of Constitutional Law* 19 (2005/2006): 236–7; *Criminal Code,* S.C., 1985, c. C-46, ss. 83.01(1)(b)(ii)(A).
30 *Immigration and Refugee Protection Act,* S.C. 2001, s. 35(1).
31 *Immigration and Refugee Protection Act,* S.C. 2001, ss. 28, 40, 41.

Process

If a permanent resident – or recognized refugee – is suspected of being inadmissible, an initial investigation is conducted by Immigration Refugees and Citizenship Canada and the Canadian Border Services Agency. Where these agencies believe there is enough evidence of a breach of law, the person will be instructed to appear at an admissibility hearing before the Immigration Division.

Detention Decisions

While awaiting an admissibility hearing the person can be detained if the government is of the view that the person may not appear at the hearing or is a danger to the public. Special provisions apply to minors, who can only be detained as a "measure of last resort."[32] Directives issued under the authority of the act elaborate that alternatives must always be considered, and if a minor is detained, it must be for the shortest duration possible and under appropriate conditions.[33]

Removal Order Hearings

Hearings before the Immigration Division are adversarial. The applicant can have legal representation, and the minister is represented by counsel for the Canada Border Services Agency. If found to be inadmissible, the person is ordered to be removed from Canada. If the person is not in Canada, the person will not be allowed to enter the country unless the decision is successfully overturned.

---

32 *Immigration and Refugee Protection Act*, S.C. 2001, s. 60.

33 For example, a detained parent or guardian may request that their child remain with them while in detention. This request can only be granted if the detaining officer determines that it is the best interests of the child and should be for the shortest time possible. Immigration and Refugee Protection Act Regulations, s. 248.1; Canadian Border Services Agency, "Arrests, Detentions and Removals – National Directive for the Detention or Housing of Minors," last updated 23 May 2024, https://www.cbsa-asfc.gc.ca/security-securite/detent/nddhm-dndhm-eng.html.

Decisions made by the Immigration Division can be appealed to the Immigration Appeal Division unless the person has been found to be inadmissible for reasons of serious criminality, organized crime, security, or violating human and international rights. The minister and the person concerned can seek leave of the Federal Court to review a decision by either division, but the person can be removed from Canada before their application is determined.

Prior to removal, the person can make an application for a Pre-Removal Risk Assessment to Immigration Refugees and Citizenship Canada. This assessment is for those who believe they would be at risk of persecution, torture, or cruel or unusual punishment if they return to the country of nationality.[34]

The application is determined by an immigration officer. Consideration entails whether there is more than "a mere possibility" that the person will face persecution, or it is "more likely than not" they would be at risk of their life, torture, or cruel and unusual treatment. If a person's Pre-Removal Risk Assessment application is approved, they receive protected status unless their removal order is based on serious criminality, organized criminality, human rights violations, or security concerns. In those cases, the removal order is stayed, but it is also subject to being reviewed again. Favourable Pre-Removal Risk Assessments are relatively rare.

If the person's Pre-Removal Risk Assessment is denied, the person can seek leave for judicial review from the Federal Court. But there is no right to remain in Canada until the court makes a decision.

The most controversial aspects of the removal process concern the detention provisions and restrictions on the rights of review of certain deportation decisions discussed below.

---

34 If deemed inadmissible on security or serious organized criminality grounds, the person cannot use the persecution basis for a Pre-Removal Risk Assessment. They can ask for a PRRA "only to screen for a substantial risk of death, torture, or cruel and unusual treatment or punishment." Graham Hudson, "Ordinary Injustices: Persecution, Punishment, and the Criminalization of Asylum in Canada," in *Immigration Policy in the Age of Punishment: Detention, Deportation, and Border Control*, ed. David C. Brotherton and Philip Kretsedemas (New York: Columbia University Press, 2018), 80.

Removal

Removal orders become enforceable once all legal recourses have been waived or exhausted. In 2020, the Auditor General released a report focusing on immigration removals, specifically assessing the Canadian Border Services Agency's handling of individuals under enforceable removal orders.

The findings revealed that the Agency's approach had not resulted in timely removals, leading to a backlog exceeding 50,000 cases. In "two thirds of these cases, the Agency did not know the whereabouts of the individual."[35] While certain situations hindered removals, such as specific medical needs of the person, perilous conditions in the country of origin, or lack of cooperation from those countries in accepting their nationals back, the primary causes for delayed removals were attributed to the management practices within the Canadian Border Services Agency. These issues included poor data quality, and deficiencies in information sharing with Immigration, Refugees, and Citizenship Canada.

Removal rates reportedly increased in 2023, although over half of those issued a deportation order between 2016 and mid-2023 remained in Canada. The immigration department explained that this was inevitable as individuals who are issued removal orders have the right to have the decision reviewed, and it can take time to exhaust all remedies. It is also the case that the government does not have formal exit controls, so it does not have accurate figures of how many people may have voluntarily left the country.[36]

Meanwhile, some advocates complain that too many people are being unfairly deported and they question why the government has not fulfilled a 2021 promise to regularize the status of

---

35 Auditor General of Canada, "Report 1," 3.
36 Marie Woolf, "Most Immigrants with Deportation Letters Are Still in Canada, CBSA Figures Show," *Globe and Mail*, 13 February 2024, https://www.theglobeandmail.com/politics/article-most-immigrants-with-deportation-letters-are-still-in-canada-cbsa/.

undocumented migrants in Canada who are contributing to Canadian communities.[37] Since then, successive ministers have said work is ongoing on a plan, with the minister indicating recently that it would not emerge soon due to disagreements within the Cabinet.[38]

Pre-Removal Detention: Length, Conditions, and Oversight

Most detention decisions must be reviewed by the Immigration Division of the Immigration and Refugee Board within forty-eight hours, then after seven days and every thirty days thereafter.[39] However, if a person is a "designated foreign national" or is named in a security certificate, ongoing reviews of their detention are only required every six months after the initial review.

The concept of a designated foreign national was introduced in 2012 by the Conservative government. It empowers the Minister of Public Safety to make such a designation if there are reasonable grounds to suspect that a person's arrival was associated with a

---

37   Holly McKenzie-Sutterholly, "Migrants across Canada Call on Ottawa for Action on Regularization, Permanent Status," *CTV News*, 18 September 2022, https://www.ctvnews.ca/canada/migrants-across-canada-call-on-ottawa-for-action-on-regularization-permanent-status-1.6073893; Jill Macyshon, "Canada Is Deporting More People Faster, Drawing Concern from Migrant Advocates," *CTV News*, 8 December 2023, https://www.ctvnews.ca/canada/canada-is-deporting-more-people-faster-drawing-concern-from-migrant-advocates-1.6678779.

38   Marie Woolf, "Ottawa Split on Plan to Let Undocumented Migrants Apply to Stay in Canada," *Globe and Mail*, 24 June 2024. The minister had announced in December 2023 that he would be presenting a plan to the Cabinet in the spring of 2024. Marie Woolf, "Ottawa Plans to Create Canadian Citizenship Path for Undocumented Immigrants," *Globe and Mail*, 14 December 2023, https://www.theglobeandmail.com/politics/article-canadas-immigration-minister-plans-broad-program-to-allow-immigrants/.

39   *Immigration and Refugee Protection Act*, S.C. 2001, s. 57 and s. 57.1; Canada Border Services Agency Government of Canada, "Detentions and Alternatives to Detention," last updated 30 May 2024, https://www.cbsa-asfc.gc.ca/security-securite/detent/menu-eng.html.

criminal organization or terrorist group involved in human smuggling.[40] The designated foreign national can be arrested without a warrant and detained. Under the Liberal government, the designation has fallen into disuse, yet it is retained in the legislation.

Detention hearings before the Immigration Division are adversarial. The detainee must be present and has the right to legal representation. The division has the authority to order the person released with or without conditions or to uphold the detention order. Detention decisions can be reviewed by the Federal Court with leave of the court. Detainees can also petition a provincial Superior Court to consider the validity of their detention.[41]

Between 2012 and 2020 more than 7,000 persons were detained annually. Detentions dropped during the COVID-19 pandemic, as detention was considered a major health risk. Numbers slowly rose again beginning in 2022, and over 5,200 persons were detained for immigration reasons in 2023.[42]

Over 80 per cent of immigration related detentions are based on the immigration officer's assessment that the person is unlikely to appear for an immigration proceeding.[43] Less than 1 per cent of detainees are detained because the person presents a danger to

---

40 As discussed in chapter 2.3: "Refugees," a designated foreign national also faces other restricted rights to review a negative decision on a claim to protection.

41 This is known as seeking habeas corpus relief. Persons detained for immigration infractions historically had been able to seek habeas corpus relief. This was curtailed by a 1989 Ontario Court of Appeal decision, which held that it could not be used to challenge an immigration matter addressed by a separate statutory scheme. However, in 2015 the Ontario Court of Appeal found that it had concurrent jurisdiction to review an indefinite detention. *Chaudhary v. Canada (Minister of Public Safety and Preparedness)* 2015 OR 127 (3rd) 401. This principle has since been upheld by the Supreme Court of Canada, *Canada (Public Safety and Emergency Preparedness) v. Chhina*, 2019 SCC 29. For a detailed discussion of these and subsequent cases, see Siena Anstis, Joshua Blum, and Jared Will, "Separate but Unequal: Immigration Detention in Canada and the Great Writ of Liberty," *McGill Law Journal* 63, no. 1 (2017), https://lawjournal.mcgill.ca /article/separate-but-unequal-immigration-detention-in-canada-and-the-great -writ-of-liberty/.

42 Canada Border Services Agency, "Annual Detention Statistics: 2012 to 2023," https://www.cbsa-asfc.gc.ca/security-securite/detent/stat-2012-2023-eng.html.

43 Canada Border Services Agency, "Annual Detention Statistics."

the public. Although proportionally smaller, persons considered a danger to the public can be detained indefinitely.

The length of detention between 2012 and 2023 fluctuated with an average of seventeen days. The number of detainees detained for over ninety-nine days fell from over 600 persons between 2013 and 2014 to 226 for the 2022–3 period. It is unclear if the fall in numbers was associated with COVID-19 precautions and therefore temporary.

Several aspects of the detention provisions have attracted considerable criticism.

Indefinite Detention

Unlike most high-income countries, Canada has no prohibition against indefinite detention.[44] Between April 2022 and April 2023, 226 individuals were detained for more than 99 days.[45] While this is a smaller number than in the 2012–16 period, critics say it is still higher than can reasonably be justified. Moreover, because there is no upper limit to immigration detention, some have been detained for several years.[46]

A Supreme Court of Canada ruling in 2007 in the case of *Charkaoui* considered in part the detention provisions of the *Immigration and Refugee Protection Act 2001*. The case involved one permanent resident and two recognized refugees detained for several years following the issuing of security certificates against them. The Court

---

44 Human Rights Watch and Amnesty International, *"I Didn't Feel Like a Human in There": Immigration Detention and the Impact on Human Health* (New York: Human Rights Watch, 2021), 5, https://www.hrw.org/sites/default/files /media_2021/06/canada0621_web.pdf; Rayer Thwaites, *The Liberty of Non-Citizens: Indefinite Detention in Commonwealth Countries* (Oxford: Hart Publishing, 2014). Thwaites argues that indefinite detention is contrary to principles of liberty and equality enshrined in the Canadian *Charter of Rights and Freedoms* and provides a comparative review of legal jurisprudence pertaining to detention of non-citizens in Australia, Canada, and the United States.

45 Canada Border Services Agency, "Annual Detention Statistics: 2012 to 2023."

46 Stephanie Silverman and Petra Molnar, "Everyday Injustices: Barriers to Access to Justice for Immigration Detainees in Canada," *Refugee Survey Quarterly* 35, no. 1 (2016): 116.

maintained the position it had earlier taken in *Chiarelli* – that deportation of a non-citizen did not "in itself" engage section 7 *Charter* rights – not to be deprived of life, liberty, and security of the person except in accordance with the principles of fundamental justice.

However, it found that "some features associated with deportation" may do so, such as detention, and the prospect of being subject to torture after removal.[47] The Court held that both the detention and security review procedures did not conform to the principles of fundamental justice. While indefinite detention could be constitutional, the detention review procedures were not. This is because they did not ensure consideration of the context and circumstances of the individual case and did not afford the detainee a meaningful opportunity to challenge the detention or the conditions of release.[48]

The Court provided examples of factors that the reviewing judge must consider. They included the length of the detention, the reasons for the delay in deportation, the anticipated future length of detention, as well as the availability of alternatives to detention. While the Court recognized that the procedures were not fair, legal commentators observed that, once again, the Court had narrowly defined rights of permanent residents and foreigners under the *Charter*. The decision in *Charkaoui* was also notable because it failed to take into consideration international law and norms concerning arbitrary detention, and interpretative guidance calling for detention to be necessary and proportionate.[49]

---

47   *Charkaoui v. Canada (Citizenship and Immigration)*, [2007] 1 SCR 350, 370.

48   *Charkaoui v. Canada (Citizenship and Immigration)*, 408.

49   As per the interpretative guidance of the United Nations Human Rights Committee regarding immigration detention and the obligations of states under the *International Covenant on Civil and Political Rights* (ICCPR). Moreover, as Catherine Dauvergne notes, the Court made several findings regarding the constitutionality of the security certificate process yet did not reference international law. This is an important omission in her view given their basis in well-established international instruments. It stresses that these rights have been extensively examined and discussed by various courts and international bodies. "This is particularly important because the core liberty rights at issue are reflected in the most well-established and long-standing international instruments that have also been interpreted and commented upon by a range of courts and international bodies." Catherine Dauvergne, "How the Charter Has Failed Non-Citizens in Canada: Reviewing Thirty Years of Supreme Court of Canada Jurisprudence," *McGill Law Journal* 58, no. 3 (2013): 696.

Detention Review

Despite the guidance provided by the Supreme Court of Canada in *Charkaoui*, scholars and advocates claim that detention review hearings continue to lack sufficient procedural safeguards, especially given the personal liberty issues at stake.[50] They argue that detainees are denied procedural fairness, since most of the evidence in support of detention is presented orally and based on hearsay. This denies the detainee a reasonable opportunity to respond. Advance disclosure is only required for documentary evidence, which is only rarely relied upon.

Critics also point to weakness in subsequent review hearings. If the initial detention review upholds the detention, the order is not reversed in subsequent reviews unless there is "clear and convincing evidence" demonstrating that detention is no longer warranted.[51] This means the detainee faces the burden to provide new evidence to justify release, rather than on the Canada Border Services Agency to establish that it remains necessary. Critics claim this means detention reviews tend to be perfunctory.

The Supreme Court has recognized that the scope of detention review under the *Immigration and Refugee Protection Act 2001* is narrower than what is available through a habeas corpus application. Habeas corpus relief is to protect individuals from unlawful deprivations of liberty by allowing them to go to a provincial superior court and demand justification for their detention. Courts are obliged to determine such applications quickly.

In its 2019 decision in *Chhina*, the Supreme Court noted that habeas corpus relief provided broader protections to individuals

---

50 Anstis et al., "Separate but Unequal," 7–12 ; Silverman and Molnar, "Everyday Injustices," 121–4; Human Rights Watch and Amnesty International, *"I Didn't Feel Like a Human,"* 14–15, 24, 31; Hanna Gros and Paloma van Groll, *"We have no Rights": Arbitrary Imprisonment and Cruel Treatment of Migrants with Mental Health Issues in Canada* (Toronto: University of Toronto International Human Rights Program, 2015), 5–6, 27–8, https://ihrp.law.utoronto.ca/We_Have_No_Rights.

51 The Federal Court jurisprudence for this is set out in Mannu Chowdhury, "Immigration Detention and Habeas Corpus: Positive Developments and Missed Opportunities in China," *Western Journal of Legal Studies* 10, no. 1 (2020): 10n84.

detained under the act. It required the government to show why ongoing detention was necessary, enabled a consideration of a broader set of factors, and was a timelier remedy. As a result, it upheld the right of detainees to challenge their ongoing detention through a habeas corpus application.[52]

Another concern about immigrant detention is that individuals detained for immigration reasons can be held in provincial jails and therefore housed with convicted and suspected criminals.[53] Canada has only three holding centres exclusively for immigration detainees located in British Columbia, Quebec, and Ontario. While these account for most detainees, between 16 and 40 per cent of others were held in provincial facilities between 2012 and 2023.[54]

Amnesty International and Human Rights Watch have urged Canada not to use provincial jails for immigration detention purposes.[55] They argue that there is less opportunity to ensure a common standard of care across different provincial institutions. However, advocates claim that often immigration detention centres themselves are like medium security prisons. Within them, detainees' privacy and liberties are severely restricted and telephone access is limited. This impedes contact with friends, family, and legal counsel. Immigration detainees reportedly have difficulty in securing legal aid services and translation services.[56]

---

52   *Canada (Public Safety and Emergency Preparedness) v. Chhina*, 2019 SCC 29, 494.

53   Anstis et al., "Separate but Unequal," 13–14.

54   Canada Border Services Agency Government of Canada, "Annual Detention Statistics: 2012 to 2023."

55   Amnesty International and Human Rights Watch, "Legal Analysis of Agreements Allowing Immigration Detention in Canadian Provincial Jails," 4 April 2022, https://www.hrw.org/news/2022/04/04/legal-analysis-agreements-allowing -immigration-detention-canadian-provincial-jails; Amnesty International, "Canada: Stop Incarcerating Immigration Detainees in Provincial Jails," 15 October 2021, https://www.amnesty.org/en/latest/news/2021/10/canada -stop-incarcerating-immigration-detainees-provincial-jails/.

56   Amnesty International and Human Rights Watch, *"I Didn't Feel Like a Human,"* 52–3; Hudson, "Ordinary Injustices," 80.

Provinces themselves have objected to holding immigration detainees in provincial institutions. Five provinces have stopped receiving immigrant detainees with the remaining announcing plans to do the same.[57]

A common critique – whether an immigration detainee is held in a dedicated immigration detention centre or a provincial jail – is the absence of a legal standard to guide where immigrants should be detained, and the absence of review of placement decisions.[58] The Immigration and Refugee Board does not have jurisdiction to review the appropriateness of the site of detention, or to order changes to the conditions under which an individual is held. As a result, immigration detainees have no recourse to appeal the decision to detain them at a particular site.

Legal and refugee advocates have also campaigned against the detention of refugees and protected persons. They point to international standards and guidance for the non-penalization of refugees who arrive without identity or travel documents. They also point to international norms for using detention only as a last resort, in exceptional circumstances, and where no alternatives exist.[59]

Amnesty International and Human Rights Watch claim in their study of Canada that many immigration detainees lose hope and become suicidal, especially refugee claimants fleeing traumatic experiences and persecution. Detention officials and Immigration Division adjudicators reportedly fail to recognize symptoms of poor mental health among immigration detainees. The situation

---

57 Nicholas Keung, "Every Canadian Province Has Now Agreed to Stop Keeping Immigration Detainees in Jail," *Toronto Star*, 21 March 2024, https://www.thestar.com/news/canada/every-canadian-province-has-now-agreed-to-stop-keeping-immigration-detainees-in-jail/article_1ce537fa-e6c7-1.

58 Amnesty International and Human Rights Watch, "Legal Analysis of Agreements."

59 Guy S. Goodwin-Gill, "Article 31 of the 1951 Convention Relating to the Status of Refugees: Non-Penalization, Detention, and Protection," in *Refugee Protection in International Law: UNHCR's Global Consultations on International Protection*, ed. Erika Feller, Volker Türk, and Frances Nicholson (Cambridge: Cambridge University Press, 2003), 184–252.

is aggravated in various centres where mental health professionals do not have regular access.[60]

Both human rights groups note that the Canada Border Services Agency is the only major law enforcement agency in Canada without independent civilian oversight.[61] They recommend that this be remedied by the creation of such an agency. We agree, given the powers of the Agency and the liberty issues at stake. Regarding detention, such an oversight body should have the authority to investigate complaints from detainees, legal counsel, civil society organizations, as well as conduct its own reviews and inspections.

We also support proposals to end indefinite detention. An outside limit on the length of detention should be imposed, as it has by many other industrialized countries. There should also be mechanisms to facilitate detainees access to legal aid services or other outside legal counsel.

Deportation: Limited Review and Consequences

The most transformational shift in Canadian deportation history was the creation of the Immigration Appeal Board, an independent review tribunal, set up in 1967 with a clarity of purpose and jurisdiction. The board could allow an appeal of a deportation order if it imposed undue hardship on the individual concerned, especially when assessed against the risk of harm the individual posed on society. The only exception to the board's jurisdiction was in cases where the individual was the subject of a security certificate.

Exceptions have since been expanded under the *Immigration and Refugee Protection Act 2001*, as noted earlier. The Immigration Appeal Division does not have jurisdiction to hear appeals of persons who were found inadmissible based on serious criminality, organized crime, security reasons, or for violating international humanitarian or human rights law.

---

60 Amnesty International and Human Rights Watch, *"I Didn't Feel Like a Human,"*
    3, 14, 35.
61 Amnesty International and Human Rights Watch, *"I Didn't Feel Like a Human,"* 79.

The Supreme Court of Canada has maintained that this restricted right of appeal is constitutional. In a 2005 case – *Medovarski* – the Court found that the act reflected a shift in priorities. The limited appeal rights of permanent residents for certain inadmissibility grounds, "communicate a strong desire to treat criminals and security threats less leniently than under the former Act."[62] As in the 1992 case of *Chiarelli*, the Court in *Medovarski* maintained that deportation of a non-citizen "cannot in itself implicate the liberty and security interests protected by [section] 7 of the Canadian *Charter of Rights and Freedoms*."

The limitations in the act and the Supreme Court of Canada jurisprudence have attracted significant and sustained critical commentary, as noted below.

Humanitarian and Compassionate Considerations

For instance, the elimination of the Immigration Appeal Division's jurisdiction to hear appeals against many deportation orders removes the opportunity to assess humanitarian and compassionate considerations that could militate against deportation. It eliminates the right to a consideration of a range of pertinent factors, including the seriousness of the actions that prompted the deportation order, the duration of the person's residence in Canada, the availability of support in the home country, the impact on dependent children, and other mitigating circumstances, including mental health issues that might have contributed to the reasons for removal.

Moreover, for removal decisions for serious criminality there is no regard to the gravity of the offence, whether it is a first offence, when it was committed and the degree to which the person may have rehabilitated.[63]

Removal to the country of origin can be to a place where the person has not resided in many years – including since early childhood – and where they may not have family or other support systems to

---

62　*Medovarski v. Canada (Minister of Citizenship and Immigration); Esteban v. Canada (Minister of Citizenship and Immigration)*, [2005] 2 S.C.R. 539, at 546.
63　Canadian Bar Association, "Bill C-43," 8.

help them re-establish themselves. It can also result in removal to countries where they face significant risk to life and security. For example, they are excluded from benefiting from a policy that suspends removals to countries considered dangerous, due to factors like armed conflict or environmental disasters.[64] Furthermore, judicial decisions have upheld the legality of removing individuals who, as decided by the minister, pose a danger to the public, even to situations where they could be at risk of torture.[65]

Without considering humanitarian and compassionate factors, it is not possible to properly evaluate the potential risk an individual poses to Canadian society compared to the harm deportation may inflict upon them and their family. Consequently, advocates contend that deportation is frequently and disproportionately harsh.

Fair Processes

Since the *Immigration and Refugee Protection Act 2001* came into force in 2002, the Supreme Court of Canada has again considered restricted appeal rights for individuals ordered deported who were also named in security certificates. Initially, the security certificate process under the act provided no opportunity for the person concerned to know the basis on which the certificate was issued, nor a meaningful opportunity for the person to respond.[66]

This was part of the constitutional challenge considered in the *Charkaoui* case, in addition to the detention review provisions discussed earlier in this chapter. The Supreme Court found that the non-disclosure provisions of the act compromised the right of a fair review. The Court held that the greater the impact on

---

64 The Administrative Deferral of Removals (ADR) temporarily defers removal in situations of humanitarian crisis. Canadian Border Security Services, "Removal from Canada," last updated 27 April 2023, https://www.cbsa-asfc.gc.ca/security -securite/rem-ren-eng.html.

65 For a review of these cases, see Graham Hudson, "As Good as it Gets? Security, Asylum, and the Rule of Law after the Certificate Trilogy," *Osgoode Hall Law Journal* 52, no. 3 (2016): 905–50.

66 This was a notable omission following the *Suresh* decision even though that case addressed provisions in the previous *Immigration Act*.

the life of the individual, "the greater the need for procedural protections to meet the common-law duty of fairness and the requirements of fundamental justice under [section] 7 of the Charter."[67]

It noted that a review before the Federal Court took place in a closed hearing, where the person concerned did not have a right to be present or to know the information upon which the security certificate was issued. In determining the reasonableness of the certificate, the Federal Court was limited to the government's evidence. As a result, the judge was required to make a ruling in the absence of all possible relevant evidence.[68] The Supreme Court decided that this amounted to an infringement of the right to fundamental justice, which could not reasonably be justified. It pointed to alternatives available to the government that infringe less on the rights of the individual concerned.[69] The Court provided as an example the use of security-cleared lawyers to act on the person's behalf in the closed hearing.

Because of the Supreme Court's decision, the act was amended in 2008. The review of security certificates remains with the Federal Court in closed hearings – and the person concerned does not have a right to be present – or to receive all the evidence upon which the certificate is based. However, the person does have the right to receive an unclassified summary of the case and can be represented by a lawyer.

The amendments provide for special advocates, appointed by the government, to protect the interest of the person, who is the subject of a security certificate, at appeal or at other immigration proceedings held in private or in the absence of their lawyer.[70] This can include inadmissibility or deportation review proceedings where the government relies on information that it says it cannot disclose without risking national security or endangering the safety of someone.

---

67 *Charkaoui v. Canada (Citizenship and Immigration)*, [2007] 1 SCR, 373, quoting from the decision in *Suresh v. Canada (Minister of Citizenship and Immigration)*.
68 *Charkaoui v. Canada (Citizenship and Immigration)*, 355.
69 *Charkaoui v. Canada (Citizenship and Immigration)*, 392–7.
70 *Immigration and Refugee Protection Act*, S.C. 2001, s. 85.

Special advocates are private lawyers with security clearance. They are entitled to review the classified information but cannot reveal the contents to the person concerned. They may not communicate with the person named in the security certificate after reviewing the classified material unless authorized by the presiding judge. The special advocate can challenge the non-disclosure of evidence and its relevance, reliability, and sufficiency before the Federal Court.[71]

The constitutional propriety of the revised process was also challenged in the courts. It was ultimately upheld by the Supreme Court of Canada in the 2014 case of *Harkat*.[72] Harkat was one of the recognized refugees from Algeria who successfully challenged the constitutionality of the detention and security certificate regime in the 2007 case of *Charkaoui*. Once the government had subsequently revised the provisions, Harkat was again named in a security certificate and deportation proceedings commenced.

Harkat claimed that as a recognized refugee he faced a serious risk of torture and/or death if deported to Algeria. He argued that he had been denied a fair hearing in the Federal Court's review of the security certificate issued against him.

Several issues were raised in the *Harkat* case, largely centring on whether the person named in the certificate had received sufficient information to ensure a fair hearing. Parts of the government's case relied on hearsay evidence and information provided by confidential sources. Summaries had been provided to Harkat, but the government had destroyed the original notes and interviews. A request by the special advocate to cross-examine the government's sources was denied.

The Supreme Court held it was up to the judge reviewing the certificate to ensure that the named person receives sufficient evidence. As part of this obligation, the judge must ensure that only evidence that raises a serious risk of injury or poses a risk to

---

71 *Immigration and Refugee Protection Act*, S.C. 2001, s. 85.
72 *Canada (Citizenship and Immigration) v. Harkat*, 2014 SCC 37.

national security or safety can be withheld. However, the Supreme Court found that the evidence provided to Harkat was sufficient to satisfy his right to know – and meet – the case against him.[73] It instructed judges to "be vigilant and skeptical with respect to the Minister's claims of confidentiality."[74]

A leading legal scholar of Canadian immigration law, Graham Hudson, acknowledges that the Supreme Court's decisions on security certificates have improved standards of due process protections. But he also points out that there are many other areas in removal proceedings where protected information is often relied upon. These include inadmissibility hearings, detention reviews, and judicial reviews, especially concerning security-based removals.[75] And while the act authorizes the Immigration and Refugee Board and/or relevant judge to appoint a special advocate in such cases, this is discretionary, as is the judge's decision on the information that must be disclosed to the person concerned.[76] This does not lead to consistency in decision-making.

Deportation to Torture

The Supreme Court of Canada's 2002 decision in *Suresh* underscored that where deportation to torture was under consideration, the person must be informed of the case to be met, subject to privilege and other valid reasons for limited disclosure. The Court acknowledged that international law prohibits deportation to torture. But it concluded that it could be constitutional in Canada nevertheless, in exceptional circumstances, including when the person poses a danger to national security.

The Court did not specify what would count as an "exceptional circumstance." It held that "danger to the security of Canada" in deportation legislation must be given a "fair, large and liberal

---

73   For a detailed review of this case and its relationship to other Supreme Court of Canada decisions, see Hudson, "As Good as it Gets?"
74   *Canada (Citizenship and Immigration) v. Harkat*, 44.
75   Hudson, "As Good as it Gets?," 1n4.
76   *Immigration and Refugee Protection Act*, S.C. 2001, s. 83(1)(c.2).

interpretation in accordance with international norms."[77] The Court was clear that such a determination is "fact-based and political" and entitled to deference.[78]

The month before the Supreme Court of Canada's decision in *Suresh*, unfolding events in another case were to have broad significance. The case involved Maher Arar, a Canadian citizen of Syrian birth, who was detained in the United States while in transit there and deported to Syria. He was removed based on unfounded suspicions linking him to terrorist groups. In Syria, he was held in prison for over eleven months and tortured, before he was eventually returned to Canada.

In 2005 Justice Dennis O'Connor was appointed to conduct an inquiry into the case. He found that Canadian law enforcement agencies shared incorrect information with the American government that may have played a role in Maher Arar's deportation and his subsequent mistreatment in Syria. He also found that Maher Arar was innocent of the allegations made against him. He recommended the implementation of improved review and accountability mechanisms for all agencies involved in matters of national security.[79]

Subsequently, the government commissioned former Supreme Court Justice Frank Iacobucci to lead an internal inquiry into the actions of Canadian officials in relation to the detention and mistreatment of three Arab Canadians abroad. Held about a year after the Arar inquiry, Commissioner Iacobucci found that Canadian officials had sent inaccurate and inflammatory intelligence to US and Middle East agencies wrongly labelling the Canadians as imminent threats. This indirectly resulted in the torture of the Canadians in Syria and Egypt.[80]

---

77 *Suresh v. Canada (Minister of Citizenship and Immigration)*, 47.

78 *Suresh v. Canada (Minister of Citizenship and Immigration)*, 49.

79 Commissioner Dennis O'Connor, *Report of the Events Relating to Maher Arar: Analysis and Recommendations*, 3 vols. (Ottawa: Public Works and Government Services Canada, 2006). A brief summary of the recommendations is found in Garry Breitkreuz, *Review of the Findings and Recommendations of the Iacobucci and O'Connor Inquiries* (Ottawa: House of Commons Canada, 2009), https://www.ourcommons.ca/Content/Committee/402/SECU/Reports/RP4004074/securp03/securp03-e.pdf.

80 Commissioner Frank Iacobucci, *Internal Inquiry into the Actions of Canadian Officials in Relation to Abdullah Almalki, Ahmed Abou-Elmaati and Muayyed Nureddin*

The Canadians that were the focus of the inquiries received formal apologies from the federal government in addition to compensation. But it took years to implement the more rigorous institutional oversight recommended by the commissions.

In 2017, legislation was passed that established the National Security and Intelligence Committee of Parliamentarians.[81] It is made up of representatives from the House of Commons and the Senate. It reviews the regulatory, policy, administrative and financial framework related to national security and intelligence, issuing regular reports on its findings.

In 2019, the Office of the National Security and Intelligence Review Agency was established. It is an independent body that reviews all government national security and intelligence activities "to ensure that they are lawful, reasonable and necessary."[82] It also investigates complaints against national security agencies.

The impact of these two institutions on how security-related intelligence affects deportation decisions is not yet clear. In the meantime, legal advocates and scholars, who are familiar with the impact of security-based allegations in removal order decisions and judicial review proceedings, claim that deportation from Canada in the context of potential torture is not as exceptional as one might expect.[83] And the risks are exacerbated by several factors.

One factor is a lack of consistency within the Federal Court regarding how it decides whether to allow a judicial review. The consequences of being denied a judicial review can be grave for those being removed to places where their lives or security may be at risk.[84] A second factor is that there have also been several instances where the Federal Court has refused to grant a stay of

---

(Ottawa: Public Works and Government Services Canada, 2008), https://publications.gc.ca/site/eng/9.699757/publication.html.

81   *National Security and Intelligence Committee of Parliamentarians Act*, S.C. 2017, c. 15.

82   *National Security and Intelligence Review Agency Act*, S.C. 2019, c. 13, s. 2; National Security Review Agency, "What We Do," last updated 6 October 2023, https://www.nsira-ossnr.gc.ca/what-we-do.

83   For a more detailed review of this issue, see Hudson, "As Good as it Gets?"

84   Sean Rehaag, "Judicial Review of Refugee Determinations: The Luck of the Draw?," *Queen's Law Journal* 38, no. 1 (2012): 1–58.

removal pending a review, even when requested by the United Nations Committee Against Torture.[85]

A third factor is that the individual who is at risk of torture must substantiate the claim with evidence concerning the human rights record in their country of nationality and their personal risk. This is a difficult burden to bear, especially for those who may be in detention or otherwise lack the resources to retain counsel. The deference accorded to the minister's opinion on whether the person has established a substantial risk of torture also makes it difficult to challenge. The Federal Court will only intervene if the opinion is unreasonable.

Among suggestions for reform are ensuring greater disclosure of evidence to the person concerned in inadmissibility proceedings, refugee determination hearings, and detention reviews. This could be through more consistent use of the special advocate system. Another aspect to reconsider is the level of judicial deference granted to ministerial discretion in determining whether an individual has demonstrated that deportation would expose them to a credible risk of torture.[86]

Proportionality: Towards a More Balanced Approach

Deportation has always been a component of Canadian immigration policy. It is a part of the sovereign right of the state to control who is allowed to enter, remain, and become a full citizen. For most of Canada's immigration history, immigrants admitted to the country and wishing to remain permanently had to acquire domicile, that is, continued residence for several years. Prior to this,

---

85 The UN Committee against Torture (CAT) is the body of ten independent experts that monitors implementation of the *Convention against Torture and Other Cruel, Inhuman or Degrading Treatment or Punishment* by its states parties. According to Hudson, "As Good as it Gets?," in "three cases Canada deported persons despite the fact that the UN CAT found there to be a substantial risk of torture" (27).

86 Hudson, "As Good as it Gets?," 26–7.

they could be deported for a wide range of reasons and with few due process protections. Deportation grounds were biased along political, social, and moral lines. Removals were carried out without regard for the consequences upon the person concerned.

The *Immigration Act, 1967* was a major watershed moment in the history of deportation from Canada. For the first time deportation orders could be reviewed by an independent appeal tribunal on questions of law and fact and on humanitarian and compassionate grounds. This helped to address the many unduly harsh consequences of previous deportation practice.

Further changes to immigration law in the 1970s specified in more detail the conduct that could lead to deportation via making a person inadmissible. The concept of domicile was removed from the *Immigration Act, 1976,* which meant that permanent residents could be deported from Canada regardless of how long they had lived in the country. The potential harshness of this open-ended vulnerability was tempered by the ability to appeal a removal order based on legal or factual errors as well on humanitarian and compassionate grounds. This enabled the consideration of mitigating factors and the ability to balance the consequences to the individual against the public interest in their removal.

Since the *Immigration and Refugee Protection Act 2001* came into force, the progressive evolution of deportation measures has been largely halted and even regressed in several respects. The grounds have been widened considerably, capturing those that pose a serious risk to others, as well as those whose removal seems to be more punitive in nature.

Today, deportation is more likely to amount to a disproportionate response than it was forty years ago, with the elimination of the jurisdiction of the Immigration Appeal Division to review a wide range of deportation orders. The change has been largely supported by jurisprudence at the Supreme Court of Canada. In the post–9/11 world, significant deference has been given to the government to determine who should be removed for constituting a security threat and a danger to the public. The individuals concerned have a reduced ability to contest the basis of such assessment, or to have the risks of harm that they face considered.

Scholars have noted that while the Supreme Court of Canada has been guided by international law in detention and removal cases involving citizens, it has been less inclined to follow it for decisions concerning foreigners and permanent residents.[87] This is noteworthy as Canada is a signatory to treaties for the protection of human rights, including some which prohibit arbitrary and indefinite detention, as well as some that prohibit removal to countries where a person faces a serious risk of torture or other forms of ill-treatment.[88]

Academics and legal advocates have also noted the ways the Supreme Court has limited the application of the *Canadian Charter of Rights and Freedoms* to non-citizens. This is evident in cases where the Court has been clear that deportation may not trigger the person's *Charter* right not to be "deprived of liberty or security of the person unless in accordance with fundamental justice." Even in situations where the right is triggered, the Court has tended to define the requirements of fundamental justice in a manner that does not guarantee the person access to full details over the case they must answer, especially if based on privileged information.

Deportation serves a valid purpose. But over the past decades, the grounds for it have been widened so far that they can now cover relatively minor infractions as well as serious violations of the law. Most importantly, the changes over the past twenty years have severely limited the scope to consider whether deportation is a proportionate response in the individual case. A person who

---

87   Dauvergne, "How the Charter Has Failed," 724. According to Dauvergne's examination spanning over thirty years of Supreme Court of Canada jurisprudence, the Court has not rendered "a single ruling in the *Charter* era that directly applies an international human rights norm to a non-citizen in Canada," with the exception of the *International Refugee Convention* (724).

88   Dauvergne, "How the Charter Has Failed," 696. Dauvergne notes that non-citizens are "required to make their arguments first and foremost in Charter terms and only secondarily in international human rights terms." She further observes that this puts non-citizens in Canada "in a different position than those in England, Australia, New Zealand, and even in some circumstances, the United States. This different position has become a worse position over time" (675).

has lived in Canada all their life, who was convicted of a criminal offence sometime in their past and has strong ties to Canada is not the same as a terrorist operative who has come to Canada to commit an act of terrorism. Provisions in deportation laws should distinguish between them.

We are of the view that deportation provisions and their associated detention practices require an in-depth, independent, and transparent review, as with many other areas of immigration policy. And for that, comprehensive data are required. The data should include specifics such as the annual count of individuals deported, the percentage of permanent residents among them, the duration of their residency in Canada, and the reasons for their removal.

Additionally, a thorough review ought to focus on rectifying the delays associated with individuals subject to enforceable removal orders, considering the Auditor General's 2020 recommendations aimed at enhancing the removal process.

Integration: Short-Term Programs, Long-Term Barriers

The successful integration of immigrants into society is vital to unlocking the benefits of immigration for the country and for the well-being of the people involved. Canada's policy is specifically designed to select the immigrants most likely to do well in a new life. Nevertheless, many of the people it chooses face difficulty in bridging gaps between their country of origin and their new life in Canada.

There are many sources of friction. It can come not only from the distinct characteristics of immigrants, in terms of their human and social capital, but also from differences in almost every human characteristic: language, culture, physical appearance, and dress. Individuals arrive having been shaped in a variety of ways by a series of forces that may or may not make for an easy transition into the Canadian setting. They have been formed by the influence of educational institutions, social practices, political processes, and economic organizations. Each person and each characteristic will have been rooted in distinctive national historical experiences.

This makes for a challenging context in which policy must operate – and one in which immigrant "integration" must be defined carefully. In this chapter, we examine which of Canada's policies encourage it and their effectiveness.

Government Responsibility for Immigrant Integration

Our focus is on immigrant integration policies in place since the passage of the *Immigration and Refugee Protection Act 2001*. The act mandates efforts to "promote the successful integration of permanent residents into Canada."[1]

Policies from Immigration and Citizenship Canada provide much needed aid to persons as they settle into Canada, including help in searching for housing and employment, and training in Canada's official languages. Collectively, these are known as "settlement programs," providing for relatively short-term needs of immigrants after their arrival. They are available to those who have not become citizens, mainly permanent residents. Immigration and Citizenship Canada's management of access to citizenship, mandated under the *Citizenship Act*,[2] is discussed in a separate chapter.

Broader policies – including over human rights, multiculturalism, and employment equity – have defined Canada's political discourse on immigrant integration, and to a considerable extent its international reputation in welcoming immigrants. These policies follow legislation separate from the *Immigration and Refugee Protection Act 2001*,[3] and collectively address aspects of integration which go beyond the limited scope of "settlement programs" it mandates. They respond to a concept of "integration" that envisions equality of participation in mainstream Canadian institutions for permanent residents and citizens, and also for their descendants. There is recognition in multiculturalism policy that maintenance of ancestral cultures may be part of successfully becoming "Canadian." And constitutional provisions in the *Canadian Charter of Rights and Freedoms* also relate both to multiculturalism and equality, and they too bear upon aspects of immigrant integration.

The objectives of the *Immigration and Refugee Protection Act 2001* also recognize these broader aspects that can help define success in integration. Its first two are "to pursue the maximum social, cultural and economic benefits of immigration,"[4] and "to enrich and strengthen the social and cultural fabric of Canadian society, while respecting

---

1   *Immigration and Refugee Protection Act*, S.C, 2001, c. 27, s. 3(1)(e).
2   Passed in 1985, frequently amended. *Citizenship Act*, R.S.C., 1985, c. C-29.
3   *Canadian Human Rights Act*, R.S.C., 1985, c. H-6; *Canadian Multiculturalism Act*, R.S.C., 1985, c. 24; *Employment Equity Act*, S.C. 1995, c. 44.
4   *Immigration and Refugee Protection Act*, S.C. 2001, s. 3 (1) (a).

the federal, bilingual and multicultural character of Canada."[5] As the legislation puts it, "integration involves mutual obligations for new immigrants and Canadian society." This implies that any feature of society may become a facilitator of – or an obstacle to – integration.

At the broadest level, immigrant integration may be affected by economic fluctuations, and the general structure of mainstream institutions and policies, such as public investment in education, the regulation of the labour market, and the provision of social welfare. These factors produce variations in immigrant integration across societies.[6] Within Canada, they change over time.[7] For example, weakening labour market protections for workers, resulting in part from technological change and globalization, may create increasing economic inequality, with distinctive effects on immigrants. Mainstream institutional policies are not generally seen as part of "integration policy," but they nevertheless may affect the difficulties immigrants face in making their way in Canada.

Clearly, the scope of policy-making affecting immigrant integration includes the mandates of the *Immigration and Refugee Protection Act 2001*. But is also considerably wider and more complex.

We begin by reviewing Canada's historical record of integrating immigrants prior to 2001, as this was shaped by the changing international environment. We see how integration raised distinctive issues for Canada's two linguistic communities, which were also affected by changes over time in the characteristics and origins of immigrants.

Our description of policy includes shorter-term settlement programs – which address the immediate needs of immigrants starting a new life in Canada – and broader policies such as those relating to equality rights and multiculturalism. We also consider the impact of wider institutional change, especially the trend towards greater economic inequality.

---

5   *Immigration and Refugee Protection Act*, S.C. 2001, s. 3 (1) (b).
6   See the review by Richard Alba and Nancy Foner, *Strangers No More: Immigration and the Challenges of Integration in North America and Western Europe* (Princeton, NJ: Princeton University Press, 2015), esp. 10–11, on "political economy" as one of the "grand narratives" in theories of immigrant integration. See also Reitz, *Warmth of the Welcome*.
7   Reitz, "Immigrant Employment Success in Canada," esp. 30–1.

We then provide a review of what is known about the impact of these policies and institutional shifts on immigrant integration. We discuss how access to citizenship affects other dimensions of integration. Debates over multiculturalism and the status of "visible minorities" often overshadow both settlement programs and the impact of policies affecting broader institutional changes, but the latter have not necessarily been less important in shaping the integration of immigrants in Canada.

Government in-house evaluations focus mainly on settlement services and include descriptions of those services and opinions of program clients. These aspects comply with Treasury Board requirements to ensure that expected outcomes of specific policies and programs are met as planned.[8] However, Canadians will also want to know the extent to which a program has a positive impact on immigrant integration overall. In addressing these issues, data from the census, labour force surveys, and special surveys, including academic publications based on these sources, can help in describing processes of immigrant integration across large populations as these may be affected or not by citizenship and integration policies over time.

Context

Over the course of Canada's experience with immigration, the question of whether or not immigrants will become good Canadians has been a constant one. Such questions are common to all countries experiencing significant immigration. Often, these concerns fade and ultimately disappear over time. Successful integration of past immigrants may even become part of a very positive, evolving national identity. Yet new waves of immigrants may have different characteristics, leading to new concerns about their integration.

A variety of terms have been used to describe the process by which immigrants become full members of society and to specify

---

8 Treasury Board of Canada, "Policy on Results," last updated 1 July 2016, https://www.tbs-sct.canada.ca/pol/doc-eng.aspx?id=31300.

what that means. Social scientists have used words such as integration, incorporation, assimilation, and acculturation. Descriptions of undesirable outcomes include marginalization and segmented assimilation. While Canada's current immigration legislation includes immigrant "integration" as an important objective, it leaves the term undefined. The previous *Immigration Act, 1976* used the word "adaptation," also without definition. Immigration, Refugees and Citizenship Canada has focused primarily on the immediate settlement needs of immigrants, and on citizenship, leaving broader aspects of integration to other government agencies operating under other legislative mandates.

Canada's Record in Welcoming Immigrants

Nineteenth-century Canadian immigration policy favoured those of British or French origins. Europeans from other parts of the continent were also recruited. But many of them – especially East Europeans and South Europeans – faced opposition on the grounds that they would detract from the character of Canadian society. In a 1909 publication that was perhaps symptomatic of the times, the progressive federal politician, labour activist, and Methodist minister James Shaver Woodsworth wrote a book called *Strangers within Our Gates, Or, Coming Canadians,*[9] which expressed serious reservations about immigrants based on negative ethnic and racial stereotypes.[10]

In the case of immigrants from Europe, subsequent experiences of integration have made the earlier concerns seem narrow-minded, if not outright bigoted. Extensive analysis of census data up to 1971 has shown that ethnic affiliations counted for little in producing inequalities of social class.[11] Despite discriminatory treatment of some, immigrants from most European origins have fared well in

---

9 James Shaver Woodsworth, *Strangers Within Our Gates, or, Coming Canadians* (1909; reprint, Toronto: University of Toronto Press, 1972). See also "Part 1: An Historical Reprise" in this volume.

10 For details and related accounts, see Reitz, *Survival of Ethnic Groups,* 5–6 ff.

11 A. Gordon Darroch, "Another Look at Ethnicity, Stratification and Social Mobility in Canada," *Canadian Journal of Sociology / Cahiers Canadiens de Sociologie* 4, no. 1 (1979): 1.

Canada, and rates of economic mobility over time have not varied greatly among groups with different origins in Europe.

Before the immigration policy reforms of the 1960s, admission of persons of non-European origins was restricted or tightly controlled, including the admission of Chinese, Japanese, other Asians, and Black people, as well as Jewish people.[12] However, unlike the evidence of successful integration of immigrants from various origins within Europe, there is little doubt that for immigrants from non-European origins, economic mobility and other aspects of integration were affected by their origins.

Government services for immigrants in the nineteenth century – when immigration was sought to populate agricultural regions in the Prairie provinces – consisted of ad hoc arrangements to assist immigrants in settling and working in the areas where they were most needed.[13] Local groups, including employers, were involved. In urban areas, immigrants themselves tended to turn for support to their own ethnic community, and where possible, to ethnic service organizations within it.[14]

Citizenship and Immigration Canada launched its official Immigrant Settlement and Adaptation Program in 1974 with a defined mandate.[15] A range of services were provided, including reception

---

12 See, for example, Robin Winks, *The Blacks in Canada: A History* (Montreal: McGill-Queen's University Press, 1971); James Morton, *In the Sea of Sterile Mountains: The Chinese in British Columbia* (Toronto: J.J. Douglas, Ltd., 1974); Abella and Troper, *None Is Too Many*.

13 Robert Vineberg, *Responding to Immigrants' Settlement Needs: The Canadian Experience* (New York: Springer, 2012). See also Kelley and Trebilcock, *Making of the Mosaic*.

14 For example, the Italian Immigrant Aid Society in Toronto was formed in 1952, based in religious organizations. COSTI is also an Italian organization, founded in 1961 to help workers unable to find employment using their trade skills. Canadian Council for Refugees, "Best Settlement Practices: Settlement Services for Refugees and Immigrants in Canada," February 1998, https://ccrweb.ca /sites/ccrweb.ca/files/static-files/bpfinal.htm#:~:text=In%201974%20the%20 federal%20government,Newcomers%20to%20Canada%20(LINC).

15 Vineberg, *Responding to Immigrants' Settlement Needs*, chap. 4; Citizenship and Immigration Canada, *Evaluation of the Immigrant Settlement and Adaptation Program (ISAP)* (Ottawa: Citizenship and Immigration Canada, 2011), https://www .canada.ca/content/dam/ircc/migration/ircc/english/pdf/research-stats /evaluation-isap2011.pdf.

facilities, language training, and assistance with employment. Over the years, this program has relied on the collaboration of community and ethnic immigrant organizations to provide settlement services to new immigrants.

Thus, the department responsible for managing levels of immigration – and the blend of skills and experience it was bringing in – was also charged with oversight of the most immediate needs of immigrants during the settlement process. But the broader and longer-term aspects of integration policy emerged separately, under the rubrics of human rights, multiculturalism, and employment equity. These policies, discussed below, were authorized by different legislation, and became the responsibility of other government departments.

Roots of Multiculturalism Policy in Canada

Multiculturalism policy was first introduced in 1971, and, at that time, it was largely unknown to most Canadians. When it came up, it did so in the context of a resurgence of French identity in Quebec and other parts of Canada. The Royal Commission on Bilingualism and Biculturalism, appointed by the Lester B. Pearson government in the mid-1960s, also covered the cultural contributions of other groups.

One of the commission's conclusions was that the *Official Languages Act* of 1969 that recognized English and French as the two official languages of Canada would receive the most support if the cultural aspirations of other groups were supported via a policy of multiculturalism. Ukrainians were among its strongest advocates, but support also came from other cultural minorities, mainly of European origins at the time.[16]

---

16 In 1971, non-European origins groups comprised just 2.3 per cent of the Canadian population. Those of British- and French-origin were 73.3 per cent of the population, and other European origins were 23.0 per cent. The remaining 1.5 per cent were "Aboriginal" peoples. Peter S. Li, *Cultural Diversity in Canada: The Social Construction of Racial Difference* (Ottawa: Department of Justice Canada, 2000), https://www.justice.gc.ca/eng/rp-pr/csj-sjc/jsp-sjp/rp02_8-dr02_8/rp02_8.pdf.

Many French Canadians saw multiculturalism policy as a setback to their own aspirations in the country. Provincial governments in Quebec have not accepted multiculturalism policy. Quebec's programs for integrating immigrants have emphasized both French language and French-Canadian culture.

Multiculturalism policy, as articulated by Prime Minister Pierre Trudeau, was a declaration of official recognition of cultural minorities in Canada, alongside an affirmation of the goals of equal treatment and integration into the mainstream.[17] Most Canadians expected that support would be provided in ways that did not affect mainstream institutions, including education, the media, or the provision of public services. Budgets for supporting cultural groups, and "heritage language" programs have always been small. Trudeau went on to create a new Ministry of Multiculturalism and spearheaded efforts at constitutional reform. This led, in 1982, to the adoption of what would become one of the pillars of the country's written constitution, the *Canadian Charter of Rights and Freedoms*. The *Charter*, in section 15, enshrines the right to equal protection and equal benefit of the law without discrimination based on race, national or ethnic origin, or gender. Section 27 provides that the *Charter* shall be interpreted in a manner consistent with the preservation and enhancement of the multicultural heritage of Canadians.

Equality rights under the *Charter* apply to "everyone," regardless of immigrant status. Extending equality rights so broadly may reach, to some extent, beyond public opinion. Not all members of the public believe that new immigrants have the same right to a job

---

17 Trudeau's oft-quoted 1971 speech in the House of Commons stated that multi-culturalism was the best means of "assuring the cultural freedom of Canadians." The goals of equity and integration are shown in his four specific government actions: support for cultural groups showing "a desire and effort" to "contribute to Canada"; overcoming barriers to "full participation" in Canadian society; promoting "creative encounters" among cultural groups "in the interest of national unity"; and supporting immigrants to acquire one of the official languages. Canada, Parliament *House of Commons Debates*, 28th Parl., 3rd Sess. (Vol. 8) (October 8, 1971), 8545–46. https://parl.canadiana.ca/view/oop.debates _HOC2803_08/811.

as native-born Canadians, for example, though acknowledgment of this right is greater for immigrants who have been in the country for longer periods of time.[18]

The *Canadian Multiculturalism Act* of 1988, enacted under the Mulroney Conservative government, in turn recognized multiculturalism as a fundamental characteristic of Canadian heritage and identity. It seeks to promote the full and equitable participation of all individuals and communities in Canadian society. Although today many Canadians see multiculturalism as part of their national identity,[19] opposition to it was expressed openly from the 1970s to the 1990s. Prominent academics and writers expressed scepticism. Eminent sociologist John Porter – who in 1965 had famously described Canada as a "Vertical Mosaic"[20] in which ethnic divisions helped maintain inequality – became an early opponent of multiculturalism in the 1970s.

Reginald Bibby, in his 1990 book, *Mosaic Madness*,[21] saw multiculturalism as an outgrowth of a toxic moral relativism. So did Richard Gwyn in *Nationalism without Walls: The Unbearable Lightness of Being Canadian* (1995).[22] The American historian Arthur Schlesinger suggested in his book *The Disuniting of America: Reflections on a Multicultural Society* (1992)[23] that multiculturalism had failed in Canada, as evidenced by the sovereigntist movement in Quebec.

Multiculturalism was originally focused on cultural retention issues among groups of European origin. It came under stress in the 1980s when increasing immigration from non-European origins had produced a substantial demographic impact. As a result,

---

18 Joseph Carens, *The Ethics of Immigration* (Oxford: Oxford University Press, 2013).

19 Michael Adams, *Unlikely Utopia: The Surprising Triumph of Canadian Pluralism* (Toronto: Viking Canada, 2007).

20 John Porter, *The Vertical Mosaic: An Analysis of Social Class and Power in Canada* (Toronto: University of Toronto Press, 1965).

21 Reginald Bibby, *Mosaic Madness: Pluralism without a Cause* (Toronto: Stoddart, 1990).

22 Richard J. Gwyn, *Nationalism without Walls: The Unbearable Lightness of Being Canadian* (Toronto: McClelland and Stewart, 1995).

23 Arthur M. Schlesinger, *The Disuniting of America: Reflections on a Multicultural Society* (New York: W.W. Norton & Co., 1998).

multicultural issues began to reflect concerns about discrimination and inequality more often affecting persons of non-European origins. Officially, the term "visible minorities" enabled government to avoid the term "race," but eventually an anti-racism component of multiculturalism policy was introduced in the late 1980s.

Criticism of multiculturalism was strengthened in a 1994 book by Neil Bissoondath, a Trinidadian-Canadian novelist living in Quebec. *Selling Illusions: The Cult of Multiculturalism in Canada* received considerable public and government attention.[24] Bissoondath argued that multiculturalism had limited his career by encouraging people to think of him primarily as a representative of a minority group, rather than as a general novelist with broader appeal. On the other hand, at about the same time, an eloquent defence of minority cultural rights by Canadian philosopher Will Kymlicka in his book *Multicultural Citizenship: A Liberal Theory of Minority Rights* became very influential internationally,[25] and may have helped tip the balance in favour of multiculturalism policy in Canada.

The concentration of numerous immigrant groups in the suburbs of Toronto, Montreal, and Vancouver – often with pivotal swing ridings in federal elections – has meant that none of the major federal political parties could afford to adopt strong anti-immigrant policy platforms.[26] Whatever else, the debate over multiculturalism has been wide-ranging,[27] and includes assertions about impacts on immigrant integration, positive and negative, which are not carefully tested with evidence.[28] Canada's multiculturalism policy has endured, and public support for the policy is understood as

---

24 Neil Bissoondath, *Selling Illusions: The Cult of Multiculturalism in Canada* (Toronto: Penguin Books, 1994).

25 Will Kymlicka, *Multicultural Citizenship: A Liberal Theory of Minority Rights* (Toronto: Oxford University Press, 1996).

26 Trebilcock, "The Puzzle of Canadian Exceptionalism."

27 Trebilcock, "The Puzzle of Canadian Exceptionalism," esp. 840–4.

28 Jeffrey G. Reitz, "Popular Multiculturalism as Social Capital: Trends and Prospects," in "Multiculturalism @50 and the Promise of a Just Society," special issue, *Canadian Issues* (Fall/Winter 2021): 39–44, https://acs-metropolis.ca/wp-content/uploads/2021/10/663_AEC-CITC_EN_V6_Web-1-1.pdf.

a general affirmation of goodwill towards immigrant minorities and their cultures.[29] But neither the policy nor public support for it are enough, necessarily, to improve immigrant integration or to address racial discrimination. Hence, their net effect on immigrant integration could be quite small.

The economic status of immigrants in Canada is clearly better than in some other countries of immigration, including the United States. But comparative evidence suggests that this difference is mostly explained by immigrant selection, and to some extent less overall inequality, not less discrimination.[30] Patterns of discriminatory disadvantage do not appear to vary consistently across countries of immigration, including Canada.[31] We return to this issue when discussing the contemporary period later in this chapter.

Human Rights and Employment Equity

Protection for equal rights and against discrimination has been part of Canadian law for decades. It has covered factors that affect immigrants, including race, national origin, colour, and religion, but enforcement has always been an issue. These protections were embodied in the *Canadian Bill of Rights*, enacted in 1960, after provinces had passed laws relating to human rights, employment, incomes, and housing, from as early as 1947.[32]

The *Canadian Human Rights Act* of 1977 extended these protections and set them out more specifically. Human rights commissions at federal and provincial levels provide a complaint-driven

---

29 Possibly forestalling an anti-immigration backlash as seen in other countries; cf. Keith Banting, "Multiculturalism Policy in Canada: Conflicted and Resilient," in *Policy Success in Canada: Cases, Lessons, Challenges*, ed. Evert Lindquist, Michael Howlett, Grace Skogstad, Geneviève Tellier, and Paul 't Hart (New York: Oxford University Press, 2022), 183–205.

30 Jeffrey G. Reitz and Raymond Breton, *The Illusion of Difference: Realities of Ethnicity in Canada and the United States* (Toronto: C.D. Howe Institute, 1994); Reitz, *Warmth of the Welcome*.

31 Alba and Foner, *Strangers No More*.

32 Morris Davis and Joseph F. Krauter, eds., *The Other Canadians: Profiles of Six Minorities* (Toronto: Methuen, 1971), 123.

process for addressing discrimination, an important idea, but they are notoriously incapable of addressing everyday racism in society.

In 1986, the federal government passed its *Employment Equity Act*. It requires large employers under federal jurisdiction to review their workforce to ascertain whether designated groups are adequately represented, and where necessary, to adopt measures to improve representation. Designated groups include "visible minorities" among three others targeted for assistance: women, the disabled, and Indigenous peoples. Provisions for enforcement are quite weak in that they rely primarily on public pressure for change. One government minister at the time called this "a persuasive rather than a coercive approach," sufficient because Canadians show more goodwill towards minorities than what is seen in other countries, as evidenced for example by its multiculturalism policies.[33]

The term "visible minorities" had been introduced in the 1980s to refer to groups of non-European origins, and a parliamentary report entitled *Equality Now!*[34] called attention to the inequities many members of those groups experienced. Visible minorities include both immigrants and the descendants of immigrants who identify with a visible minority.

The *Employment Equity Act* exists only in the federal jurisdiction, and thus affects less than 10 per cent of the workforce. In 1996, the federal public service became subject to it. The objectives and procedures embodied in the act have not been adopted in any provincial jurisdiction.

"Affirmative action" was addressed in the *Charter of Rights and Freedoms*. It stated that policies to improve the condition of disadvantaged persons should not be prevented by laws covering

---

33 Jeffrey G. Reitz, "Less Racial Discrimination in Canada, or Simply Less Racial Conflict?: Implications of Comparisons with Britain," *Canadian Public Policy* 14, no. 4 (1988): 425.

34 Bob Daudlin, *Equality Now! Report of the Special Committee on Visible Minorities in Canadian Society* (Ottawa: Department of Supply and Services Canada, 1984), https://parl.canadiana.ca/view/oop.com_HOC_3202_15_2.

equality and mobility rights.[35] This provision has not been used to extend affirmative action for immigrants or racialized minorities, including at the provincial level. An *Employment Equity Act* was adopted in Ontario in 1993, covering visible minorities as in the federal law. This act was likened to "race quotas"[36] by the subsequent Ontario Progressive Conservative government of Mike Harris, and was repealed as one of the first actions taken following its election in 1995.

Reviews of the *Employment Equity* Act are mandated to occur every five years. One of them, published in 2002,[37] revealed the weakness of equity enforcement criteria. It found that visible minority "representation" was assessed essentially as an overall employment rate only. No distinction was drawn along the lines of occupational skill levels or remuneration. As a result, no inferences regarding equality of opportunity can be drawn.

Representation of visible minorities improved over the period 1987 to 2000 in the federally regulated private sector – including banking, transportation, communications, and most Crown corporations – though change in the federal public service[38] has been slower. Independent research has shown that the federal *Employment Equity Act* has had modest positive impacts,

---

35 Section 15 of the *Charter* sets forth "Equality Rights," with two subsections. Subsection 1 entitled "Equality before and under law and equal protection and benefit of law" describes the equality rights themselves, and subsection 2 entitled "Affirmative action programs" states that "Subsection (1) does not preclude any law, program or activity that has as its object the amelioration of conditions of disadvantaged individuals or groups including those that are disadvantaged because of race, national or ethnic origin, colour, religion, sex, age or mental or physical disability." *Canadian Charter of Rights and Freedoms*, https://laws-lois.justice.gc.ca/eng/const/page-12.html.

36 *Job Quotas Repeal Act*, 1995 (Bill 8), https://www.ola.org/en/legislative-business/bills/parliament-36/session-1/bill-8.

37 Judi Longfield, *Promoting Equality in the Federal Jurisdiction: Review of the Employment Equity Act. Report of the Standing Committee on Human Resources Development and the Status of Persons with Disabilities* (Ottawa: Public Works and Government Services Canada, 2022), https://www.ourcommons.ca/DocumentViewer/en/37-1/HUMA/report-9/.

38 Longfield, *Promoting Equality in the Federal Jurisdiction*, chap. 1.

though substantial disadvantages remain in key areas, including management.[39]

In 2005, the Liberal government of Paul Martin announced its "National Action Plan against Racism."[40] The accompanying document, published by the Department of Canadian Heritage, attempted to be comprehensive. It presented evidence of racism in the country affecting immigrants, visible minorities, and Indigenous peoples, and listed a series of measures to address it. Many such measures were already part of Canadian policy in various departments, including not only Canadian Heritage but also Justice Canada, Citizenship and Immigration Canada, Health Canada, Human Resources and Skills Development Canada, among others.

Immigrants in the Emerging Knowledge Economy

In our chapter on the economic stream, we discussed the impact that technological change and the emerging knowledge economy has had on immigrant selection since the 1960s. We also described the difficulties posed by obstacles to recognition of immigrants' foreign education and work experience. Other labour market challenges, such as globalization and technological innovation, also appear to have affected both immigrants and the Canadian-born population, making labour market entry more difficult.[41]

In the two decades prior to 2001, the poverty rate among newly arriving immigrants and their families rose relative to the Canadian-born population, in part because of the changing economic

---

39 Harish Jain and John J. Lawler, "Visible Minorities Under the Canadian Employment Equity Act, 1987–1999," *Relations Industrielles/Industrial Relations* 59, no. 3 (2004): 585–611.

40 Department of Canadian Heritage, *A Canada for All: Canada's Action Plan against Racism* (Ottawa: Public Works and Government Services Canada, 2005), https:// publications.gc.ca/collections/Collection/CH34-7-2005E.pdf. See also Vineberg, *Responding to Immigrants' Settlement Needs*, 61.

41 Green and Worswick, "Entry Earnings of Immigrant Men in Canada."

environment.[42] These economic trends potentially affect the social, cultural, and political integration of immigrants. They set the stage for related provisions in the immigration legislation passed in 2001.[43]

Relevant Legislative Provisions

The *Immigration and Refugee Protection Act 2001* mandates efforts to "promote the successful integration of permanent residents into Canada,"[44] but leaves the term "integration" undefined. Policies of the department of Immigration, Refugees and Citizenship Canada have addressed the integration objective mainly by providing for the most immediate needs of immigrants, as outlined earlier in this chapter. It provides settlement services and official language training to all permanent residents. Broader integration objectives are reflected in the policies that Immigration, Refugees and Citizenship Canada uses to select candidates for immigration based on their ability to become "established" in Canada.[45] It leaves other aspects to other government policies and programs.

There is an exception: the act's objective to work with provinces to remove barriers to immigrant employment arising from inadequate recognition of foreign credentials.[46] At the time the

---

42 Eden Crossman, *Low-Income and Immigration: An Overview and Future Directions for Research* (Ottawa: Citizenship and Immigration Canada, 2013), https://www.canada.ca/content/dam/ircc/migration/ircc/english/resources/research/documents/pdf/r21-2012-low-income-ec-eng.pdf. The author states that the term "low income" is equivalent to an indicator of "poverty," 6.

43 Crossman, *Low-Income and Immigration*, 4. "Many immigration policy changes have taken place since 2002, starting with the implementation of the Immigration and Refugee Protection Act (IRPA), and it is important to understand how these changes have influenced the income situation of recent immigrants" (4).

44 *Immigration and Refugee Protection Act*, S.C. 2001, s. 3(c).

45 *Immigration and Refugee Protection Act*, S.C. 2001, s. 12(2)

46 *Immigration and Refugee Protection Act*, S.C. 2001, s. 3 (j). Objective (j) is "to work in cooperation with the provinces to secure better recognition of the foreign credentials of permanent residents and their more rapid integration into society." This wording also implies that citizens would not be among those whose further integration is a priority, but as will be seen, most integration policies target all immigrants, not only those who have not acquired citizenship. This is the only specific policy priority explicitly linked to the work "integration."

legislation was passed, this was a salient issue. Since employment is constitutionally a provincial responsibility, the act limits federal actions to collaboration with the provinces.

In the sections that follow, we first address settlement programs mainly covered under provisions of the act, and then address the broader policies mandated under other legislation during the same time period. Evaluation of the impact of these policies is discussed, where relevant analyses are available. A separate section considers the overall picture of immigrant integration in Canada today, identifying successes, and noting potential priority areas for future policy.

Settlement Services

Settlement services can be grouped into three broad categories: employment-related services; those related to development of skills in an official language; and services providing immigrants with information, orientation, and referrals that may help them find housing, employment, and social services in the community. Internationally, Canada is thought of as having a quite extensive and robust set of immigrant settlement services.[47] Nonetheless, providing a description and assessment of them is an extremely complex task. In some respects, it is impossible.

One reason for this difficulty is the prevalence of local initiatives. Many of the federal government's specific programs are operated by a variety of entities, selected in a competitive grants process. Each has its own specific goals and activities. These include social service agencies, educational institutions, community ethnic or civic organizations, and health care

---

47   Myer Siemiatycki and Triadafilos Triadafilopoulos, "International Perspectives on Immigrant Service Provision" (Toronto: Mowat Centre for Policy Innovation, 2010); John Shields, Julie Drolet, and Karla Valenzuela, *Immigrant Settlement and Integration Services and the Role of Nonprofit Providers: A Cross-National Perspective on Trends, Issues and Evidence*, RICS Working Paper No. 2016/1 (Toronto: Ryerson Centre for Immigration and Settlement, 2016); Jessica Praznik and John Shields, *An Anatomy of Settlement Services in Canada: A Guide* (Toronto: Ryerson University, 2018).

organizations. They vary in size and in the range of services. Many organizations provide a variety of services, including those related to information and orientation, language, and employment. Language instruction services have relatively standardized procedures and criteria of operation, while information and referral services, or related social programs, may have little or no standardization.

Policy is also decentralized. While Immigration, Refugees and Citizenship Canada is the most prominent federal agency responsible for immigrant integration, others have relevant policies and programs, including those related to multiculturalism and human rights. Quebec handles its own system of immigrant settlement, guided by its priorities for interculturalism and integration of immigrants into francophone society, and with significant financial contributions from the federal government as defined by the Quebec-Canada Accord relating to immigration.[48] Other provincial governments have their own relevant policies. Municipalities are also active. These policies are interconnected in various ways, and Immigration, Refugees and Citizenship Canada provides grants to other levels of government in support of their policies.

As a result, these programs lack any clearly stated common objectives that could be used to assess either their goals or their actual outcomes. As immigration numbers rise, so do settlement costs. Overall budget trends for settlement programs are difficult to identify, because of the complexity of funding, and the multiplicity of sources.

Concerns have been expressed that federal government allocations for settlement funding do not match provincial needs – particularly as immigration numbers have increased – and that the overall financial viability of organizations providing settlement

---

48 Canada–Québec Accord relating to Immigration and Temporary Admission of Aliens, 5 February 1991, https://www.canada.ca/en/immigration-refugees -citizenship/corporate/mandate/policies-operational-instructions-agreements /agreements/federal-provincial-territorial/quebec/canada-quebec-accord -relating-immigration-temporary-admission-aliens.html.

services has been weakened by rising costs and reductions in other government programs, at both the federal and provincial levels.[49] Addressing this, federal-provincial immigration agreements have included provisions related to budgets for immigration services. For 2023–6, the federal government plans to spend more than $2 billion annually for grants and contributions to settlement services, up from the roughly $1.5 billion announced for 2019–22.[50]

Overall Evaluation

Evaluation studies find that while many immigrants use settlement services, many do not.[51] Use tends to occur in the first few years after arrival, more often by refugees and sponsored family members than by economic immigrants or their dependents. Women use the services more often than men. Information and referral services were the most-used category of settlement services, followed by language training. Employment services, considered a

---

49 Sophia Lowe, Ted Richmond, and John Shields, "Settling on Austerity: ISAs, Immigrant Communities and Neoliberal Restructuring," *Alternate Routes: A Journal of Critical Social Research* 28 (2017): 14–46. See also chapter 2.2: "Family Sponsorship: Raising Requirements."

50 Sean Fraser, *Immigration, Refugees and Citizenship Canada 2023–2024 Departmental Plan* (Ottawa: Immigration, Refugees and Citizenship Canada, 2023), 51, https://www.canada.ca/en/immigration-refugees-citizenship/corporate/publications-manuals/departmental-plan-2023-2024/departmental-plan.html; Ahmed Hussen, *Immigration, Refugees and Citizenship Canada Departmental Plan 2019–2020* (Ottawa: Immigration, Refugees and Citizenship Canada, 2019), 24, https://www.canada.ca/en/immigration-refugees-citizenship/corporate/publications-manuals/departmental-plan-2019-2020/departmental-plan.html.

51 About 50 per cent of adult immigrants admitted between 2016 and 2020 used at least one federally funded settlement service. See Statistics Canada, "Settlement Services Provided to Immigrants to Canada, 2020," *The Daily*, 2 June 2022, https://www150.statcan.gc.ca/n1/daily-quotidien/220602/dq220602e-eng.htm. See also Immigration, Refugees and Citizenship Canada, *Evaluation of the Immigrant Settlement and Adaptation Program (ISAP)*, 20–1; and Immigration, Refugees and Citizenship Canada, *Evaluation of the Settlement Program* (Ottawa: Immigration, Refugees and Citizenship Canada, 2017), 8–9, https://www.canada.ca/en/immigration-refugees-citizenship/corporate/reports-statistics/evaluations/settlement-program.html.

provincial responsibility, were least frequently used, though their impact may be greater than this suggests.[52]

Levels of satisfaction with services among those who use them are high. In surveys conducted among service recipients as part of government evaluation studies, appreciation is expressed for the support and help they have received. What is not known is whether services meet the most pressing needs of immigrants, and what role settlement services play in the overall process of immigrant integration. While the existing programs are arguably significant, there may well be important unmet needs.

We do not know why many immigrants do not use government funded services, or whether their needs are being met through other means, for example drawing on informal resources in their community.[53] Just as the COVID-19 pandemic impacted the admission of immigrants, it also affected settlement services, including the shift from direct in-person delivery to hybrid service delivery. As a result, there has been an opening up of access to services in traditionally underserved areas, and at the same time the creation of new staffing concerns for service providers. Learning from this experience will be helpful, not least as part of responding to the expansion of immigration numbers.[54]

Language Assessment and Training

Language training is distinctive among settlement services in that it is managed by Immigration, Refugees and Citizenship Canada through contribution agreements with service-providing

---

52 Statistics Canada, "Settlement Services Provided to Immigrants to Canada, 2020."

53 There is also the issue of settlement services being offered to primary applicants but not necessarily to other family members. See chapter 2.2: "Family Sponsorship: Raising Requirements," and specifically the section "Family: A Cornerstone of Effective Integration."

54 Victoria Esses et al., "Supporting Canada's COVID-19 Resilience and Recovery through Robust Immigration Policy and Programs," *FACETS* 6, no. 1 (2021): 686–759, https://doi.org/10.1139/facets-2021-0014; Ashika Niraula, Anna Triandafyllidou, and Marshia Akbar, "Navigating Uncertainties: Evaluating the Shift in Canadian Immigration Policies during the COVID-19 Pandemic," *Canadian Public Policy* 48, no. S1 (2022): 49–59, https://doi.org/10.3138/cpp.2022-010.

organizations. The agreements are intended to ensure that national priorities and standards are maintained, while accommodating regional and local needs. The language training facilities are identified nationally as Language Instruction for Newcomers to Canada, or "LINC," in English. The French equivalent is Cours de langue pour immigrants au Canada, or "CLIC."

Despite a standardized language knowledge test for most immigrant applicants, many immigrants begin life in Canada lacking fluency in an official language, particularly refugees or family class immigrants.[55] Evaluation data on immigrants arriving between 2015 and 2017 indicate that about one in four immigrants received language assessments, and about 18 per cent took some form of language training after arrival.[56] These tended to be less educated persons and those lacking work permits. Language training, though costly relative to other settlement services, undoubtedly helps immigrants to be better prepared for economic and social integration in Canada. Nonetheless, evaluations conducted by the government have not proven the extent of the contribution.

Those who enrol in language courses have lower levels of language knowledge, which does improve over the course of instruction, particularly in reading and writing. Whether they have learned more than those not in language instruction remains a critical issue.[57] Longitudinal survey data show that time spent in

---

55   Immigration, Refugees and Citizenship Canada, *Evaluation of Language Training Services 2020* (Ottawa: Immigration, Refugees and Citizenship Canada, 2020), 24, https://www.canada.ca/content/dam/ircc/documents/pdf/english/corporate/reports-statistics/evaluations/E4-2018_LanguageTrain_Eng.pdf.

56   Immigration, Refugees and Citizenship Canada, *Evaluation of Language Training Services 2020*, 23.

57   Citizenship and Immigration Canada, *Evaluation of the Language Instruction for Newcomers to Canada (LINC) Program* (Ottawa: Citizenship and Immigration Canada, 2010), 32–6, https://www.canada.ca/content/dam/ircc/migration/ircc/english/resources/evaluation/linc/2010/linc-eval.pdf. The 2020 evaluation showed no difference in objective measures of language knowledge progression in the short-term for those in LINC classes, though subjective measures over the longer term showed better results for those having taken LINC classes. See Immigration, Refugees and Citizenship Canada, *Evaluation of Language Training Services 2020*, 48.

language courses yields higher wages in later employment, particularly for the highly skilled.[58] The longitudinal survey covered immigrants arriving in 2000–1 and followed three waves through the next four years.

Employment Services and Credential Recognition

When the *Immigration and Refugee Protection Act 2001* was passed, the issue of foreign credential recognition had taken on added importance. It is acknowledged in one of the act's objectives, and it was the only specific policy priority explicitly linked to the word "integration."[59] The Liberal government quickly established a "Foreign Credential Recognition Program" with a modest $68 million budget.[60] Deferring to provincial responsibility for employment, the federal program has been limited to promoting national standards, and sponsoring projects to improve practices across the country. Employment counselling services also make referrals to provincial credential recognition services.

Immigrant selection has been part of the effort to address the problem of foreign credential recognition. Shortly after winning the federal election in 2006, the Conservative government launched an effort to improve immigrant employment with several revisions to selection policy, as described in the chapter on the economic stream. One of its initiatives, introduced in 2013, was to verify the Canadian equivalence of prospective immigrants' educational credentials before approving applications for permanent

---

58 George Orlov, "The Impact of Language Training on the Transfer of Pre-Immigration Skills and the Wages of Immigrants," *SSRN Electronic Journal*, 2018, https://ssrn.com/abstract=3412195.

59 The act's objective (j) is "to work in cooperation with the provinces to secure better recognition of the foreign credentials of permanent residents and their more rapid integration into society." This wording also implies that citizens would not be among those whose further integration is a priority, but as will be seen, most integration policies target all immigrants, not only those who are permanent residents rather than citizens.

60 Vineberg, *Responding to Immigrants' Settlement Needs*, 57.

residence.[61] Experience showed that selecting immigrants based on the Canadian equivalence of their qualifications led to better labour market integration. But even after the policy was implemented, new immigrants remained underemployed, particularly those who came from outside Europe.[62] This indicates that there remains a need to improve employer recognition of immigrant qualifications.

Reviews are available for the Foreign Credential Referral Office in 2013, and the Foreign Credential Recognition Program in 2020.[63] The Foreign Credential Referral Office directs immigrants to relevant services and is administered as part of Immigration, Refugees and Citizenship Canada. The Foreign Credential Recognition Program funds provincial and territorial governments and other organizations in support of credential recognition, including efforts to harmonize procedures across Canada, and is under Employment and Social Development Canada.

Reviews noted that for the nursing profession, some aspects of foreign credential assessments were harmonized, but that significant inconsistencies remained. They also noted that while national harmonization would increase the mobility of immigrants, an inherent difficulty in coordinating provincial credential recognition processes arises because of their distinctive regulatory regimes.

---

61 Jeffrey G. Reitz, "Canada: New Initiatives and Approaches to Immigration and Nation-Building," in *Controlling Immigration: A Global Perspective*, ed. James F. Hollifield, Philip L. Martin, and Pia M. Orrenius, 3rd ed. (Stanford, CA: Stanford University Press, 2014), 88–116; Reitz, "Canada: Continuity and Change in Immigration for Nation-Building"; Rupa Banerjee, "Introduction to the Special Issue: Canada's Economic Immigration Policy: Opportunities and Challenges for the Road Ahead," *Journal of International Migration and Integration* 24, Supplement 3 (2023): 585–97, https://doi.org/10.1007/s12134-023-01068-y; Ferrer, Picot, and Riddell, "New Directions in Immigration Policy."

62 Banerjee et al., "Evaluating Foreign Skills."

63 Citizenship and Immigration Canada, *Evaluation of the Foreign Credentials Referral Office* (Ottawa: Citizenship and Immigration Canada, 2013), https://www.canada.ca/content/dam/ircc/migration/ircc/english/pdf/pub/fcro-eng.pdf; Employment and Social Development Canada, *Evaluation of the Foreign Credential Recognition Program: Report*.

Integration Policies and Programs under Other Legislation

Popularity and Limited Effects of Multiculturalism

During the last two decades, while several countries in Europe staged a "retreat of multiculturalism,"[64] the majority of Canadians continue to support the policy. And yet over the same time, developments in Canada regarding multiculturalism have focused mainly on whether there is need to reinforce support for mainstream culture.[65] The history of multiculturalism in Canada suggests its popular significance does not mean it can generate new initiatives to address racial inequalities.[66] This has been borne out in more recent experience. Multiculturalism in Canada is popular as a symbol of national distinctiveness but there is a lack of any clear evidence that this support improves immigrant integration.

In the federal jurisdiction, some changes were made by the Harper Conservative government to reinforce mainstream culture, only to be reversed by the subsequent Trudeau Liberal government. Regarding the *Zero Tolerance for Barbaric Cultural Practices Act* in 2015, the Conservative government's immigration minister Chris Alexander stated, "We need to stand up for our values ... We need to do that in citizenship ceremonies. We need to do that to protect women and girls from forced marriage and other barbaric practices."[67] The offensive feature of the legislation, referring to the proscribed barbaric practices already illegal under other legislation as "cultural," was repealed by the subsequent Liberal government.

---

64 Christian Joppke, "The Retreat of Multiculturalism in the Liberal State: Theory and Policy," *British Journal of Sociology* 55, no. 2 (2004): 237–57, https://doi.org/10.1111/j.1468-4446.2004.00017.x.

65 See also Abu-Laban, Tungohan, and Gabriel, *Containing Diversity*.

66 Reitz, "Popular Multiculturalism as Social Capital."

67 John Barber, "Canada's Conservatives Vow to Create 'Barbaric Cultural Practices' Hotline," *The Guardian*, 2 October 2015, https://www.theguardian.com/world/2015/oct/02/canada-conservatives-barbaric-cultural-practices-hotline.

Beginning in 2010, the Conservative government strengthened requirements for acquiring Canadian citizenship, including those related to language and knowledge of Canada, and raised the fees for citizenship applications significantly. The rate of naturalization in the country reportedly declined markedly as a result.[68] These moves reflect a relative reluctance among many Conservative Party supporters to embrace immigration. But this is rooted in their conservative social values rather than in negative views on the economic impact of immigration.[69] The Conservative government deferred to its supporters' social conservatism by emphasizing more restrictive views on multicultural issues, while maintaining the previous Liberal government's commitment to numbers of immigrants, possibly because of support for immigration among business leaders.

Concern about whether immigrants accept mainstream values is also reflected in public attitudes towards Muslims. A major survey showed that two-thirds of Canadians in 2010 agreed that "there are too many immigrants coming into this country who are not adopting Canadian values," and a majority said that Muslims "want to be distinct from the larger Canadian society." In Quebec, this perception of Muslims as a threat to collective values is stronger, leading to majority support for banning Muslim women from wearing a headscarf in public places.[70] A provincial commission set to investigate the question of what constitutes "reasonable accommodation" of minority religious practices submitted a report in 2007, with recommendations aimed at reconciliation of inter-group differences.[71]

---

68   Andrew Griffith, "What the Census Tells Us about Citizenship," *Toronto Star*, 20 March 2018, https://policyoptions.irpp.org/magazines/march-2018/what-the-census-tells-us-about-citizenship/. See also chapter 3.3, "Citizenship: Raising the Bar" and specifically the section "Tightening the Requirements: 2010–2022."

69   Reitz, *Pro-Immigration Canada*.

70   Reitz, *Pro-Immigration Canada*, 15–16.

71   Gérard Bouchard and Charles Taylor, *Building the Future: A Time for Reconciliation* (Quebec: Commission de consultation sur les pratiques d'accommodement reliées aux différences culturelles, 2007).

The report received extensive coverage but did little to promote cultural flexibility in Quebec. In 2019 the province adopted measures to highlight its secular nature with the *Act respecting the laicity of the State* (Bill 21),[72] prohibiting the wearing of the headscarf and other religious symbols by certain public employees. While no other province has taken such a measure, this debate in Quebec has echoes across Canada.

Understanding of the impact of multiculturalism in Canada is aided by comparisons with other countries that lack such a policy. Most comparative analyses have expressed scepticism that multiculturalism policy has much influence on immigrant integration.[73] Compared to other countries, immigrant integration in Canada generally is assessed in more positive terms; however, the difference seems mainly due to more effective immigrant selection rather than to multiculturalism policies.

A Multiculturalism Policy Index has been developed which ranks countries according to the robustness of policies considered supportive of multiculturalism.[74] The index includes an affirmation of the principle of multiculturalism in policy as well as seven others: school curriculum, media, exemption of minorities from dress codes, dual citizenship, funding of ethnic groups, bilingual education, and affirmative action. Compilation of policy data across countries shows that when all of the components are considered, despite the alleged "retreat" from multiculturalism, most

---

72 *Act respecting the laicity of the State*, chapter L-0.3, https://www.legisquebec.gouv
    .qc.ca/en/document/cs/l-0.3.
73 See Rogier van Reekum, Jan Willem Duyvendak, and Christoph Bertossi, "National
    Models of Integration and the Crisis of Multiculturalism: A Critical Comparative
    Perspective," *Patterns of Prejudice* 46, no. 5 (2012): 417–538, https://doi.org/10.1080
    /0031322X.2012.718162. The effort to include a wider range of policies in the mix
    resulted in the creation of the more general Migrant Integration Policy Index
    (https://www.mipex.eu), but it also has not been shown to relate directly to immi-
    grant integration outcomes.
74 Will Kymlicka, *Multiculturalism: Success, Failure, and the Future* (Washington, DC:
    Migration Policy Institute, 2012); Keith Banting, Richard Johnston, Will Kymlicka,
    and Stuart Soroka, "Do Multiculturalism Policies Erode the Welfare State? An
    Empirical Analysis," in *Multiculturalism and the Welfare State*, ed. Keith Banting
    and Will Kymlicka (Oxford: Oxford University Press, 2006), 48–91.

countries with significant immigrant populations have strengthened their multiculturalism policies over past decades. Overall, Canada has been rated highly for its multiculturalism policies but was downgraded in 2010 for adopting dress codes for minorities.[75]

Canada's "Action Plan Against Racism" introduced in 2005 has not been abandoned, but it is seriously neglected. It still exists within the Department of Canadian Heritage. However, the plan to ensure continuity and reports on progress has not materialized. The most recent plan, released in 2019,[76] reads very much like the one published in 2005. It too emphasizes the need for a government-wide plan and lists a series of measures the government is taking to address racism. There is little reference to past activities or to attempts to assess progress. The 2019 plan included a new "anti-racism secretariat," but the initial annual budget of $11.2 million shrank to about $1.5 million.[77]

From Visible Minorities to Racialized Canadians

Policies to address racial inequality and discrimination have advanced little in recent years. As mentioned, though Employment Equity legislation mandates reviews every five years, after the review published in 2002,[78] there was a two-decade hiatus. In

---

75 Rebecca Wallace, Erin Tolley, and Madison Vonk, *Multiculturalism Policy Index: Immigrant Minority Policies, Third Edition* (Kingston: School of Policy Studies, Queen's University, 2021), https://www.queensu.ca/mcp/sites/mcpwww/files/uploaded_files/immigrantminorities/evidence/Immigrant%20Minorities%20Index%20Evidence%202021-Web0122.pdf. The index is debatable both for what it includes and how countries are rated. The inclusion of affirmative action as part of multiculturalism seems out of step with popular Canadian views, since multiculturalism is popular in Canada, while employment equity is not. And rating Canada highly for its employment equity policies seems inappropriate given the limited applicability of Canadian employment equity policy, as described above.

76 Department of Canadian Heritage, *Building a Foundation for Change: Canada's Anti-Racism Strategy* (Ottawa: Canadian Heritage, 2019), https://www.canada.ca/en/canadian-heritage/services/combatting-racism-discrimination/anti-racism-strategy-2019-2022.html.

77 The 2005 plan allocated $56 million over five years (see above); the 2019 plan indicated a budget of $4.6 million for the three-year period 2019–22.

78 Longfield, *Promoting Equality in the Federal Jurisdiction.*

2022, a new review task force was commissioned, and its report was released in 2023.[79]

Official terminology has become part of the debate. The term "visible minorities," introduced to avoid the language of race, has come under attack. The United Nations Committee on the Elimination of Racial Discrimination has said the phrase is discriminatory and recommended that Canada reconsider its use of the term.[80] Recently, Statistics Canada has begun to use the term "racialized minorities" in its publications. Whereas the term "visible minority" reflects the perspective of the dominant population, using the term "racialized" minority reflects an acknowledgment that race is a category imposed by a dominant population.

One objection to the term "visible minorities" has been that it is too broad, ignoring the distinctive experiences of specific racialized groups such as Black people, Chinese, and others. However, in this respect the definition of "racialized" minority has been identical to the definition of "visible minority." To address the objection, it will be necessary to consistently distinguish among racialized groups with distinctive experiences in Canada.

In response to the recent Employment Equity Review released in December 2023, the government indicated support for the Task Force recommendation to treat Black workers (as well as

---

79 Adelle Blackett, *A Transformative Framework to Achieve and Sustain Employment Equity: A Report of the Employment Equity Act Review Task Force* (Ottawa: Employment and Social Development Canada, 2023), https://www.canada.ca /content/dam/esdc-edsc/documents/corporate/portfolio/labour/programs /employment-equity/reports/act-review-task-force/EEA-Review-Task-Force -Report-2023-v2.pdf. The Public Service Alliance of Canada, one of Canada's largest unions, and with a long history of engagement with employment equity policy, released a report on its consultations with the Task Force. See Public Service Alliance of Canada, "Employment Equity Act Review Report: What We Heard," 2022, https://psacunion.ca/sites/psac/files/2022-psac-employmentequityactreview _en_0.pdf.

80 CBC News, "Term 'Visible Minorities' May Be Discriminatory, UN Body Warns Canada," *CBC News*, 8 March 2007, https://www.cbc.ca/news/canada /term-visible-minorities-may-be-discriminatory-un-body-warns-canada-1.690247.

LGBTQ workers) as an employment equity group distinct from "visible minorities."[81] While the change requires legislative amendment not yet proposed, a group pursuing a "Black Class Action" lawsuit against the federal government had included a similar demand to recognize Black workers in the *Employment Equity Act*, and claimed victory based on reports of government support.[82]

Race and Policing

Significant public discussions of policies towards equal opportunity have occurred in connection with policing, which is mainly a provincial or local responsibility. Among the situations in which Black people report unfair or discriminatory treatment, those involving the police are among those most frequently mentioned. In recent years, attention has focused on perceptions of unfairness at the hands of the police and the criminal justice system generally, by members of the Black community in cities including Toronto and Montreal.[83] Police mistreatment of members of other groups, including undocumented immigrants and asylum seekers, has also been reported.[84]

Public attention is most quickly aroused by instances in which police appear to use excessive force in dealing with minorities, in some cases leading to death. Regarding more everyday experiences, research has shown that police disproportionately subject

---

81 David Thurton, "Ottawa Backs Listing Black and LGBTQ Workers under Canada's Workplace Equity Laws," *CBC News*, 11 December 2023, https://www.cbc.ca/news/politics/workplace-equity-black-lgbtq-1.7055067.

82 Black Class Action, "Black Class Action Secures Major Victory for Workers," News Release, 14 December 2023, https://www.blackclassaction.ca/post/black-class-action-secures-major-victory-for-workers.

83 Scot Wortley and Akwasi Owusu-Bempah, "Unequal before the Law: Immigrant and Racial Minority Perceptions of the Canadian Criminal Justice System," *Journal of International Migration and Integration / Revue de l'integration et de La Migration Internationale* 10, no. 4 (2009): 447–73, https://doi.org/10.1007/s12134-009-0108-x.

84 Sarah Marsden, *Enforcing Exclusion: Precarious Migrants and the Law in Canada* (Vancouver: UBC Press, 2018).

Black people to stop-and-search procedures, creating an impression that they engage in "racial profiling," that is, targeting Black people for surveillance.[85]

Survey research shows that Black people are disproportionately affected even after adjustments are made for a series of variables, including gang membership, drug and alcohol use, public leisure activities, and even self-reported criminal activity. Two provincial Human Rights Commissions in Canada – in Ontario[86] and Nova Scotia[87] – have reviewed data and found evidence confirming that Black people are subjected to racial profiling and racial discrimination from police in a way that is consistent with systemic racism and anti-Black racial bias.

Studies also indicate that discriminatory treatment by police extends into the courts. A review of 1,800 criminal cases in the Toronto courts in the mid-1990s showed that Black people were less likely to be released on bail, after taking account of a variety of legal factors, and based largely on negative character assessments of defendants by police.[88] Further, while detention without bail often leads to a guilty plea, this was not the case for Black defendants; instead, the charges against Black defendants were more often withdrawn, suggesting the prosecution expected greater difficulty proving them in court. These studies show that the impact of negative police treatment of Black people extends beyond the simple question of surveillance.

---

85 Scot Wortley and Julian Tanner, "Data, Denials, and Confusion: The Racial Profiling Debate in Toronto," *Canadian Journal of Criminology and Criminal Justice* 45, no. 3 (2003): 367–90, https://doi.org/10.3138/cjccj.45.3.367.

86 Ontario Human Rights Commission, *A Disparate Impact Second Interim Report on the Inquiry into Racial Profiling and Racial Discrimination of Black Persons by the Toronto Police Service* (Toronto: Ontario Human Rights Commission, 2020), https://www3.ohrc.on.ca/sites/default/files/A%20Disparate%20Impact%20-%20TPS%20inquiry%20%28updated%20January%202023%29.pdf.

87 Scot Wortley, *Halifax, Nova Scotia: Street Checks Report* (Halifax: Nova Scotia Human Rights Commission, 2019), https://cdn.halifax.ca/sites/default/files/documents/city-hall/boards-committees-commissions/230911adacinfo3.pdf.

88 Gail Kellough and Scot Wortley, "Remand for Plea: Bail Decisions and Plea Bargaining as Commensurate Decisions," *British Journal of Criminology* 42, no. 1 (2002): 186–210, https://doi.org/10.1093/bjc/42.1.186.

Assessing Immigrant Integration

Ultimately, the successful integration of immigrants depends on the relationships that develop among the diverse population groups that their arrival creates. Today, this is mainly a question about "visible minorities," the racialized populations of non-European backgrounds. The historical record shows that immigrants to Canada from European backgrounds have been to a considerable degree successfully integrated in Canadian society, including economic, social, political, and cultural domains.

Earlier negative distinctions among persons of German, Italian, Polish, and other European backgrounds have faded to insignificance, while cultural traditions continue to be celebrated. In today's world, the distinctions that matter are those between these groups, now often referred to collectively as "whites" – both colloquially and in official government statistics – and the various immigrant groups of non-European origins considered as racialized: Chinese, South Asian, and Black peoples being the largest among a host of others.

This leads us to a key question: Are immigrants within the definition of racialized populations in Canada on course towards successful integration? It is useful to ask this as part of policy development on immigrant integration to help understand the scope of the problem. Various answers are given. They reveal both problems of integration and promising signs of progress towards greater integration. There is evidence of widespread discrimination of new immigrants and racialized minorities in the country. At least since the 1980s, academic research has demonstrated this, and the fact has been officially recognized by the federal government.

Disadvantages have persisted over time, and vary among racialized groups, according to 2021 census data.[89] Rates of poverty – defined as disposable family income below basic living costs in one's local community – were higher in 2020 across most racialized minorities compared to the white population, and they remained

---

89 Christoph Schimmele, Feng Hou, and Max Stick, "Poverty among Racialized Groups across Generations," *Economic and Social Reports* 3, no. 8 (2023), https://www150.statcan.gc.ca/n1/pub/36-28-0001/2023008/article/00002-eng.htm.

higher even after adjustments for socio-demographic characteristics,[90] and higher also among the children of immigrants.[91]

Although surveys show many Canadians remain positive about the state of race relations, minority groups themselves often see things differently. A 2019 national survey found that while most – 64 per cent – felt race relations were generally good, perspectives among minority groups were less positive.[92] Black and Indigenous peoples were the least positive, compared to those of South Asian and Chinese origins.

Among Black people, 83 per cent thought that people in their group experienced unfair treatment either often or at least sometimes. For Indigenous people it was 73 per cent, for South Asian people 64 per cent, and for Chinese people 63 per cent.

In addition, the impacts of discrimination were seen as substantial. For both Black and Indigenous peoples, 29 per cent said that people in their groups were affected "to a great extent," and another 40 per cent said they were affected "somewhat." These two groups also were the most likely to say that discrimination is the main reason why members of their group cannot get ahead.

When the mainstream population was asked which racial groups were most frequently targeted for discrimination, they were most likely to mention Indigenous peoples, Black people, and Muslims. Perceptions of the direction of change over time also varied. Among Canadians generally, 32 per cent thought that relations among racial groups in Canada had improved over the

---

90 The characteristics considered in the statistical adjustments were sex, age, education, language, generational co-residence, household type, number of earners in the economic family, population size of the economic family and geographic distribution.

91 An exception to low poverty rates for racialized minorities is the case of Filipinos. In the second generation, after statistical adjustments, poverty rates were higher than whites for Chinese, Blacks, Latin Americans, Arabs, Southeast Asians, West Asians, and Koreans.

92 Environics Institute for Survey Research and Canadian Race Relations Foundation, *Race Relations in Canada 2019: A Survey of Canadian Public Opinion and Experience* (Toronto: Environics Institute for Survey Research, 2019), https://www.environicsinstitute.org/projects/project-details/race-relations-in-canada-2019.

previous ten years, while 39 per cent thought they had remained about the same, and 24 per cent thought they were worse.[93]

Despite these problems, many Canadians regard intergroup issues as less difficult than in other countries because minorities are treated more fairly. Comparative research has not provided strong evidence that this is the case. A comprehensive review of evidence from Canada, the United States, and four European countries – UK, France, Germany, and the Netherlands – showed that while attitudes towards immigration vary greatly across countries, there are few substantial differences in immigrant integration that could be attributed to differences in discriminatory treatment within institutions such as labour markets or housing markets.[94]

Better results on some indicators were generally offset by less positive results on others. For example, immigrants in Canada usually tend to have much higher rates of early citizenship (at least until recently), but often have lower voting rates. Minorities in Canada are more often elected to federal Parliament, but less often to office at the municipal level.

Increasing Inequality and Immigrant Integration

If immigrants are obliged to take the least well-paid jobs, it matters how poorly paid those jobs are, relative to a mainstream standard. The extent of inequality in Canada has increased, with consequences for immigrants. Overall income inequality has increased significantly in Canada in recent years.[95] For Toronto, an initial analysis of census data for the period 1970 to 2005 showed that growing inequality had affected immigrant minorities, who have become concentrated in low-income areas of the city where

---

93 Environics Institute for Survey Research and Canadian Race Relations Foundation, *Race Relations in Canada*, 7.

94 Alba and Foner, *Strangers No More*.

95 David A. Green, W. Craig Riddell, and France St-Hilaire, "Income Inequality in Canada: Driving Forces, Outcomes and Policy," in *Income Inequality: The Canadian Story*, ed. David A. Green, W. Craig Riddell, and France St-Hilaire (Montreal: Institute for Research on Public Policy, 2016), 1–73.

incomes were falling, while whites were concentrated in high-income areas where incomes were rising. Middle-income populations have become more concentrated in suburban areas.[96] Based on subsequent analyses of data to 2021, these trends continue and have not been reversed.[97]

Immigrants and temporary foreign workers are increasingly concentrated in low-skill occupations that are slowly disappearing, adding to their economic uncertainty. Census data over the period 2001 to 2021 show that Canadian-born workers have shifted to expanding higher-skilled occupations, where their economic prospects are enhanced.[98] The role of temporary foreign workers in filling the low-skill jobs also is increasing.

In a comparative context, the extent of inequality in Canada has been found to affect integration. For example, there is less income inequality in Canada compared to the United States, related to Canada's stronger labour movement, which has supported incomes at the bottom end, helping immigrants, including those who do not hold unionized jobs. Improvement to the minimum wage in Canada has helped immigrants as much as, or more than, Canadian-born persons, because immigrants are more often represented among workers in minimum-wage jobs. On the other hand, immigrants in Canada face a more difficult challenge in the labour market than is typical in Europe, where labour standards provide stronger protection for low-end wages, benefiting immigrants there.

---

96 John David Hulchanski, *The Three Cities within Toronto: Income Polarization among Toronto's Neighbourhoods, 1970–2005* (Toronto: Cities Centre Press, University of Toronto, 2010).

97 Green, Riddell, and St-Hilaire, "Income Inequality in Canada." See also Statistics Canada, "Distributions of Household Economic Accounts for Income, Consumption, Saving and Wealth of Canadian Households, First Quarter 2023", *The Daily*, 4 July 2023, https://www150.statcan.gc.ca/n1/daily-quotidien/230704/dq230704a-eng.pdf.

98 Garnett Picot and Feng Hou, "Immigration and the Shifting Occupational Distribution in Canada, 2001 to 2021," *Economic and Social Reports* 4, no. 3 (2024), https://www150.statcan.gc.ca/n1/en/pub/36-28-0001/2024003/article/00006-eng.pdf?st=DiOd1riE.

Ethno-Racial Diversity and Social Belonging

Does immigration itself undermine social cohesion? This question is often raised in connection with the concentration of ethnic minorities in particular neighbourhoods. Do ethnic communities, and their maintenance of ethnic cultures over time, hinder effective minority integration? Potentially negative consequences of diversity were identified in a study in the United States that found that intergroup trust was undermined, the so-called hunkering down hypothesis.[99]

A comparative study across nineteen countries, including Canada and the United States, showed that the impact of immigration on social cohesion varies according to context. Based on data from the period 1981 to 2000, the study found that greater income inequality, such as exists in the United States, makes immigration a more divisive issue.[100] More equality, and the impact of strong multicultural policies,[101] seemed to produce higher levels of social cohesion as indicated by interpersonal trust, and by organizational and social participation. Within Canada, survey data from members of minority groups show that concentrations of immigrants in ethnic neighbourhoods, and the retention of ties to an ethnic community, promotes integration in Canada in some respects, while slowing it somewhat in others.[102]

On the positive side, minorities with stronger community attachments have a greater sense of belonging in Canada, and higher overall life satisfaction. They are more likely to participate

---

99 Robert D. Putnam, "*E Pluribus Unum*: Diversity and Community in the Twenty-First Century," *Scandinavian Political Studies* 30, no. 2 (2007): 137–74, https://doi.org/10.1111/j.1467-9477.2007.00176.x.

100 Christel Kesler and Irene Bloemraad, "Does Immigration Erode Social Capital? The Conditional Effects of Immigration-Generated Diversity on Trust, Membership, and Participation across 19 Countries, 1981–2000," *Canadian Journal of Political Science* 43, no. 2 (2010): 319–47, https://www.jstor.org/stable/20743152.

101 Countries were classified as having strong, medium, or weak multiculturalism policies based on the Multiculturalism Policy Index as described above.

102 Jeffrey G. Reitz, "Assessing Multiculturalism as a Behavioural Theory," in *Multiculturalism and Social Cohesion*, ed. Jeffrey G. Reitz et al. (Dordrecht: Springer Netherlands, 2009), 1–47.

in community life. These are important aspects of well-being. On the other hand, these minority-focused persons are somewhat slower to develop an identity as a "Canadian," and slower to acquire Canadian citizenship. And they also are somewhat less trusting in others.

Muslims and Religious Accommodation

Concerns about the integration of Muslim minorities intensified following the terrorist attacks of 11 September 2001, in the United States, and subsequent acts of violence by perpetrators claiming a global Islamic agenda. Canadians shared these concerns to some extent, though Canada has been spared severe attacks.[103] Social research evidence clearly refutes these concerns about Muslim integration. Muslim communities in Western countries represent a variety of cultural and national backgrounds. Each such community tends to reflect these different backgrounds as much as or more than a common Muslim identity. Moreover, Muslim experience in the community or the workplace differs little from that of other religious minorities such as Hindus, Sikhs, and others. Their main problems centre on employment opportunity, recognition of qualifications, and discrimination problems of visible minority immigrants in general, not Muslims specifically.[104]

---

103   A 2010 Environics Focus Canada survey asked, "Do you think most Muslims coming to our country today want to adopt Canadian customs and way of life or do you think they want to be distinct from the larger Canadian society?" Most respondents (55 per cent) thought Muslims "want to be distinct." Far fewer (28 per cent) thought Muslims want *to* adopt Canadian customs. Jeffrey G. Reitz, "The Status of Muslim Minorities Following the Paris Attacks," in *After the Paris Attacks*, ed. Edward M. Iacobucci and Stephen J. Toope (Toronto: University of Toronto Press, 2015), 21–8. For a study comparing the economic well-being of Muslims in Canada and France, see Jeffrey G. Reitz, Emily Laxer, and Patrick Simon, "National Cultural Frames and Muslims' Economic Incorporation: A Comparison of France and Canada," *International Migration Review* 56, no. 2 (June 2022): 499–532, https://doi.org/10.1177/01979183211035725.

104   Abdolmohammad Kazemipur, *The Muslim Question in Canada* (Vancouver: UBC Press, 2014).

Black Experience

It is increasingly recognized that the Black experience in Canada is distinctive among racialized minorities, at least in part related to the history of slavery in North America. While slavery's legacy is less important in Canada than in the United States, both were shaped by a British colonial system in which slavery flourished. The initial Black setters in Canada were former slaves from the United States, and the isolation of Black people in these communities was not entirely different from what was observed for Black people in northern US cities following the "Great Migration" from the south beginning in about 1910.

Discrimination against Black people in Canada is more severe than against other immigrant minorities, a pattern noted in virtually every study distinguishing between racialized groups. Some studies have indicated worsening Black disadvantage over time.[105] A unique survey of the Black community in Toronto found that while relations with the police cause serious distress and affect the everyday experiences, particularly of young Black men, experiences of discrimination are prevalent across the social and economic spectrum within the Black community.[106]

Second-generation Black youth are more aware of discrimination than are their immigrant parents, a distinction that also appears in other minority groups. Despite rates of higher education in line with those of the mainstream population, the employment prospects of the Black second-generation are less positive than for second-generation Chinese or South Asians.

A Black-led Philanthropic Fund was proposed by the Liberal Party in the federal election campaign of 2021. The $200 million

---

105 René Houle, *Changes in the Socioeconomic Situation of Canada's Black Population, 2001 to 2016* (Ottawa: Statistics Canada, 2020), https://www150.statcan.gc.ca/n1/en /pub/89-657-x/89-657-x2020001-eng.pdf?st=DNVuOlCC; Anne-Marie Livingstone and Morton Weinfeld, "Black Families and Socio-economic Inequality in Canada," *Canadian Ethnic Studies/Études ethniques au Canada* 47, no. 3 (2015): 1–23.

106 Environics Institute, *The Black Experience Project in the GTA – Overview Report* (Toronto: Environics Institute for Survey Research, 2017), https://www.torontomu.ca/content /dam/diversity/reports/black-experience-project-gta---1-overview-report.pdf.

fund would support organizations in the Black community. The stated purpose of the fund was to address distinctive disadvantages of Black people in Canada. The platform stated: "Data show that Canada's Black community is one of the most disadvantaged, with a higher prevalence of low-income households, lower employment rates, and a much higher likelihood of enduring discrimination at work. Inequality of any kind holds us all back."[107] The promise was to "swiftly implement" the fund, and in 2022 a "Supporting Black Canadian Communities Initiative" was established with funding of $25 million over five years.[108]

The integration of many immigrant groups in Canadian society faces significant obstacles, and difficulties experienced by Black and Muslim immigrants remain among the most serious. Progress over the past two decades has been slow, so much so that successful immigrant integration will remain on the agenda in Canada well into the future.

Holistic Strategies: A More Comprehensive Approach

Since the enactment of the *Immigration and Refugee Protection Act 2001*, successive federal governments have emphasized selection policy as the means to improve immigrant integration. The focus has been on employment, because economic success has significant implications across other areas of life. If carefully selected immigrants can integrate more rapidly in Canada, then less attention is needed over efforts to assist them after their arrival.

---

107   Liberal Party Platform, "Forward for Everyone," accessed 21 July 2024, https:// liberal.ca/our-platform/supporting-black-canadian-communities/#0.

108   The terms of reference and composition of the "external reference group" are outlined by Employment and Social Development Canada, "Supporting Black Canadian Communities Initiative," last updated 25 June 2024, https://www .canada.ca/en/employment-social-development/programs/social-development-partnerships/supporting-black-communities/supporting-black-canadian-communities-initiative.html. A Canadian Institute for People of African Descent has also been announced.

Yet significant problems of immigrant integration remain, particularly for racialized groups, and most seriously for Black people and for Muslims. Efforts to remove barriers to the integration of racialized immigrants have not clearly made significant progress, and in fact some data suggest that difficulties may have increased due to lack of resources in minority communities, along with ineffectiveness of public policy over time.

To some extent, the Canadian practice to address policy to "visible minorities" in general is giving way to a recognition that needs vary across minority groups, and that policies should be sensitive to differences among groups such as Blacks, Asians, and others. Likewise, evaluation of policy also should take account of these differences.

The settlement programs that address the immediate needs of newly arriving immigrants are challenged by the expansion of immigrant numbers. These programs will require much more support, and it will be important to ensure that resources are allocated to create the greatest impact. For example, housing referral services may be of limited use if available and affordable housing exists only at great distances from settlement cities. Attention to broader social policies may be required.

While the practice of responding to community initiatives has many advantages, evaluation review studies should give significantly more attention to finding out what works in assisting immigrants during the settlement process, and which specific types of programs lead to more effective outcomes. With their limited resources, community organizations providing settlement services cannot be expected to conduct this type of evaluation themselves. An expansion of participation by immigrant minorities in the development processes of these programs may help with the policy innovation needed to bring longer-term outcomes.

Evaluation of the effectiveness of policies addressing immigrant integration require more attention to the ultimate objectives of such policies: ensuring full and equal participation of immigrant minorities in Canadian society. Because responsibility for immigrant integration is spread across government departments and among provinces, greater coordination is needed. Effective research also requires special data sources. Statistics Canada's "Ethnic Diversity Survey" conducted in 2002 has been of considerable value in meeting its objective to "help us to better understand how people's backgrounds affect their participation in the social, economic and cultural life of Canada."[109] It should be repeated to establish trend lines in immigrant integration.

Recent renewal of assessment of the *Employment Equity Act* is welcome after the decades-long deferral of this mandated scrutiny. Furthermore, since the act applies only to the limited federal jurisdiction, more effective policy to address disadvantages within immigrant and minority employment at the provincial levels would also be helpful.

Objections that employment equity imposes undue bureaucratic requirements on employers – or that it mandates "race quotas" – have not been supported by experience with the policy at the federal level. In fact, some employers subject to the federal employment equity legislation, such as banks, have emerged as among the most ardent supporters of equal opportunity in hiring. Their experience could be examined in detail to indicate further directions in policy development. Canada's multiculturalism policy may be ripe for renewal.

While the substantial support for multiculturalism in Canada is associated with support for immigration, the impact that either the policy – or its public support – has on the longer-term integration of immigrants in Canada is not well researched. Most comparative studies have not indicated multiculturalism policy is among the most important determinants of immigrant integration.

This chapter has shown how researchers have identified several specific components of multicultural policies, of which simple affirmation of multiculturalism in national policy is only one.[110]

---

109   Statistics Canada, "Ethnic Diversity Survey," last updated 24 October 2007,
       https://www23.statcan.gc.ca/imdb/p2SV.pl?Function=getSurvey&Id=4077.

110   Wallace, Tolley, and Vonk, "Multiculturalism Policy Index." Canada was downgraded in 2010 for adopting dress codes for minorities. Some ratings might be questioned. For example, Canada was given full marks for affirmative action, based on its anti-discrimination policies generally, with mention of the federal *Employment Equity Act* but with no acknowledgment of the limited application of that policy.

Any review of multiculturalism in Canada should consider the possibility that the policy might become more comprehensive.

Overall integration of immigrants in Canada proceeds even in the absence of comprehensive policies. But it is not yet clear whether minority communities with the most negative experiences will overcome disadvantages without a change in policy direction. Immigrant integration is a long-term process – extending over decades and even generations –and yet governments tend to react to short-term political forces and trends. Canada's lack of serious racial conflict has left racial inequality unaddressed and unaffected.[111] If policy development waits for more visible social problems to emerge, the opportunity to prevent them will have been lost.

111   Keith Banting and Debra Thompson, "The Puzzling Persistence of Racial Inequality in Canada," *Canadian Journal of Political Science* 54, no. 4 (2021): 870–91, doi:10.1017/S0008423921000585.

Citizenship: Raising the Bar

Securing Canadian citizenship is the end of a long journey for immigrants. It is official recognition, guaranteeing a range of rights unavailable to others who have arrived in the country, from voting to holding public office. A Canadian passport grants its holder the ability to live outside national borders for an indefinite period with the right to freely return.

Citizenship status has been tightly guarded for most of Canada's history. The authority to grant it to immigrants was discretionary and exercised by the government's executive branch for much of that time. The way these powers were exercised was driven by politics and wielded without impartiality, excluding races and classes of people deemed unsuitable.

In 1946, Canada passed the *Canadian Citizenship Act*,[1] which for the first time recognized Canadian citizenship as a status distinct from that of a British subject. The opportunity for an immigrant to become a Canadian citizen through naturalization was open to all who met the requirements of the act. Executive discretion was reduced in favour of a more transparent and less arbitrary process. Ever since, the rules for acquiring Canadian citizenship have been adjusted, often alongside shifts in immigration policy. This has also been the case for the period between 2002 and 2022.

---

1 *Canadian Citizenship Act*, S.C., c. 15. It came into effect in 1947.

Significant amendments to citizenship legislation came after the Conservative government was elected in 2006. Some of these changes regularized the status of many thousands of persons whose status was uncertain due to previous alterations to citizenship legislation over many years. However, in other respects, the new rules tightened naturalization requirements and broadened the grounds for revoking citizenship. Some of those changes were reversed by the subsequent Liberal government. Others remain in place – and continue to be controversial.

This chapter is concerned with the policy shifts around citizenship in the twenty-first century and their underlying rationale. We examine some of the possible implications of the change in policies and point to areas where more information is needed to properly assess impact.

The link between citizenship and integration warrants further study in Canada, not least since obtaining Canadian citizenship has traditionally marked a significant stride towards complete immigrant integration. Government pronouncements continue to espouse this ideal, noting that by "enabling civic participation, citizenship supports the ability of newcomers to contribute to public life and integrate into society."[2] Moreover, an objective of the *Immigration and Refugee Protection Act 2001* is "to promote the successful integration of permanent residents into Canada, while recognizing that integration involves mutual obligations for new immigrants and Canadian society."[3]

Despite the rhetoric, naturalization rates among immigrants have plummeted over the past several years alongside stricter requirements for obtaining citizenship. More analysis is needed to further isolate the causes, the impact this has on different immigrant groups, and the consequences in terms of facilitating immigrant integration.

The way Canada links immigration with a path to citizenship is reflected in how the system is run. The Minister of Immigration,

---

2 Immigration and Refugees Citizenship Canada, "Regulations Amending the Citizenship Regulations (Oath of Citizenship)," *Canada Gazette*, Part I, Volume 157, Number 8, 15 February 2023, https://www.canadagazette.gc.ca/rp-pr/p1/2023/2023-02-25/html/reg1-eng.html.

3 *Immigration and Refugee Protection Act*, S.C. 2001, c. 27, s. 3(1)(e).

Refugees and Citizenship is responsible for overseeing policies and programs under the *Citizenship Act, 1985*[4] and the *Immigration and Refugee Protection Act 2001*. Both are administered by the Department of Immigration, Refugees and Citizenship.

Specific rules and procedures associated with citizenship are set out in the *Citizenship Act*'s regulations.[5] There are also operational manuals, instructions, and guidelines covering the work of officials administering the *Citizenship Act*. The rules governing who can become a citizen have changed significantly since the post–Second World War period, which are discussed in the following sections.[6]

Context

Evolution: 1866–1946

With the passage of the *Canadian Citizenship Act* in 1946, Canada became the first Commonwealth nation to create its own class of citizenship separate from Britain. Before it became law, the highest status available to born or naturalized Canadians was being a British subject. Rights to enter and remain in Canada were specified in immigration legislation. For these purposes, beginning in 1910, immigration acts included a definition of who was a Canadian citizen. For example, the *Immigration Act* of 1910 defined a Canadian citizen as persons born in Canada, British subjects with three years residence in Canada (domicile), and persons naturalized under Canadian law.[7]

---

4 *Citizenship Act*, R.S.C., 1985, c. C-29.

5 *Citizenship Regulations*, S.O.R./93-246, ss. 12–15.

6 For an insightful review of the evolution of Canadian citizenship law, see Elke Winter and Adina Madularea, "Quo Vadis Canada? Tracing the Contours of Citizenship in a Multicultural Country," in *Immigration, Racial and Ethnic Studies in 150 Years of Canada: Retrospects and Prospects*, ed. Shibao Guo and Lloyd Wong (Leiden: Brill Sense, 2018), 191–208.

7 *Immigration Act*, S.C. 1910, c. 27, s. 2(f). Domicile was later raised to five years in 1914. As mentioned in Part 1: An Historical Reprise, not all British subjects were admissible to Canada. Those that were had acquired domicile after a specified period of years.

Hundreds of thousands of immigrants came to Canada in the first part of the twentieth century. To stay permanently, they needed to become naturalized. Immigrants did not all have an equal opportunity to do so. The process was informed by the same racial, political, and socio-economic preferences that governed immigration policy. It was also administered in a similar way, with the minister responsible having broad discretion to establish guidelines, accept naturalization applications, and even revoke citizenship.

Until the twentieth century, the requirements for naturalization were straightforward. Applicants had to swear an oath that they had resided in Canada for three years and take an oath of allegiance to the British Crown.[8] In the early 1900s, naturalization requirements were tightened alongside immigration admission criteria. Notice of naturalization applications had to be published, members of the public could object to the application, and presiding judges had great latitude to reject applications.[9] Asian applicants were routinely rejected.

By 1914, a new *Naturalization Act* required applicants to demonstrate they were of "good character" and raised the period of prior residency in Canada to five years. Adequate knowledge of English or French was another requirement and remains so to this day.[10] The minister responsible was given broad discretion to revoke naturalization if obtained by fraud or misrepresentation.[11] Wives and children could not apply for naturalization and had to be included

---

8 *Naturalization Act*, 1868, S.C. 22. For a review and analysis of how naturalization requirements changed between Confederation and the *Nationality Act, 1914*, see Peter Price "Naturalising Subjects, Creating Citizens: Naturalisation Law and the Conditioning of 'Citizenship' in Canada, 1881–1914," *The Journal of Imperial and Commonwealth History*, 45, no. 1 (2017): 1–21, https://doi.org/10.1080/03086534.2016.1262646.

9 Some of these changes were introduced in the 1903 amendments to the *Naturalization Act*. Price, "Naturalising Subjects," 11–12.

10 *An Act Respecting British Nationality, Naturalization, and Aliens*, 1914, S.C. c. 44, s. 2 (*Naturalization Act*, 2014). This act was part of measures taken to unify naturalization laws across the British Empire. For more on that and how the notion of a distinct Canadian citizen evolved, see J. Donald Galloway, "The Dilemmas of Canadian Citizenship Law," *Georgetown Immigration Law Journal* 13, no. 2 (1999): 201–31; Price, "Naturalising Subjects," 13.

11 *Naturalization Act*, 2014, s. 7.

in the application of their husband/father.[12] For the following several decades, naturalization remained a highly discriminatory and arbitrary process. It was denied to persons of certain races as well as to political or labour activists deemed unsuitable.[13]

Also, the grounds for revocation were broadened. During the 1930s, naturalization certificates could be revoked if a person was of bad character. This could be applied to persons who demonstrated disloyalty or disaffection to the Crown, communicated with national enemies, or had received criminal fines over $500 or terms of imprisonment of over a year.[14]

Distinct Canadian Status: 1947–2001

The *Canadian Citizenship Act* of 1946 came into effect in 1947. It gave new meaning to Canadian citizenship. It also gave the Canadian government autonomy from the British system that recognized all British subjects as nationals.[15] The act defined who was a Canadian citizen – delinking the definition from British subject status – although British residents who at the time of the act had domicile in Canada were recognized as citizens.

In addition to persons born or naturalized in Canada, the act broadened the definition to include persons born abroad to a Canadian father.[16] Also, for the first time, Canadian women

---

12 *Naturalization Act*, 2014, s. 33(d). They were defined as persons with disabilities along with "lunatics." Married women and children could be included in the application of the husband/father.

13 Naturalization revocations in these circumstances are discussed in Kelley and Trebilcock, *Making of the Mosaic*, chaps. 5 and 6.

14 Kelley and Trebilcock, *Making of the Mosaic*, 229; *Naturalization Act*, 1927, R.S.C. (vol II) c. 93, s. 9.

15 The *Canadian Citizenship Act* coincided with increased migration of British subjects within the Commonwealth. The United Kingdom began to receive higher levels of immigrants from its former colonies in the Caribbean and Africa. See Reitz, "The Institutional Structure of Immigration." In Canada, immigration admission criteria limited British immigration of individuals born or naturalized in Great Britain, Newfoundland, New Zealand, Australia, and South Africa. See, for example, Orders in Council, P.C. 1931-695 and P.C 1953-859.

16 A Canadian woman could only confer nationality to a foreign-born child if the woman was unmarried at the time of birth.

did not lose their citizenship if they married a foreign spouse.[17] The act also set out the grounds for which citizenship could be lost. These included circumstances in which a person became naturalized elsewhere, served in the Armed Forces of another country, or lived outside Canada for over ten years since being naturalized.

The transition towards a redrawn Canadian system and away from its British predecessor came with difficulties. Thousands of individuals who were considered citizens prior to the 1946 legislation were severely affected by the new *Canadian Citizenship Act*. Many were either not recognized as citizens or were required to take measures within a certain period to retain their status. The new rules were not communicated well. As a result, many thousands of persons who thought they were Canadian discovered they were not. Known as the "lost Canadians," their number would grow. It would take almost sixty years to resolve their problems.

By the mid-twentieth century, naturalization requirements included continued Canadian residence of four of the preceding six years, evidence of good character and adequate knowledge of English or French.[18] The federal Cabinet retained the authority to revoke naturalization certificates on relatively broad grounds. The list included acts of disloyalty, residing outside of Canada for more than six years, or having obtained naturalization fraudulently.[19]

In the 1970s, immigration and citizenship laws were relaxed. The *Immigration Act* of 1976 was not only less racially selective but also more transparent and publicly accountable than any other

---

17 In "Quo Vadis Canada?," Winter and Madularea note that another way the new act was a break from the past was that it removed the distinction between those born in Canada and those naturalized in the country. "All individuals living permanently in Canada (except Indigenous Peoples, who could not vote in federal elections until 1960 without losing their status as "Indians") were now to be 'Canadian citizens' regardless of their place of birth" (194).

18 *Canadian Citizenship Act*, 1946, s. 10. More relaxed provisions applied to persons who had resided in Canada for twenty years or who had served in the Canadian Armed Forces during the First and Second World Wars.

19 Acts of disloyalty included disloyalty to the British Crown and being found guilty of treason or sedition; *Canadian Citizenship Act*, 1946, s. 21.

legislation of its kind enacted up to that time.[20] Laws on citizenship and naturalization also took a progressive turn.

In 1977, a new *Citizenship Act* replaced the 1946 legislation.[21] The special status of British subjects was withdrawn.[22] The length of residency required for naturalization was reduced to three years. Children born of Canadian mothers after the act came into force were recognized as citizens, eliminating the previous gendered discrimination that recognized only children born of Canadian fathers. Canadians were for the first time permitted to hold more than one nationality. Foreign children adopted by Canadian parents were recognized as citizens.[23]

The 1977 changes gave the Minister of Citizenship discretion to waive language requirements and rules covering knowledge of Canada on compassionate grounds. The Cabinet could also direct the minister to award citizenship to any person to help them avoid undue hardship or as a reward for exceptional conduct.[24] Revocation of citizenship was limited to situations where it was obtained by fraud, misrepresentation, or by concealing a material fact.[25]

Although the *Citizenship Act* of 1977 was more inclusive than its predecessor, it failed to resolve the problem of the lost Canadians – individuals excluded from citizenship due to legislative changes since the passing of the 1946 legislation. It also exacerbated the problem by imposing new rules on citizenship by inheritance.

Children born abroad before the act came into force could only claim citizenship as a right if their father was a Canadian. A similar child of a Canadian mother had to apply for citizenship, swear an oath of allegiance, and pass security and criminal checks. The Supreme

---

20 Discussed in Part 1: An Historical Reprise.

21 *Citizenship Act*, 1976, S.C., c. 108.

22 This was consistent with making Canadian law less discriminatory. By this time there were many more immigrants to Canada from non-British countries who were frustrated at the disparity of treatment. See Julius Grey and John Gill, "Canadian Citizenship," *The Canadian Encyclopedia*, 16 September 2020, last edited 16 September 2020, https://www.thecanadianencyclopedia.ca/en/article/citizenship.

23 *Citizenship Act*, 1976, ss. 3, 5(1).

24 *Citizenship Act*, 1976, s. 5(3)(4).

25 *Citizenship Act*, 1976, s. 9.

Court of Canada held this to be unconstitutional in 1997.[26] Nonetheless, the situation remained unaddressed for another decade.

The 1977 act also required all children born abroad to a Canadian parent who was also born abroad to take steps to retain citizenship before their twenty-eighth birthday.[27] As with previous changes to citizenship legislation, it was not well communicated. Many were unaware of the requirement, missed the deadline, and ended up among the lost Canadians.

Over subsequent years, naturalization requirements have expanded. In addition to residency and language requirements, applicants have to pass a citizenship test to show a basic understanding of Canada's history, geography, political system, and economic, social, and cultural characteristics. Persons who are not eligible for citizenship include those incarcerated or on parole, as well as those convicted of war crimes or crimes against humanity or under investigation into them. Individuals guilty of a serious criminal offence cannot be considered for citizenship for several years following conviction.[28]

Between 1970 and 1996, citizenship rates among immigrants with eleven to fifteen years residence in Canada steadily rose from 59 per cent to 83 per cent. This period corresponded to relatively robust public investment in promoting citizenship, supporting settlement services, and advancing Canada's multicultural policies.[29] When the *Immigration and Refugee Protection Act 2001* was passed in Parliament, about three quarters of immigrants to Canada were Canadian citizens.[30] As will be discussed more fully below, rates of citizenship acquisition have fallen since then.

---

26 *Benner v. Canada (Secretary of State)*, [1997] 1 SCR 358.
27 *Canadian Citizenship Act*, S.C. 1974-75-76, c. 108, s. 8(1)(c).
28 *Citizenship Act* S.C., 1985, c. 29, ss. 21 and 22. Also, until more recent provisions, the Cabinet had the authority to declare certain persons ineligible for citizenship if there were reasonable grounds to believe they were a threat to national security or they would engage in organized criminal activity.
29 Irene Bloemraad, "Becoming a Citizen in the United States and Canada: Structured Mobilization and Immigrant Political Incorporation," *Social Forces* 85, no. 2 (2006): 670, https://www.jstor.org/stable/4494935.
30 Bloemraad, "Becoming a Citizen," 667.

Citizenship in the Twenty-First Century

Resolving Status and Limiting Access: 2002–2009

At the beginning of the twenty-first century, the rules pertaining to citizenship and naturalization had remained relatively stable for over twenty years. Then, as it had been under the 1977 legislation, Canadian citizenship was defined as a person born in Canada,[31] born abroad to Canadian parents, or naturalized in Canada.

Immigration and citizenship reform was part of the Conservative Party's 2006 election platform. In 2008, it introduced amendments to the *Citizenship Act*.[32] These focused on two main issues that had received considerable media coverage. The first was designed to resolve the situation of the lost Canadians. The second was aimed at limiting rights to the inheritance of Canadian citizenship.

Lost Canadians

An early campaigner for the lost Canadians was someone whose own citizenship unwittingly ended when his father became an American citizen. Don Chapman lobbied extensively throughout the 1990s for people like himself, whose citizenship had been lost due to changes in citizenship legislation. He convinced the Canadian Broadcasting Corporation to investigate the issue. The CBC found that over 200,000 individuals in Canada may have lost their citizenship due to gaps left by successive *Citizenship Acts* and regulations.[33] Many were unaware they were not Canadian, and only found out when they applied for a passport, claimed social security, or were required to undergo a security check for a new job.

---

31 Excluding children of foreign diplomats, consular officers, and their employees and employees of a United Nations agency. *Citizenship Act*, 1977, s. 3(2).

32 Bill C-37, "An Act to Amend the *Citizenship Act*," which came into force on 17 April 2009.

33 CBC News, "Lost Canadians," *CBC News*, last updated March 2007, https://www.cbc.ca/news2/background/lostcanadians/index.html.

There were some very eye-catching names among these individuals. Senator Romeo Dallaire, a former Canadian Forces Lieutenant General, only found out he was one of the lost Canadians on being appointed to the Canadian Senate in 2005.[34] The government granted him citizenship, but thousands of other cases remained unresolved.

Among those whose stories made the news were those affected by new travel requirements imposed by the United States following the 2001 terrorist attacks. After the destruction of the World Trade Center left America in shock, the United States tightened border controls and required Canadians to have passports to enter. A growing number of Canadians applied for a passport for the first time, some only to find out that they did not count as citizens, despite having lived in Canada all their lives. Many of these newfound lost Canadians were ordered to leave the country.

By this time, other examples of lost Canadians were becoming well known.[35] They included women who had married Canadian foreign servicemen during the Second World War and their foreign-born children.[36] Regulations passed at that time recognized them as citizens but many did not know they had to reaffirm their citizenship in order to be recognized.

Nor was the rule that any Canadian citizens born abroad would lose their citizenship if they were not living in Canada on their twenty-fourth birthday.[37] Another group among the lost Canadians

---

34 Richard Foot and Peggy Ann Osborne, "Lost Canadians," *The Canadian Encyclopedia*, 25 July 2017, https://www.thecanadianencyclopedia.ca/en/article/lost-canadians.

35 The Economist, "Lost in Kafkaland: When Is a Canadian Not a Canadian?," 1 February 2007, https://www.economist.com/the-americas/2007/02/01/lost-in-kafkaland.

36 It was estimated that between 43,000 and 48,000 wives of Canadian servicemen and thousands of war babies (born to Canadian servicemen and foreign mothers) came to Canada at the conclusion of the Second World War. See Don Chapman, "History – Lost Canadians: War Brides," accessed 22 July 2024, https://lostcanadian.com/history_page/war-brides/; and Don Chapman, "History – Lost Canadians: War Babies," accessed 22 July 2024, https://lostcanadian.com/history_page/war-babies/.

37 Don Chapman, "Who Are the Lost Canadians?," *The Lost Canadians* (blog), 1 December 2008, https://blog.lostcanadian.com/2008/12/who-are-lost-canadians.html.

were certain children born out of wedlock before the *Citizenship Act* of 1977. They were only considered Canadian if their mother was Canadian. Those born to a Canadian father and foreign mother were excluded.

The gaps in legislation that created the problem of lost Canadians were addressed in 2009 amendments to the *Citizenship Act*. Most of the lost Canadians were recognized as citizens.[38] But the amendments also imposed a rule that created a new group of persons who could no longer claim citizenship as a right: second-generation children born abroad. This new rule became known as the "first-generation limitation."

First-Generation Limitation

The conflict between Israel and Lebanon of 2006 brought this issue over the inheritance of citizenship to light. In July of that year, Israeli Defense Forces invaded Lebanon in response to Hezbollah incursions into Israel. One million Lebanese were displaced during the five-week conflict. At that time, there were some 40,000 to 50,000 Canadian citizens visiting or residing in Lebanon.[39] Most registered with the Canadian embassy during the conflict. Within weeks, Canada conducted an intensive operation assisting over 15,000 individuals to leave Lebanon at a cost of $94 million.[40]

Critics complained that many of those being evacuated had minimal connections to Canada. Labelled by commentators as

---

38 Francine Compton, "Lost Canadians," *APTN News*, 12 April 2014, https://
   www.aptnnews.ca/investigates/lost-canadians/#:~:text=Bill%20C%2D37%20
   granted%20citizenship,individuals%20out%20of%20the%20loop. An estimated
   95 per cent were recognized, affecting approximately 750,000 individuals.

39 Standing Senate Committee on Foreign Affairs and International Trade, *The
   Evacuation of Canadians from Lebanon in July 2006: Implications for the Government of
   Canada* (Ottawa: Senate of Canada, 2007), 1, https://sencanada.ca/content/sen
   /Committee/391/fore/rep/rep12may07-e.pdf.

40 CBC News, "$94M for Lebanon Rescue, but Canadian Evacuee Grateful," *CBC News*,
   24 November 2006, https://www.cbc.ca/news/canada/94m-for-lebanon-rescue
   -but-canadian-evacuee-grateful-1.627646.

"citizens of convenience," some questioned why Canadian tax-payers should foot the bill for rescuing people who were not making a meaningful contribution to the country. It was also reported that over half of those evacuated returned to Lebanon within a month.[41] Other commentators have noted that these claims were largely speculative.[42] Prime Minister Harper promised to investigate the matter. His response was included in the 2009 amendments to the *Citizenship Act*.

The changes remain in place. Canadian citizenship for children born abroad goes only to those whose parents were born in Canada, or naturalized in the country, hence the term "first-generation limitation." It means that Canadians who acquired citizenship by descent [i.e., born abroad to Canadian citizens] are not entitled to pass on Canadian citizenship to their children unless those children are born in Canada.[43] There is an exception for Canadian public servants, and for children who would otherwise be stateless.[44]

The first-generation limitation was drawn up during a controversy and remains controversial. Critics claim that it is unnecessarily broad and excludes those who may have a substantial connection to Canada. As observed by Pal and Ryder-Bunting, the "rule does not consider the amount of time the parent has spent in Canada or how they retain a connection to the country."[45] It is viewed as unfairly prejudicing children of Canadian parents who were born abroad but who maintain close ties with Canada, many of whom serve in United Nations agencies, non-governmental organizations, or are employed by national and multinational corporations.

---

41   Allan Woods, "Dual Citizenship Faces Review," *National Post*, 29 September 2007, https://web.archive.org/web/20070929111734/http://www.canada.com/national-post/news/story.html?id=fb2d75ab-8880-4945-8537-1508186a4964&k=61921#.

42   Audrey Macklin and François Crépeau, *Multiple Citizenship, Identity and Entitlement in Canada*, IRPP Study, No. 6 (Montreal: Institute for Research on Public Policy, 2010), 21.

43   Michael Pal and Luka Ryder-Bunting, "Citizenship and the First-Generation Limitation in Canada," *Dalhousie Law Journal* 45, no. 1 (2022): 4.

44   This protection against statelessness was included in the 2017 amendments passed by the Liberal government.

45   Pal and Ryder-Bunting, "Citizenship and the First-Generation Limitation," 8.

According to Statistics Canada, there were approximately 4 million Canadians living abroad in 2016. Around half of these citizens were Canadian "by descent" as defined above: born abroad to Canadian citizens.[46] Their children, if born abroad, would not obtain Canadian citizenship under the first-generation limitation. Commentators have observed that the first-generation limitation runs counter to more expansive and somewhat comparable provisions in the *Canada Election Act*.

Until 2019, Canadians who had lived for five years outside Canada, other than public servants, were prohibited from voting in federal elections. The Supreme Court of Canada held that this was unconstitutional. The Court characterized the right to vote as a fundamental right, and the cornerstone of democracy. It found no evidence to support the government's claim that the restriction was necessary to ensure electoral fairness.[47]

Writing for the majority, Justice Wagner made the following observations: "… the world has changed. Canadians are both able and encouraged to live abroad, but they maintain close connections with Canada in doing so. The right to vote is no longer tied to the ownership of property and bestowed only on select members of society. And citizenship, not residence, defines our political community and underpins the right to vote."[48]

Other states that have first-generation limitations tend to allow for some flexibility, such as an opportunity for the second

---

46 Julien Bérard-Chagnon and Lorena Canon, *The Canadian Diaspora: Estimating the Number of Canadian Citizens Who Live Abroad* (Ottawa: Statistics Canada, 2022), https://www150.statcan.gc.ca/n1/pub/91f0015m/91f0015m2022001-eng .htm#a10.

47 The Court characterized the restriction as targeting those who are deemed less deserving of the vote than other Canadians. It noted previous decisions where the Court has foreclosed the use of worthiness to justify restrictions on the right to vote. *Frank v. Canada (Attorney General)*, 2019 SCC 1, para. 82.

48 *Frank v. Canada (Attorney General)*, para. 35. For a review of the competing political philosophies of belong that underpinned the decision of the majority and dissenting justices, see Sarah Burton, "Locating the People: An Exploration of Non-Resident Enfranchisement and Political Belonging in 'Frank v. Canada (Attorney General),'" *McGill Law Journal* 66, no. 4 (2021): 637–72.

generation to subsequently acquire nationality.[49] Most commentators agree that Canada should do the same.[50]

Change is in the wind. In December 2023 the Ontario Superior Court found the second-generation limitations unconstitutional.[51] In May 2024 the government introduced to Parliament amendments that would remove the limitation.[52]

Tightening the Requirements: 2010–2022

The 2009 changes were a prelude to more extensive changes that followed in 2010 and 2014. These next set of changes fell broadly within two categories: more rigorous conditions for naturalization and broader powers to revoke citizenship by birth or naturalization. These came at a time of sweeping changes to immigration and refugee processes and were similarly based on allegations that the system was plagued by fraud. As explained by Jason Kenny, Immigration and Citizenship Minister in 2010, "these amendments are intended to simplify the process of revoking the citizenship of people who acquired it by making false statements, by fraud, or by hiding important facts,

49 Pal and Ryder, "Citizenship and the First-Generation Limitation," 20–1. They looked at laws in Australia, France, Germany, New Zealand, Switzerland, the United Kingdom, and the United States. Aside from New Zealand, Canada had the most restrictive law.

50 Pal and Ryder also provide a very helpful summary of current academic debates around whether citizenship should be accorded by being born in the country (*jus soli*), assigned based on the citizenship of the parents (*jus sanguine*), or by establishing a real and substantial connection to the country (*jus nexi*). See Pal and Ryder, "Citizenship and the First-Generation Limitation,"15–19. See also Lois Harder, *Canadian Club: Birthright Citizenship and National Belonging* (Toronto: University of Toronto Press, 2022). Harder takes a critical view of birth right citizenship and proposes other alternatives that may be more consistent with democratic and socially just principles.

51 *Bjorkquist et al. v. Attorney General of Canada*, 2023 ONSC 7152 (CanLII).

52 "Bill C-71: An Act to amend the Citizenship Act (2024)." The bill has yet to proceed to second reading. For more on its progress, see https://www.parl.ca /legisinfo/en/bill/44-1/c-71.

including war crimes."[53] Like immigration fraud allegations, no evidence of widespread citizenship fraud came to light.

Conditions for Naturalization

The 2014 amendments to the *Citizenship Act* increased the required length of time a permanent resident must live in Canada prior to applying for citizenship from three years to four years. Time spent in Canada before becoming a permanent resident, such as a refugee applicant or as a temporary resident, would no longer qualify. This restriction was later modified by the Liberal government in 2017, with amendments that take account of a portion of the time spent as a temporary resident or a protected person.[54] The Liberal government also reduced the residency requirement to three years.

The 2014 amendments imposed more stringent proof of residency, which remains in force. Among them, applicants must provide proof of income tax filings for three consecutive years prior to their application. Although the 2014 changes also required applicants to show that they intend to reside in Canada if granted citizenship, this was subsequently repealed by the Liberal government in 2017.

The 2014 amendments required all applicants between sixteen and sixty-four years of age to provide proof with their application of their proficiency in English or French and required them to pass a citizenship exam. Previously, adults over fifty-four were exempt, as were children under eighteen. The Liberals subsequently reverted to the eighteen to fifty-four year old age bracket for meeting these requirements.

---

53 Citizenship and Immigration Canada, "Speaking Notes for The Honourable Jason Kenney, P.C., M.P. Minister of Citizenship, Immigration and Multiculturalism to Announce Legislation Regarding Citizenship," 10 June 2010, https://web.archive.org/web/20131222213321/http://www.cic.gc.ca/english/department/media/speeches/2010/2010-06-10.asp.

54 Each day as a temporary resident or protected person accounts for a half a day for the purpose of residency for citizenship, up to a total of 365 days. *Citizenship Act*, 1985, s. 5(1.001)(a).

To satisfy the language requirement, applicants must provide documentary proof of their ability to speak and listen in English or French at a sufficient level to understand and communicate on daily matters, take instruction, and use basic grammar.[55] The documentary evidence must come from a government approved agency, which is often a private provider that offers this service for a substantial fee.[56] The applicants' language is also assessed at a citizenship interview, which all adult applicants must attend.

The citizenship exam was made more rigorous, the citizenship study guide more complex,[57] and a higher test score required. With the increased difficulty of the citizenship test, failure rates rose from less than 4 per cent in 2009 to nearly 15 per cent in 2011.[58] Several polls over recent years show that less than a quarter of Canadians would pass the test. One online survey of over 1,500 Canadians in 2023 showed that only 23 per cent would pass the test.[59]

Application fees were also raised substantially. Between 2014 and 2015 the processing fee rose from $100 to $530 for each adult applicant.[60] An additional citizenship fee brought the total to $630 per adult and $100 for each additional family member under

55 The Canadian Language Benchmarks Level 4 or higher. Immigration, Refugees and Citizenship Canada, "What Language Level Do I Need When I Apply for Citizenship?," accessed 22 July 2024, https://ircc.canada.ca/english/helpcentre/answer.asp?qnum=569&top=5.

56 Other acceptable forms of proof include a certificate from certain government-funded language training programs or a certificate confirming completion of secondary or post-secondary education in French or English.

57 Winter and Madularea, "Quo Vadis Canada?," 200.

58 Carys Mills, "How Applicants Are Stumbling on the Final Step to Becoming Canadians," *Globe and Mail*, 29 June 2012, https://www.theglobeandmail.com/news/national/how-applicants-are-stumbling-on-the-final-step-to-becoming-canadians/article4382633/.

59 Laura Osman, "Think You Could Pass the Canadian Citizenship Test?," *National Post*, 29 June 2023, https://nationalpost.com/news/canada/canadian-citizenship-test. This was better compared to a 2019 poll that showed only 12 per cent of Canadians would pass the test. Forum Research, "Most Canadians Would Fail Citizenship Test," July 2019, http://poll.forumresearch.com/post/2990/canada-day-2019/.

60 Winter and Madularea, "Quo Vadis Canada?," 201.

eighteen years of age.[61] The government claimed that the fee hikes were necessary to cover costs.[62] But many observers pointed out that the new fees were particularly onerous for those of limited financial means. In 2019, the Liberal government committed to waiving the fees, although this has not yet been done.[63]

Andrew Griffith, a former senior official in the immigration department, cautioned in 2013 that the reforms have raised barriers to citizenship and risk leading to widespread immigrant disengagement with Canada.[64] The subsequent steep decline in naturalization rates correspond to the more onerous and costly conditions for naturalization, impacting especially low-income immigrants and those who do not have English or French as their mother tongue.[65]

While the COVID-19 global pandemic disrupted Canadian citizenship and immigration processing, the decline in naturalization rates preceded it, according to Statistics Canada. In 1996, over 75

---

61 Immigration, Refugees and Citizenship Canada, "Fee List," last updated 22 July 2024, https://www.ircc.canada.ca/english/information/fees/fees.asp.

62 Madalina Chesoi and Eleni Kachulis, *Canadian Citizenship: Practice and Policy* (Ottawa: Library of Parliament, 2020), 4–5, https://lop.parl.ca/staticfiles/Pub-licWebsite/Home/ResearchPublications/BackgroundPapers/PDF/2020-64-E.pdf. Application fees are listed on the Government of Canada website, https://ircc.canada.ca/english/information/fees/fees.asp.

63 Maan Alhmidi, "Ottawa Plans to Eliminate Citizenship Application Fees," *Globe and Mail*, 24 December 2019, https://www.proquest.com/docview/2330006745/citation/E5D6A5B1CEF845BBPQ/1.

64 Nicholas Keung, "Canada Faces Dramatic Drop in Citizenship, Prompting Concerns about Disengaged Immigrants," *Toronto Star*, 24 March 2015, https://www.thestar.com/news/immigration/canada-faces-dramatic-drop-in-citizenship-prompting-concerns-about-disengaged-immigrants/article_1e5f2410-03d1-53a8-8a78-54e1dc5a0d9d.html.

65 Feng Hou and Garnett Picot, *Trends in the Citizenship Rate among New Immigrants to Canada* (Ottawa: Statistics Canada, 2019), 5, https://www150.statcan.gc.ca/n1/en/pub/11-626-x/11-626-x2019015-eng.pdf?st=1H19l_c7. See also Feng Hou and Garnett Picot, "The Decline in the Naturalization Rate among Recent Immigrants in Canada: Policy Changes and Other Possible Explanations," *Migration Studies* 9, no. 3 (2021): 1030–53; Chesoi and Kachulis, *Canadian Citizenship*, 8–10; Alex Nanoff, "Newcomers Falling Out of Love with Canadian Citizenship," Institute for Canadian Citizenship, 15 February 2023, https://inclusion.ca/article/newcomers-falling-out-of-love-with-canadian-citizenship/.

per cent of permanent residents who had been in Canada for five to nine years became naturalized: one of the highest rates in the world. This dropped to 60 per cent in 2016, with the most significant decline taking place between 2011 and 2016.[66]

Subsequently, with the onset of the global pandemic, naturalization rates for immigrants within ten years of acquiring permanent residency dropped to 46 per cent in 2021.[67] Although the annual count of naturalizations began to recover, by 2023,[68] the rate of naturalization remained a concern.

The decline has been larger for those with lower levels of education, language skills, and family income.[69] Many analysts attribute the fall in naturalization rates to the increased stringency of citizenship prerequisites and the higher fees. Researchers also note that conditions and policies in the countries of origin could also contribute. For example, China and India do not acknowledge dual nationality, and are major sources of immigrants to Canada. In the latest census, permanent residents from these nations stood out among the prominent responders who indicated they did not have Canadian citizenship.[70] The fact that they are required to relinquish their original nationality might play a part in their hesitation to attain Canadian citizenship.

66   Hou and Picot, *Trends in the Citizenship Rate*, 2; Feng Hou and Garnett Picot, *The Decline in the Citizenship Rate among Recent Immigrants to Canada: Update to 2021* (Ottawa: Statistics Canada, 2024), https://www150.statcan.gc.ca/n1/pub/36-28-0001/2024002/article/00002-eng.htm.
67   Nanoff, "Newcomers Falling out of Love"; Collington, "Percentage of Permanent Residents Becoming Canadian Citizens in Decline"; Institute for Canadian Citizenship, "Citizenship and Immigration Dashboard," accessed 22 July 2024, https://inclusion.ca/research-ideas/citizenship-and-immigration-dashboard/.
68   Institute for Canadian Citizenship, "Citizenship and Immigration Dashboard." For example, from January to April 2023, there was a 20 per cent reduction in the naturalization of permanent residents compared to the same period in 2022, with an upswing in the last quarter.
69   Hou and Picot, *Decline in the Citizenship Rate*, 1.
70   Catherine Tuey and Hélène Maheux, *A Portrait of Citizenship in Canada from the 2021 Census* (Ottawa: Statistics Canada, 2022), 7–8, https://www12.statcan.gc.ca/census-recensement/2021/as-sa/98-200-X/2021008/98-200-X2021008-eng.cfm.

More research is needed to understand the reasons for the declining naturalization rates and their impact. The decrease of the last decade is disturbing because empirical evidence from several European countries and the United States suggests that faster access to citizenship improves economic, educational, political, and social integration of immigrants.[71]

Processing times for citizenship applications are persistently below the ministry's service standards. In 2015 the ministry introduced a service standard. The service standard for citizenship applications is twelve months from the time a completed application is received to when a decision is made. However, for 2021 to 2022, just 9 per cent of applications were serviced within the standard and, in 2023, processing times were sixteen months.[72] The ministry reports it is dealing with this backlog and aiming to improve processing times through greater use of digital and online initiatives. One of the initiatives concerns taking of the oath of citizenship.

For decades part of the citizenship ceremony has been the taking of a citizenship oath before an authorized official. During the COVID-19 pandemic, the ceremonies were moved online. Then, in February 2023, the government announced it was introducing a self-administering option, to enable individuals to forego a formal

---

71 See Christina Gathmann and Julio Garbers, "Citizenship and Integration,"
    IZA Institute of Labor Economics, December 2022, https://papers.ssrn.com
    /abstract=4298821; Jens Hainmueller, Dominik Hangartner, and Giuseppe
    Pietrantuono, "Naturalization Fosters the Long-Term Political Integration of
    Immigrants," *Proceedings of the National Academy of Sciences of the United States of
    America* 112, no. 41 (2015): 12651–6; Madeleine Sumption and Sarah Flamm, "The
    Economic Value of Citizenship for Immigrants in the United States," Migration
    Policy Institute, September 2012, https://www.migrationpolicy.org/research
    /economic-value-citizenship-immigrants-united-states.

72 Immigration, Refugees and Citizenship Canada, "Immigration, Refugees
    and Citizenship Canada Service Standards," last updated 19 December 2023,
    https://www.canada.ca/en/immigration-refugees-citizenship/corporate/man-
    date/service-declaration/service-standards.html; and Immigration, Refugees
    and Citizenship Canada, "Apply for Citizenship: After You Apply," last updated
    1 May 2024, https://www.canada.ca/en/immigration-refugees-citizenship/ser-
    vices/canadian-citizenship/become-canadian-citizen/after-apply-next-steps
    .html.

proceeding in favour of taking the oath through an online portal. The government's rationale is that this will speed up processing times.[73]

The decision was resisted by the opposition in Parliament, as well as dissent from a significant portion of individuals who participated in the consultation process before it was unveiled. And the change was announced in a low-key manner – published in *The Gazette*, the government newspaper – without a more widely circulated press release. Critics argue that the change diminishes the significance of the citizenship ceremony for new Canadians and the wider community. They assert that the cost-saving benefits are relatively marginal, particularly when weighed against the loss of a long-standing symbol that has welcomed new citizens for generations.[74]

In July 2023, Andrew Griffith launched a public petition opposing the change. This petition swiftly gained support from other prominent figures, including former Governor General Adrienne Clarkson and former Minister of Immigration Sergio Marchi. Within months, the petition had over 1,500 signatures, urging the government to reconsider its plan and reinstate in-person ceremonies. The government's response indicated its commitment to further explore the utilization of the online tool, while acknowledging the strides made in reducing the backlog of approved applications awaiting the conferral of citizenship.[75]

Revocation

Among the most controversial changes to citizenship law imposed by the Conservative government in 2014 were those made to the

---

73 Immigration, Refugees Citizenship Canada, "Regulations Amending the Citizenship Regulations (Oath of Citizenship)."

74 Andrew Griffith, "A One-Click Citizenship Oath Isn't the Way to Go," *Policy Options*, 21 June 2023, https://policyoptions.irpp.org/magazines/june-2023/a-one-click-citizenship-oath-isnt-the-way-to-go/; Parliament of Canada, "Petition to the Minister of Immigration, Refugees and Citizenship," https://www.ourcommons.ca/petitions/en/Petition/Details?Petition=e-4511.

75 Parliament of Canada, "Petition to the Minister of Immigration, Refugees and Citizenship."

removal of citizenship, known as revocation. The changes were both substantive and procedural.

The substantive changes expanded the grounds for revoking citizenship. Prior to 2014, citizenship could only be revoked for conduct prior to becoming a citizen. For example, citizenship could be revoked if the person engaged in fraud or misrepresentation in the application process.

In 2014, three new grounds were added, covering conduct after a person became a citizen. One concerned individuals convicted of serious crimes related to national security. Another related to persons convicted outside Canada of a crime recognized in Canada as a terrorism offence. The third concerned Canadian citizens who had served in foreign forces or in other groups engaged in armed conflict with Canada.[76]

Revocation was prohibited if the person would be made stateless. In effect, this made the changes applicable only to Canadian citizens who also had another nationality.

Procedural protections for person's whose citizenship was being revoked were reduced. Previously, the federal Cabinet had the power to revoke citizenship once the legal basis for revocation was established. This had to be set out in a report prepared by the Minister of Citizenship. The person concerned had the right to know the basis for which revocation was being considered, and an opportunity to make submissions at a hearing before the Federal Court prior to the report being finalized and forwarded to the Cabinet. Even where the requirements of the *Citizenship Act* were met, Cabinet could decide not to revoke citizenship for humanitarian and compassionate reasons.[77]

The 2014 amendments limited due process requirements. The person in question had a right to be notified and to make representations in writing prior to citizenship being revoked. However, the person was not entitled to an oral hearing. The decision to revoke

---

76 *Strengthening Canadian Citizenship Act*, S.C. 2014, c. 22, s. 8. This latter ground did not require a conviction.

77 *Citizenship Act*, 1985, (2009-04-17 to 2014-02-05) s. 18.

was the minister's, as opposed to the Cabinet's.[78] The person could request that it be reviewed by the Federal Court, but had to first seek leave of the Federal Court, which is reserved for cases the court certifies are of "general importance."[79] A further appeal to the Federal Court of Appeal could only be made with permission of the Federal Court.

The 2014 changes came amidst the rise of the Islamic State of Syria and Iraq ("Daesh"), which by mid-2014 controlled significant parts of Syria and Iraq. Known for committing massive human rights violations and atrocities, Daesh was considered a threat to both regional and global security. Its large social media presence helped it to recruit foreign fighters, estimated to number at least 40,000 persons.[80] These recruits came from all corners of the world, including Canada.[81]

The expanded 2014 citizenship revocation rules were designed to deter terrorism at home, prevent terrorist recruitment of Canadians, and stop repatriation of Canadians who had served with Daesh and other terrorist groups. They also came after several Western democracies had amended their laws to strip citizenship

78 An exception was if the citizenship revocation was for engaging in military service with an enemy force. In that case, the minister had to refer the case to a Federal Court judge. If the court declared that the person came within the provision, citizenship was revoked. *Strengthening Canadian Citizenship Act*, S.C. 2014, s. 10.1(2).

79 For a thorough review of the revocation amendments and critical commentary, see Audrey Macklin, "Citizenship Revocation, the Privilege to Have Rights and the Production of the Alien," *Queen's Law Journal* 40, no. 1 (2015): 1–54.

80 Lila Hassan, "Countries Don't Want Their ISIS Foreign Fighters Back: A Review," *FRONTLINE*, 6 April 2021, https://www.pbs.org/wgbh/frontline/article /repatriating-isis-foreign-fighters-key-to-stemming-radicalization-experts-say -but-many-countries-dont-want-citizens-back/.

81 Benmelech and Klor, "Where Are ISIS's Foreign Fighters Coming From?," NBER Working Paper 22190, https://www.nber.org/system/files/working_papers /w22190/w22190.pdf. In tabling the legislation in Parliament, Minister of Citizenship and Immigration Chris Alexander claimed that there were 130 Canadians fighting with extremists throughout the world. Quoted in Sangeetha Pillai and George Williams, "The Utility of Citizenship Stripping Laws in the UK, Canada and Australia," *Melbourne University Law Review* 41, no. 2 (2017): 845–89.

on terrorism-related grounds after the terrorist attacks of 9/11.[82] The Canadian Minister of Citizenship and Immigration said the changes "will ensure that those who wish to do us harm will not be able to exploit their Canadian citizenship to endanger Canadians or our free and democratic way of life."[83]

The amendments also had a punitive and symbolic element. When the changes were tabled in Parliament, the minister said that they would help maintain the integrity of citizenship, by discouraging disloyalty. In introducing the legislation to the Senate, Senator Nicole Eaton said it underscored that betrayal "comes at a price."[84]

Vigorous critiques of the provisions swiftly followed.[85] Commentators noted that the changes meant that various Canadian citizens were now treated differently, because the new provisions only applied to persons with more than one nationality. Some also questioned the strength of the security rationale because the national security grounds required a conviction for offences that generally carried a sentence of life imprisonment. Therefore, a person who was incarcerated could not be considered a security threat.

Critics argued that the reduced procedural protections were unconstitutional given the gravity of the consequences to the person whose citizenship was revoked. They became foreign nationals

---

82 Including Australia, Austria, France, Germany, the Netherlands, Norway, and the United Kingdom. For more on this, see Audrey Macklin, "A Brief History of the Brief History of Citizenship Revocation in Canada," *Manitoba Law Journal* 44, no. 1 (2021): 443, https://heinonline.org/HOL/P?h=hein.journals/manitob44&i=472.

83 Citizenship and Immigration Canada, "Protecting Canadians–Government of Canada Now Able to Revoke Citizenship of Dual Citizens Convicted of Terrorism," 29 May 2015, https://www.newswire.ca/news-releases/protecting-canadians---government-of-canada-now-able-to-revoke-citizenship-of-dual-citizens-convicted-of-terrorism-517764271.html.

84 Quoted in Pillai and Williams, "The Utility of Citizenship Stripping Laws," 866. These authors claim that this "symbolic rationale" seemed more important that the security justification.

85 See Macklin, "Citizenship Revocation"; Patti Tamara Lenard, "Democracies and the Power to Revoke Citizenship," *Ethics and International Affairs* 30, no. 1 (2016): 73–91, doi:10.1017/S0892679415000635; Ben Lerer and Alex Bogach, "Citizenship Revocation in Canada: Dialogue or Defiance?," *Canadian Journal of Administrative*

and subject to removal.[86] Commentators were also critical of the impact on other countries arguing that Canada was inappropriately offloading its problems onto others.

Instead, they argued that a preferable strategy would be to prosecute individuals who are suspected of terrorism under criminal law – while simultaneously implementing measures to mitigate the risk of radicalization within Canadian society.[87] Such measures included programs to counter violence and extremism, deradicalization programs, community engagement, the monitoring of online and social media, and research and early intervention initiatives.[88]

The Liberal Party included repeal of the additional grounds for revocation in its 2015 campaign promises. This commitment was fulfilled in 2017 with amendments to the *Citizenship Act* that restricted revocation once again to situations where Canadian citizenship was obtained by fraud, false representation, or by concealing material circumstances.[89] However, the Liberal government left the procedures for citizenship revocation intact. It was also quick to use them. Within ten months of the Liberal election win, over 165 individuals had their

---

Law and Practice 35, no. 3 (2022): 311–23; Canadian Council for Refugees, "Bill C-6: An Act to amend the Citizenship Act and to make consequential amendments to another Act Submission of the Canadian Council for Refugees," April 2016, https://ccrweb.ca/sites/ccrweb.ca/files/bill-c6-citizenship-submission.pdf.

86 Macklin notes that the procedures for citizens facing citizenship revocation on grounds of misrepresentation were less than required for permanent residents facing loss of status on the same grounds. The latter had a right to an oral hearing before an independent, quasi-judicial tribunal, the Immigration Appeal Division of the Immigration and Refugee Board. Macklin, "Citizenship Revocation," 27.

87 Macklin, "A Brief History," 452.

88 See, for example, Public Safety Canada, "National Strategy on Countering Radicalization to Violence," 21 December 2018, https://www.publicsafety.gc.ca/cnt/rsrcs/pblctns/ntnl-strtg-cntrng-rdclztn-vlnc/index-en.aspx.

89 *An Act to Amend the Citizenship Act and to Make Consequential Amendments to Another Act*, S.C 2017, c. 14. The changes introduced by this act are comprehensively covered in Julie Béchard and Sandra Elgersma, *Bill C-6: An Act to Amend the Citizenship Act and to Make Consequential Amendments to Another Act* (Ottawa: Library of Parliament, 2016), https://lop.parl.ca/sites/PublicWebsite/default/en_CA/ResearchPublications/LegislativeSummaries/421C6E.

citizenship revoked without a hearing. This was close to the total number of revocations made in the previous twenty-five years.[90]

In 2017, the Federal Court held that the practice was unlawful.[91] The court considered whether the procedures violated the *Canadian Charter of Rights and Freedoms* and the *Canadian Bill of Rights*. It reasoned that the *Charter* did not apply because revocation of citizenship did not on its own violate the person's right to life, liberty, or security of freedom. It held that the *Bill of Rights* was relevant, specifically its guarantee of a right to "fair hearing" in matters concerning a person's "rights and obligations."[92] Since the revocation of citizenship directly affected a person's rights, the person was entitled to an oral hearing before an impartial decision-maker. The revocation procedures of the *Citizenship Act* fell short.

The 2017 amendments to the *Citizenship Act* provided expanded procedural protections. These included advance notice of the request for revocation, the basis of the request and an opportunity to present written evidence for why the certificate should not revoked. The person could also request special relief for humanitarian and compassionate reasons. Unless the person consented to the minister making the decision, all cases had to be referred to the Federal Court for an oral hearing. The decision to revoke or not rested with the court. A revocation decision could only be appealed to the Federal Court of Appeal with leave of the court.

A person whose citizenship is revoked becomes a permanent resident. This too changed from the 2014 provisions that deemed any person whose citizenship was revoked for national security reasons to be a foreign national. They could then be removed from Canada without the procedural protections afforded to permanent residents.

Lawyers have since noted a possible procedural loophole that could erode the 2017 procedural protections. It is through a parallel

---

90 Evan Dyer, "Trudeau Government Revoking Citizenship at Much Higher Rate than Conservatives," *CBC News*, 9 October 2016, https://www.cbc.ca/news/politics/citizenship-revocation-trudeau-harper-1.3795733.

91 *Hassouna v. Canada (Citizenship and Immigration)*, 2017 FC 473. Citizenship was restored to those caught in the former procedure.

92 *Canadian Bill of Rights*, S.C. 1960, c. 44, ss. 1(a) and 2(e).

regulatory procedure found in the *Citizenship Regulations,* which permits the registrar to cancel or compel a person to surrender a certificate. The registrar is authorized to do this "if there are reasons to believe" that the person is not entitled to a citizenship certificate. There is no corresponding obligation to disclose the basis of the belief, or to provide an oral hearing before an independent tribunal.

The wording of this relatively open procedure has been used since the 2017 amendments to the act. It was applied in a situation where a citizenship certificate was issued to an individual who failed to make required disclosures that he was the subject of an immigration proceeding when he applied for citizenship.[93]

In other words, the use of this administrative procedure came despite specific provisions in the act and its regulations regarding due process requirements. Whether this will become less of an exception is to be seen.

Repatriation Assistance

One of the benefits of Canadian citizenship is the right to Canadian consular services when outside the country. This includes replacing lost, stolen, damaged, or expired passports and providing other forms of emergency assistance.[94] The limits of consular assistance were tested in a case brought before the Federal Court in 2020, regarding Canadian citizens detained in camps in north-west Syria. The Canadian government had not assisted them to return to Canada.[95]

The camps are in the area under the *de facto* control of the non-state entity, the Autonomous Administration of North and East

---

93 The decision was upheld by the Federal Court in *Ortiz v. Canada (Citizenship and Immigration)*, 2020 FC 188, although the court did not consider whether the process violated the *Canadian Bill of Rights*. For more on this case, and the legal arguments for limiting the cancellation provisions to situations involving administrative errors, see Ben and Bogach, "Citizenship Revocation in Canada: Dialogue or Defiance."

94 Global Affairs Canada, "Canadian Consular Services Charter," last updated 11 July 2024, https://travel.gc.ca/assistance/emergency-info/consular /canadian-consular-services-charter.

95 *Boloh 1(a), Boloh 2(a)* (male only), *Boloh 12,* and *Boloh 13,* v. *Canada,* Federal Court of Canada, 20 January 2023.

Syria (AANES). The camps hold men, women, and children suspected of being affiliated with Daesh, most of whom are from Iraq and Syria. Canadians make up a relatively small number. The case before the Federal Court was brought on behalf of four men, thirteen women, and thirteen children, all Canadian citizens. None of them had been charged with an offence but were held indefinitely on the suspicion that they fought for or aided Daesh.

The uncontested evidence before the Federal Court included observations by a senior United Nations official, among others, on the dire condition of the camps. They were described as overcrowded, insecure, and unsanitary.[96] Children were at particular risk of death due to malnutrition and lack of medical care. Violence was rife in the camp where the men were incarcerated. It was undisputed that other countries had repatriated their nationals.

The Canadian government argued that it had discharged its consular responsibilities, including by verifying the whereabouts and well-being of the detainees, requesting available medical care, and conveying Canada's expectations that they be treated humanely.[97]

The Federal Court held that more was required, and failing to assist in their repatriation was a violation of every Canadian citizen's "right to enter, remain in and leave Canada" as set out in the *Canadian Charter of Rights and Freedoms*.[98] It was also a violation of international law.[99] Prior to the court's ruling, the government agreed to repatriate the women and children. The court's decision mandated that the government do the same for the four Canadian men.

The decision was, however, overturned on appeal.[100] The Federal Court of Appeal acknowledged the abysmal conditions in

---

96 Fionnuala Ní Aoláin, "Letter of the Special Rapporteur on the promotion and protection of human rights and fundamental freedoms while countering terrorism to Mr. Lawrence Greenspon," 3 January 2023, United Nations Human Rights Special Procedures, https://www.ohchr.org/sites/default/files/documents/issues/terrorism/sr/2023-01-25/Letter-Canada-repatriations.pdf.

97 *Boloh 1(A)et al v. Canada*, 2023 FC, para. 50.

98 *Canadian Charter of Rights and Freedoms*, s. 6.

99 *Boloh 1(A)et al v. Canada*, 2023 FC, paras. 114–40.

100 *Canada v. Boloh 1(a) et al.*, 2023 FCA 120, 31 May 2023.

the camps, yet found that there was no constitutional require-ment obliging the Canadian government to repatriate Canadians held there. The court held that *Charter*'s right of citizens to "enter, remain in and leave Canada" does not give rise to a right to "to be returned to Canada." The Supreme Court of Canada refused leave to appeal the decision.[101]

Advancing Equity in Citizenship Acquisition

Canadian citizenship rules today are very close to what they were in 2002, despite the various changes made in between. But there are two significant areas where they diverge, and which need reform.

The first relates to the acquisition of citizenship. For over sixty years, a person born abroad to a Canadian parent was also consid-ered Canadian. Then, in response to a single and rather anomalous circumstance, citizenship by inheritance was limited to a single generation. The intention was to prevent citizenship from being inherited by persons whose parents had no substantial connection to Canada. Its application had a much broader reach.

Millions of Canadians live and work abroad. Many of them advance Canada's international, humanitarian, and economic interests. The government's proposed amendments are important to respond flexibly to these circumstances and not remain an abso-lute bar to citizenship by second-generation inheritance.

The second area of significant change concerns citizenship requirements, which have become more onerous and costly. A recent statistical analysis found that changes in fees, language, and knowledge requirements for citizenship are significantly responsible for declining naturalization rates. Moreover, the decline has been most evident "among immigrants with low income, low educational levels, and low official language abili-ties."[102] Changes to the language and knowledge requirements

---

101 *Boloh 1(a) et al. v Canada*, 2023 SCC, 16 November 2023.
102 Hou and Picot, "Decline in the Naturalization Rate," 1050.

were made without evidence that the more stringent standards were a good proxy for determining who is worthy of citizenship. This should be examined, especially since some groups of permanent residents are more adversely impacted by the changes than others.

Further study on the causes and rates of naturalization are needed. This can help shed light on the extent to which Canadian policies are determinative or whether other factors – such as source country conditions and policies – play a role. Furthermore, low naturalization rates may reflect that immigrants are waiting longer to become naturalized. More longitudinal study is needed to ascertain this, and more analysis is needed on how slow/low rates of citizenship acquisition in Canada impact on integration.

Canada removed overt racial barriers to citizenship a half a century ago. But if current requirements unjustifiably impose greater hurdles on some groups than others, then we have not succeeded in ensuring that all permanent residents have an equal opportunity to become citizens. Without citizenship, persons are not able to vote, or freely return to Canada once they have left. They are vulnerable to the revocation of their status and removal from the country. Their integration is incomplete, and the facilitation of the integration goal of immigration policy is not fully realized.

Conclusion: Where to from Here?

We began this review of contemporary Canadian immigration policy by looking back to the immigration policies that preceded it. The history of Canadian immigration policy shows a progression from narrow nativist policies to policies that are far more open, inclusive, and accountable compared to years past. Efforts were made to limit the unchecked exercise of executive discretion, embedding greater due process protections in immigration processes, and ensuring robust parliamentary oversight and meaningful public consultation on major changes to immigration policy.

While current immigration policy remains relatively open and non-discriminatory, our review also highlights that since the *Immigration and Refugee Protection Act 2001*, elements of past practices have resurfaced by which policy initiatives were adopted in an arbitrary manner with only cursory public discussion and debate. For example, since 2001 economic and family class immigration together averaged 85 per cent of Canada's annual admissions. Within these streams, since 2008, ministerial authority has expanded to a degree not witnessed in nearly half a century. This includes the authority to change assessment criteria, ranking systems, quotas, and processing measures and to cancel and initiate new programs.

Major changes have not been required to first go before Parliament for review. This has reduced the level of legislative and public scrutiny. Because Ministerial Instructions are frequently altered, there is less certainty on how immigration policy is applied now, and in the future, and less opportunity for careful evaluation and assessment.

Another noteworthy feature of the contemporary era is the difficulty for the public to get access to data necessary to properly assess immigration programs. Even descriptive data on the characteristics of immigrants are significantly less detailed and not as systematically provided as they had been in the past. The once-readily accessible longitudinal data, collected consistently over an extended period, is no longer predictably made available by the government. The government's poor record of responding to requests for information, as it is legally mandated to do, has exacerbated the problem of acquiring data and evidence to evaluate immigration policy. Government-commissioned assessments of immigration programs tend to lack systematic rigour, primarily concentrating on whether the programs were executed as intended rather than evaluating their effectiveness in achieving the desired outcomes.

From the 1970s to the 1990s, significant changes to immigration policies were typically preceded by thorough studies and reviews, which were subsequently open to nationwide public consultations. However, in the twenty-first century, even though the changes introduced have been equally significant, they have not undergone meaningful open review and public comment. The government frequently refers to new changes as having been subjected to prior "stakeholder" consultations. But these are poorly described and given their vagueness are unconvincing evidence of support for new policies, including rapid expansion of annual admissions.

This lack of transparency may help explain why future planned immigration levels are now being questioned in the press on an almost daily basis and why public support for high levels of annual immigration has waned.

Beyond overall immigration levels, our review has shown that there are many significant questions regarding policy changes in each of the major immigration streams: economic, family, and refugee. In the following section we summarize some of our key observations regarding these streams as well as developments in deportation policy, integration efforts, and citizenship acquisition.

Detailed recommendations are set out in earlier chapters of this book and reflect our best reading of the scholarship on the various topics and taking into account reactions from invited reviewers – both academics and eminent practitioners – on earlier drafts of these chapters. The following is an overview of the most notable changes in Canadian immigration policy over the last two decades, coupled with observations of how the policy-making process has progressively become less transparent. The scale, scope, and selection criteria for immigrants to Canada have significantly evolved with the intent to positively influence all facets of society. To uphold this objective and maintain public backing for immigration, the rationale behind many changes should be provided and open for comment and review. Moreover, impact evaluations should become standard practice and broader public engagement solicited in future policy formulation.

Key Substantive Changes

Economic Class: Dramatic Redesign, Employer and Provincial Involvement, More Temporary Workers

The number of immigrants admitted to Canada through the economic stream and as temporary foreign workers has seen substantial growth. Annual permanent arrivals within the economic stream rose from approximately 152,000 in 2001 to nearly 273,000 in 2023. The number of temporary foreign workers experienced an even more dramatic increase, soaring from 73,000 to 1,270,000 during the same period.[1]

This increase in numbers coincided with significant changes in selection criteria and processes. The emphasis has shifted from selecting individuals primarily based on their general employability and adaptability to a changing economic environment – indicated for example by levels of education and other forms of

---

1 See figures 3 and 5. Note that the number of temporary foreign workers represents all those with valid temporary work permits at the end of the indicated year, including those whose permits were issued in previous years.

human capital – to more often favouring those who can meet short-term labour market employer demand in specific occupational categories. Current policy also privileges candidates with prior Canadian work experience and those who meet criteria set by provincial governments.

There has been no comprehensive and systematic analysis of whether the changes in selection criteria have influenced the characteristics of admitted immigrants or effectively tackled the problems of immigrant skill underutilization or of skill shortages, which they were intended to address. The available information indicates that the changes have not significantly achieved either goal. Furthermore, existing studies suggest that they may not necessarily lead to long-term labour market success for immigrants.

For many years, employment bias and the failure to recognize immigration qualifications have presented significant obstacles to the economic progress of racialized immigrant communities. Regrettably, there has been little noticeable improvement over the past two decades. Similarly, despite substantial public criticism directed towards the Temporary Foreign Worker Program, research commissioned by the government indicates that policy reforms have had minimal impact on addressing the areas of concern.

Family Class: More Restrictive Eligibility Criteria

Since the enactment of the *Immigration and Refugee Protection Act 2001*, the family sponsorship stream has been significantly adjusted. Canadian citizens and permanent residents can sponsor spouses, common-law partners, conjugal partners, and dependent biological children relatively easily. Processing times for these family members have improved in recent years. At the same time, the sponsorship of other family members has become more difficult. It has become much harder to sponsor parents and the sponsorship of other close relatives is only permissible in limited circumstances.

The restriction of eligible family members for sponsorship has been grounded in the notion that reuniting more than immediate family members places an undue financial burden on the public purse. However, this assumption has not been thoroughly examined. Like various aspects of Canadian immigration policy, the family class stream has received limited attention when it comes to conducting comprehensive longitudinal impact assessments.

More in-depth assessment would help to gain a deeper understanding of the role that immediate and extended family play in immigrant integration and whether existing rules have a disproportionately negative impact on individuals of modest financial means who might stand to benefit the most from family reunification.

Refugees: Greater Numbers, Changing Selection Priorities

In the refugee sphere, the contemporary period has seen both progressive developments and setbacks regarding Canada's international and domestic commitments regarding refugee protection. Positively, Canada has consistently remained a top donor to international humanitarian refugee relief efforts and the number of refugees it has resettled from abroad has risen in line with increased immigration levels generally. However, the proportion of government-sponsored refugees, which prioritizes the neediest refugees, is declining. This threatens to erode Canada's commitment to offering protection to the most vulnerable.

Canada's inland refugee determination process has changed significantly over the past two decades. The establishment of the Refugee Appeal Division of the Immigration and Refugee Board in 2012 has introduced a more meaningful review process for those whose refugee claims have been denied. However, in parallel, the grounds for finding a person ineligible to have their claim determined have expanded, and appeal rights reduced for certain groups. Such changes have increased the probability of genuine refugees being denied international protection and removed to countries where their lives may be at risk.

Each year the number of people forced to migrate because of conflict, climate, and economic hardship grows. Harsh policies to prevent irregular arrivals are often ineffective, inhumane, and tend to overburden transit countries with the least resources. Countries like Canada, which are relatively far removed from large irregular migration routes, are among the least affected. And while Canada has a system for protecting refugees, its role in addressing the needs of distressed migrants who do not land at our borders is ill-defined. Participation in global discussions like those around the Global Compact on Migration is not enough.

Over the coming years, Canada should have a clear and comprehensive strategy for concretely supporting development efforts to reduce the need for distressed migration. This includes development efforts in countries of origin and transit, support for climate adaptation and relocation programs, and mechanisms that can match our immigration needs to migrants who are compelled to move.

The World Bank Group's *World Development Report 2023* recommends ways to enhance bilateral and multilateral cooperation to help ensure that international migration can be "a force for growth and shared prosperity" in all countries.[2] Establishing an expert group familiar with international migration and the Canadian domestic context would be worthwhile.

Integration: Diffusion of Responsibility

Promoting the successful integration of permanent residents into Canada is a key objective of the *Immigration and Refugee Protection Act 2001*. Various programs and policies have a bearing on successful integration. Immigration admissions criteria aim to select those that will establish easily in Canada. Post-arrival settlement support is also aimed to facilitate this. These programs are delivered by different government and non-governmental organizations. They are frequently underfunded. Moreover, they are not guided by overarching clear policy objectives nor are their programs well coordinated. Importantly, their impact is not systematically evaluated.

In addition, there are a myriad of other policies and programs that have a bearing on successful integration related to advancing

---

2 World Bank Group, *World Development Report 2023: Migrants, Refugees, and Societies* (Washington, DC: World Bank Group, 2023), xxiii.

human rights, multiculturalism, and employment equity policies. Despite the decades of work in these areas, significant problems of immigrant integration remain, particularly for racialized groups. Efforts to remove barriers to their integration have not been shown to be fully effective. Further, increases in overall economic inequality in Canada have disproportionately affected immigrants.

Immigrant integration is a complex, long-term endeavour that unfolds over decades and across generations. Paradoxically, governmental responses often succumb to the pressures of short-term political considerations and transient trends. To rectify this, there is a compelling need for increased investment in understanding the multifaceted barriers to integration and adequately resourced approaches to program design and coordinated delivery, aimed at dismantling these impediments.

Annual Admissions: Doubling in Ten Years

In 2016, the government opted for a significant expansion in annual admissions, close to doubling by 2024. The Canadian immigration program was already one of the most aggressively expansionist among states in the Organisation for Economic Co-operation and Development (OECD). One would expect that a decision to double the size of immigration would be preceded by considerable public discussion and debate.

An expansion of immigration numbers of this magnitude would by itself be a major policy change. What is particularly disturbing, however, is that it comes in the wake of numerous changes in the design and operation of the immigration program. While in some instances these new features show promise, most have yet to receive careful evaluation in relation to program objectives. In fact, since the success of each immigration cohort is not known before the passage of a significant amount of time, meaningful evaluation cannot occur in just one or two years. This means that public discussion and debate about the implications of all the changes are limited and based on little evidence.

In effect, the program that is being expanded is not the program that the public had come to know. Public mistrust of high immigration levels has grown, and if the various program changes turn out to have negative unanticipated consequences, Canada's immigration program will have been damaged in a way that will be difficult to correct.

Removal

Permanent residents do not possess an unconditional right to remain in Canada. Their status can be revoked for various reasons, including criminal activities, posing a threat to national security, or obtaining their status through fraudulent means or misrepresentation. For many decades individuals facing removal orders have had the right to appeal the decision for errors of law or fact in the decision or on the basis of humanitarian and compassionate considerations.

Under the *Immigration and Refugee Protection Act 2001*, the grounds for removal have broadened to encompass those who pose a significant risk to individuals and society, as well as others who do not pose such risks. Furthermore, the right to appeal removal orders has been restricted.

As a result, a significantly larger group of individuals, including long-term residents with strong ties to Canada and no threat to society, can now find themselves at risk of deportation. If their removal is for a reason that excludes a hearing before the Immigration Appeal Division, the consequences of deportation to the person and resident family members cannot be assessed against the risk the person poses to Canadian society. Deportation today is more likely to be a disproportionate response compared to forty years ago.

Citizenship

Beginning in 2006, a series of changes were made to rules whereby permanent residents can become naturalized Canadian citizens. Some resulted in conferring citizenship on many thousands of

individuals whose status was uncertain due to previous alterations to citizenship legislation over many years. However, in most
respects, the new rules tightened requirements and broadened
the grounds for revoking citizenship. Some of those changes were
eased in subsequent years while others remain in place and continue to be controversial.

Higher fees and more rigorous language and knowledge
requirements are among the changes. Permanent residents wishing to become a Canadian citizen must provide proof of language
proficiency in English and French and pass a citizenship exam,
which has become more difficult and one in which most Canadians recently polled would fail. Taken together, changes in fees,
language, and knowledge requirements for citizenship have contributed to declining naturalization rates especially among immigrants with low income and education levels.

While studies in other countries have shown a link between citizenship and successful immigrant integration, this issue remains
largely unexplored in Canada.

Policy Process

In this book, our aim has been to illuminate ways in which Canadian immigration policy formulation and implementation can be
enhanced. Each of the preceding chapters presents comprehensive recommendations concerning policies that govern the selection of immigrants, those designed to foster enduring connections
between immigrants and their new society, and policies that mandate the removal of immigrants who breach their terms of stay.

In addition to those recommendations, we provide the following
general proposals of relevance to all aspects of Canadian immigration policy and programs.

Public Accountability

The greater reliance on ministerial authority to determine the size,
composition, and criteria for the two largest immigration streams

permits flexibility and responsiveness to emerging issues. However, it forecloses serious public debate over crucial features of our current and future immigration policies. This reduces transparency and accountability and inhibits the formation of a robust public consensus on future levels of immigration to Canada.

Throughout the contemporary period and until very recently, public opinion polls showed that a substantial majority of Canadians were supportive of existing levels and patterns of immigration. The government has used this as public endorsement for the path it set even though the polling did not reflect any serious engagement with crucial aspects of current policies and the potential for errors of judgment in their formulation and administration.

Public polls also did not reflect the often-negative experience of many Canadians, permanent residents, and aspiring immigrants directly engaged with the system. Processing backlogs have been a perennial problem, as has been the difficulty in knowing why many immigration applications are rejected.

The complex and constantly evolving policies within the immigration system create challenges for individuals trying to navigate it and for public accountability for these changes.[3] Additionally, heightened eligibility requirements for aspiring immigrants, barriers confronting refugees seeking asylum, and limited rights to appeal adverse immigration decisions for certain groups have considerably diminished the due process protections that Canada previously prided itself on within its immigration system. In a liberal democracy, foreclosing serious public debate about a constellation of policies that will profoundly shape the character and future of the country is difficult if not impossible to defend.

We propose that setting projected immigration targets and the policies designed to achieve these targets should, at a minimum, adhere to a consistent "notice and comment principle." This would involve a widely accessible public website where

---

3 Triadafilopoulos and Taylor, "The Domestic Politics of Selective Permeability: Disaggregating the Canadian Migration State."

government proposals and solicited responses to them are available. This approach aligns with best practices observed in various other aspects of Canadian public policy-making, economic regulations, and social governance in Canada and around the world.[4]

In addition, we consider that there is a strong case for the appointment of a small advisory council to the Minister of Immigration, Refugees and Citizenship Canada. It could consist of some ten to twelve persons representative of a broadly cast range of constituencies, including, for example, both business and labour, as well as housing and health care sectors, law and integration services – constituencies that are most impacted by significant increases in immigration admission policies. The council's scope would recognize that all Canadians are in some ways stakeholders in the immigration system.

The responsibility of the advisory council could include responding to proposed policy changes and overseeing a systematic rolling cycle of policy evaluations conducted by qualified third parties. All such evaluations should be placed in the public domain, and along with the council's responses to proposed policy changes, be subject to a public notice and comment regime. Setting up a committee of experts, as we have suggested, regarding Canada's contributions to global migration policy could also be part of the advisory council's responsibilities.

However, we doubt that these proposals in themselves go far enough. In his *2023 Annual Report to Parliament on Immigration*, the minister mentioned that the government launched a Strategic Immigration Review in 2002, which elicited more than 17,000 responses.[5] However, most Canadians are probably unaware that such a review was undertaken or of its consequences.

Also in 2023, Immigration, Refugees, and Citizenship Canada published a report titled "An Immigration System for Canada's

---

4 Steven Croley, *Regulation and Public Interests: The Possibility of Good Regulatory Government* (Princeton, NJ: Princeton University Press, 2008); Jeremy D. Fraiberg and Michael J. Trebilcock, "Risk Regulation: Technocratic and Democratic Tools for Regulatory Reform," *McGill Law Journal* 43, no. 4 (1998): 835–87.

5 Miller, *2023 Annual Report to Parliament on Immigration*, 8–9.

Future."[6] The document presents numerous valuable suggestions, most of which we support. Specifically, we endorse the initiative to digitalize departmental processes, aiming to enhance user-friendliness and accessibility of information. However, the plan does not address many substantive, procedural, and evaluative concerns highlighted in this book and reflected in scholarly and expert discourse in the field.

The report also notes that the *Immigration and Refugee Protection Act 2001* came into force over twenty-years ago and that it will be examined to assess the need for legislative amendments or reform. The aim is to "ensure the legislation continues to reflect the goals of our immigration system, and that it provides a sufficiently flexible framework to meet them while keeping Canadians safe."[7]

In the omnibus budget bill presented to Parliament in April 2024, significant changes to existing policies were proposed, including reducing temporary worker admissions, implementing new regulations to cap international student numbers, and simplifying and streamlining asylum and deportation processes. However, these changes do not foresee the broad-ranging and inclusive public consultation process that we argue is necessary to strengthen public commitments to prevailing policies.

As Nobel Laureate Amartya Sen has famously argued, engaging a broad range of citizens as active agents – not passive patients – in the policy-making process is essential, particularly on issues that will shape the future character of their country.[8] In our view, nothing short of a full-blown, high-profile public review is called for at this time. This must draw on the knowledge and experience of all relevant stakeholders engaging broad segments of society.

In this respect, past experience is informative. Prior to the enactment of the *Immigration Act, 1976* and the *Immigration and Refugee*

---

6   Immigration, Refugees and Citizenship Canada, "An Immigration System for Canada's Future: Strengthening Our Communities," last modified 15 November 2023, https://www.canada.ca/en/immigration-refugees-citizenship/campaigns/canada-future-immigration-system/plan.html.

7   Immigration, Refugees and Citizenship Canada, "An Immigration System," 43.

8   Amartya Sen, *Development as Freedom* (New York: Alfred Knopf, 1999); and Amartya Sen, *The Idea of Justice* (Boston, MA: Harvard University Press, 2009).

Protection Act 2001, the government commissioned detailed thematic studies reviewed in public hearings. In that spirit, we propose that Immigration, Refugees, and Citizenship Canada prepare a discussion paper identifying major substantive, procedural, and evaluation issues and invite written responses and public discussion. Written submissions should be on a public website, along with reactions from the advisory council we have proposed.

Moreover, we propose that the House of Commons Standing Committee on Citizenship and Immigration hold public hearings on issues raised in the discussion paper across Canada. Its findings and recommendations would also be made available on the same public website. The government would then issue its policy responses to issues raised in its discussion paper and the public reactions that it has elicited.[9]

Enhanced Data, Evidence, and Analysis

Empirical evidence of how well or poorly a policy or program is meeting its ostensible objectives is often unclear or non-existent. Government-commissioned evaluations of immigration programs and processes are not systematic. Those that are undertaken frequently focus on whether the program was implemented as planned and not on whether it has had the desired impact. The lack of publicly accessible data inhibits the ability of academics, researchers, and policy analysts from being able to conduct independent informed analysis of government programs.

As noted earlier, we propose that periodic impact evaluations be systematically required of all major immigration programs and be placed in the public domain pursuant to a notice and comment process, and that the detailed longitudinal data required be made more accessible. Following are some of the issues that need further study.

Overall economic success of immigrants: Studies are needed to better track the economic success of immigrants over time, by

---

9 Michael Trebilcock, *Public Inquiries: A Scholar's Engagements with the Policy-Making Process* (Toronto: University of Toronto Press, 2022), Part C.

category. For example, currently there is no evidence to shed light on whether the shift in selection priorities in the economic stream have resulted in better economic outcomes for economic immigrants. Similarly, we do not know what effect the narrowing of family class sponsorships has had on family incomes. And we have very little evidence of how immigrants admitted in the contemporary period are faring relative to the Canadian population.

Optimal immigration levels for the immediate and longer term: The levels the government sets are announced but not subject to informed public discussion. We recommend that proposed targets be accompanied by detailed evidence in support of them which should be subject to the review and comment mechanisms and public review suggested above.

Integration: Successful immigrant integration is an objective of immigration policy. However, there is no definition or agreed indicia of successful integration. This requires clarification, and audits undertaken of the different federal, provincial, and municipal programs dedicated towards facilitating integration. Public funding for programs should be tied to the completion of systematic impact evaluations over time.

Retention: Recent reports suggest that the number of immigrants who do not remain in Canada has risen steadily since the 1980s. On average, 5 per cent of immigrants who received permanent residence between 1982 and 2017 left after five years. This rate increases to over 17 per cent after twenty years. "The annual probability of emigrating peaks three to seven years after admission."[10] According to the Conference Board of Canada, the emigration rate has surged in recent years with the rate of immigrants leaving Canada being the highest in two decades.[11]

Greater effort is needed to address the reasons for outward migration. We also endorse the Conference Board's recommendation that retention rates should be a key performance indicator for Canadian immigration strategy.

---

10 Bérard-Chagnon et al., *Emigration of Immigrants*.
11 Dennler, *The Leaky Bucket*; Lone, "Canada's Surging Cost of Living Fuels Reverse Immigration."

Overstaying: Also not well known is the extent to which temporary residents leave Canada at the expiry of their visas. The government has admitted to publishing incorrect data on the number of temporary workers for some time. In rectifying the problem, it should also better track and publish how many temporary workers overstay their visas.

Federal Provincial Coordination

We acknowledge the important role provincial involvement plays in helping provinces secure the immigrants they need. Provincial Nominee Programs have grown rapidly in recent years and now account for 27 per cent of total economic admissions compared to just 10 per cent in 2006. Provincial admission criteria differ from the criteria used in federal and other provincial selection policies. This creates several challenges.

First, prospective immigrants are confronted with a complex and confusing labyrinth of policies. Second, provincial nominees are free to move to other provinces after they arrive in Canada, which creates a risk of undermining the objective of the policy that governed their admission. Third, the absence of a more coordinated system renders more challenging the task of evaluating the impact of Canadian immigration policies.

Significant integration and settlement programs, although frequently funded by the federal government, are usually decentralized and managed by the provinces and, more commonly, by a diverse array of community organizations. The latter organizations possess the advantage of being closely connected to their constituents and their specific needs. However, these programs encounter challenges due to short-term and unpredictable funding, which hinders ongoing evaluation of their effectiveness. Addressing these coordination issues requires more systematic attention.

Role of Artificial Intelligence in Program Administration

Serious and open consideration is required into the role of artificial intelligence (AI) in making immigration decisions. The rapidly expanding capacity of AI has the potential to facilitate and expedite much decision-making in the immigration domain. However, there are legitimate due process, human rights, and humanitarian concerns that demand case-specific judgments that cannot be readily reduced to algorithms, regardless of their sophistication.

The future role of AI-assisted decision-making requires a delicate and ongoing balancing of competing considerations.[12] Again, this is an area where an advisory council could offer valuable advice.

The Case for Incrementalism

A major strength of Canadian immigration policy has been its high level of support by the general population. In contrast to individuals in many other nations, Canadians exhibit a notably pro-immigration stance. On a per capita basis, Canada admits more immigrants than any other country and yet majorities support immigration. Our commitment to immigration has been maintained even as more are questioning the number of immigrants Canada should annually admit.

The facts of recent expansion bear repeating. Between 1991 and 2015 Canada admitted around 235,000 immigrants annually on a permanent basis. This figure then began to climb. By 2023, Canada was admitting close to twice that number with 471,000 permanent residents arriving and 485,000 anticipated for 2024.[13] The

---

12 For discussions of the potential application of AI to immigration decisions, see Abdi Aidid and Benjamin Alarie, *Legal Singularity: How Artificial Intelligence Can Make Law Radically Better* (Toronto: University of Toronto Press, 2023), 173–5; Mario Bellissimo, "Application Backlogs and Processing Times: Brief submitted to the House of Commons Standing Committee on Citizenship and Immigration," 30 May 2022, https://www.ourcommons.ca/Content/Committee/441/CIMM/Brief /BR11845890/br-external/BellissimoLawGroupProfessionalCorporation-e.pdf; Petra Molnar and Lex Gill, *BOTS AT THE GATE: A Human Rights Analysis of Automated Decision-Making in Canada's Immigration and Refugee System* (Toronto: University of Toronto International Human Rights Program, 2018), https://citizenlab.ca/wp-content/uploads/2018/09/IHRP-Automated-Systems-Report-Web-V2.pdf.

13 See figure 3; see also Immigration, Refugees and Citizenship, *Annual Report to Parliament on Immigration* (Ottawa: 2023), https://publications.gc.ca/collections /collection_2023/ircc/Ci1-2023-eng.pdf.

number of temporary foreign workers in the country experienced more spectacular growth, from some 322,000 in 2025 to 1,270,360 in 2023.[14] The number of international students in the country also grew rapidly, from 219,000 in 2015 to 1,040,000 in 2023.[15]

The rapid expansion has stirred controversy. In the fall of 2022, 69 per cent of Canadians polled voiced support for annual immigration levels. However, within a year, that support declined by 18 percentage points.[16]

This current unease about annual immigration levels has focused primarily on the impact that large numbers of arrivals have on the housing, health, and labour sectors.[17] Often the distinction is not made between the impact of permanent and temporary immigration on these sectors.[18] While Canadians continue to support immigration, they increasingly question the annual number of immigrants that the country can absorb.

Various factors contribute to Canada's long-standing pro-immigration stance. Many would point to our multicultural policy and decades-old tradition of welcoming immigrants. While these are important, economic factors have also been crucial. Canada has consistently sought immigration to drive economic growth, and our immigration program has been managed with this objective in mind. Canada's skill-selected immigrants are predominantly

14 See figure 5; see also Parisa Mahboubi and Mikal Skuterud, "Canada Must Stem the Surge in Temporary Foreign Workers and International Students," *Globe and Mail*, 7 February 2024.

15 See figure 7.

16 Environics Institute, *Canadian Public Opinion about Immigration and Refugees, Focus Canada* (Fall 2023), 7.

17 See, for example, Jack Jedwab, "What Underlies Concern over Canada's Immigration Numbers?" Metropolis Institute, 11 March 2024, https://acsmetropolisca-wpuploads.s3.ca-central-1.amazonaws.com/wp-content/uploads/2024/03/20094653/Immigration-concerns-remain-high.pdf.

18 See, for example, Meggs and Fortin, "Are We Heading for 100 Million Canadians?" https://inroadsjournal.ca/are-we-heading-for-100-million-canadians/, and the response from Century Initiative CEO Lisa Lalande, "The Century Initiative Does Not Advocate Massive Temporary Immigration," *Inroads: The Canadian Journal of Opinion*, no. 53 (Summer/Fall 2023), https://inroadsjournal.ca/inroads-special/.

highly educated and capable workers, with almost half now holding university degrees.

Our history and geography have helped shape a positive stance towards immigrants. Unlike the United States, Canada does not have a border with Mexico, whose undocumented migrants are the main source of controversy in the United States. And unlike many European countries, Canada is a settler society without former colonies whose citizens have grown up expecting a welcome in the "mother country." When Canadians talk positively about "immigration," they refer to something different from "immigration" as understood elsewhere. We are principally talking about skilled workers arriving with an official government invitation in hand.

Canadian belief in immigration for economic growth has been sustained through many trials. Many predicted that 9/11 and the resulting War on Terror would force Canadians to abandon both immigration and multiculturalism. Despite worries about the loyalties of some groups of immigrants, overall support for immigration remains high. While many immigrants struggle more in the job market, rather than turn against them on that basis, Canadians have rallied, mounting programs to help immigrants find jobs and help employers see the value of foreign-acquired education and experience.

But it would be short-sighted to think Canadians will always support immigration unconditionally. Rapid expansion of annual admissions alone will not improve Canada's domestic productivity per capita. High rates of immigration are thought to contribute to strained health care services and exacerbate housing shortages. A surge in refugee claims also threatens to weaken public confidence in the system as Canadians are highly suspicious of "bogus refugee claims," despite our high acceptance rates. And notwithstanding our high ideals, minority groups still face racism and discrimination. For example, employment audits show job applicants with Asian names have about a 40 per cent lower chance of being invited for an interview, even with Canadian education and experience.

In essence, Canadian backing for immigration is robust but not unconditional. Planned annual immigration levels must align with policies that facilitate newcomers' integration without burdening Canadians seeking employment, housing, or health care. This is crucial for upholding broader public trust in the system's ability to serve all Canadians.

Ensuring public support for immigration must be a high priority and public accountability should be a major feature of immigration policy-making. Canadians will support immigration policy only if they see it as in the national interest, and not something designed to serve the interests of a select few. Taking that support for granted would be very unwise.[19]

In writing about the recent dramatic decline in public approval for current immigration levels, Keith Neuman and Michael Adams observed that the decline in support represents the most "significant one-year change in this indicator in four decades of research":

> Up until now, we would have considered anyone who says there is too much immigration to Canada to be expressing a xenophobic sentiment, reflecting fear or rejection of those seen as too different because of race, religion, or culture. This still applies for some, but we must now recognize that the public discourse has changed – that it is increasingly about the country's capacity to receive the numbers of newcomers arriving as well as who it is we are admitting.[20]

---

19 Despite recent criticism of immigrant policy in the media, the government appears unconcerned about maintaining public support for permanent immigration numbers. For example, early in 2024, the housing minister and former immigration minister Sean Fraser expressed confidence that permanent immigration numbers were "in the right place" even after the dramatic increases over previous years. This view appears to assume that the declining support for immigration numbers found in the series of Environics polls cited earlier (Environics "Focus Canada – Fall 2022," and "Focus Canada – Fall 2023") reflected only the growing public concerns about temporary immigration, even though the interview question has normally been interpreted as applying to permanent immigration numbers. See Spencer Van Dyk, "Permanent Immigration Levels 'in the Right Place': Fraser," *CTV News*, 3 April 2024, https://www.ctvnews.ca/politics/permanent-immigration-levels-in-the-right-place-fraser-1.6832085.

20 Keith Neuman and Michael Adams, "The Conversation around Immigration in Canada Is Shifting," *Globe and Mail*, 3 November 2023, https://www.theglobeandmail.com/opinion/article-the-conversation-around-immigration-in-canada-is-shifting/.

We, like many Canadians, support liberal immigration policies for various economic, social, political, and humanitarian reasons. However, we are concerned that the rapid shifts in numbers, criteria, and processes over the past two decades have not been properly evaluated and have been imposed with very limited participation by the Canadian public.

It is not sufficient to conduct "stakeholder surveys" or to repeat platitudes in support of immigration that may appear to be reflecting the interests of a few. The case for liberal economic, family, and refugee policies is not strengthened by wonder-working claims that increased immigration will solve our relatively poor performance on economic productivity measures in recent years.

Improving our productivity depends on many factors, not least of which is significant investment in retraining and technological innovation. Without such investments, immigration alone is unlikely to raise average Canadian incomes. Reports of "labour shortages" are met by calls for more immigration, yet they may reflect deeper problems that deserve attention, including (according to testimony before a Senate committee) "low wages, improved benefits and job stability, and productivity enhancing technological change."[21]

Nor is it all clear that immigration will dramatically reduce dependency ratios (ratio of income earners to elderly or young dependents) in an aging society. This is because immigrants are not substantially younger than the current resident population, and the projected increase in young immigrants will not be enough to substantially change the overall dependency ratio.

Alongside this, future immigration levels should also consider the capacity of housing markets, health care systems, and integration services to accommodate major population increases (at least in the short term). Uncertainties in these areas render long-term immigration targets hazardous and suggest major virtues to incrementalism.

---

21 Jim Stamford, "Interrogating the Labour Shortage Hypothesis," Center for Future Work, 11 October 2023, https://centreforfuturework.ca/2023/10/11/interrogating-the-labour-shortage-hypothesis/.

We close by posing a question: Is Canada's approach to immigration "a beacon to the world" or is it "a disaster in the making"? There is no shortage of proponents of both views. In our view, Canada's immigration and multiculturalism policies have largely served us well. But the factors that have influenced the shape of Canada's success in immigration policy must be widely understood and maintained.

To date, Canadian immigration policies have not generated a dysfunctional social, economic, and political environment that immigration has provoked in other countries. However, there is no case for complacency. There remains considerable room for improvement in current policies as this book has sought to demonstrate. With a commitment to continuous review and improvement, now and hopefully for the future, the prevailing political and public sentiment supporting immigration can be sustained and strengthened.

Epilogue

Shortly after this book went to print, the Canadian government announced a 27 per cent reduction in the annual intake of permanent residents over the next three years, decreasing the target from 500,000 to 365,000 by 2027. The prime minister explained that previous immigration projections had not anticipated the added strain on housing, healthcare, and social services. This policy adjustment, he stated, would give the government time to "catch up" by investing in these sectors to better accommodate newcomers in the future.[1]

Government statements suggested that growing public concerns about immigration levels had influenced this decision. An Environics poll published just three days before the prime minister's announcement indicated that, "for the first time in a quarter century, a clear majority of Canadians say there is too much immigration."[2]

Alongside the permanent resident reduction, the government also lowered the annual number of temporary foreign workers

---

1 The Canadian Press, "Trudeau Announces Massive Drop in Immigration Targets as Liberals Make Major Pivot," *CTV News*, 24 October 2024, https://www.ctvnews.ca/politics/trudeau-announces-massive-drop-in-immigration-targets-as-liberals-make-major-pivot-1.7085333.

2 Environics Institute for Survey Research, "Canadian Public Opinion about Immigration and Refugees," Focus Canada Series, 17 October 2024, Introduction. Fifty-eight per cent of Canadians agreed that overall "there is too much immigration in Canada." This represented an increase of 14 percentage points over the 2023 findings, which in itself was 17 percentage points over the previous 2022 survey results.

allowed entry and set new caps on how many temporary workers each employer could hire.[3]

Additionally, the issuance of international study permits, already reduced by 35 per cent in 2024, was set to drop by a further 10 per cent. Financial requirements for prospective international students were raised, admission verification standards were tightened, and work options for students were limited.[4]

In justifying these changes, the prime minister criticized employers for using the temporary foreign worker program to suppress wages and blamed educational institutions, under provincial oversight, for bringing in more international students than communities could reasonably support. He called their behaviour unacceptable, treating students as "an expendable means to line their own pockets."[5]

This shift in policy marked yet another abrupt change, made in response to public pressure. However, like other adjustments noted in this book, these new measures were introduced swiftly, without substantial public debate. There was no transparent, evidence-based review to guide the setting of annual immigration targets, address labour market needs, or plan for sustainable population growth. Similarly, the criteria for setting limits on temporary foreign workers and the projected impact of the new regulations remained vague.

While there was significant evidence of misuse in the international student visa process, provinces and universities warned that an overcorrection could severely impact the financial stability of Canadian universities and colleges.[6] Moreover, the announcement

---

3 Government of Canada, "Minister Boissonnault Reducing the Number of Temporary Foreign Workers in Canada," 26 August 2024, https://www.canada.ca/en/employment -social-development/news/2024/08/minister-boissonnault-reducing-the-number -of-temporary-foreign-workers-in-canada.html.

4 Immigration and Citizenship Canada, "Strengthening Temporary Residence Programs for Sustainable Volumes," 18 September 2024, https://www.canada.ca /en/immigration-refugees-citizenship/news/2024/09/strengthening-temporary -residence-programs-for-sustainable-volumes.html.

5 The Canadian Press, "Trudeau Announces Massive Drop."

6 ICEF Monitor, "Canada: Mid-year Data Indicates that International Student Commencements Could Drop by Nearly 50% for 2024," 11 September 2024, https:// monitor.icef.com/2024/09/canada-mid-year-data-indicates-that-international -student-commencements-could-drop-by-nearly-50-for-2024/.

did not include any commitment to a transparent evaluation of the changes' impacts over the coming years.

The way these policy shifts were introduced – and the absence of a clear understanding of their implications – underscores this book's central argument: Canada urgently needs an open, informed public review of its immigration policies. In the past, similar periods of reflection have proven invaluable for shaping the country's immigration future. Today, such a reflection is long overdue. President-elect Donald Trump's recent threat to impose a 25 per cent tariff on all imports from Canada unless tighter security measures are implemented at the shared border may add a new sense of urgency to such a comprehensive review.

Appendix

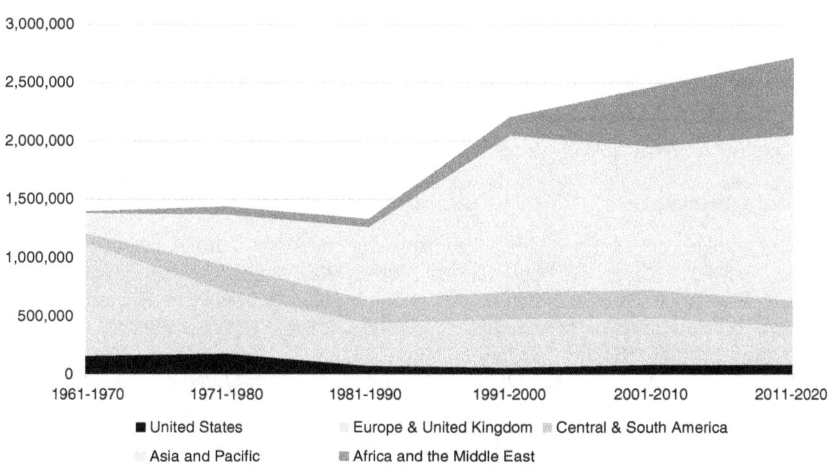

Source: Immigration, Refugees and Citizenship Canada. 1961–2000: compiled in Reitz, 2022,[1] 2001–2010: Facts and Figures 2010;[2] 2011–2016: Facts and Figures 2016;[3] 2016–2020: Canada "Open Government" website: Permanent Residents by Country of Citizenship, January 2015–September 2023, https://open.canada.ca/data/en/dataset/f7e5498e-0ad8 -4417-85c9-9b8aff9b9eda/resource/d1c1f4f3-2d7f-4e02-9a79-7af98209c2f3 File url: https://www.ircc.canada.ca/opendata-donneesouvertes/data/EN_ODP-PR-Citz.xlsx Note: For 1961–2010, origin refers to country of last permanent residence; for 2011–2020, origin refers to country of citizenship. Comparison of data from years for which both indicators are available shows only small differences.

---

1 Reitz, "Canada: Continuity and Change in Immigration for Nation-Building."
2 Citizenship and Immigration Canada, *Canada Facts and Figures: Immigration Overview – Permanent and Temporary Residents* (Ottawa: Citizenship and Immigration Canada, 2010), 124.
3 Citizenship and Immigration Canada, *Facts and Figures 2016 – Immigration Overview – Permanent Residents* (Ottawa: Citizenship and Immigration Canada, 2016).

Figure 2. Immigration to Canada by Origins and Year, 2001–2023

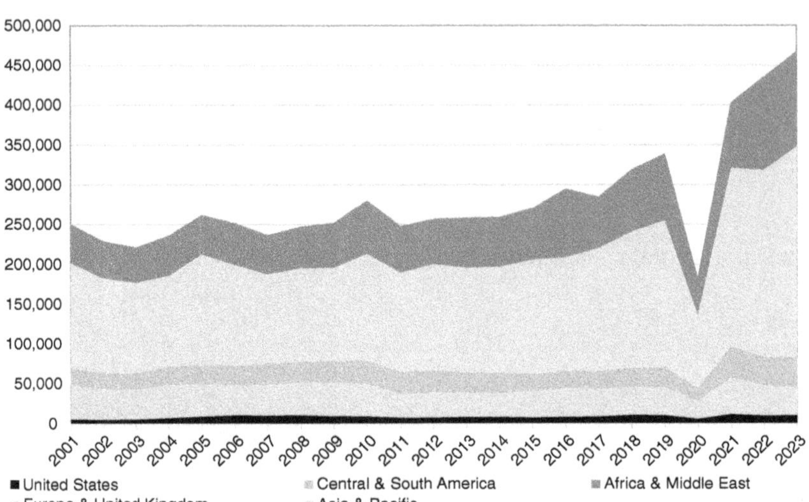

Source: Immigration, Refugees and Citizenship Canada. 2001–2010: Facts and Figures 2010;[4] 2011–2016: Facts and Figures 2016;[5] 2016–2020: Canada "Open Government" website: Permanent Residents by Country of Citizenship, January 2015–February, 2024, https://open.canada.ca/data/en/dataset/f7e5498e-0ad8-4417-85c9-9b8aff9b9eda /resource/d1c1f4f3-2d7f-4e02-9a79-7af98209c2f3
File url: https://www.ircc.canada.ca/opendata-donneesouvertes/data/EN_ODP-PR-Citz .xlsx.
Accessed April 2024
Note: For 2001–2010, origin refers to country of last permanent residence; for 2011–2023, origin refers to country of citizenship. Comparison of data from years for which both indicators are available shows only small differences.

---

4 Citizenship and Immigration Canada, *Canada Facts and Figures: Immigration Overview – Permanent and Temporary Residents.*
5 Citizenship and Immigration Canada, *Facts and Figures 2016 – Immigration Overview – Permanent Residents.*

Figure 3. Immigration to Canada by Class of Entry, 1980–2023

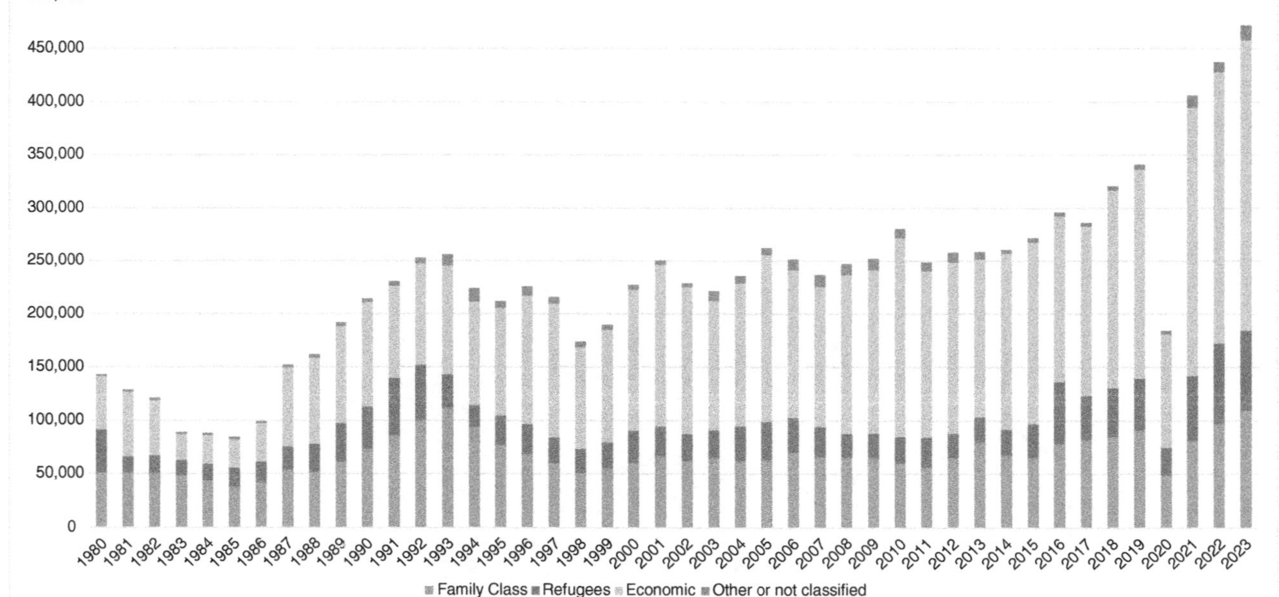

Source: Immigration, Refugees and Citizenship Canada. 1980–2006: Facts and Figures 2006,[6] 2007–2016: Facts and Figures 2016,[7] 2017–2023: Canada "Open Government" website, "Canada – Admissions of Permanent Residents by Province/Territory and Immigration Category, January 15–February 2024," https://open.canada.ca/data/en/dataset/f7e5498e-0ad8-4417-85c9-9b8aff9b9eda/resource/5582034d-8f89-49d5-8597 -483d628078a1, file url: https://www.ircc.canada.ca/opendata-donneesouvertes/data/EN_ODP-PR-ProvImmCat.xlsx
Accessed April 2024

6 Citizenship and Immigration Canada, *Facts and Figures 2006: Immigration Overview – Permanent and Temporary Residents* (Ottawa: Citizenship and Immigration Canada, 2006).
7 Citizenship and Immigration Canada, *Facts and Figures 2016 – Immigration Overview – Permanent Residents.*

Figure 4. Per cent in Each Admission Category, Economic Class, 2006–2023

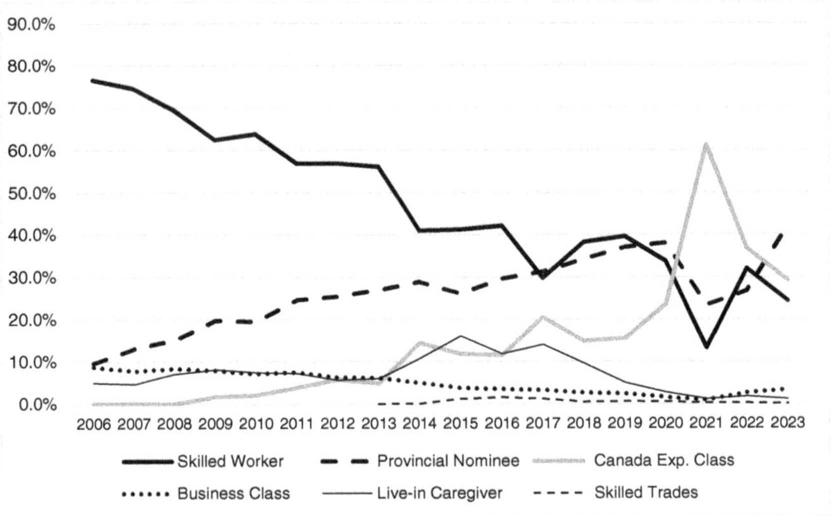

Source: Immigration, Refugees and Citizenship Canada. Government of Canada,
Open Government website. Accessed April 2024.
https://open.canada.ca/data/en/dataset/f7e5498e-0ad8-4417-85c9-9b8aff9b9eda
Canada – Permanent Residents by Immigration Category
Note: Provincial Nominees include Atlantic Immigration Programs and Pilot Programs
(new in 2016), and Canada Experience Class includes Temporary Resident to Permanent
Resident Pathway (created as a temporary program to help meet immigration targets
during pandemic, extended: https://www.canada.ca/en/immigration-refugees-citizenship
/services/application/application-forms-guides/guide-5069-temporary-resident-permanent
-resident-pathway.html#eligibility). Quebec selection classes not included.

Figure 5. Temporary Work Permit Holders in Canada at Year End, by Program, 2000–2023

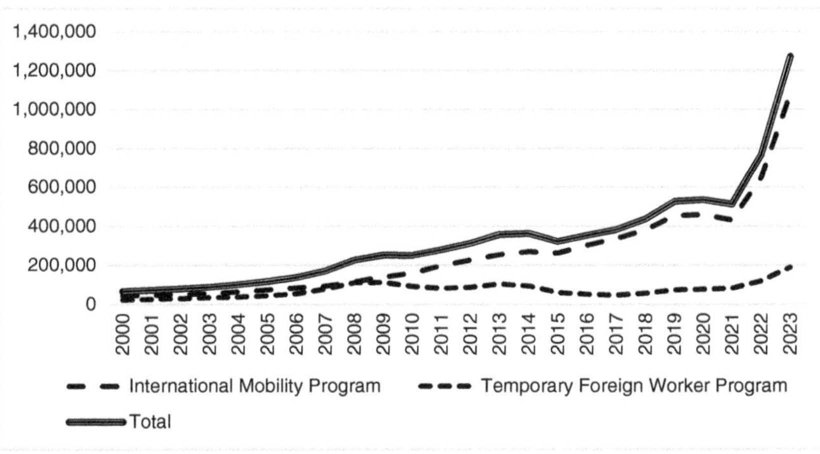

Source: Government of Canada, Open Government website, accessed April 2024. Canada–Temporary Foreign Worker Program (TFWP) work permit holders on December 31st by Province/Territory of intended destination and program, 2000–2023 (EN_ODP_annual-TR-work-TFW_CITZ_year_end.xlsx); https://www.ircc.canada.ca/opendata-donneesouvertes/data/EN_ODP_annual-TR-work -TFW_PT_program_year_end.xlsx
Canada–International Mobility Program (IMP) work permit holders on December 31st by province/territory of intended destination and program, 2000–2023 (EN_ODP _annual-TR-work-IMP_CITZ_year_end.xlsx); https://www.ircc.canada.ca/opendata-donneesouvertes/data/EN_ODP_annual-TR-work -IMP_PT_program_year_end.xlsx
Note: Work permit holders in Canada at each year end include those whose permits became effective in that year or in previous years. Data on the International Mobility Program prior to its creation in 2014 have been adjusted to match the program definition, as covering work permits holders not requiring a Labour Market Impact Assessment. Data on work permits under the Temporary Foreign Worker Program include those for whom Labour Market Impact Assessments were required. See *Annual Report to Parliament on Immigration, 2014*, pp. 2, 6, 16. On 22 June, IRCC announced that data previously published on work permit holders in the International Mobility Program were incorrect (*Globe and Mail*, 22 June 2023); data here are the corrected data currently posted.

Figure 6. Temporary Work Permit Holders by Year Permit Became Effective, 2015–2023

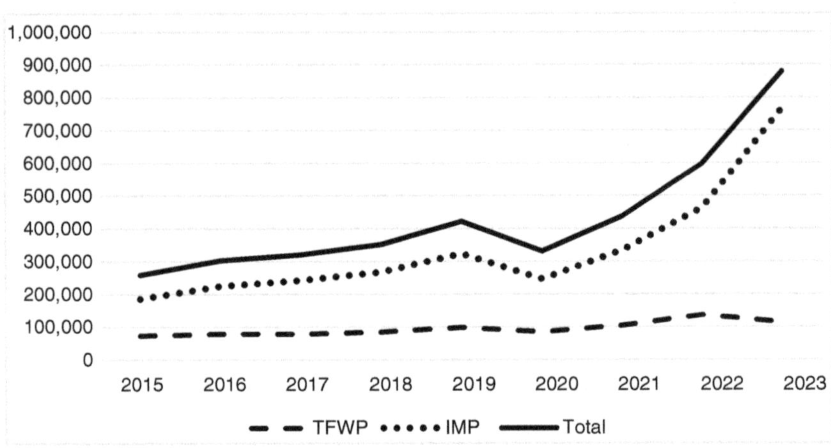

Source: Government of Canada, Open Government website, accessed April 2024.
Canada–International Mobility Program (IMP) work permit holders by province/
territory of intended destination, program and year in which permit(s) became effective,
January 2015–February 2024.
EN_ODP-TR-Work-IMP_PT_program_sign (1).xlsx
https://www.cic.gc.ca/opendata-donneesouvertes/data/EN_ODP-TR-Work-IMP_PT
_program_sign.xlsx
Canada–Temporary Foreign Worker Program (TFWP) work permit holders by province/
territory of intended destination, program and year in which permit(s) became effective,
January 2015–June 2023
EN_ODP-TR-Work-TFWP_PT_program_sign.xlsx
https://www.cic.gc.ca/opendata-donneesouvertes/data/EN_ODP-TR-Work-TFWP_PT
_program_sign.xlsx

Figure 7. Study Permit Holders in Canada by Year End, 2000–2023, and by Year Permit Became Effective 2015–2023

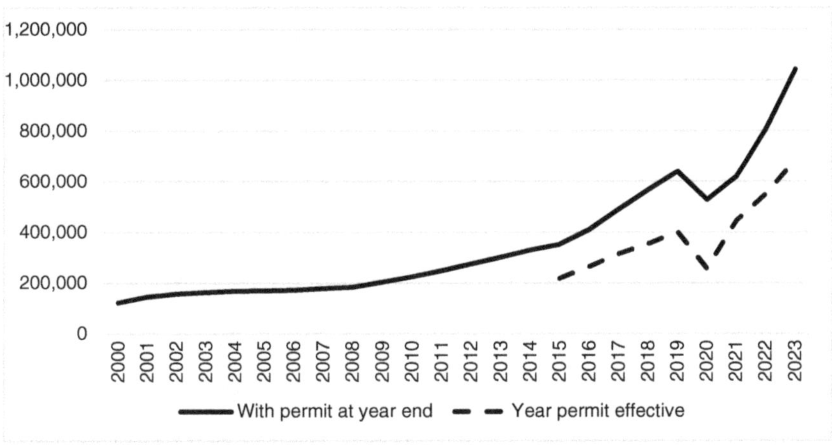

Source: Government of Canada, "Open Government" Website.
Canada–Study permit holders with a valid permit on December 31st by Province/Territory of intended destination and study level, 2000–2023.
EN_ODP-TR-Study-IS_PT_study_level_sign.xlsx
https://open.canada.ca/data/en/dataset/90115b00-f9b8-49e8-afa3-b4cff8facaee/resource/b663a97c-61d4-4e17-af51-0cba01ef3a44
https://www.cic.gc.ca/opendata-donneesouvertes/data/EN_ODP_annual-TR-Study-IS_PT_study_level_year_end.xlsx
Accessed April 2024
Canada–Study permit holders by province/territory of intended destination, gender and year in which permit(s) became effective, January 2015–June 2023.
EN_ODP-TR-Study-IS_PT_gender_sign.xlsx
https://open.canada.ca/data/en/dataset/90115b00-f9b8-49e8-afa3-b4cff8facaee/resource/a26ab6fd-c51a-4cd2-8da5-77d0ac41fb81
https://www.cic.gc.ca/opendata-donneesouvertes/data/EN_ODP-TR-Study-IS_PT_gender_sign.xlsx
Accessed April 2024

Figure 8. Refugees Resettled in Canada 1979–2023

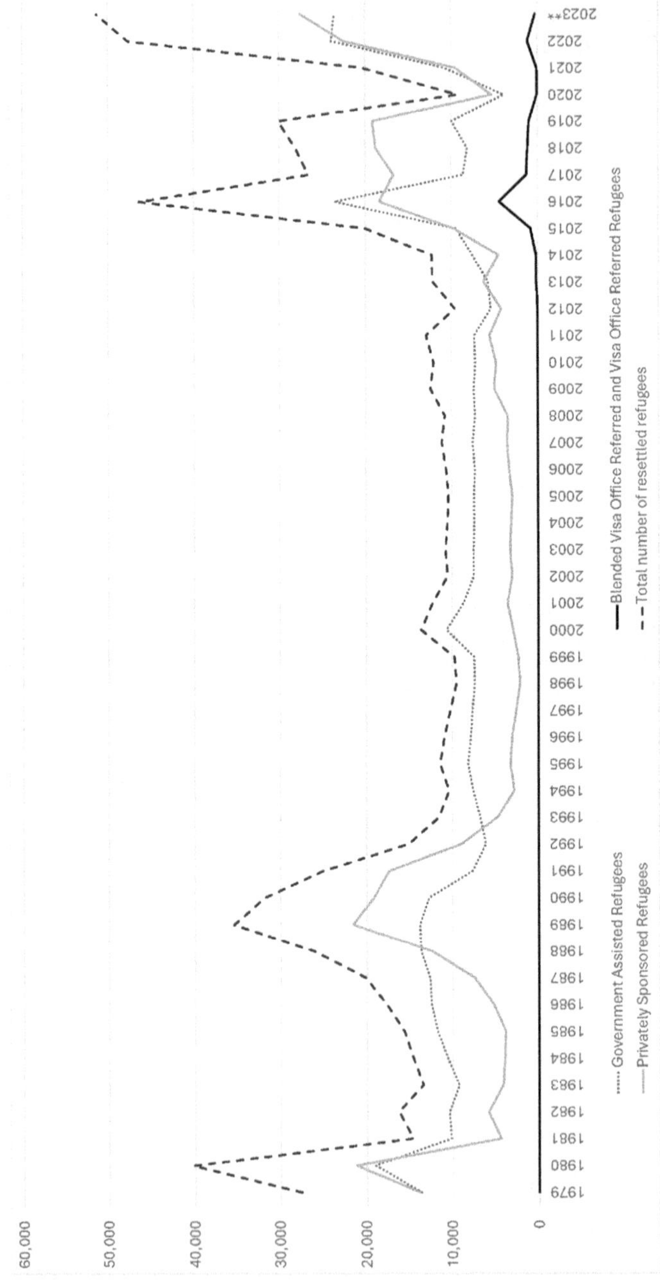

Source: UNHCR Canada, statistics compiled from various reports and publications of Immigration, Refugees and Citizenship Canada.

Figure 9. Asylum Claims in Canada 2001–2023

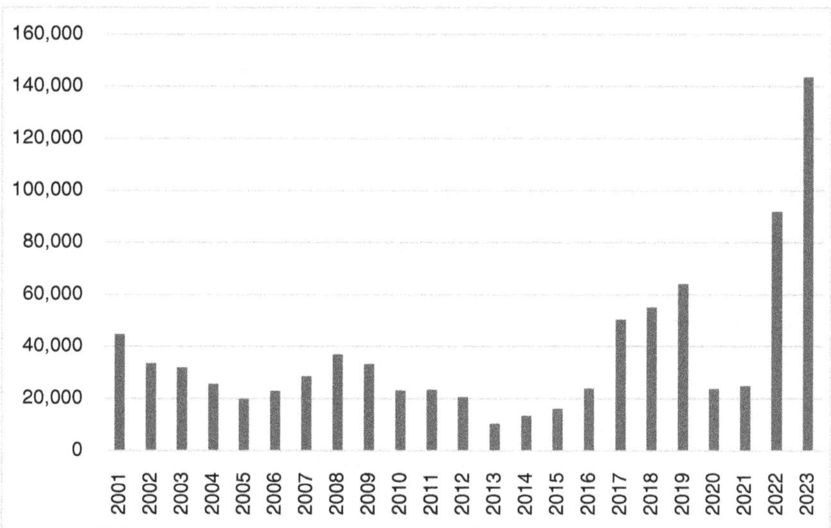

Source: Immigration Refugees and Citizenship Canada, Total Asylum Claims processed by CBSA and IRBC, https://www.canada.ca/en/immigration-refugees-citizenship/services/refugees/asylum-claims.html; and Immigration Refugees and Citizenship Canada, Refugee Claimants - Years 2001-2016, https://publications.gc.ca/collections/collection_2017/ircc/Ci44-21-2017-eng.pdf

Figure 10. Asylum Claims: Acceptance and Rejection Rates on the Merits 2011–2023

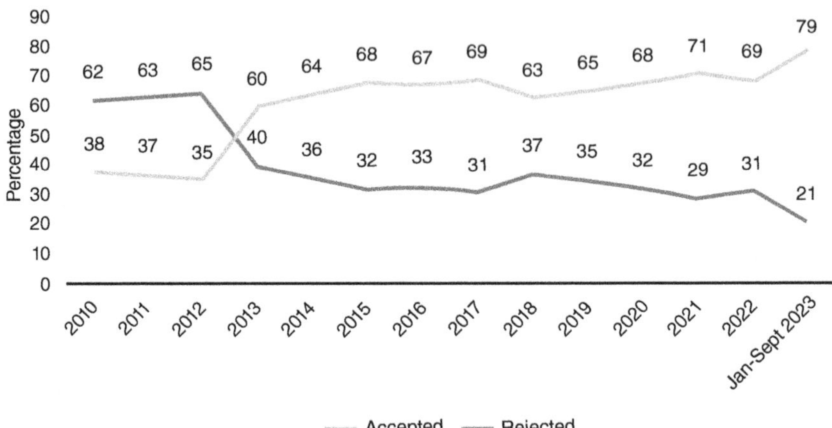

Source: UNHCR Canada, statistics for 2010–2012 compiled from Statistics Canada, "Asylum Claimants," May 2019, https://www150.statcan.gc.ca/n1/pub/89-28-0001 /2018001/article/00013-eng.htm; Statistics from 2012-2023 from Immigration, Refugees and Citizenship Canada, "Refugee Claim Statistics (2013–2023)," https://www.irb-cisr.gc .ca/en/statistics/protection/Pages/index.aspx

Categories of Admission	Skilled Worker[2]			Other Federal Program	Provincial Nominee Program	Quebec[3]
	Federal Skilled Worker Program	Canada Experience Class	Federal Skilled Trades Program	Business, Care-giver, and other small programs[4]	Each province has its own programs	Parallel to federal
Criteria for Eligibility	Language, education, and work experience requirements (similar to traditional points system)	Language, and work experience in Canada (as temporary immi-grant) in designated occupations	Language, secondary education, work experi-ence in designated trades, and job offer or certificate of qualification in Canada	Varies by program	Established by province (may be available to temporary immigrants in the province)	Parallel to federal, for those plan-ning to settle in Quebec
Selection Process	Express Entry, using Comprehensive Ranking Scheme	Express Entry, using Comprehensive Ranking Scheme	Express Entry, using Comprehensive Ranking Scheme	Varies by program	Varies; Express Entry available for those eligible as a Skilled Worker	Parallel to federal, leading to Quebec certification

1. Includes partners and dependents of principal applicant.
2. In addition to the three categories indicated, a "public policy" category for "temporary resident to permanent resident pathways" was introduced during the COVID-19 pandemic, initially for refugees in the health care field, and described as "time-limited," but later renewed and described as applying to undocumented construction workers.
3. Quebec's immigration system includes categories similar to the federal system; its Expression of Interest process is similar to Express Entry.
4. Includes pilot programs. Sources: Immigration and Citizenship Canada, "Immigrate to Canada," https://www.canada.ca/en/immigration-refugees-citizenship/services/immigrate-canada.html. Accessed November 25, 2024. Government of Québec, "Immigrate permanently to Québec," https://www.quebec.ca/en/immigration/permanent. Accessed November 25, 2024. See also note 38 on p. 111.

Bibliography

Abella, Irving, and Troper, Harold. *None Is Too Many: Canada and the Jews of Europe 1933–1948*. 4th ed. Toronto: University of Toronto Press, 2024.

Adachi, Ken. *The Enemy That Never Was: A History of Japanese Canadians*. Toronto: McClelland and Stewart, 1976.

Adams, Michael. *Unlikely Utopia: The Surprising Triumph of Canadian Pluralism*. Toronto: Viking Canada, 2007.

Advisory Council on Economic Growth. *Attracting the Talent Canada Needs through Immigration*. Ottawa: Government of Canada, 2016.

Aidid, Abdi, and Benjamin Alarie. *Legal Singularity: How Artificial Intelligence Can Make Law Radically Better*. Toronto: University of Toronto Press, 2023.

Alba, Richard, and Nancy Foner. *Strangers No More: Immigration and the Challenges of Integration in North America and Western Europe*. Princeton, NJ: Princeton University Press, 2015.

Alboim, Naomi, and Karen Cohl. "Shaping the Future: Canada's Rapidly Changing Immigration Policies." Toronto: The Maytree Foundation, October 2012. https://maytree.com/wp-content/uploads/shaping-the-future.pdf.

Alhmidi, Maan. "Ottawa Plans to Eliminate Citizenship Application Fees." *Globe and Mail*, 24 December 2019. https://www.proquest.com/docview/2330006745/citation/E5D6A5B1CEF845BBPQ/1.

Ali, Mehrunnisa Ahmad, and Assel Baitubayeva. "Immigrant Women's Roles in Family Settlement." In *Putting Family First: Migration and Integration in Canada*, edited by Harald Baude, 177–97. Vancouver: UBC Press, 2019.

Ali, Mehrunnisa Ahmad, Marc Yvan Valade, and Tania Dargy. "How Families Shape Settlement Trajectories." In *Putting Family First: Migration and Integration Canada*, edited by Harald Bauder, 158–73. Vancouver: UBC Press, 2019.

Anstis, Siena, Joshua Blum, and Jared Will. "Separate but Unequal: Immigration Detention in Canada and the Great Writ of Liberty." *McGill Law Journal* 63, no. 1 (2017). https://lawjournal.mcgill.ca/article/separate-but-unequal-immigration-detention-in-canada-and-the-great-writ-of-liberty.

Atkinson, Michael M. *Governing Canada: Institutions and Public Policy*. Toronto: Harcourt Brace & Company Canada, 1993.

Auditor General of Canada. "Chapter 2 – The Governor in Council Appointment
     Process." *2009 March Status Report of the Auditor General of Canada.* Ottawa: Office
     of the Auditor General of Canada, 2009. https://www.muskratfallsinquiry.ca
     /files/P-01777.pdf.
– "Chapter 2 – Selecting Foreign Workers under the Immigration Program." *Report
     of the Auditor General of Canada.* Ottawa: Office of the Auditor General of Canada,
     2009.
– "Chapter 3 – Citizenship and Immigration Canada – The Economic Component
     of the Canadian Immigration Program." *Report of the Auditor General of Canada.*
     Ottawa: Office of the Auditor General of Canada, 2009.
– "Citizenship and Immigration Canada – The Economic Component of the Canadian
     Immigration Program." *Report of the Auditor General of Canada.* Ottawa: Office of the
     Auditor General of Canada, 2000.
– "Report 1 – Immigration Removals." *Report of the Auditor General of Canada.* Ottawa:
     Office of the Auditor General of Canada, 2020. https://www.oag-bvg.gc.ca
     /internet/english/parl_oag_202007_01_e_43572.html.
– "Report 2 – Processing of Asylum Claims." *Report of the Auditor General of Canada.*
     Ottawa: Office of the Auditor General of Canada, 2019. https://www.oag-bvg
     .gc.ca/internet/English/parl_oag_201905_02_e_43339.html.
– "Report 5 – Temporary Foreign Worker Program – Employment and Social
     Development Canada." *Report of the Auditor General of Canada.* Ottawa: Office of the
     Auditor General of Canada, 2017. https://www.oag-bvg.gc.ca/internet/English
     /att__e_42263.html.
– "Report 9 – Processing Applications for Permanent Residence – Immigration,
     Refugees and Citizenship Canada." *Report of the Auditor General of Canada.* Ottawa:
     Office of the Auditor General of Canada, 2023.
Axworthy, Lloyd, and Allan Rock. "The Safe Third Country Agreement Is Unsafe – and
     Unconstitutional." *Globe and Mail,* 11 October 2022. https://www.theglobeandmail.
     com/opinion/article-the-safe-third-country-agreement-is-unsafe-and
     -unconstitutional/.
Aydemir, Abdurrahman, and Chris Robinson. *Return and Onward Migration among
     Working Age Men.* Ottawa: Statistics Canada, 2006.
Badets, Jane, and Tina W.L. Chui. *Canada's Changing Immigrant Population.* Ottawa:
     Statistics Canada, and Toronto: Prentice Hall Canada, 1994.
Banerjee, Rupa. "Introduction to the Special Issue: Canada's Economic Immigration
     Policy: Opportunities and Challenges for the Road Ahead." *Journal of International
     Migration and Integration* 24, Supplement 3 (2023): 585–97. https://doi.org/10.1007
     /s12134-023-01068-y.
Banerjee, Rupa, Feng Hou, Jeffrey G. Reitz, and Tingting Zhang. "Evaluating Foreign
     Skills: Effects of Credential Assessment on Skilled Immigrants' Labour Market
     Performance in Canada." *Canadian Public Policy* 47, no. 3 (2021): 358–72.
Banting, Keith. "Multiculturalism Policy in Canada: Conflicted and Resilient." In
     Policy Success in Canada: Cases, Lessons, Challenges, edited by Evert Lindquist,
     Michael Howlett, Grace Skogstad, Geneviève Tellier, and Paul 't Hart, 183–205.
     New York: Oxford University Press, 2022.
Banting, Keith, and Debra Thompson. "The Puzzling Persistence of Racial Inequality in
     Canada." *Canadian Journal of Political Science* 54, no. 4 (2021): 870–91. doi:10.1017
     /S0008423921000585.

Banting, Keith, and Will Kymlicka. "Introduction: The Political Sources of Solidarity in Diverse Societies." In *The Strains of Commitment: The Political Sources of Solidarity in Diverse Societies*, edited by Keith Banting and Will Kymlicka, 1–58. New York: Oxford University Press, 2017.

Banting, Keith, Richard Johnston, Will Kymlicka, and Stuart Soroka. "Do Multiculturalism Policies Erode the Welfare State? An Empirical Analysis." In *Multiculturalism and the Welfare State*, edited by Keith Banting and Will Kymlicka, 48–91. Oxford: Oxford University Press, 2006.

Barber, John. "Canada's Conservatives Vow to Create 'Barbaric Cultural Practices' Hotline." *The Guardian*, 2 October 2015. https://www.theguardian.com/world/2015/oct/02/canada-conservatives-barbaric-cultural-practices-hotline.

Barry, Brian. *Culture and Equality: An Egalitarian Critique of Multiculturalism*. Boston: Harvard University Press, 2002.

Beaujot, Roderic. "Effect of Immigration on Demographic Structure." In *Canadian Immigration Policy for the 21st Century*, edited by Charles M. Beach, Alan G. Green, and Jeffrey G. Reitz, 49–91. Montreal: Queen's University Press, and John Deutsch Institute for the Study of Economic Policy, 2003.

Beaujot, Roderic P., and Kevin McQuillan. *Growth and Dualism: The Demographic Development of Canadian Society*. Toronto: Gage, 1982.

Becerra-Valdivia, Lorena, and Thomas Higham. "The Timing and Effect of the Earliest Human Arrivals in North America." *Nature* 584 (2020): 93–7.

Beiser, Morton. *Strangers at the Gate: The "Boat People's" First Ten Years in Canada*. Toronto: University of Toronto Press, 1999.

Bélanger, Danièle, and Guillermo Candiz. "The Politics of 'Waiting' for Care: Immigration Policy and Family Reunification in Canada." *Journal of Ethnic and Migration Studies* 46, no. 16 (2019): 3472–90.

Bell, Stewart. "Passenger Wanted in Sri Lanka." *National Post*, 22 October 2009. https://immigrationwatchcanada.org/2009/10/22/passenger-wanted-in-sri-lanka/.

Belshaw, John Douglas. *Canadian History: Pre-Confederation*. 2nd ed. Victoria, BC: BCampus, 2020. https://opentextbc.ca/preconfederation2e/.

Benmelech, Efram, and Esteban F. Klor. "Where Are ISIS's Foreign Fighters Coming From?" NBER Working Paper 222190. National Bureau of Economic Research. April 2016.

Benslimane, Souheil, and David Moffette. "The Double Punishment of Criminal Inadmissibility for Immigrants." *Journal of Prisoners on Prisons* 28, no. 1 (2019): 44–65. https://doi.org/10.18192/jpp.v28i1.4351.

Bérard-Chagnon, Julien, and Lorena Canon. *The Canadian Diaspora: Estimating the Number of Canadian Citizens Who Live Abroad*. Ottawa: Statistics Canada, 2022. https://www150.statcan.gc.ca/n1/pub/91f0015m/91f0015m2022001-eng.htm#a10.

Bérard-Chagnon, Julien, Stacey Hallman, and Genevieve Caron. *Recent Immigrants and Non-Permanent Residents Missed in the 2011 Census*. Ottawa: Statistics Canada, 2019. https://www150.statcan.gc.ca/n1/pub/89-657-x/89-657-x2019008-eng.htm.

Bérard-Chagnon, Julien, Stacey Hallman, Marc-Antoine Dionne, Jackie Tang, and Benoit St-Jean. *Emigration of Immigrants: Results from the Longitudinal Immigration Database*. Ottawa: Statistics Canada, 2024. https://www150.statcan.gc.ca/n1/pub/91f0015m/91f0015m2024002-eng.htm.

Bibby, Reginald. *Mosaic Madness: Pluralism without a Cause*. Toronto: Stoddart, 1990.

Bissoondath, Neil. *Selling Illusions: The Cult of Multiculturalism in Canada*. Toronto: Penguin, 1994.

Black, Warren. "Novel Features of the Immigration Act, 1976." *Canadian Bar Review* 56, no. 4 (1978): 561–78.

Blackett, Adelle. *A Transformative Framework to Achieve and Sustain Employment Equity: A Report of the Employment Equity Act Review Task Force*. Ottawa: Employment and Social Development Canada, 2023.

Bloemraad, Irene. "Becoming a Citizen in the United States and Canada: Structured Mobilization and Immigrant Political Incorporation." *Social Forces* 85, no. 2 (2006): 667–95. https://www.jstor.org/stable/4494935.

– *Understanding "Canadian Exceptionalism" in Immigration and Pluralism Policy*. Washington, DC: Migration Policy Institute, 2012.

Bloom, Michael. *Brain Gain: The Economic Benefits of Recognizing Learning and Learning Credentials in Canada*. Ottawa: The Conference Board of Canada, 2001.

Bonikowska, Aneta, Feng Hou, and Picot, Garnett. *Which Human Capital Characteristics Best Predict the Earnings of Economic Immigrants?* Ottawa: Statistics Canada, 2015.

Borjas, George J. "The Economic Benefits from Immigration." *Journal of Economic Perspectives* 9, no. 2 (1995): 3–22. https://doi.org/10.1257/jep.9.2.3.

Bouchard, Gérard, and Charles Taylor. *Building the Future: A Time for Reconciliation*. Quebec: Commission de consultation sur les pratiques d'accommodement reliées aux différences culturelles, 2007.

Bourgeon, Lauriane, Ariane Burke, and Thomas Higham. "Earliest Human Presence in North America Dated to the Last Glacial Maximum: New Radiocarbon Dates from Bluefish Caves, Canada." *PLoS One* 12, no. 1 (2017): e0169486.

Bouvier, Leon F. "Replacement Migration: Is It a Solution to Declining and Aging Populations?" *Population and Environment* 22, no. 4 (2001): 377–81.

Boyd, Monica. "Immigration Policies and Trends: A Comparison of Canada and the United States." *Demography* 13, no. 1 (1976): 83–104.

Boyd, Monica, and Michael Vickers. "100 Years of Immigration in Canada." *Canadian Social Trends*, 58 (2000): 2–12.

Bradimore, Ashley, and Harald Bauder. "Mystery Ships and Risky Boat People: Tamil Refugee Migration in the Newsprint Media." *Canadian Journal of Communication* 36, no. 4 (2012): 637–61. https://doi.org/10.22230/cjc.2011v36n4a2466.

Bragg, Bronwyn, and Lloyd L. Wong. "'Cancelled Dreams': Family Reunification and Shifting Canadian Immigration Policy." *Journal of Immigrant & Refugee Studies* 14, no. 1 (2016): 46–65. https://doi.org/10.1080/15562948.2015.1011364.

Breitkreuz, Garry. *Review of the Findings and Recommendations of the Iacobucci and O'Connor Inquiries*. Ottawa: House of Commons Canada, 2009. https://www.ourcommons.ca/Content/Committee/402/SECU/Reports/RP4004074/securp03/securp03-e.pdf.

Brimelow, Paul. *Alien Nation: Common Sense about America's Immigration Disaster*. New York: Random House, 1995.

Brosseau, Laurence. *Immigration Policy Primer*. Ottawa: Library of Parliament, 2019. https://lop.parl.ca/sites/PublicWebsite/default/en_CA/ResearchPublications/202005E.

Buchanan, Patrick. *The Death of the West: How Dying Populations and Immigrant Invasions Imperil Our Country and Civilization*. New York: St. Martin's Press, 2002.

Burton, Sarah. "Locating the People: An Exploration of Non-Resident Enfranchisement and Political Belonging in 'Frank v. Canada (Attorney General).'" *McGill Law Journal* 66, no. 4 (2021): 637–72.

Business Council of British Columbia. "OECD Predicts Canada Will Be the Worst Performing Advanced Economy over the next Decade … and the Three Decades after That." *Business Council of British Columbia* (blog), 14 December 2021. https://bcbc.com/insight/oecd-predicts-canada-will-be-the-worst-performing-advanced-economy-over-the-next-decade-and-the-three-decades-after-that/.

Canada, Department of Canadian Heritage. *Building a Foundation for Change: Canada's Anti-Racism Strategy*. Ottawa: Canadian Heritage, 2019.

– *Canada's Action Plan against Racism: A Canada for All: An Overview*. Ottawa: Canadian Heritage, 2005.

Canada, Department of Employment and Immigration. *The Live-In Caregiver Program*. Ottawa: Ministry of Supply and Services, 1992.

Canada, Department of Manpower and Immigration. *Report of the Canadian Immigration and Population Study (The Green Paper)*. Ottawa: Information Canada, 1974.

Canada, House of Commons. *Equality Now! Report of the Special Committee on the Participation of Visible Minorities in Canadian Society*. Ottawa: Supply and Services Canada, 1984.

– *House of Commons Debates*. Third Session, Twenty-Eighth Parliament, 8545–46. Ottawa: Queen's Printer, 1971.

– *Report to Parliament by the Special Joint Committee on Immigration Policy*. First Session, Thirtieth Parliament. Ottawa: Information Canada, 1975.

– "The State of Canada's Access to Information System." Report of the Standing Committee on and Access to Information, Privacy and Ethics (John Brassard, Chair). 44th Parliament, 1st session. Ottawa: House of Commons, June 2023.

Canada, Royal Commission on Aboriginal Peoples. *Report of the Royal Commission on Aboriginal Peoples*. Ottawa: The Commission, 1996.

Canadian Council for Refugees. "Best Settlement Practices: Settlement Services for Refugees and Immigrants in Canada." Montreal: Canadian Council for Refugees, 1998.

Capurri, Valentina. *Not Good Enough for Canada: Canadian Public Discourse around Issues of Inadmissibility for Potential Immigrants with Diseases and/or Disabilities, 1902–2002*. Toronto: University of Toronto Press, 2020.

Cardoso, Miguel, Michael Haan, Federico Lombardo, and Yoko Yoshida. "Research on Labour Market Impacts of the Temporary Foreign Worker Program." Working Paper Series. Canadian Labour Economics Forum, 2023.

Cardoso, Tom, and Robyn Doolittle. "Canada's Immigration System Is Overwhelmed with Information Requests. Ottawa Was Warned – but Did Nothing." *Globe and Mail*, 16 June 2023. https://www.theglobeandmail.com/canada/article-immigration-applications-access-requests/.

Carens, Joseph. *The Ethics of Immigration*. Oxford: Oxford University Press, 2013.

Carmona, Magdalena Sepúlveda. *A Contemporary View of "Family" in International Human Rights Law and Implications for the Sustainable Development Goals (SDGs)*. New York: UN Women, 2017. https://www.unwomen.org/sites/default/files/Headquarters/Attachments/Sections/Library/Publications/2017/Discussion-paper-A-contemporary-view-of-family-in-international-human-rights-law-en.pdf.

Carver, Peter. "A Failed Discourse of Distrust and Significant Procedural Change: The Harper Government's Legacy in Immigration and Refugee Law." *Review of Constitutional Studies* 21, no. 2 (2016): 209–34.

CBC News. "Beyond 94: Truth and Reconciliation in Canada." *CBC News*, 19 March 2018. Last updated 1 May 2024. https://www.cbc.ca/newsinteractives/beyond-94//child-welfare.

– "Lost Canadians." *CBC News,* last updated March 2007. https://www.cbc.ca/news2/background/lostcanadians/index.html.

– "$94M for Lebanon Rescue, but Canadian Evacuee Grateful." *CBC News*, 24 November 2006. https://www.cbc.ca/news/canada/94m-for-lebanon-rescue-but-canadian-evacuee-grateful-1.627646.

– "Term 'Visible Minorities' May Be Discriminatory, UN Body Warns Canada." *CBC News*, 8 March 2007. https://www.cbc.ca/news/canada/term-visible-minorities-may-be-discriminatory-un-body-warns-canada-1.690247.

Chapman, Don. "Who Are the Lost Canadians?" *The Lost Canadians* (blog), 1 December 2008. https://blog.lostcanadian.com/2008/12/who-are-lost-canadians.html.

Chen, Xiaobei, and Sherry Xiaohan Thorpe. "Temporary Families? The Parent and Grandparent Sponsorship Program and the Neoliberal Regime of Immigration Governance in Canada." *Migration, Mobility, & Displacement* 1, no. 1 (2015): 81–97. https://doi.org/10.18357/mmd11201513308.

– "Temporary Families? The Parent and Grandparent Sponsorship Program and the Neoliberal Regime of Immigration Governance in Canada." *Migration, Mobility, & Displacement* 1, no. 1 (June 2015): 81–98.

Chesoi, Madalina, and Eleni Kachulis. *Canadian Citizenship: Practice and Policy.* Ottawa: Library of Parliament, 2020. https://lop.parl.ca/staticfiles/PublicWebsite/Home/ResearchPublications/BackgroundPapers/PDF/2020-64-E.pdf.

Chin, Rita. *The Crisis of Multiculturalism in Europe: A History.* Princeton, NJ: Princeton University Press, 2017.

Chowdhury, Mannu. "Immigration Detention and Habeas Corpus: Positive Developments and Missed Opportunities in China." *Western Journal of Legal Studies* 10, no. 1 (2020): 1–31. https://doi-org.myaccess.library.utoronto.ca/10.5206/uwojls.v10i1.8544.

Citizenship and Immigration Canada. *Annual Report to Parliament on Immigration 2014.* Ottawa: Citizenship and Immigration Canada, 2014.

– *A Broader Vision: Immigration and Citizenship Plan, 1995-2000, Annual Report to Parliament.* Ottawa: Citizenship and Immigration Canada, 1995.

– *Canada Facts and Figures: Immigration Overview Permanent and Temporary Residents 2010.* Ottawa: Public Works and Government Services Canada, 2011. https://publications.gc.ca/collections/collection_2011/cic/Ci1-8-2010-eng.pdf.

– *The Economic Performance of Immigrants: Immigration Category Perspective.* Ottawa: Citizenship and Immigration Canada, 1998.

– "Evaluation of the Family Reunification Program." Evaluation Division. Government of Canada, February 2014.

– "Evaluation of the Foreign Credentials Referral Office (FCRO)." Ottawa: CIC Research and Evaluation, 2013.

– "Evaluation of the Immigrant Settlement and Adaptation Program (ISAP)." Ottawa: Citizenship and Immigration Canada, September 2011.

– "Evaluation of the Language Instruction for Newcomers to Canada (LINC) Program." Research and Evaluation. Ottawa: Citizenship and Immigration Canada, March 2010.
– *Facts and Figures 2005: Immigration Overview - Permanent and Temporary Residents.* Ottawa: Citizenship and Immigration Canada, 2006.
– *Facts and Figures 2006: Immigration Overview – Permanent and Temporary Residents.* Ottawa: Citizenship and Immigration Canada, 2006.
– *Facts and Figures 2010: Immigration Overview – Permanent and Temporary Residents.* Ottawa: Citizenship and Immigration Canada, 2010.
– *Facts and Figures 2016: Immigration Overview – Permanent Residents.* Ottawa: Citizenship and Immigration Canada, 2016.
– "Government of Canada to Cut Backlog and Wait Times for Family Reunification – Phase I of Action Plan for Faster Family Reunification." Government of Canada, 4 November 2011.
Citizenship and Immigration Canada. *The Economic Performance of Immigrants: Immigration Category Perspective.* Ottawa: Citizenship and Immigration Canada, 1998. https://publications.gc.ca/collections/Collection/MP22-18-2-2000E.pdf.
– "Protecting Canadians – Government of Canada Now Able to Revoke Citizenship of Dual Citizens Convicted of Terrorism," 29 May 2015.
Collier, Paul. *Exodus: How Migration Is Changing Our World.* New York: Oxford University Press, 2013.
Collington, Christian. "Percentage of Permanent Residents Becoming Canadian Citizens in Decline, Statscan Data Shows." *Globe and Mail,* 15 February 2023. https://www.theglobeandmail.com/canada/article-percentage-of-permanent-residents-becoming-canadian-citizens-in.
Compton, Francine. "Lost Canadians." *APTN News,* 12 April 2014. https://www.aptnnews.ca/investigates/lost-canadians/#:~:text=Bill%20C%2D37%20granted%20citizenship,individuals%20out%20of%20the%20loop.
Consky, Mitchell. "Mortgages, Inflation and Immigration among Top Concerns for Canadians in 2024: Nanos Survey." *CTV News,* 3 January 2024. https://www.ctvnews.ca/canada/mortgages-inflation-and-immigration-among-top-concerns-for-canadians-in-2024-nanos-survey-1.6708433.
Corbett, David. *Canada's Immigration Policy: A Critique.* Toronto: University of Toronto Press, 1957.
Croley, Steven. *Regulation and Public Interests: The Possibility of Good Regulatory Government.* Princeton, NJ: Princeton University Press, 2008.
Cross, Phillip. "Canada's Per-Person GDP Growing at Slowest Rate since the Great Depression." *The Quarterly* (2023): 2–3. https://www.fraserinstitute.org/sites/default/files/quarterly-fall-2023.pdf.
Crossman, Eden. *Low-Income and Immigration: An Overview and Future Directions for Research."* Ottawa: Citizenship and Immigration Canada, 2013. https://www.canada.ca/content/dam/ircc/migration/ircc/english/resources/research/documents/pdf/r21-2012-low-income-ec-eng.pdf.
Crossman, Eden, Choi, Youjin, Lu, Yuqian, and Hou, Feng. "International Students as a Source of Labour Supply: A Summary of Recent Trends." Ottawa, ON: Statistics Canada, 2022. https://www150.statcan.gc.ca/n1/pub/36-28-0001/2022003/article/00001-eng.htm.
Crossman, Eden, Feng Hou, and Garnett Picot. "Are the Gaps in Labour Market Outcomes between Immigrants and Their Canadian- Born Counterparts Starting to

Close?" *Economic and Social Reports* 1, no. 4 (2021). https://doi.org/10.25318
/362800012021004000004-eng.

Cryderman, Kelly. "Alberta, and the Rest of Canada, Are Woefully Unprepared for
the Coming Immigration Boom." *Globe and Mail*, 25 July 2023. https://www
.theglobeandmail.com/opinion/article-alberta-and-the-rest-of-canada-are-woefully
-unprepared-for-the-coming.

Darroch, A. Gordon. "Another Look at Ethnicity, Stratification and Social Mobility
in Canada." *Canadian Journal of Sociology / Cahiers Canadiens de Sociologie* 4, no. 1
(1979): 1–25.

Daudlin, Bob. *Equality Now! Report of the Special Committee on Visible Minorities in
Canadian Society*. Ottawa: Department of Supply and Services Canada, 1984. https://
parl.canadiana.ca/view/oop.com_HOC_3202_15_2.

Dauvergne, Catherine. "How the Charter Has Failed Non-Citizens in Canada:
Reviewing Thirty Years of Supreme Court of Canada Jurisprudence." *McGill Law
Journal* 58, no. 3 (2013): 663–728. https://doi.org/10.7202/1018393ar.

Davis, Morris, and Joseph F. Krauter, eds. *The Other Canadians: Profiles of Six Minorities*.
Toronto: Methuen, 1971.

Davis, Susan, Roslyn Kunin, and Robert Trempe. *Not Just Numbers: A Canadian
Framework for Future Immigration*. Ottawa: Minister of Public Works and
Government Services Canada, 1997.

Dawson, Tyler. "Half of all Canadians Say There Are Too Many Immigrants: Poll."
National Post, 12 March 2024. https://nationalpost.com/news/canada/half
-of-all-canadians-say-there-are-too-many-immigrants-poll.

Dennler, Kathryn. *The Leaky Bucket: A Study of Immigrant Retention Trends in Canada*.
Ottawa: The Conference Board of Canada, 2023.

DeShaw, Rell. "The History of Family Reunification in Canada and Current Policy."
Canadian Issues (2006): 9–14. https://acs-metropolis.ca/wp-content/uploads
/2019/05/CITC-2006-Spring-Printemps-2.pdf.

Desiderio, Maria Vincenza, and Kate Hooper. *The Canadian Expression of Interest
System: A Model to Manage Skilled Migration to the European Union?* Brussels:
Migration Policy Institute Europe, 2016.

DeVoretz, Don J., ed. *Diminishing Returns: The Economics of Canada's Recent Immigration
Policy*. Toronto: C.D. Howe Institute, 1995.

– "Immigration and Employment Effects." Discussion Paper 89.B.3. Ottawa: Institute
for Research on Public Policy, 1989.

Dickson, Janice. "Stranded in Pakistani Hotels for Months, Afghan Refugees Struggle
with Hopelessness While Awaiting Word from Canada." *Globe and Mail*, 14
December 2022. https://www.theglobeandmail.com
/politics/article-afghan-refugees-waiting-canada-pakistan/.

Dirks, Gerald E. *Canada's Refugee Policy: Indifference or Opportunism?* Montreal: McGill-
Queen's University Press, 1977.

– *Controversy and Complexity: Canadian Immigration Policy during the 1980s*. Montreal:
McGill-Queen's University Press, 1995.

Dodge, David. "Economic Outlook: The Long Term Is Now." Bennett Jones, 11
December 2023. https://www.bennettjones.com/Events-Section/Economic
-Outlook-The-Long-Term-is-Now.

Dolin, Benjamin, and Margaret Young. "Canada's Immigration Program." Background
Paper. Ottawa: Parliamentary Information and Research Service, 2004.

Domestic Bureau of Statistics. *The Canada Year Book 1932*. Ottawa: Ministry of Trade and Commerce, 1932.

Doyle, Matther, Mikal Skuterud, and Christopher Worswick. "Optimizing Immigration for Economic Growth." C.D. Howe Institute Commentary No. 662. Toronto: C.D. Howe Institute, 2024.

Dungan, Peter, Tony Fang, and Morley Gunderson. "Macroeconomic Impacts of Canadian Immigration: Results from a Macro Model." *British Journal of Industrial Relations* 51, no. 1 (2013): 174–95.

Dyer, Evan. "Trudeau Government Revoking Citizenship at Much Higher Rate than Conservatives." *CBC News*, 9 October 2016. https://www.cbc.ca/news/politics /citizenship-revocation-trudeau-harper-1.3795733.

Dyson, Diane, Ezekiel Roos-Walker, and Charity-Ann Hannan. "A Systems Approach to Immigrant Families and the Labour Market." In *Putting Family First: Migration and Integration Canada*, edited by Harald Bauder, 92–106. Vancouver: University of British Columbia Press, 2019.

Economist, The. "Lost in Kafkaland: When Is a Canadian Not a Canadian?" *The Economist*, 1 February 2007. https://www.economist.com/the-americas/2007/02 /01/lost-in-kafkaland.

Editorial Board. "Canada's Immigration Plan Should Involve More than Just Big Numbers." *Globe and Mail*, 7 January 2023. https://www.theglobeandmail.com /opinion/editorials/article-canadas-immigration-plan-should-involve-more -than-just-big-numbers/.

Edo, Anthony, Lionel Ragot, Hillel Rapoport, Sulin Sardoschau, Andreas Steinmayr, and Arthur Sweetman. "An Introduction to the Economics of Immigration in OECD Countries." *Canadian Journal of Economics* 53, no. 4 (2020): 1365–1403. https://doi.org/10.1111/caje.12482.

Employment and Social Development Canada. *Evaluation of the Foreign Credential Recognition Program: Report*. Ottawa: Employment and Social Development Canada, 2020.

Environics Institute. *The Black Experience Project in the GTA – Overview Report*. Toronto: Environics Institute for Survey Research, 2017. https://www.torontomu.ca/content /dam/diversity/reports/black-experience-project-gta---1-overview-report.pdf.

– *Canadian Public Opinion about Immigration and Refugees, Focus Canada (Fall 2022)*. Toronto: Environics Institute for Survey Research, 2022.

– "Focus Canada – Fall 2023: Canadian Public Opinion About Immigration and Refugees." Toronto: Environics Institute for Survey Research, 2023.

Environics Institute for Survey Research and Canadian Race Relations Foundation. *Race Relations in Canada 2019: A Survey of Canadian Public Opinion and Experience*. Toronto: Environics Institute for Survey Research, 2019. https://www .environicsinstitute.org/projects/project-details/race-relations-in-canada-2019.

Esipova, Neli, Julie Ray, and Dato Tsabutashvili. "Canada No. 1 for Migrants, U.S. in Sixth Place." *Gallup*, 23 September 2020. https://news.gallup.com/poll/320669 /canada-migrants-sixth-place.aspx.

Esses, Victoria, Jean McRae, Naomi Alboim, Natalya Brown, Chris Friesen, Leah Hamilton, Aurélie Lacassagne, Audrey Macklin, and Margaret Walton-Roberts. "Supporting Canada's COVID-19 Resilience and Recovery through Robust Immigration Policy and Programs." *FACETS* 6, no. 1 (2021): 686–759. https://doi .org/10.1139/facets-2021-0014.

Ferrer, Ana M., Garnett Picot, and William Craig Riddell. "New Directions in Immigration Policy: Canada's Evolving Approach to the Selection of Economic Immigrants." *International Migration Review* 48, no. 3 (2014): 846–67. https://doi.org/10.1111/imre.12121.

Feze, Ida Ngueng, Gabriel Marrocco, Miriam Pinkesz, Jacqueline Lacey, and Yann Joly, "Flying under the Radar: Two Decades of DNA Testing at IRCC." *Canadian Journal of Law and Technology* 17, no. 2 (2019): 226–75. https://digitalcommons.schulichlaw.dal.ca/cgi/viewcontent.cgi?article=1257&context=cjlt.

FitzGerald, David Scott, and David Cook-Martín. *Culling the Masses: The Democratic Origins of Racist Immigration Policy in the Americas.* Cambridge, MA: Harvard University Press, 2014.

Fitzpatrick, Meagan. "Don't Bring Parents Here for Welfare, Kenney Says." *CBC News*, 10 May 2013. https://www.cbc.ca/news/politics/don-t-bring-parents-here-for-welfare-kenney-says-1.1351002.

Flecker, Karl. "Building 'The World's Most Flexible Workforce': The Harper Government's 'Double-Doubling' of the Foreign Worker Program." *Briarpatch*, 1 November 2007. https://briarpatchmagazine.com/articles/view/building-the-worlds-most-flexible-workforce.

Foot, Richard, and Peggy Ann Osborne. "Lost Canadians." *The Canadian Encyclopedia*, 25 July 2017. https://www.thecanadianencyclopedia.ca/en/article/lost-canadians.

Fraiberg, Jeremy D., and Michael J. Trebilcock. "Risk Regulation: Technocratic and Democratic Tools for Regulatory Reform." *McGill Law Journal* 43, no. 4 (1998): 835–87.

Francis, R. Douglas, Richard Jones, and Donald B. Smith. *Destinies: Canadian History Since Confederation.* Toronto: Holt, Rinehart, and Winston, 1988.

Fraser, Sean. *2022 Annual Report to Parliament on Immigration.* Ottawa: Immigration, Refugees and Citizenship Canada, 2022. https://publications.gc.ca/collections/collection_2022/ircc/Ci1-2022-eng.pdf.

– *Immigration, Refugees and Citizenship Canada 2023–2024 Departmental Plan.* Ottawa: Immigration, Refugees and Citizenship Canada, 2023. https://www.canada.ca/en/immigration-refugees-citizenship/corporate/publications-manuals/departmental-plan-2023-2024/departmental-plan.html.

Frenette, Marc, and René Morissette. "Will They Ever Converge? Earnings of Immigrant and Canadian-Born Workers over the Last Two Decades." Analytical Studies Branch – Research Paper Series. Ottawa: Statistics Canada, 2003.

Gagnon, Philippe, Robert Mason, and Madalina Chesoi. "Overview of the Canada–United States Safe Third Country Agreement." Library of Parliament HillStudies, Publication No. 2020-70-E, 1 September 2023.

Galloway, J. Donald. "The Dilemmas of Canadian Citizenship Law." *Georgetown Immigration Law Journal* 13, no. 2 (1999): 201–31.

Gaucher, Megan. *A Family Matter: Citizenship, Conjugal Relationships, and Canadian Immigration Policy.* Vancouver: UBC Press, 2018.

Goldring, Luin, and Patricia Landolt. *Producing and Negotiating Non-Citizenship: Precarious Legal Status in Canada.* Toronto: University of Toronto Press, 2013.

Gonzales-Barrera, Ana, and Philipp Connor. "Around the World, More Say Immigrants Are a Strength Than a Burden." Pew Research Center, 14 March 2019. https://www.pewresearch.org/global-migration-and-demography/2019/03/14/around-the-world-more-say-immigrants-are-a-strength-than-a-burden/.

Goodwin-Gill, Guy S. "Article 31 of the 1951 Convention Relating to the Status of Refugees: Non-Penalization, Detention, and Protection." In *Refugee Protection in International Law: UNHCR's Global Consultations on International Protection*, edited by Erika Feller, Volker Türk, and Frances Nicholson, 184–252. Cambridge: Cambridge University Press, 2003.

Government of Canada. *Report of the Royal Commission on Aboriginal Peoples*. 5 vols. Ottawa: Canada Communication Group, 1996. https://www.bac-lac.gc.ca/eng /discover/aboriginal-heritage/royal-commission-aboriginal-peoples/Pages/final -report.aspx.

– *White Paper on Immigration*. Ottawa: Queen's Printer, 1966.

Green, David. "No, Immigration Is Not Some Magic Pill for Saving the Economy." *Globe and Mail*, 25 December 2022. https://www.theglobeandmail.com/business /commentary/article-no-immigration-is-not-some-magic-pill-for-saving-the -economy/.

Green, David, and Christopher Worswick. "Entry Earnings of Immigrant Men in Canada: The Roles of Labour Market Entry Effects and Returns to Foreign Experience." In *Canadian Immigration: Economic Evidence for a Dynamic Policy Environment*, edited by Ted McDonald, Elizabeth Ruddick, Arthur Sweetman, and Christopher Worswick, 77–110. Montreal: McGill-Queen's University Press, 2010.

Green, David A., W. Craig Riddell, and France St-Hilaire. "Income Inequality in Canada: Driving Forces, Outcomes and Policy." In *Income Inequality: The Canadian Story*, edited by David A. Green, W. Craig Riddell, and France St-Hilaire, 1–73. Montreal: Institute for Research on Public Policy, 2016.

Grey, Julius, and John Gill. "Canadian Citizenship." *The Canadian Encyclopedia*, 7 February 2006; last edited 16 September 2020.

Griffith, Andrew. "A One-Click Citizenship Oath Isn't the Way to Go." *Policy Options*, 21 June 2023. https://policyoptions.irpp.org/magazines/june-2023/a-one-click -citizenship-oath-isnt-the-way-to-go/.

– "What the Census Tells Us about Citizenship." *Toronto Star*, 20 March 2018. https:// policyoptions.irpp.org/magazines/march-2018/what-the-census-tells-us-about -citizenship/.

Gros, Hanna, and Paloma van Groll. *"We have no Rights": Arbitrary Imprisonment and Cruel Treatment of Migrants with Mental Health Issues in Canada*. Toronto: University of Toronto International Human Rights Program, 2015.

Guillemette, Yvan, and David Turner. "The Long Game: Fiscal Outlooks to 2060 Underline Need for Structural Reform." *OECD Economic Policy Papers*, No. 29. Paris: OECD Publishing, 2021. https://doi.org/10.1787/a112307e-en.

Gure, Yasmine, and Feng Hue. *The Short-Term Labour Market Outcomes of Blended Visa Office-Referred Refugees*. Ottawa: Statistics Canada, 2024. https://www150.statcan .gc.ca/n1/pub/36-28-0001/2024001/article/00003-eng.htm.

Gwyn, Richard J. *Nationalism without Walls: The Unbearable Lightness of Being Canadian*. Toronto: McClelleand and Stewart, 1995.

Hainmueller, Jens, Dominik Hangartner, and Giuseppe Pietrantuono. "Naturalization Fosters the Long-Term Political Integration of Immigrants." *Proceedings of the National Academy of Sciences of the United States of America* 112, no. 41 (2015): 12651–6.

Harder, Lois. *Canadian Club: Birthright Citizenship and National Belonging*. Toronto: University of Toronto Press, 2022.

Hassan, Lila. "Countries Don't Want Their ISIS Foreign Fighters Back: A Review." *FRONTLINE*, 6 April 2021. https://www.pbs.org/wgbh/frontline/article/repatriating-isis-foreign-fighters-key-to-stemming-radicalization-experts-say-but-many-countries-dont-want-citizens-back/.

Hawkins, Freda. *Canada and Immigration: Public Policy and Public Concern.* 2nd ed. Montreal: McGill-Queen's University Press, 1988.

– *Critical Years in Immigration: Canada and Australia Compared.* 2nd ed. Montreal: McGill-Queen's University Press, 1991.

Hennebry, Jenna. *Permanently Temporary? Agricultural Migrant Workers and Their Integration in Canada.* IRPP Study, No. 26. Montreal: Institute for Research on Public Policy, 2012.

Henry-Dixon, Natasha. "Underground Railroad." *The Canadian Encyclopedia*, last edited 3 March 2023. https://www.thecanadianencyclopedia.ca/en/article/underground-railroad.

Hiebert, Daniel. *The Canadian Express Entry System for Selecting Economic Immigrants: Progress and Persistent Challenges.* Washington, DC: Migration Policy Institute, 2019.

– *What's So Special about Canada? Understanding the Resilience of Immigration and Multiculturalism?* Washington, DC: Migration Policy Institute, 2016.

Honohan, Iseult. "Reconsidering the Claim to Family Reunification in Migration." *Political Studies* 57, no. 4 (2009): 768–87. https://doi.org/10.1111/j.1467-9248.2008.00761.x.

Hood, Joe. "Housing Affordability Woes Have Spilled over to Rental Market, CMHC Report Finds." *Financial Post*, 26 January 2023, sec. Real Estate. https://financialpost.com/real-estate/cmhc-rental-vacancy-rate-lowest-two-decades.

Hopper, Tristen. "How Record-High Immigration Could Be Hurting Canadian Productivity." *National Post*, 13 December 2023. https://nationalpost.com/opinion/first-reading-how-record-high-immigration-could-be-hurting-canadian-productivity.

Horn, Michiel. "The Great Depression: Past and Present." *Journal of Canadian Studies* 11, no. 1 (1976): 41–50.

Hou, Feng, and Aneta Bonikowska. "Selections before the Selection: Earnings Advantages of Immigrants Who Were Former Skilled Temporary Foreign Workers in Canada." *International Migration Review* 52, no. 3 (2018): 695–723.

Hou, Feng, and Garnett Picot. "Annual Levels of Immigration and Immigrant Entry Earnings in Canada." *Canadian Public Policy* 40, no. 2 (2014): 166–81.

– "Changing Immigrant Characteristics and Pre-Landing Canadian Earnings: Their Effect on Entry Earnings over the 1990s and 2000s." *Canadian Public Policy* 42, no. 3 (2016): 308–23.

– *The Decline in the Citizenship Rate among Recent Immigrants to Canada: Update to 2021.* Ottawa: Statistics Canada, 2024. https://www150.statcan.gc.ca/n1/pub/36-28-0001/2024002/article/00002-eng.htm.

– "The Decline in the Naturalization Rate among Recent Immigrants in Canada: Policy Changes and Other Possible Explanations." *Migration Studies* 9, no. 3 (2021): 1030–53.

– *Trends in the Citizenship Rate among New Immigrants to Canada.* Ottawa: Statistics Canada, 2019. https://www150.statcan.gc.ca/n1/en/pub/11-626-x/11-626-x2019015-eng.pdf?st=1H19l_c7.

Hou, Feng, Eden Crossman, and Garnett Picot. "Two-Step Immigration Selection: An Analysis of Its Expansion in Canada." *Economic Insights*, no. 112 (2020). https://www150.statcan.gc.ca/n1/pub/11-626-x/11-626-x2020010-eng.htm.

– "Two-Step Immigration Selection: Recent Trends in Immigrant Labour Market Outcomes." *Economic Insights*, no. 113 (2020). https://www150.statcan.gc.ca/n1/pub/11-626-x/11-626-x2020011-eng.htm.

Houle, René. *Changes in the Socioeconomic Situation of Canada's Black Population, 2001 to 2016*. Ottawa: Statistics Canada, 2020. https://www150.statcan.gc.ca/n1/en/pub/89-657-x/89-657-x2020001-eng.pdf?st=DNVuOlCC.

Hudson, Graham. "As Good as It Gets? Security, Asylum, and the Rule of Law after the Certificate Trilogy." *Osgoode Hall Law Journal* 52, no. 3 (2016): 905–50.

– "Ordinary Injustices: Persecution, Punishment, and the Criminalization of Asylum in Canada." In *Immigration Policy in the Age of Punishment: Detention, Deportation, and Border Control*, edited by David C. Brotherton and Philip Kretsedemas, 75–96. New York: Columbia University Press, 2018.

Hulchanski, John David. *The Three Cities within Toronto: Income Polarization among Toronto's Neighbourhoods, 1970–2005*. Toronto: Cities Centre Press, University of Toronto, 2010.

Human Rights Watch. "Sri Lanka: Events of 2009." In *World Report 2010*, edited by Ian Gorvin, 347–54. New York: Human Rights Watch, 2010.

Human Rights Watch and Amnesty International. *"I Didn't Feel Like a Human in There": Immigration Detention and the Impact on Human Health*. New York: Human Rights Watch, 2021.

Huntington, Samuel. *Who Are We? Challenges to America's National Identity*. New York: Simon and Schuster, 2005.

Hussen, Ahmed. *Immigration, Refugees and Citizenship Canada Departmental Plan 2019–2020*. Ottawa: Immigration, Refugees and Citizenship Canada, 2019. https://www.canada.ca/en/immigration-refugees-citizenship/corporate/publications-manuals/departmental-plan-2019-2020/departmental-plan.html.

Hyndman, Jennifer. "Gender and Canadian Immigration Policy: A Current Snapshot." *Canadian Woman Studies* 19, no. 3 (1999): 6–10.

Hynie, Michaela, Susan McGrath, Jonathan Bridekirk, Anna Oda, Nicole Ives, Jennifer Hyndman, Neil Arya, Yogendra Shakya, Jill Hanley, Kwame McKenzie, and SyRIA.Ith. "What Role Does Type of Sponsorship Play in Early Integration Outcomes? Syrian Refugees Resettled in Six Canadian Cities." *Refuge: Canada's Journal on Refugees* 35, no. 2 (2019): 36–63. https://refuge.journals.yorku.ca/index.php/refuge/article/view/40600.

Iacobucci, Frank. *Internal Inquiry into the Actions of Canadian Officials in Relation to Abdullah Almalki, Ahmed Abou-Elmaati and Muayyed Nureddin*. Ottawa: Public Works and Government Services Canada, 2008. https://publications.gc.ca/site/eng/9.699757/publication.html.

Imai, Shin. "Deportation in the Depression." *Queen's Law Journal* 7, no. 1 (1981): 66–94.

Immigration, Refugees and Citizenship Canada. "An Immigration Plan to Grow the Economy." News Release, 1 November 2022. https://www.canada.ca/en/immigration-refugees-citizenship/news/2022/11/an-immigration-plan-to-grow-the-economy.html.

- "An Immigration System for Canada's Future: Strengthening Our Communities." October 2023. https://www.canada.ca/en/immigration-refugees-citizenship/campaigns/canada-future-immigration-system.html.
- *Annual Reports to Parliament on Immigration*, 2014–2023. https://www.canada.ca/en/immigration-refugees-citizenship/corporate/publications-manuals/annual-reports-parliament-immigration.html.
- "Canada Welcomes Historic Numbers of Newcomers in 2022." News Release, 3 January 2023. https://www.canada.ca/en/immigration-refugees-citizenship/news/2022/12/canada-welcomes-historic-number-of-newcomers-in-2022.html.
- *Evaluation of Express Entry: Early Impacts on Economic Outcomes and System Management*. Research and Evaluation Branch. Ottawa: IRCC, 2020.
- *Evaluation of Language Training Services*. Research and Evaluation Branch. Ottawa: IRCC, 2020.
- *Evaluation of the Pre-Removal Risk Assessment Program*. Evaluation Division. Ottawa: IRCC, 2016.
- *Evaluation of the Provincial Nominee Program*. Research and Evaluation Branch. Ottawa: IRCC, 2017. https://www.canada.ca/content/dam/ircc/documents/pdf/english/evaluation/e1-2015-pnp-en.pdf.
- *Evaluation of the Settlement Program*. Research and Evaluation Branch. Ottawa: IRCC, 2017.
- *Express Entry Year-End Report 2016*. Ottawa: IRCC, 2016.
- *Express Entry Year-End Report 2019*. Ottawa: IRCC, 2019.
- *Express Entry Year-End Report 2021*. Ottawa: IRCC, 2021.
- *Facts and Figures 2016 – Immigration Overview – Temporary Residents*. Ottawa: IRCC, 2016.

Jackman, Barbara. "Charter Rights to Privacy and Security: The Impact of International Terrorism and Globalization: Impact on Charter Rights in Immigration Law." *National Journal of Constitutional Law* 19 (2005/2006): 229–61.

Jain, Harish, and Lawler, John J. "Visible Minorities under the Canadian Employment Equity Act, 1987–1999." *Relations Industrielles/Industrial Relations* 59, no. 3 (2004): 585–611.

Jasanoff, Maya. *Liberty's Exiles: American Loyalists in the Revolutionary World*. New York: Vintage Books, 2012.

Jean-Nicolas Beuze, Erla. "UNHCR's Statement to the Committee on Citizenship and Immigration – 7 May 2019." UNHCR Canada, 7 May 2019.

Jedwab, Jack. "What Underlies Concern over Canada's Immigration Numbers?" Metropolis Institute and the Associates for Canadian Studies, 11 March 2024. https://acs-metropolis.ca/studies/what-underlies-concern-over-canadas-immigration-numbers/.

Jewell, Eva, and Ian Mosby. *Calls to Action Accountability: A 2022 Status Update on Reconciliation*. Toronto: Yellowhead Institute, 2022. https://yellowheadinstitute.org/wp-content/uploads/2023/12/YI-TRC-C2A-2023-Special-Report-compressed.pdf.

Joeck, Molly. "Canadian Exclusion Jurisprudence Post-Febles." *International Journal of Refugee Law* 33, no. 1 (2021): 54–88. https://doi.org/10.1093/ijrl/eeab034.

Joly, Yann, Shahad Salman, Ida Ngueng Feze, Palmira Granados Moreno, Michèle Stanton-Jean, Jacqueline Lacey, Micheline Labelle, et al. "DNA Testing for Family Reunification in Canada: Points to Consider." *Journal of International Migration and Integration* 18, no. 2 (2017): 391–404. https://doi.org/10.1007/s12134-016-0496-7.

Jonas, Sabrina. "Ottawa Says It Will Bypass Quebec's Immigration Cap to Speed Up Family Reunification." *CBC News*, 4 March 2024. https://www.cbc.ca/news /canada/montreal/family-reunification-federal-minister-quebec-1.7132823.

Joppke, Christian. "The Retreat of Multiculturalism in the Liberal State: Theory and Policy." *British Journal of Sociology* 55, no. 2 (2004): 237–57. https://doi.org/10.1111 /j.1468-4446.2004.00017.x.

Kaida, Lisa, Max Stick, and Feng Hou. *The Long-Term Economic Outcomes of Refugee Private Sponsorship*. Ottawa: Statistics Canada, 2020. https://www150.statcan.gc .ca/n1/pub/11f0019m/11f0019m2019021-eng.htm.

Kaplan, Robert. *The Revenge of Geography: What the Map Tells Us About Coming Conflicts and the Battle Against Fate*. New York: Random House, 2012.

Kaprielian-Churchill, Isabel. "Armenian Refugees and Their Entry into Canada, 1919–30." *Canadian Historical Review* 71, no. 1 (1990): 80–108. https://muse-jhu-edu.myaccess .library.utoronto.ca/article/573505/pdf.

Kazemipur, Abdolmohammad. *The Muslim Question in Canada*. Vancouver: UBC Press, 2014.

Keller, Tony. "Canada Has a Doctor Shortage. But If Governments Wanted, We Could Have a Doctor Surplus." *Globe and Mail*, 4 August 2023. https://www.theglobeandmail .com/business/commentary/article-canada-has-a-doctor-shortage-but-if-governments -wanted-we-could-have-a/.

– "How Can the Trudeau Government Fix Its Immigration Mess? Press 'Rewind.'" *Globe and Mail*, 9 August 2024.

Kelley, Ninette. *People Forced to Flee: History, Change and Challenge*. Oxford: Oxford University Press, 2022.

Kelley, Ninette, and Michael Trebilcock. *The Making of the Mosaic: A History of Canadian Immigration Policy*. 2nd ed. Toronto: University of Toronto Press, 2010.

Kellough, Gail, and Scot Wortley. "Remand for Plea: Bail Decisions and Plea Bargaining as Commensurate Decisions." *British Journal of Criminology* 42, no. 1 (2002): 186–210. https://doi.org/10.1093/bjc/42.1.186.

Kesler, Christel, and Irene Bloemraad. "Does Immigration Erode Social Capital? The Conditional Effects of Immigration-Generated Diversity on Trust, Membership, and Participation across 19 Countries, 1981–2000." *Canadian Journal of Political Science* 43, no. 2 (2010): 319–47. https://www.jstor.org/stable/20743152.

Keung, Nicholas. "Every Canadian Province Has Now Agreed to Stop Keeping Immigration Detainees in Jail." *Toronto Star*, 21 March 2024. https://www.thestar. com/news/canada/every-canadian-province-has-now-agreed-to-stop-keeping -immigration-detainees-in-jail/article_1ce537fa-e6c7-1.

Koch, Eric. *Deemed Suspect: A Wartime Blunder*. Toronto: Methuen, 1980.

Kymlicka, Will. *Multicultural Citizenship: A Liberal Theory of Minority Rights*. New York: Oxford University Press, 1996.

– *Multiculturalism: Success, Failure, and the Future*. Washington, DC: Migration Policy Institute, 2012.

Labman, Shauna, and Adèle Garnier. "A Necessary Re-assertion of Government Resettlement." In *Canada and the Global Refugee Regime: Continuity, Change, Challenges and Critiques*, edited by Nathan Benson, James Milner, and Delphine Nakache. Montreal: McGill-Queen's University Press, forthcoming.

Lafleur, Steve, and Josef Filipowicz. "Canada's Housing and Immigration Policies Are at Odds." *Globe and Mail*, 10 April 2023. https://www.theglobeandmail.com

/opinion/article-canadas-housing-and-immigration-policies-are-at
-odds/.

Lalande, Lisa. "The Century Initiative Does Not Advocate Massive Temporary Immigration." *Inroads: The Canadian Journal of Opinion*, no. 53 (Summer/Fall 2023). https://inroadsjournal.ca/inroads-special/.

Lenard, Patti Tamara. "Democracies and the Power to Revoke Citizenship." *Ethics and International Affairs* 30, no. 1 (2016): 73–91. doi:10.1017/S0892679415000635.

Lerer, Ben, and Alex Bogach. "Citizenship Revocation in Canada: Dialogue or Defiance?" *Canadian Journal of Administrative Law and Practice* 35, no. 3 (2022): 311–23.

Leslie, John F. "Indigenous Suffrage." *The Canadian Encyclopedia*, 31 March 2016. https://www.thecanadianencyclopedia.ca/en/article/indigenous-suffrage.

Levinson-King, Robin. "Canada: Why the Country Wants to Bring in 1.5m Immigrants by 2025." *BBC News*, 22 November 2022. https://www.bbc.com/news/world-us -canada-63643912.

Li, Peter S. *Cultural Diversity in Canada: The Social Construction of Racial Difference.* Ottawa: Department of Justice Canada, 2000.

– "The Market Worth of Immigrants' Educational Credentials." *Canadian Public Policy* 27, no. 1 (2001): 23–38.

Livingstone, Anne-Marie, and Morton Weinfeld. "Black Families and Socio-economic Inequality in Canada." *Canadian Ethnic Studies/Études ethniques au Canada* 47, no. 3 (2015): 1–23.

Lone, Wa. "Canada's Surging Cost of Living Fuels Reverse Immigration." *Reuters*, 10 December 2023. https://www.reuters.com/world/americas/canadas-surging -cost-living-fuels-reverse-immigration-2023-12-09/.

Longfield, Judi. *Promoting Equality in the Federal Jurisdiction: Review of the Employment Equity Act. Report of the Standing Committee on Human Resources Development and the Status of Persons with Disabilities.* Ottawa: Government Services Canada, 2022.

Lowe, Sophia, Ted Richmond, and John Shields. "Settling on Austerity: ISAs, Immigrant Communities and Neoliberal Restructuring." *Alternate Routes: A Journal of Critical Social Research* 28 (2017): 14–46.

Lu, Yuqian, and Feng Hou. "Foreign Workers in Canada: Changing Composition and Employment Incidences of Work Permit Holders." *Economic and Social Reports* 3, no. 10 (2023). https://www150.statcan.gc.ca/n1/pub/36-28-0001/2023010 /article/00004-eng.htm.

Lundy, Matt. "Asylum Claims Jump at Canadian Airports after Ottawa Eases Some Visitor Visa Requirements." *Globe and Mail*, 23 October 2023. https://www .theglobeandmail.com/business/article-canada-airports-asylum-claims/.

– "Canada Stuck in 'Population Trap,' Needs to Reduce Immigration, Bank Economists Say." *Globe and Mail*, 15 January 2024. https://www.theglobeandmail .com/business/article-canada-stuck-in-population-trap-needs-to-reduce- immigration-bank.

– "Canada Wants to Welcome Immigrants." *Globe and Mail*, 26 November 2022. https:// www.theglobeandmail.com/business/article-canada-immigration-population -boom/.

– "Ottawa Revises Downward Two Decades of Data on Temporary Foreign Workers." *Globe and Mail*, 22 June 2023. https://www.theglobeandmail.com/business/article -temporary-foreign-workers-data-revision.

MacIntosh, Constance. "Medical Inadmissibility, and Physically and Mentally Disabled Would-Be Immigrants: Canada's Story Continues." *Dalhousie Law Journal* 42, no. 1 (2019): 125–51.

Macklin, Audrey. "A Brief History of the Brief History of Citizenship Revocation in Canada Canadian Terror: Multi-Disciplinary Perspectives on the Toronto 18 Terrorism Trials: Part Four: Sentencing, Parole, Reintegration, and an Unknown Future: Chapter 16." *Manitoba Law Journal* 44, no. 1 (2021): 434–67.

– "And Just like That, You're an Illegal Immigrant: Thanks to a Bad Regulation, Thousands of People Living and Working Here Are about to Become Outlaws." *National Post*, 19 March 2015. https://nationalpost.com/opinion/audrey-macklin-poof-now-youre-an-illegal-immigrant.

– "Citizenship Revocation, the Privilege to Have Rights and the Production of the Alien." *Queen's Law Journal* 40, no. 1 (2015): 1–54.

Macklin, Audrey, and François Crépeau. *Multiple Citizenship, Identity and Entitlement in Canada*. IRPP Study, No. 6. Montreal: Institute for Research on Public Policy, 2010.

MacLeod, Marsha. "Ottawa Capped Immigration Program for Afghans Who Worked with Canada since Its Launch." *Globe and Mail*, 14 December 2022. https://www.theglobeandmail.com/politics/article-canada-afghan-resettlement/.

Macyshon, Jill. "Canada Is Deporting More People Faster, Drawing Concern from Migrant Advocates." *CTV News*, 8 December 2023. https://www.ctvnews.ca/canada/canada-is-deporting-more-people-faster-drawing-concern-from-migrant-advocates-1.6678779.

Mahboubi, Parisa. *Quality over Quantity: How Canada's Immigration System Can Catch Up with Its Competitors*. Commentary No. 654. Toronto: C.D. Howe Institute, 2024. https://www.cdhowe.org/sites/default/files/2024-02/For%20advance%20release%20Immigration%20Commentary_654.pdf.

Mahboubi, Parisa, and Mikal Skuterud. "Canada Must Stem the Surge in Temporary Foreign Workers and International Students." *Globe and Mail*, 7 February 2024.

Major, Darren, Louis Blouin, and Romain Schué. "Canada Bringing Back Visa Requirements for Mexican Nationals to Curb Asylum Seekers." *CBC News*, 28 February 2024. https://www.cbc.ca/news/politics/mexico-canada-visas-asylum-1.7128408.

Marsden, Sarah. *Enforcing Exclusion: Precarious Migrants and the Law in Canada*. Vancouver: UBC Press, 2018.

Martin, Beth. "Immigrants are Family Members, Too." In *Putting Family First: Migration and Integration in Canada*, edited by Harald Bauder, 23–44. Vancouver: UBC Press, 2019.

Mason, Gary. "Opinion: It's Not Racist or Xenophobic to Question Our Immigration Policy." *Globe and Mail*, 5 January 2023. https://www.theglobeandmail.com/opinion/article-its-not-racist-or-xenophobic-to-question-our-immigration-policy/.

May, Bryan. *Temporary Foreign Worker Program: Report of the Standing Committee on Human Resources, Skills and Social Development and the Status of Persons with Disabilities*. Ottawa: House of Commons, 2016. https://publications.gc.ca/collections/collection_2016/parl/xc67-1/XC67-1-1-421-4-eng.pdf.

Maynard, Carolyn. *Access at Issue: the Unsustainable Status Quo*. Special Report to Parliament. Ottawa: Information Commissioner to Canada, 2024. https://www.oic-ci.gc.ca/en/resources/reports-publications/access-issue-unsustainable-status-quo.

McKenzie-Sutterholly, Holly. "Migrants across Canada Call on Ottawa for Action on Regularization, Permanent Status." *CTV News*, 18 September 2022. https://www.ctvnews.ca/canada/migrants-across-canada-call-on-ottawa-for-action-on-regularization-permanent-status-1.6073893.

McKie, David. "Backlog of Refugee Claims Has Grown under Conservatives." *CBC News*, 4 December 2009. https://www.cbc.ca/news/politics/backlog-of-refugee-claims-has-grown-under-conservatives-1.863218.

Medianu, Stelian, Alina Sutter, and Victoria Esses. "The Portrayal of Refugees in Canadian Newspapers: The Impact of the Arrival of Tamil Refugees by Sea in 2010." *Idées d'Amériques*, no. 6 (2015). https://doi.org/10.4000/ideas.1199.

Meggs, Michèle, and Pierre Fortin. "Are We Heading for 100 Million Canadians?" *Inroads: The Canadian Journal of Opinion* 53 (2023). https://inroadsjournal.ca/are-we-heading-for-100-million-canadians/.

Mehrunnisa Ahmad Ali, and Marc Yvan Valade. "How Families Shape Settlement Trajectories." In *Putting Family First: Migration and Integration Canada*, edited by Harald Bauder, 153–77. Vancouver: UBC Press, 2019.

Mertins-Kirkwood, Hadrian. "The Hidden Growth of Canada's Migrant Workforce." In *The Harper Record 2008–2015*, edited by Teresa Healy and Stuart Trew, 149–58. Ottawa: Canadian Centre for Policy Alternatives, 2015.

Miller, Marc. *2023 Annual Report to Parliament on Immigration*. Ottawa: Immigration, Refugees and Citizenship Canada, 2023. https://publications.gc.ca/collections/collection_2023/ircc/Ci1-2023-eng.pdf.

Mills, Carys. "How Applicants Are Stumbling on the Final Step to Becoming Canadians." *Globe and Mail*, 29 June 2012. https://www.theglobeandmail.com/news/national/how-applicants-are-stumbling-on-the-final-step-to-becoming-canadians/article4382633/.

Molinaro, Dennis G. *Deportation from Canada*. Immigration and Ethnicity in Canada Series, Booklet No. 36. Ottawa: Canadian Historical Association, 2018.

Molnar, Petra, and Lex Gill. *BOTS AT THE GATE: A Human Rights Analysis of Automated Decision-Making in Canada's Immigration and Refugee System*. Toronto: University of Toronto International Human Rights Program, 2018. https://citizenlab.ca/wp-content/uploads/2018/09/IHRP-Automated-Systems-Report-Web-V2.pdf.

Moreno, Palmira Granados, Ida Ngueng Feze, and Yann Joly. "Does the End Justify the Means? A Comparative Study of the Use of DNA Testing in the Context of Family Reunification." *Journal of Law and the Biosciences* 4, no. 2 (2017): 250–81. https://doi.org/10.1093/jlb/lsx012.

Morton, James. *In the Sea of Sterile Mountains: The Chinese in British Columbia*. Vancouver: J.J. Douglas, Ltd., 1974.

Moscrop, David. "Canada Must Support the Migrants It's Letting in to Fill Jobs." *Washington Post*, 18 November 2022. https://www.washingtonpost.com/opinions/2022/11/18/canada-migrants-economy-jobs.

Nanos. "Canadians Prefer that Canada Accepts Fewer Immigrants and International Students than What Is Projected for 2023." 11 September 2023. https://nanos.co/canadians-prefer-that-canada-accepts-fewer-immigrants-and-international-students-than-what-is-projected-for-2023-globe-nanos/.

Naomi Alboim, and Karen Cohl. "Shaping the Future: Canada's Rapidly Changing Immigration Policies." Maytree Foundation, October 2012.

Neuman, Keith, and Michael Adams. "The Conversation around Immigration in Canada Is Shifting." *Globe and Mail*, 3 November 2023. https://www.theglobeandmail.com /opinion/article-the-conversation-around-immigration-in-canada-is-shifting/.

Nicholson, Frances. *The Right to Family Life and Family Unity of Refugees and Others in Need of International Protection and the Family Definition Applied*. New York: UNHCR, 2018.

Niraula, Ashika, Anna Triandafyllidou, and Marshia Akbar. "Navigating Uncertainties: Evaluating the Shift in Canadian Immigration Policies during the COVID-19 Pandemic." *Canadian Public Policy* 48, no. S1 (2022): 49–59. https://doi .org/10.3138/cpp.2022-010.

Norrie, Kenneth, and Douglas Owram. *A History of the Canadian Economy*. Toronto: Harcourt Brace Jovanovich, 1991.

Norrie, Kenneth, Douglas Owram, and J.C. Herbert Emery. *A History of the Canadian Economy*. 4th ed. Toronto: Thomson/Nelson, 2007.

Nuttall, J.J. "Increase in Foreign Workers through Federal Program Still a Problem, Says Union." *Tyee*, 17 July 2017. https://thetyee.ca/News/2017/07/27/Increase -in-Foreign-Workers-Still-a-Problem/.

O'Connor, Dennis. *Report of the Events Relating to Maher Arar: Analysis and Recommendations*. 3 vols. Ottawa: Public Works and Government Services Canada, 2006.

Omatsu, Maryka. *Bittersweet Passage: Redress and the Japanese Canadian Experience*. Toronto: Between the Lines, 1992.

Ontario Human Rights Commission. *A Disparate Impact Second Interim Report on the Inquiry into Racial Profiling and Racial Discrimination of Black Persons by the Toronto Police Service*. Toronto: Ontario Human Rights Commission, 2020.

– *Policy on Removing the "Canadian Experience" Barrier*. Toronto: Ontario Human Rights Commission, 2013. https://www.ohrc.on.ca/sites/default/files /policy%20on%20removing%20the%20Canadian%20experience%20barrier _accessible.pdf.

Organisation for Economic Co-operation and Development. *International Migration Outlook 2022*. Paris: OECD, 2022. https://doi.org/10.1787/30fe16d2-en.

Organisation for Economic Co-operation and Development and European Commission. *Indicators of Immigrant Integration 2023: Settling In*. Paris: OECD Publishing, 2023. https://doi.org/10.1787/1d5020a6-e.

Orlov, George. "The Impact of Language Training on the Transfer of Pre-Immigration Skills and the Wages of Immigrants." *SSRN Electronic Journal*, 2018. https://ssrn .com/abstract=3412195.

Ortega-Araiza, Javier. "Canada Invests $6.2M to Help Skilled Refugees Find Jobs." *New Canadian Media*, 22 December 2022. https://newcanadianmedia.ca/canada-invests -6-2m-to-help-skilled-refugees-find-jobs/.

Osman, Laura. "Think You Could Pass the Canadian Citizenship Test?" *National Post*, 29 June 2023. https://nationalpost.com/news/canada/canadian-citizenship-test.

Otis, Daniel. "'Super Visa' Allows Some People to Stay in Canada for up to 7 Years, Here's Who Is Eligible to Apply." *CTV News*, 7 June 2022, https://www.ctvnews .ca/canada/super-visa-allows-some-people-to-stay-in-canada-for-up-to-7-years -here-s-who-is-eligible-to-apply-1.5936961.

Oziewicz, Estanislao. "Ottawa Reconsidering Refugee Process: Immigration Act Provision Allowing for Multiple Claims under Review." *Globe and Mail*, 6 November 1999.

Pal, Michael, and Luka Ryder-Bunting. "Citizenship and the First-Generation Limitation in Canada." *Dalhousie Law Journal* 45, no. 1 (2022): 1–26.

Paperny, Anna Mehler, and Ted Hesson. "Insight: Canada Immigration: Why Asylum Seekers Are Crossing the Border." *Reuters*, 14 March 2023. https://www.reuters.com/world/americas/canada-immigration-why-record-asylum-seekers-are-crossing-us-border-2023-03-11/.

Parai, Louis. "Canada's Immigration Policy, 1962–74." *International Migration Review* 9, no. 4 (1975): 449–77.

Parliament of Canada. "M-62 Uyghurs and Other Turkic Muslims 44th Parliament, 1st Session – Members of Parliament – House of Commons of Canada." 1 February 2023. https://www.ourcommons.ca/members/en/54157/motions/11892002.

Pew Research Center. "Around the World, More Say Immigrants Are a Strength Than a Burden." Washington, DC: Pew Research Center, 2019.

Picot, Garnett, and Andrew Heisz. "The Performance of the 1990s Canadian Labour Market." Business and Labour Market Analysis Division. Ottawa: Statistics Canada, 2000.

Picot, Garnett, and Feng Hou. "The Effect of Pre-immigration Canadian Work Experience on the Returns to Human Capital among Immigrants." *Journal of International Migration and Integration* 24, no. 3 (2023): 661–79. doi:10.1007/s12134-023-01025-9.

– *Immigrant Characteristics, the IT Bust, and Their Effect on Entry Earnings of Immigrants.* Ottawa: Statistics Canada, 2009.

– "Immigration and the Shifting Occupational Distribution in Canada, 2001 to 2021." *Economic and Social Reports* 4, no. 3 (2024). https://www150.statcan.gc.ca/n1/en/pub/36-28-0001/2024003/article/00006-eng.pdf?st=DiOd1riE.

Picot, Garnett, Eden Crossman, and Feng Hou. "Provincial Nominee Program: Recent Trends and Provincial Differences in Earnings Outcomes." *Economic and Social Reports* 3, no. 12 (2023). https://www150.statcan.gc.ca/n1/pub/36-28-0001/2023012/article/00004-eng.htm.

Picot, Garnett, Feng Hou, and Eden Crossman. "The Provincial Nominee Program: Its Expansion in Canada." Statistics Canada, 26 July 2023. https://www150.statcan.gc.ca/n1/pub/36-28-0001/2023007/article/00004-eng.htm.

Picot, Garnett, Feng Hou, Eden Crossman, and Yuqian Lu. "Transition to Permanent Residency by Lower- and Higher-Skilled Temporary Foreign Workers." *Economic and Social Reports* 2, no. 1 (2022). https://www150.statcan.gc.ca/n1/en/pub/36-28-0001/2022001/article/00002-eng.pdf?st=YCPN-IQW.

Picot, Garnett, Feng Hou, Li Xu, and Aneta Bonikowska. *Which Immigration Selection Factors Best Predict the Earnings of Economic Principal Applicants?* Ottawa: Immigration, Refugees and Citizenship Canada, 2020. https://www.canada.ca/content/dam/ircc/documents/pdf/english/corporate/reports-statistics/research/immigration-selection-factors-predict-earnings-economic-principal-applicants/r3c-2020_ee_eng.pdf.

Pillai, Sangeetha, and George Williams. "The Utility of Citizenship Stripping Laws in the UK, Canada and Australia." *Melbourne University Law Review* 41, no. 2 (2017): 845–89.

Plaut, W. Gunther. *Refugee Determination in Canada.* Ottawa: Minister of Supply and Services, 1985.

Porter, John. *The Vertical Mosaic: An Analysis of Social Class and Power in Canada.* Toronto: University of Toronto Press, 1965.

Praznik, Jessica, and John Shields. *An Anatomy of Settlement Services in Canada: A Guide.* Toronto: Ryerson University, 2018.

Price, Peter. "Naturalising Subjects, Creating Citizens: Naturalisation Law and the Conditioning of 'Citizenship' in Canada, 1881–1914." *The Journal of Imperial and Commonwealth History*, 45, no. 1 (2017): 1–21. https://doi.org/10.1080/03086534.2016.1262646.

Public Service Alliance of Canada. "Employment Equity Act Review Report: What We Heard." Ottawa: Public Service Alliance of Canada, 2022.

Pugliese, Anita, and Julie Ray. "Nearly 900 Million Worldwide Wanted to Migrate in 2021." *Gallup*, 24 January 2023. https://news.gallup.com/poll/468218/nearly-900-million-worldwide-wanted-migrate-2021.aspx.

Putnam, Robert D. "E Pluribus Unum: Diversity and Community in the Twenty-First Century." *Scandinavian Political Studies* 30, no. 2 (2007): 137–74. https://doi.org/10.1111/j.1467-9477.2007.00176.x.

Raska, Jan. "1973: Canada's Response to the Chilean Refugees." Canadian Museum of Immigration at Pier 21. Accessed 22 July 2023. https://pier21.ca/research/immigration-history/canadas-response-chilean-crisis.

– "Recruiting Domestic Workers and Live-in Caregivers in Canada." Canadian Museum of Immigration at Pier 21. Accessed 8 July 2024. https://pier21.ca/recruiting-domestic-workers-and-live-caregivers-canada.

Ratushny, Ed. *A New Refugee Status Determination Process for Canada.* Ottawa: Minister of Supply and Services, 1984.

Redmond, Melissa, and Beth Martin. "All in the (Definition of) Family: Transnational Parent–Child Relationships, Rights to Family Life, and Canadian Immigration Law." *Journal of Family Issues* 44, no. 3 (2021): 766–84. https://doi.org/10.1177/0192513X211054461.

Rehaag, Sean. "Judicial Review of Refugee Determinations: The Luck of the Draw?" *Queen's Law Journal* 38, no. 1 (2012): 1–58.

Reitz, Jeffrey G. "Assessing Multiculturalism as a Behavioural Theory." In *Multiculturalism and Social Cohesion*, edited by Jeffrey G. Reitz, Raymond Breton, Karen K. Dion, and Kenneth L. Dion, 1–47. Dordrecht: Springer Netherlands, 2009.

– "Canada: Continuity and Change in Immigration for Nation-Building." In *Controlling Immigration: A Comparative Perspective*, edited by James F. Hollifield, Philip L. Martin, Pia M. Orrenius, and François Héran, 4th ed., 123–67. Stanford, CA: Stanford University Press, 2022.

– "Canada: New Initiatives and Approaches to Immigration and Nation Building." In *Controlling Immigration: A Global Perspective*, edited by James F. Hollifield, Philip L. Martin, and Pia M. Orrenius, 2nd ed., 88–116. Stanford, CA: Stanford University Press, 2014.

– "The Distinctiveness of Canadian Immigration Experience." In "National Models of Integration and the Crisis of Multiculturalism: A Critical Comparative Perspective," edited by Christophe Bertossi and Jan Willem Duyvendak. Special issue, *Patterns of Prejudice* 46, no. 5 (2012): 418–35.

– "Immigrant Employment Success in Canada, Part I: Individual and Contextual Causes." *Journal of International Migration and Integration* 8, no. 1 (2007): 11–36.

– "Immigrant Skill Utilization in the Canadian Labour Market: Implications of Human Capital Research." *Journal of International Migration and Integration* 2, no. 3 (2001): 347–78.

– "Immigrant Success in the Knowledge Economy: Institutional Change and the Immigrant Experience in Canada, 1970–1995." *Journal of Social Issues* 57, no. 3 (2001): 579–613.
– "The Institutional Structure of Immigration as a Determinant of Inter-Racial Competition: A Comparison of Britain and Canada." *International Migration Review* 22, no. 1 (1988): 117–46.
– "Less Racial Discrimination in Canada, or Simply Less Racial Conflict?: Implications of Comparisons with Britain." *Canadian Public Policy* 14, no. 4 (1988): 424–41.
– "Popular Multiculturalism as Social Capital: Trends and Prospects." In "Multiculturalism @50 and the Promise of a Just Society." Special issue, *Canadian Issues* (Fall/Winter 2021): 39–44. https://acs-metropolis.ca/wp-content/uploads/2021/10/663_AEC-CITC_EN_V6_Web-1-1.pdf.
– "Pro-Immigration Canada: Social and Economic Roots of Popular Views." IRPP Study, No. 20. Montreal: Institute for Research on Public Policy, 2011.
– "The Role of Employers in Selecting Highly Skilled Immigrants: Potentials and Limitations." *Journal of International Migration and Integration* 24 (2023): S621–39. https://doi.org/10.1007/s12134-023-01030-y.
– "Selecting Immigrants for the Short Term: Is It Smart in the Long Run?" *Policy Options* 31, no. 7 (2010): 12–16.
– "The Status of Muslim Minorities Following the Paris Attacks." In *After the Paris Attacks*, edited by Edward M. Iacobucci and Stephen J. Toope, 21–8. Toronto: University of Toronto Press, 2015.
– *The Survival of Ethnic Groups.* Toronto: McGraw Hill-Ryerson, 1980.
– *Warmth of the Welcome: The Social Causes of Economic Success for Immigrants in Different Nations and Cities.* Boulder, CO: Westview Press, 1998.
Reitz, Jeffrey G., and Raymond Breton. *The Illusion of Difference: Realities of Ethnicity in Canada and the United States.* Toronto: C.D. Howe Institute, 1994.
Reitz, Jeffrey G., Josh Curtis, and Jennifer Elrick. "Immigrant Skill Utilization: Trends and Policy Issues." *Journal of International Migration and Integration* 15, no. 1 (2014): 1–26.
Reitz, Jeffrey G., Emily Laxer, and Patrick Simon. "National Cultural Frames and Muslims' Economic Incorporation: A Comparison of France and Canada." *International Migration Review* 56, no. 2 (2022): 499–532. https://doi.org/10.1177/01979183211035725.
Richardson, Ben, Yadullah Hussain, and Naomi Powell. "Canada Needs More Doctors – and Fast." RBC Thought Leadership, 23 November 2022. https://thoughtleadership.rbc.com/proof-point-canada-needs-more-doctors-and-fast/.
Robinson, Walter G. *The Refugee Status Determination Process: A Report of the Task Force on Immigration Practices and Procedures.* Ottawa: Minister of Supply and Services, 1981.
Robitaille, Edana. "IRCC Inventory Stands at 2 Million Applications." *CIC News*, 27 May 2023. https://www.cicnews.com/2023/05/ircc-inventory-stands-at-2-million-applications-0535128.html.
Sampat-Mehta, Ramdeo. *International Barriers: A Critique.* Ottawa: Canada Research Bureau, 1973.
Satayana, George. *The Life of Reason: The Phases of Human Progress.* Vol. 1, *Reason in Common Sense.* N.p., 1905.
Satzewich, Victor. *Racism and the Incorporation of Foreign Labour: Farm Labour Migration to Canada since 1945.* New York: Routledge, 1991.

Saunders, Doug. *Maximum Canada: Why 35 Million Canadians Are Not Enough*. Toronto: Knopf, 2017.

Schimmele, Christoph, Feng Hou, and Max Stick. "Poverty among Racialized Groups across Generations." *Economic and Social Reports* 3, no. 8 (2023). https://www150.statcan.gc.ca/n1/pub/36-28-0001/2023008/article/00002-eng.htm.

Schinnerl, Sandra, and Antje Ellermann. "The Education-Immigration Nexus: Situating Canadian Higher Education as Institutions of Immigrant Recruitment." *Journal of International Migration and Integration* 224 (2023): 599–620. https://doi.org/10.1007/s12134-023-01043-7.

Schlesinger, Arthur M. *The Disuniting of America: Reflections on a Multicultural Society*. New York: W.W. Norton, 1998.

Schuck, Peter H. "The Transformation of Immigration Law." *Columbia Law Review* 84, no. 1 (1984): 1–90. https://www.jstor.org/stable/1122369.

Schuster, A., M.V. Desiderio, and G. Urso, eds. *Recognition of Qualifications and Competences of Migrants*. Brussels: International Organization for Migration, 2013.

Seidle, F. Leslie. *Canada's Provincial Nominee Immigration Programs: Securing Greater Policy Alignment*. IRPP Study, No. 43. Montreal: Institute for Research on Public Policy, 2013.

Sen, Amartya. *Development as Freedom*. New York: Alfred Knopf, 1999.

– *The Idea of Justice*. Boston, MA: Harvard University Press, 2009.

Shephard, Ben. *The Long Road Home: The Aftermath of the Second World War*. New York: Anchor Books, 2012.

Shields, John, Julie Drolet, and Karla Valenzuela. *Immigrant Settlement and Integration Services and the Role of Nonprofit Providers: A Cross-National Perspective on Trends, Issues and Evidence*. RICS Working Paper No. 2016/1. Toronto: Ryerson Centre for Immigration and Settlement, 2016.

Siemiatycki, Myer, and Triadafilos Triadafilopoulos. *International Perspectives on Immigrant Service Provision*. Toronto: Mowat Centre for Policy Innovation, 2010.

Silverman, Stephanie, and Petra Molnar. "Everyday Injustices: Barriers to Access to Justice for Immigration Detainees in Canada." *Refugee Survey Quarterly* 35, no. 1 (2016): 109–27.

Singer, Colin R. "Canada Express Entry Draws to Target 82 Occupations in 5 Fields Starting in Summer 2023." Immigration.ca, 31 May 2023. https://www.immigration.ca/canada-express-entry-draws-to-target-82-occupations-in-5-fields-starting-in-summer-2023/.

Skuterud, Mikal. "Canada's Missing Workers: Temporary Residents Working in Canada." E-Brief 345. Toronto: C.D. Howe Institute, 2023.

– "Canadian Stats and Two-Step Immigration." *Policy Options*, 19 December 2016. https://policyoptions.irpp.org/magazines/december-2016/in-search-of-better-statistics-on-immigration.

Stamford, Jim. "Interrogating the Labour Shortage Hypothesis." The Center for Future Work. 11 October 2023. https://centreforfuturework.ca/2023/10/11/interrogating-the-labour-shortage-hypothesis/.

Statistics Canada. "150 Years of Immigration in Canada." Last updated 17 May 2018. https://www150.statcan.gc.ca/n1/pub/11-630-x/11-630-x2016006-eng.htm.

– "Canada's Population Estimates: Record-High Population Growth in 2022." *The Daily*, 22 March 2023. https://www150.statcan.gc.ca/n1/daily-quotidien/230322/dq230322f-eng.htm.

– *Immigrants in Canada: Selected Highlights*. Ottawa: Statistics Canada, 1990. https:// publications.gc.ca/site/eng/9.816566/publication.html.
– "Longitudinal Survey of Immigrants to Canada: A Portrait of Early Settlement Experiences." Ottawa: Special Surveys Division, Statistics Canada, 2005.
– "A Portrait of Citizenship in Canada from the 2021 Census." Ottawa: Statistics Canada, 2022.
– "Settlement Services Provided to Immigrants to Canada, 2020." *The Daily*. Ottawa: Statistics Canada, 2 June 2022.
Stone, Laura. "Groups Representing Canadian Universities and Colleges Raise 'Significant Concerns' about International Student Cap." *Globe and Mail*, 31 January 2024.
Strik, Tineke, Betty de Hart, and Ellen Nissen. *Family Reunification: A Barrier or Facilitator of Integration? A Comparative Study*. Brussels: European Commission, 2013.
Sunahara, Ann Gomer. *The Politics of Racism: The Uprooting of Japanese Canadians during the Second World War*. Toronto: Lorimer, 1981.
Swann, Neil, Ludwig Auer, Denis Chénard, Angélique dePlaa, Arnold DeSilva, Douglas Palmer, and John Serjak. *The Economic and Social Impacts of Immigration: A Research Report Prepared for the Economic Council of Canada*. Ottawa: Minister of Supply and Services, 1991.
Sweetman, Arthur, and Casey Warman. "Canada's Immigration Selection System and Labour Market Outcomes." *Canadian Public Policy* 39, Supplement 1 (2013): S141–64. https://doi.org/10.3138/CPP.39.Supplement1.S141.
Thevenot, Shelby. "Canadians See Family Reunification as Biggest Priority in 2020." *Canada Immigration News*, 1 September 2020. https://www.cicnews.com/2020/09 /canadians-see-family-reunification-as-biggest-priority-in-2020-0915631.html.
Thornton, Russell. "Population History of North American Indians." In *A Population History of North America*, edited by Michael R. Haines and Richard H. Steckel, 9–51. Cambridge: Cambridge University Press, 2000.
Thurton, David. "Ottawa Backs Listing Black and LGBTQ Workers under Canada's Workplace Equity Laws." *CBC News*, 11 December 2023. https://www.cbc.ca/news /politics/workplace-equity-black-lgbtq-1.7055067.
Thwaites, Rayer. *The Liberty of Non-Citizens: Indefinite Detention in Commonwealth Countries*. Oxford: Hart Publishing, 2014.
Trafford, Brittany. "Update on the Economic Mobility Program for Refugees (Phase 2): The Economic Mobility Pathways Project ('EMPP)." In *Beyond the Border: Immigration Update July 2022*, 12–13. Halifax: Stewart McKelvey, 2022. https:// www.stewartmckelvey.com/thought-leadership/update-on-the-economic -mobility-program-for-refugees-phase-2-the-economic-mobility-pathways-project -empp/.
Trebilcock, Michael. *Public Inquiries: A Scholar's Engagements with the Policy-Making Process*. Toronto: University of Toronto Press, 2022.
– "The Puzzle of Canadian Exceptionalism in Contemporary Immigration Policy." *Journal of International Migration and Integration* 20, no. 3 (2019): 823–49.
Triadafilopoulos, Triadafilos. *Becoming Multicultural: Immigration and the Politics of Membership in Canada and Germany*. Toronto: University of Toronto Press, 2012.
Triadafilopoulos, Triadafilos, and Zack Taylor. "The Domestic Politics of Selective Permeability: Disaggregating the Canadian Migration State." *Journal of Ethnic and Migration Studies* 50, no. 3 (2023): 702–25. https://doi.org/10.1080/13691 83X.2023.2269785.

Trudeau, Justin. "How to Fix the Broken Temporary Foreign Worker Program." *Toronto Star*, 5 May 2014. https://www.thestar.com/opinion/commentary/2014/05/05 /how_to_fix_the_broken_temporary_foreign_worker_program_justin_trudeau .html.

Truth and Reconciliation Commission of Canada. *Calls to Action*. Winnipeg: Truth and Reconciliation Commission of Canada, 2015. https://ehprnh2mwo3.exactdn.com /wp-content/uploads/2021/01/Calls_to_Action_English2.pdf.

Tuey, Catherine, and Nicolas Bastien. "Non-Permanent Residents in Canada: Portrait of a Growing Population from the 2021 Census." Statistics Canada, Catalogue no. 75-006-X, 2021. https://www150.statcan.gc.ca/n1/pub/75-006-x/2023001 /article/00006-eng.htm.

Tuey, Catherine, and Hélène Maheux. *A Portrait of Citizenship in Canada from the 2021 Census*. Ottawa: Statistics Canada, 2022. https://www12.statcan.gc.ca/census -recensement/2021/as-sa/98-200-X/2021008/98-200-X2021008-eng.cfm.

United Food and Commercial Workers and the Agricultural Workers Alliance. *The Status of Migrant Farm Workers in Canada*. Toronto: UFCW and AWA, 2015. https:// www.ufcw.ca/templates/ufcwcanada/images/directions15/october/1586 /MigrantWorkersReport2015_EN_email.pdf.

United Nations. *Replacement Migration: Is It a Solution to Declining and Ageing Populations?* New York: United Nations, Population Division, Department of Economic and Social Affairs, 2000.

– *United Nations Charter*. United Nations Conference on International Organization, 1945. https://www.un.org/en/about-us/un-charter/full-text.

United Nations General Assembly. *Draft Convention Relating to the Status of Refugees*. A/RES/429, UN General Assembly, 14 December 1950. https://www.refworld .org/legal/resolution/unga/1950/en/7683.

– *Convention on the Rights of the Child*, 20 November 1989. https://www.ohchr.org/ en/instruments-mechanisms/instruments/convention-rights-child.

– *Protocol Relating to the Status of Refugees*. A/RES/2198, UN General Assembly, 16 December 1966. https://www.refworld.org/legal/resolution/unga/1966 /en/9990.

– *Universal Declaration of Human Rights*. United Nations General Assembly, 10 December 1948. https://www.un.org/en/about-us/universal-declaration-of -human-rights#:~:text=Article%2012,against%20such%20interference%20or%20 attacks.

United Nations High Commissioner for Refugees. "Complementary Pathways for Admission to Third Countries." Accessed 20 December 2022. https://www.unhcr .org/complementary-pathways.html.

– *Effective Processing of Asylum Applications: Practical Considerations and Practices*. Geneva: UNHCR, 2022.

– *Guidelines on International Protection No. 5: Application of the Exclusion Clauses: Article 1F of the 1951 Convention relating to the Status of Refugees*, HCR/GIP/03/05. 4 September 2003.

– *Legal Considerations Regarding Access to Protection and a Connection between the Refugee and the Third Country in the Context of Return or Transfer to Safe Third Countries*. Geneva: UNHCR, 2018.

– "Mid-Year Trends 2023." Accessed 1 November 2023. https://www.unhcr.org/mid -year-trends-report-2023.

– *UNHCR Resettlement Handbook*. Geneva: UNHCR, 2023. https://www.unhcr.org
   /resettlement-handbook/.

Valenti, Fabrizio, and Susan Bennet. *Labour Market Impact of the Temporary Foreign
   Worker Program: Final Report*. Ottawa: KSAR Consulting Group, 2022.

VanderPlaat, Madine, Yoko Yoshida, and Howard Ramos. "The Role of Spouses and
   Children in the Decision to Settle or Not to Settle into a Certain Community: A
   Focus on Cities Outside of Montréal, Toronto, and Vancouver." Research Brief,
   Research and Evaluation. Ottawa: Citizenship and Immigration Canada, 2013.

Van Dyk, Spencer. "Permanent Immigration Levels 'in the Right Place': Fraser." *CTV
   News*, 3 April 2024. https://www.ctvnews.ca/politics/permanent-immigration
   -levels-in-the-right-place-fraser-1.6832085.

van Reekum, Rogier, Jan Willem Duyvendak, and Christophe Bertossi. "National
   Models of Integration and the Crisis of Multiculturalism: A Critical Comparative
   Perspective." *Patterns of Prejudice* 46, no. 5 (2012): 417–538. https://doi.org/10.1080
   /0031322X.2012.718162.

Villiers, Janice D. "Brave New World: The Use and Potential Misuse of DNA
   Technology in Immigration Law." *Boston College Third World Law Journal* 30, no. 2
   (2010): 239–72.

Vineberg, Robert. *Responding to Immigrants' Settlement Needs: The Canadian Experience*.
   New York: Springer, 2012.

Vinokur, David. "30 Years of Changes at the Immigration and Refugee Board of
   Canada." The Canadian Immigration Historical Society, *CIHS Bulletin*, no. 88
   (2019): 6–12. https://cihs-shic.ca/wp-content/uploads/2019/04/Bulletin-88
   -Final.pdf.

Wallace, Rebecca, Erin Tolley, and Madison Vonk. *Multiculturalism Policy Index:
   Immigrant Minority Policies, Third Edition*. The Multiculturalism Policy Index
   Project. Kingston, ON: Queen's University, School of Policy Studies, 2021.

Wang, Shuguang, and Skylar Maharaj. "Community Support for Immigrants and their
   Families." In *Putting Family First: Migration and Integration in Canada*, edited by
   Harald Bauder, 67–91. Vancouver: UBC Press, 2019.

Ward, W. Peter. *The Japanese in Canada. Canada's Ethnic Groups*, Booklet No. 3. Ottawa:
   Canadian Historical Association, 1982.

Warr, W.L., and M.B. Percy. "Immigration Policy and Canadian Economic Growth."
   In *Domestic Policies in the International Economic Environment*, edited by John
   Walley, 57–110. Toronto: University of Toronto Press, 1985.

Whitaker, Reg. *Double Standard: The Secret History of Canadian Immigration Policy*.
   Toronto: Lester and Orpen Dennys, 1987.

– "Official Repression of Communism during World War II." *Labour/Le Travail* 17
   (1986): 135–66. https://www.lltjournal.ca/index.php/llt/article/view/2492.

Wilkinson, Lori, and Joseph Garcea. *The Economic Integration of Refugees in Canada: A
   Mixed Record?* Washington, DC: Migration Policy Institute, 2017.

Wilton, Robert, Stine Hansen, and Edward Hall. "Disabled People, Medical
   Inadmissibility, and the Differential Politics of Immigration." *The Canadian
   Geographer* 61, no. 3 (2017): 389–400. https://doi.org/10.1111/cag.12361.

Winks, Robin. *The Blacks in Canada: A History*. Montreal: McGill-Queen's University
   Press, 1971.

Winter, Elke, and Adina Madularea. "Quo Vadis Canada? Tracing the Contours of
   Citizenship in a Multicultural Country." In *Immigration and Ethnic Studies in 150*

Years of Canada: Retrospects and Prospects, edited by Shibao Gao and Lloyd Wong, 191–208. Leiden: Brill Sense, 2018.

Woolf, Marie. "Federal Program Matching Refugees with Jobs set to be Made Permanent." *Globe and Mail*, 7 May 2024.

– "Most Immigrants with Deportation Letters Are Still in Canada, CBSA Figures Show." *Globe and Mail*, 13 February 2024. https://www.theglobeandmail.com/politics /article-most-immigrants-with-deportation-letters-are-still-in-canada-cbsa/.

– "Ottawa Plans to Create Canadian Citizenship Path for Undocumented Immigrants." *Globe and Mail*, 14 December 2023. https://www.theglobeandmail. com/politics/article-canadas-immigration-minister-plans-broad-program-to -allow-immigrants/.

– "Ottawa Split on Plan to Let Undocumented Migrants Apply to Stay in Canada." *Globe and Mail*, 24 June 2024.

– "Poll Finds More than Half of Canadians Want Fewer Immigrants than Ottawa's Target." *Globe and Mail*, 11 September 2023. https://www.theglobeandmail.com /politics/article-poll-finds-more-than-half-of-canadians-want-fewer-immigrants-than/.

– "Spike in International Student Asylum Claims an Abuse of Study Permits, Experts Warn." *Globe and Mail*, 22 April 2024.

Woods, Allan. "Dual Citizenship Faces Review." *National Post*, 29 September 2007. https:// web.archive.org/web/20070929111734/http://www.canada.com/nationalpost /news/story.html?id=fb2d75ab-8880-4945-8537-1508186a4964&k=61921#.

Woodsworth, James Shaver. *Strangers Within Our Gates, or, Coming Canadians*. 1909. Reprint, Toronto: University of Toronto Press, 1972.

World Bank. 2023. *World Development Report 2023: Migrants, Refugees, and Societies*. Washington, DC: World Bank, 2023.

Wortley, Scot. *Halifax, Nova Scotia: Street Checks Report*. Halifax: Nova Scotia Human Rights Commission, 2019.

Wortley, Scot, and Akwasi Owusu-Bempah. "Unequal before the Law: Immigrant and Racial Minority Perceptions of the Canadian Criminal Justice System." *Journal of International Migration and Integration* 10, no. 4 (2009): 447–73. https://doi.org /10.1007/s12134-009-0108-x.

Wortley, Scot, and Julian Tanner. "Data, Denials, and Confusion: The Racial Profiling Debate in Toronto." *Canadian Journal of Criminology and Criminal Justice* 45, no. 3 (2003): 367–90. https://doi.org/10.3138/cjccj.45.3.367.

Wright, Teressa. "Canada's Backlog of 'Legacy' Refugee Claims Soon to Be Cleared – but a New List Is Growing." *Global News*, 30 April 2019. https://globalnews.ca /news/5220024/refugee-legacy-claims-cleared/.

Wrzesnewskyj, Borys. *Family Reunification: Report of the Standing Committee on Citizenship and Immigration*. Ottawa: House of Commons Canada, 2017. https:// www.ourcommons.ca/Content/Committee/421/CIMM/Reports/RP8810563 /cimmrp08/cimmrp08-e.pdf.

Young, Rebekah. "Raising the Bar, Not Just Lowering the Number: Canada's Immigration Policy Confronts Critical Choices." Scotia Bank, 21 March 2024. https://www.scotiabank.com:443/content/scotiabank/ca/en/about/economics /economics-publications/post.other-publications.insights-views.canada-s- immigration-policy--march-21--2024-.html.

Index

Page numbers in italics refer to figures and tables.

Books in the Series

- Ninette Kelley, Jeffrey G. Reitz, and Michael J. Trebilcock, *Reshaping the Mosaic: Canadian Immigration Policy in the Twenty-first Century*
- Peter MacKinnon, *Confronting Illiberalism: A Canadian Perspective*
- Aisha Ahmad (ed.), *Securing Canada's Future: Vital Insights from Women Experts*
- Ingrid Leman Stefanovic (ed.), *Conversations on Ethical Leadership: Lessons Learned from University Governance*
- Sue Winton, *Unequal Benefits: Privatization and Public Education in Canada*
- David A. Detomasi, *Profits and Power: Navigating the Politics and Geopolitics of Oil*
- Michael J. Trebilcock, *Public Inquiries: A Scholar's Engagement with the Policy-making Process*
- Andrew Green, *Picking up the Slack: Law, Institutions, and Canadian Climate Policy*
- Peter MacKinnon, *Canada in Question: Exploring Our Citizenship in the Twenty-First Century*
- Harvey P. Weingarten, *Nothing Less than Great: Reforming Canada's Universities*
- Allan C. Hutchinson, *Democracy and Constitutions: Putting Citizens First*
- Paul Nelson, *Global Development and Human Rights: The Sustainable Development Goals and Beyond*
- Peter H. Russell, *Sovereignty: The Biography of a Claim*
- Alistair Edgar, Rupinder Mangat, and Bessma Momani (eds.), *Strengthening the Canadian Armed Forces through Diversity and Inclusion*
- David B. MacDonald, *The Sleeping Giant Awakens: Genocide, Indian Residential Schools, and the Challenge of Conciliation*
- Paul W. Gooch, *Course Correction: A Map for the Distracted University*
- Paul T. Phillips, *Truth, Morality, and Meaning in History*

- Stanley R. Barrett, *The Lamb and the Tiger: From Peacekeepers to Peacewarriors in Canada*
- Peter MacKinnon, *University Commons Divided: Exploring Debate and Dissent on Campus*
- Raisa B. Deber, *Treating Health Care: How the System Works and How It Could Work Better*
- Jim Freedman, *A Conviction in Question: The First Trial at the International Criminal Court*
- Christina D. Rosan and Hamil Pearsall, *Growing a Sustainable City? The Question of Urban Agriculture*
- John Joe Schlichtman, Jason Patch, and Marc Lamont Hill, *Gentrifier*
- Robert Chernomas and Ian Hudson, *Economics in the Twenty-First Century: A Critical Perspective*
- Stephen M. Saideman, *Adapting in the Dust: Lessons Learned from Canada's War in Afghanistan*
- Michael R. Marrus, *Lessons of the Holocaust*
- Roland Paris and Taylor Owen (eds.), *The World Won't Wait: Why Canada Needs to Rethink Its International Policies*
- Bessma Momani, *Arab Dawn: Arab Youth and the Demographic Dividend They Will Bring*
- William Watson, *The Inequality Trap: Fighting Capitalism Instead of Poverty*
- Phil Ryan, *After the New Atheist Debate*
- Paul Evans, *Engaging China: Myth, Aspiration, and Strategy in Canadian Policy from Trudeau to Harper*